Experimental Film and Queer Materiality

Experimental Film and Queer Materiality

JUAN A. SUÁREZ

OXFORD
UNIVERSITY PRESS

Oxford University Press is a department of the University of Oxford. It furthers
the University's objective of excellence in research, scholarship, and education
by publishing worldwide. Oxford is a registered trade mark of Oxford University
Press in the UK and certain other countries.

Published in the United States of America by Oxford University Press
198 Madison Avenue, New York, NY 10016, United States of America.

© Oxford University Press 2024

All rights reserved. No part of this publication may be reproduced, stored in
a retrieval system, or transmitted, in any form or by any means, without the
prior permission in writing of Oxford University Press, or as expressly permitted
by law, by license, or under terms agreed with the appropriate reproduction
rights organization. Inquiries concerning reproduction outside the scope of the
above should be sent to the Rights Department, Oxford University Press, at the
address above.

You must not circulate this work in any other form
and you must impose this same condition on any acquirer.

Library of Congress Cataloging-in-Publication Data
Names: Suárez, Juan Antonio, author.
Title: Experimental film and queer materiality / Juan A. Suárez.
Description: New York : Oxford University Press, 2024. |
Includes bibliographical references and index.
Identifiers: LCCN 2023054946 (print) | LCCN 2023054947 (ebook) |
ISBN 9780197773802 (paperback) | ISBN 9780197566992 (hardback) |
ISBN 9780197567012 (epub)
Subjects: LCSH: Experimental film—History. | Sexual minorities in motion pictures.
Classification: LCC PN1995.9.E96 S823 2024 (print) | LCC PN1995.9.E96 (ebook) |
DDC 791.43/611—dc23/eng/2024/eng/20240119
LC record available at https://lccn.loc.gov/2023054946
LC ebook record available at https://lccn.loc.gov/2023054947

DOI: 10.1093/oso/9780197566992.001.0001

Paperback printed by Marquis Book Printing, Canada
Hardback printed by Bridgeport National Bindery, Inc., United States of America

Contents

Acknowledgments	vii
1. Introduction: Sexuality on the Outside: Experimental Film and Queer Materiality	1
2. Ruins, Magical Objects, Litter, Synthetics: The Queer Materials of Postwar Avant-Garde Film	24
3. Amphetamine and Queer Materiality in Andy Warhol's Factory Films	62
4. Crashing Bodies, Excrement, and Plastics: The Kuchar Brothers in the Sixties	91
5. Glitter and Queer Embodiment in 1960s and 1970s Experimental Film and Performance	116
6. Film Grain, Discontinuous Representation, and the Queer Corporealities of Underground Cinema	151
7. The Afterlives of Film Grain: Precarious Bodies and Poor Images	180
8. Synthetic, Exotic, Magnetic: The Noise of Queer Experimental Film	208
Notes	253
Index	297

Acknowledgments

While the bulk of the writing that follows was done between April 2020 and October 2022, I have been mulling over this project for the last decade. In this time, I have many to thank for friendship, support, encouragement, fun times, and for making that cumulus of activities that we call research communal, affective, and cooperative. Marc Siegel is directly responsible for many of these pages and was among the first to respond to the ideas in them. Lucas Hilderbrand gave suggestions and advice. Federico Windhausen has been a great interlocutor and sharer of information and resources. Ara Osterweil hosted me during a stay at McGill University in the summer of 2012, during which I worked on what eventually became one of the chapters of this book, and she has been unfailingly generous and appreciative. Celestino Deleyto and Marimar Azcona have invited me to present parts of this project at the University of Zaragoza and have long been close coconspirators. Michele Pierson invited me to give a talk at King's College in the early stages of this work and has long been a source of ideas and encouragement. It has been a privilege to share research projects and interests with Glyn Davis. Because every encounter with them is memorable and inspiring and there are traces of their conversations scattered all over the book, I warmly thank: Henri Abelove, Rodrigo Andrés, Alberto Berzosa, Rosalyn Deutsche, Miguel Fernández Labayen, Jonathan Flatley, Rosalind Galt, Elena Gorfinkel, Ron Gregg, Juan Guardiola, Nguyen Tan Hoang, Kathleen McHugh, Pedro Ortuño, Michele Pierson, Veronica Pravadelli, Ann Reynolds, Karl Schoonover, and Chris Straayer. Stephanie Schulte-Strathaus and Vinzenz Hediger kindly hosted me at different times at Arsenal (Berlin) and at the Deutsches Filmmuseum (Frankfurt), respectively. Gloria Vilches is immensely knowledgeable and stimulating and has frequently invited me to Aula X-Céntric (CCCB), where I presented some of these ideas to wonderfully receptive audiences. P. Adams Sitney has replied to queries with astonishing generosity. After all these years, Jim Naremore and Richard Dyer remain crucial inspirations. Juanfra Cerdá and Clara Calvo are great colleagues and pop sensations. Pedro Férez adds that spark. David Moore waves from the other side. I wish I had been able to celebrate the completion

viii ACKNOWLEDGMENTS

of this project with Douglas Crimp and David Vilaseca; their friendship, conversation, and the interests we shared are (will always be) woven into my writing and thinking.

A lot of this work would not have been possible without the help of individuals at various archives, museums, and galleries. I owe a big thank you to M. M. Serra and Tom Day, at the Film-Makers' Cooperative; Ashley Swinnerton at MoMA Film Study Center; Jon Shibata, Antonella Bonfanti, and Michael Campos-Quinn at Pacific Film Archive; Todd Wiener at the UCLA Film and Television Archive; Orson Sieverding, on behalf of Studio 111a (Düsseldorf) (and Colin Lang for putting us in touch); Alexis Constantin at the Centre Pompidou; Andrew Lampert, John Mhiripiri, and the late Roger Haller, at Anthology Film Archives; Patrick Seymour at the Andy Warhol Museum; Fernando Chaves Espinach at LUX; Eike Dürrfeld, at Gallery Thomas Schulte (Berlin); Photios Giovanis, formerly of Callicoon Fine Arts (New York); Ramón Romero Coma at Filmoteca de Catalunya (Barcelona); and Lilly Bajraktari at Gladstone Gallery (New York). A very special thank you goes to Jim Hubbard, who gave me access to Tom Chomont's films and to his own. William E. Jones, Jim Hubbard, Jerry Tartaglia, Ashley Hans Scheirl, Peggy Ahwesh, Jennifer Reeves, and David Domingo generously granted permission for the use of their images and gave me access to their films. Michel Nedjar and Marcel Cifré Pérez graciously allowed me to permit images from Teo Hernández's *Salomé* and Carles Comas's *Fosca*, respectively. I am especially thankful to Jennifer Reeves for letting me use one of her images on the cover.

Norm Hirschy, my editor at Oxford University Press, has been totally supportive from the start; I cannot thank him enough for his generosity and patience. The anonymous readers provided great suggestions that have improved the book enormously.

My parents, Juan Antonio Suárez and Maruja Sánchez del Valle, passed away shortly before this work was in full swing and would surely have liked to see it finished. The memory of Fernando Suárez is indelible. My sister Rosaura is always there and so are, on the other side of the family, Pepita Avila, María José Belmonte, and Sandra Fueyo. I was lucky to know Juan Belmonte before he left us. My nephew and niece, Fernando and Martina, may never read this, but I'm sure it is better because they are around.

Finally, my partner Juanfran Belmonte has seen me through a time of considerable losses and difficulties, but also of travel, fun, play, and change. He has given invaluable feedback, has often restored my tottering confidence, and has good-humoredly endured that ominous unspecified "everything" that living with someone struggling with long-term writing involves. I thank him for his constant support and love.

This research was supported by project PGC2018-095393 "Queer Temporalities in Contemporary Anglophone Cultures" (2019–2023); Ministerio de Ciencia, Investigación y Universidades, Gobierno de España. I have been accompanied in this project by a fantastic team full of collegiality and cheer, where there are also some long-term friends: Carolina Sánchez-Palencia, Pedro Férez, Juan Francisco Belmonte, Estíbaliz Encarnación, Adriana Serón, Ángela López, Cristina Hurtado, María Piqueras, Corpus Navalón, Irene Rodríguez Pintado, and Inmaculada Parra.

Early versions of Chapters 3 and 4 have appeared, respectively, as: "Warhol's 1960s Films, Amphetamine, and Queer Materiality," *Criticism* 56, no. 3, special issue: Andy Warhol, ed. Jonathan Flatley and Anthony Gruden (Summer 2014): 623–652; and "The Kuchars, The 1960s, and Queer Materiality," *Screen* 56, no. 1 (Spring 2015): 25–45.

1

Introduction: Sexuality on the Outside

Experimental Film and Queer Materiality

Queer Materiality

So long as the impulse to write a book is traceable, this one owes its existence to a deep-seated fascination with the circuitous functioning of sexuality. This came alive for me in the work of sexually heterodox filmmakers who have occasionally produced reticent, discreet images that, while embedded in a sexual context, cannot be easily interpreted through the usual protocols applied to the study of sexuality on the screen. One instance of this obliquity, is the moment in Kenneth Anger's *Fireworks* (1947), one of the pinnacles of post–World War II experimental film and of queer film at large, when the protagonist is bashed by a gang of sailors, his chest cut open with broken glass, and a pulsing gas meter appears among his entrails where we would expect a heart. What can be made of this technological irruption? The most opaque element in a relatively explicit film about the sadomasochistic fantasies of a young man, it is quickly passed over in the critical literature. Is it a joke? An attempt to undercut the pathos of the scene? An ironic jab at the well-worn image of the heart as organic seat of the emotions? What is its connection with the brutal sexual awakening that is the main subject of the work? And with the illumination and fulfillment that follow the assault? The gauge remains a recalcitrant element that resists integration. The same could be said of Marie Menken's fondness for glitter, dust, sand, paper shreds, and other scraps that dance animatedly in her films. One could easily connect these materials, and Menken's pixilated images, to various traditions in art and film history. But it would be harder to factor in sexuality and affect into these accounts, even knowing that these films were the work of an unconventional heterosexual woman many of whose most intense relationships were with gay men, from Anger himself to her husband Willard Maas. And what role does sexuality play in Harry Smith's *Heaven and Earth Magic*? Its dizzyingly mutable ensembles of late nineteenth-century furnishings, clothes, ornaments,

Experimental Film and Queer Materiality. Juan A. Suárez, Oxford University Press. © Oxford University Press 2024.
DOI: 10.1093/oso/9780197566992.003.0001

2 EXPERIMENTAL FILM AND QUEER MATERIALITY

and mechanical parts reference Jewish mysticism, magic, astronomy, and the memoirs of Dr. Daniel Schreber, the famous schizophrenic studied by Sigmund Freud; but no attention has been paid to the sexual and gender politics of the film's unstable corporealities. The same could be said about Mike and George Kuchar: they have seldom been explored as "queer" filmmakers even if their work clamors for such an approach. But where does their queerness lie? Sexuality is the object of bemused parody in their work, which evinces a strong fixation with the excremental and with the delirious quality of the material culture of their childhood, dominated by low-grade plastics in colorful designs. While not transparently sexual, these elements are integral to their queer aesthetic and would therefore need to be considered when elucidating the sexual politics of their work—but what is the sexuality of plastics and gaudy bric-a-brac? And what is the queer import of the material, nonhuman aspects of Warhol's films—the grain, the unusual durations, the zooming and strobe cuts, the abundant noise? How do these contribute to the queerness of queer film at large? In many ways these components remain out of the range of queer analysis because until recently this last has tended to favor subjectivity while failing to address elements such as Anger's meter, Menken's glitter and sand, Smith's deranged mechanisms and esoteric objects, the Kuchar's plastics, and Warhol's emphasis on grain, duration, or noise—elements that are material, contingent, nonhuman, and apparently peripheral to sexuality. But should one so limit inquiry? Is it legitimate to confine sex to subjectivity and human corporeality while eliding its contingent material incarnations, solicitations, and detours?

The notion that experimental film has been a crucial vehicle for the articulation and dissemination of queer identities and communities is a familiar one and has driven much extraordinary work in both film and cultural studies in recent decades. Scholars, such as Richard Dyer and others working in his wake, have shown how the experimental screen, under cover of marginality and the alibi of artistic value, delved into proscribed sexual iconography and experience.[1] Not only what was on screen but screenings themselves, which gathered bohemians and unconventionals of all stripes in search of unusual visual fare, frequently provided an occasion for queer communal affirmation.[2] A less familiar claim, which I am making the central point of this book, is that experimental film channeled a particular perception of the modern everyday that I am calling "queer materiality." Queer materiality designates the material side of queerness—the manner in which the mixture of sexual and social alterity that we have been calling "queer" for over three decades now is intimately embedded in the objects, technologies, substances, and spaces that make up the hardware of experience. Conversely, "queer materiality" also denotes the queer side of material: an odd animacy in the things of the world, manifest in the way in which substances and materials have acted as catalysts, conduits, or relays for sexual and corporeal dissent, prompting, inspiring, or invoking wayward bodies and behaviors.[3] Due to its discrepant aesthetic, to its marginality, which allowed it to escape strict supervision, and to the camera's ability to capture or simulate life's unfolding, experimental film has been a privileged medium for foregrounding the materiality of queerness and the queerness of material.

Such heightened attention to matter runs counter to most studies of experimental film and to much queer analysis. Both fields have privileged various types of subjectivity in their approaches—the exalted individuality of the independent auteur or the intricacies of queer identification. Queer analysis in particular—whether of film or of other media—has tended to treat "queerness" under the rubrics of identity, subjectivity, and community, giving it a thoroughly anthropomorphic outline that has only recently begun to be contested. This contestation was spearheaded by material feminism's engagement with science studies and ecocritical perspectives—in work by Karen Barad, Elizabeth Grosz, and Stacy Alaimo, among others—and has been continued in explorations of the queer nonhuman—by Jack Halberstam, Susan Stryker, Jeffrey J. Cohen, or Mel Y. Chen, to name just a few—that have sought to distance themselves from "the anthropic"—Stryker's term—in search of expanded conceptions of agency, relationality, and community.[4] In line with these critiques, a recurring argument in the pages that follow is that alongside its involvement with the notion of the singular self, queer sexuality involves as well a material and experiential horizon beyond individual bodies, subjects, and identities. Experimental cinema has provided multiple figurations of a nonhuman (queer) libido, and the overall goal of this book will be to explore some of these depictions in order to establish their intellectual and artistic genealogies, analyze their formal contours, assess their politics, and ascertain their usefulness for imagining a more emancipated present and future.

Most of my examples belong to a formative period in the development of both experimental cinema and queer culture: the years running from World War II to the early eighties. This period spans the emergence and institutional consolidation of a second wave of experimental filmmaking in North America, Europe, and parts of Latin America—notably Argentina,

Brazil, and Mexico—and the increase of gay and lesbian visibility, a trend that culminates with the launching of the Gay Liberation Movement in the early 1970s. While this is my primary temporal frame, I will also look beyond this relatively self-contained era at more recent work that prolongs and inflects the styles and concerns of that earlier moment. Most of my examples come from the United States, yet in keeping with the transnational quality of the avant-garde and queer cultures, they will be considered in a global network of connection and influence. Some of the filmmakers I will be studying are well-known figures, such as Andy Warhol, Jack Smith, Kenneth Anger, Marie Menken, Ken Jacobs, Barbara Hammer, Harry Smith, and the Kuchar brothers, while others have yet to receive significant critical attention—as in the case of Ron Rice, Sara Kathryn Arledge, Jim Davis, Tom Chomont, Teo Hernández, Jim Hubbard, Ashley Hans Scheirl, and Ursula Pürrer. By regarding their work through the prism of queer materiality, I will provide new readings of their work and will place them in a strand of film and queer culture that remains to be thoroughly theorized and historicized.

One of my conclusions will be that the queerness of experimental film has little to do with identity politics, that is, with the struggle for self-definition and self-assertion of much of 1970s and 1980s gay, lesbian, and feminist militancy. Furthermore, because of its non-anthropomorphism and its investment in the object world, the queer register of avant-garde cinema has little to do even with the "queerness" postulated by much queer inquiry, a queerness that has taken subjectivity (however contingent, historicized, mediated, and materialized) as pivot of analysis.

Queer experimental cinema imagines a world where sexuality does not start or end in subjects, even if subjects are certainly *there*, caught in the networks as way stations and junctions. Queer experimental film pictures sexuality as a connective force that brings together human and nonhuman, animate and inanimate—merely heuristic distinctions—in complex hybrid configurations. Sexuality originates in and activates materials that are peripheral to the (human) body and the self-enclosed subject but contain and involve both. A short list of the materials featured at some length in this book are plastics, dust, glitter, fabrics, excrement, photographic grain, television scan lines and pixels, amphetamine, garbage, mechanical ensembles, and several kinds of noise (visual, aural, cybernetic). Their importance to queer cinema—to cinema at large—has not been sufficiently shown, and neither has been their importance to a radical theory of sexuality. Experimental film forces us to conceptualize the queer potential of these peripheries of

INTRODUCTION. SEXUALITY ON THE OUTSIDE 5

sexuality: their ability to produce and sustain eccentric erotic alignments and desires and to reconfigure our understanding of our immediate environment and our modes of inhabiting it. Rather than focus on subjects and their desires—which we have done long enough—we may want to follow the example of experimental artists and filmmakers in giving serious consideration to the libidinal intensities triggered off by the promiscuous solicitations of the object world.

This slight change of optic will help to expand current paradigms in queer thought. It seems fair to say that, from the beginning, queer studies has pursued a remapping of subjectivity and a revolutionary recasting of gender and sexuality: of gender as a performative act lacking substantive essence (Judith Butler's famous contention) and of sexuality as a central category in the definition of the modern subject, a category that has been crucial to the arbitration of citizenship, civil rights, and legal status (as demonstrated most influentially by Michel Foucault and Gayle Rubin).[5] More recently, queer scholarship has been concerned with class, ethnicity, and nationality; with the temporalities and spatialities of heterodox sexuality; with the transnational and global dimensions of queerness; and with its (mis)alignment with the scientific and health apparatuses.[6]

Whatever the differences in methodology and scope between these lines of inquiry, practically all of them share a number of assumptions: that sexuality is an attribute of subjects; that it is primarily staged on and by human bodies; and that it is an intersubjective transaction that may involve at times material-technological interfaces (in cybersex, telephone sex). What is often missing from this picture is the nonhuman horizon of the sexual: the fact that alongside subjects, sexuality involves an expansive rapport with substances, objects, and locations, and therefore constantly engages, and is engaged by, horizons that are not exclusively (trans)subjective or corporeal. As Jeffrey J. Cohen put it in *Medieval Identity Machines*, it is somewhat puzzling that "a critical movement predicated upon the smashing of boundary should limit itself to the small contours of the human form, as if the whole of the body could be contained in the porous embrace of the skin."[7] In many ways, Sara Ahmed's queer phenomenology broke important ground by showing that sexual orientation is never a merely subjective trait, but involves as well an orientation toward the material horizon, which queerness in particular has a way of rearranging and rendering oblique, puzzling, opaque, and newly traversable.[8] And more recently, in their introduction to the "Queer Inhumanisms" special issue of *GLQ*, Dana Luciano and Mel Y. Chen have

6 EXPERIMENTAL FILM AND QUEER MATERIALITY

pointed out that the tendency to identify sexuality with genitality and to locate queerness primarily in relation to the human body and sexuality hinders our ability to imagine other forms of "intrahuman connection" and "trans/material attachment."[9]

There are important reasons to go beyond the comfortable, if self-limiting, embrace of the human form. In a well-known interview given to the French magazine *Gai pied* in 1981, Michel Foucault pointed out that the most radical effects of unorthodox sexuality do not lie in the practice of sex itself nor in "identifying with the psychological traits and the visible masks of the homosexual" (or lesbian, or transgender, or transsexual, or sadomasochist, we might add).[10] Insisting on these has the strategic value of emphasizing visibility and self-affirmation. However, visibility, affirmation, and sexual openness locate sexuality in a precisely circumscribed terrain from where it speaks endlessly about itself, yielding knowledge that, in the last instance, might facilitate the production and control of deviant communities by the medical and political establishments. Rather than confine and circumscribe homosexuality to "the ready-made formulas of the pure sexual encounter and the lovers' fusion of identities," which the fabric of conventional society could easily accommodate, Foucault proposed using the desires that homosexuality unleashed to unravel this fabric—to generate unscripted, noninstitutionalized affective links and produce, ultimately, an alternative "way of life."[11] A "way of life" based on unprecedented styles of friendship and community still remains inside an intersubjective frame. Yet the "affective and relational virtualities" that "homosexuality"—any unorthodox sexuality—might bring about could well extend to matter and materiality and to libidos, eroticisms, and relations no longer exclusively dependent on people but also relayed, catalyzed, or generated through things. Across this intermediate human-material horizon spreads, to return to Ahmed, "the 'nonresidence' of queer": its failure to reside in either particular bodies or objects and its dependence instead on what she named a "mutuality of support."[12]

A benefit from the awareness of matter at large (a queer *parti pris de choses*, to invoke François Ponge) is a more accurate knowledge of the workings of sexuality, which always responds to changes in the material horizon of everyday life. If sex is, to recall Judith Butler, "part of a regulatory practice that produces the bodies it governs" and makes them intelligible in relation to the social norm, it is hard to see how this regulatory production, which she describes as a "materialization," would operate untouched by fashions,

INTRODUCTION. SEXUALITY ON THE OUTSIDE   7

technology, pharmaceuticals, materials, or things.[13] The materiality that Butler contemplates is that of human bodies called into being by discursive injunction (bodies properly sexed, gendered, and socialized) *and* their refuted obverse: an "excluded domain that comes to bound and to haunt the field of intelligible body life" (51). She exemplifies this obverse as an unformalized, unsignifiable corporeality at times embodied in the animal, the woman, the slave, as well as in various national, racial, and geographical others (52). To this realm would also belong the world's mundane materiality, but it is not acknowledged in Butler's account. Its tacit suppression keeps Butler's characterization of sexuality and gender human- or at least bio-centered, (inter)subjective, and psychological.[14] From her anthropomorphic perspective, sexual and gender performativity internalize "hegemonic norms," always described as speech acts; drag performs "*the sign*"—but not the materials—of gender (237); gender is a play "between psyche and appearance," where the latter includes "what appears *in words*" (234) but apparently in little else; the body is an inscription surface only inscribed through citations of the law but not worked over by its dispersed instrumentality (107–111); and the subject's assumption and subversion of the existing sexual imaginary seems to operate in a material void. This is not, however, to reject Butler's incisive analysis, which, to be fair, was a theoretical elucidation of sexuality and therefore entitled to a degree of abstraction and not a material ethnography in the style of Daniel Miller and his school.[15] I am only drawing attention to what Butler's discourse excludes—the material horizon—in order to attempt, following her words, "to refigure the necessary 'outside'" of her critique as "a future horizon . . . in which the violence of exclusion is perpetually in the process of being overcome" (53). Such overcoming would require, first, drawing attention to the exclusion that grounds the terms of her analysis and, second, letting the excluded other—the repressed thing-horizon; "what is merely material"—"begin to signify" so that we can redefine sexuality, materiality, and the relations between both.[16]

Matter did signify eloquently in the intensely aestheticized consumer capitalism that emerged in North Atlantic societies after World War II. The centrality of design, commodity display, advertising, packaging, and brand identity, and the profusion of new materials (e.g. the boom in plastics and synthetics during the middle decades of the twentieth century) effectively reinvented the quotidian and heightened what Walter Benjamin had called in the 1930s "the sex appeal of the inorganic."[17] To this sex appeal bear witness contemporaneous art and literary movements such as the *nouveau rèalisme*,

8 EXPERIMENTAL FILM AND QUEER MATERIALITY

junk and installation art, pop art, the French *nouveau roman*, minimalism—which made ample use of industrial materials—and concrete and electronic music, but also semiotics—Roland Barthes's and Jean Baudrillard's captivating dissections of everyday objects and icons—and critical theory—Henri Lefebvre's studies of everyday life in the modern world.[18] Lefebvre notes in one of these volumes: "Now it is the object that plays the lead, not in its objectivity (which had meaning only in relation to the subject) but as a thing, almost a pure form."[19]

The complex, alluring, at times exasperatingly banal material horizon explored by post-World War II artists and intellectuals was not a mere neutral backdrop against which sexuality unfolded. On the contrary, this new world of things triggered off many pleasures, fantasies, investments, and affects. "The spontaneous androgyny of [1960s] unisex fashions did more for the boundless expansion of masculine pleasure than all the demonstrations," claims the (brazenly male-centered) off-screen commentary in Guy Hocquenghem and Lionel Soukaz's film *Race d'Ep* (1979). Warhol recalls that by the end of the 1960s "[m]achinery had already taken over people's sex lives—dildos and all kinds of vibrators."[20] In a classic study of female impersonators researched roughly around the same years Warhol evokes, Esther Newton noticed that many of her subjects were using hormone shots—a product of postwar medical technology—and plastic inserts to change the shape of their bodies.[21] To a great extent both Warhol and Newton's drag queens inhabited a new regime of bodies and pleasures forged during the war and immediate postwar years. Susan Stryker and Paul B. Preciado have shown that these decades ushered in what Preciado has called a "pharmaco-pornographic" capitalism in which the body and sexual energy became main raw materials to be meted out and regulated.[22] New chemicals and surgical techniques allowed the fine-tuning of mood, hormonal balance, sexual rhythm, and corporeal morphology; they brought about new idioms in sexuality and personality and created new bodily configurations—the post-op transsexual, most famously embodied at the time by Christine Jorgensen.

These examples show that it is not always easy to determine where sex, bodies, or subjects start and chemicals and materials end in recent history; that one cannot possibly talk about sexuality—let alone queer sexuality—in late modernity and still remain in the embrace of (organic, human) skin or even in the ideality of such categories as subjectivity and identity. If early modernity put sex at the center of individual definition, as Michel Foucault once showed, mid-twentieth century material culture propitiated its scattering and

INTRODUCTION. SEXUALITY ON THE OUTSIDE   9

dissolution across the world. And in this centrifugal push, subjects and sex endlessly knocked against matter, forever losing their recognizable outlines in the scrimmage. Pitching Bruno Latour in a queer key, one could state that sexuality in late modernity turned out to be full of things, while things were themselves full of desires and sexual possibility.[23] Michael Warner accurately sized up the situation: "new fields of sexual autonomy come about through new technologies: soap, razors, the pill, condoms, diaphragms, Viagra, lubricants, implants, steroids, videotape, vibrators, nipple clamps, violet wands, hormones, sex assignment surgeries, and others we can't yet predict."[24]

We may stand to gain much from applying to the study of sexuality— and to the sexuality of experimental cinema—the kind of re-centering that actor-network theory and so-called new materialisms have applied to the study of sociology and science. Such re-centering consists in granting material mediators—physical objects, architectural structures, laboratory equipment, animals, chemical substances, environments—the ability to generate practices and knowledge. To recall Latour's and Michel Serres's terms, social practice does not result from autonomous active subjects acting on passive objects; it arises from "collectivities" of "quasi-subjects" and "quasi-objects" operating together in collaborative networks.[25] Because "one cannot construct the social with the social," we need things, states Latour.[26] Similarly, because one does not have sex with sexuality alone, sexual fantasies and acts involve a thick web of actuality—sites, fabrics, objects, styles of bodily and material habitation, sounds, images, and texts.

These elements are not simply inert. In sexuality, as in other realms of practice, it is important to keep in mind what Jane Bennett has called "thing power": "the material agency or effectivity of nonhuman or not-quite-human things."[27] Brushing against objects, queerness not only evinces its dependence on matter; it also brings out certain oddness in things. This "oddness" could be described as a sort of residue that exists beyond recognizable appearance and use, an instability manifest, for example, in objects' sexual valence—the way in which things may become part of complex networks of relation and affect. This uncertain aspect in things and materials is translated in the films I will be exploring in this book into various forms of nonlinear motility such as oscillation, quiver, and intermittence—forms of movement-in-place that evoke a subterranean agitation in matter. Examples are Marie Menken's animated objects, sand, beads, and light; the grain that boils on the surface of the image in underground films of the sixties and seventies and

10   EXPERIMENTAL FILM AND QUEER MATERIALITY

later examples of queer cinema; the morphing machinery and humanoids in Harry Smith's films; the spastic, tumbling bodies that populate the films of the Kuchar brothers; the plastic discards and disreputable materials that Jack Smith used to forge his queer tropicalist fantasies; the glitter that covers films by Teo Hernández, Stéphane Marti, or Carles Comas; and the noise that envelops the work of Lionel Soukaz, Abigal Child, and Asheley Hans Scheirl and Ursula Pürrer, among others. The intense, nonpurposive vibrations of these elements evoke the libidinal power of matter, the fact that all things and textures may become quickened by sexual energy.

Sexuality Outside

Psychoanalysis provided ample evidence of the sexual latency of the material world, a latency that traverses Sigmund Freud and Melanie Klein's writings. Freud's *The Psychopathology of Everyday Life* (1900) showed that the speech, props, and routes of daily existence were the signs of an unceasing utterance that bespoke unavowed desires and emotions.[28] "Fetishism" (1927) explained how sexual intensity was transferred from the genital area to pieces of clothing or body parts (hair, feet).[29] And the foundational "Analysis of a Phobia in a Five-Year Old Boy" (1909), an early formulation of the Oedipus complex, revealed that the sexuality of a young analysand involved a human cast (his immediate family and relations), but also animals, riding implements, vehicles, locations (loading docks, the zoo, the bedroom, the bathroom), excrement, and movement (train travel but also the movement of the body at play and of horses in the streets).[30] Similarly, Klein's early writings proposed that school activities, teachers, school subjects, the streets leading to the school, and school buildings and fixtures (daises, blackboards, desks) frequently become charged with "sexual" or "coitus" significance for children.[31]

The mechanism that underpins these associations is symbol-formation, which, in Ernest Jones's influential summation, connects disparate entities through a perceived similarity that is sexually motivated and (therefore) unconscious.[32] For Klein, as for much classical psychoanalysis, symbolization is the central procedure in sublimation—the mechanism that divests libidinal fixations of their explicit sexual character. But rather than as divestment, it may be more accurate to regard symbolization and sublimation as sexuality in a different register: as the transfer of sensual and affective intensity (Klein's

INTRODUCTION. SEXUALITY ON THE OUTSIDE 11

"sum of affect") to purportedly non-sexual body parts, activities, locations, or objects.[33]

Transfers, connections, and displacements are indeed all there is in sexuality. While in his *Three Essays on the Theory of Sexuality* (1905), Freud recalled that the turn of sexuality toward the material world was widely regarded a "perversion"—a deviation of the sexual instinct from its "natural" genital goal—he also pointed out that "perversion" is merely an extension of "normal" sexual behavior.[34] Genitality is itself a displacement from an earlier libidinal fixation on the earliest locations of pleasure: the mouth and the anus ("orifices lined with mucus"). Moving from the mouth and the anus to the genitals, and from there, through the power of Klein's "coitus significance," to virtually anything, sexuality is the most labile of instincts, as it may be satisfied with a great variety of objects.[35] It is also the most abstract: not defined by goal or direction, it is, at its most elemental, sheer intensity—the "overvaluation" of a particular object that becomes the target of psychic investment.[36] In this light, "perversion" turns out to express the truth of sexuality as an intensity that may be located in any body part or in any *thing* and can be endlessly transferred and repositioned in expansive relational chains. This is the ultimate reason why Lacan claimed that there is no such a thing as a sexual relationship, since sexuality—at least for humans—is endlessly mediated through symbolic stand-ins that impede limpid access to a purported organic core of sex.[37] And this is why at the same time, in apparent contradiction, nothing escapes the pull of sexuality since anything may become an object of desire—from the most sublime face to a pile of excrement.[38]

Useful as psychoanalysis is for its inventory of sexual effects, it also has considerable limitations that stem from its conceptual provisos (it regarded sexuality on subjective and inter-subjective terms only) and historicity (it emerged at a time when the traditional nuclear family was much more central than it is today). Because of these biases, classical psychoanalysis tended to refer the material attachments of the libido back to the structure of the family, the confines of the self, and to organic bodies marked by a binary gender economy. Thing affections and libidinal projections always end up symbolizing the family circle, dominated by its Oedipal dynamics and bodies concerned with shoring up their own phallic completeness and warding off castration. And yet, the libido's extraordinary capacity to create endless lines of connection across the world can only with considerable interpretive violence be brought back to family, anthropomorphic embodiment, and intrapsychic drama.

12 EXPERIMENTAL FILM AND QUEER MATERIALITY

This is the criticism that Gilles Deleuze and Félix Guattari leveled against psychoanalysis more than five decades ago: that it reduced the multiple affects of the libido to the family triangle, discrete subjectivity, and binary sexual difference. Psychoanalysis remained fixated on Oedipal development and linear libidinal evolution, sanctioning these concepts with the same gestures that it used to criticize and relativize them. And it disconnected the subject and its sexuality from the social, political, and material worlds. In the last instance, psychoanalysis offered, in Deleuze and Guattari's colorful terms: "The dirty little secret in place of the wide-open spaces glimpsed for a moment. . . Interiority in place of a new relationship to the outside."[39] What was necessary to keep track of the material, supra-subjective quality of the libido was a theory of sexuality that remained "outside": that would not read desire in terms of transcendental tropes of subjectivity, interiority or anthropomorphic corporeality, nor turn libidinal investment into a key to subjective truth or to some sort of identity.

Deleuze and Guattari's *Anti-Oedipus* sought to provide such a theory. According to them, the libido operates by means of endless, unpredictable junctions with no beginning, end, or direction. Its dominant trope is the machine, a conjunction of interlocking parts driven by energies that traverse it and open it up to other mechanisms. Libidinal machines do not make up discrete wholes but molecular ensembles that might, however, be coerced back into unitary entities, or, in Deleuze–Guattari's contagious jargon, into "molarities," "paranoid reinscriptions," or "reterritorializations." The task of a critical project that takes seriously the boundless productivity of the libido— a project they call "schizoanalysis"—would be to show that even the most apparently stable, self-enclosed units are in fact machine-like polymorphs engineered by the connective force of desire, whose procreant character is designated by Deleuze and Guattari as "desiring-production" (*AO* 322 and ff.).

Libidinal machines are not ideal or metaphorical, but real and material. They emerge on the surface of the world, or socius—the "body without organs" (without organization and coordinates) or "plane of immanence" on which desire inscribes its paths (*AO* 327) or "lines of the universe."[40] These paths involve the small and the large: discrete elements, such as things, sounds, spaces, languages, and images as well as the collective repertoires resulting from the conjunctions of these elements, such as ethnicities, industrial processes, economic forces, social classes, and "history"—not a chronological record but an image reservoir and a source of intensities relocated

INTRODUCTION. SEXUALITY ON THE OUTSIDE   13

("plugged") onto the body. The libido is "the direct investment of masses, of large aggregates, and of social and organic fields" and desire is always "group desire": an omnivorous collective formation that metabolizes the things and histories of the world and the "flows of life and society" (*AO* 292–293).

A schizoanalytic take on fetishism, for example, would eschew the binary Freudian schematic of the phallic and the castrated, the penis and its substitutes, the male and the female, the reality of the flesh and its phantasmatic projections, and might look very much like Gayle Rubin's description of the concept: a molecular formation where histories, iconographic repertoires, and objects intersect, where singular bodies give way to intensities scattered across a plurality of material supports.

> I do not see how one can talk about fetishism, or sadomasochism, without thinking about the production of rubber, the techniques and gear used for controlling and riding horses, the high polished gleam of military footwear, the history of silk stockings, the cold authoritative qualities of medical equipment, or the allure of motorcycles and the elusive liberties of leaving the city for the open road. For that matter, how can we think about fetishism without the impact of cities, of certain streets and parks, of red-light districts and "cheap amusements," or the seductions of department store counters, piled high with desirable and glamorous goods? To me fetishism raises all sorts of issues concerning shifts in the manufacture of objects, the historical and social specificities of control and skin and social etiquette, or ambiguously experienced body invasions and minutely graduated hierarchies. If all of this complex social information is reduced to castration or the Oedipus complex or knowing or not knowing what one is not supposed to know, I think something important has been lost.[41]

Molecular, material, non-anthropomorphic, and historical, the machines engineered by desire do not have a gender, but a plurality of ever-shifting genders, nor a predetermined sexuality beyond the desire for connection: "Sexuality is badly explained by the binary organization of the sexes, and just as badly by a binary organization within each sex. . . [It] is the production of a thousand sexes, which are so many uncontrollable becomings."[42] It is all a matter of temporary affiliations, "unnatural alliances," and passages through intensive states. Yet all this mobility is frequently brought back to stabilities of identity or sexual orientation. At times, such reduction is justified in the name of political pragmatism, yet the price to pay is a hardening of supple possibilities for invention and action. This is why the revolutionary or reactionary character of a particular sexual community or emancipatory movement cannot be decided on the basis of their allegiance to a particular practice or object choice, but on the basis of their respect for the molecular functioning of the libido. (*AO* 350) Deleuze and Guattari saw already in the early years of gay and lesbian liberation that homosexuality or lesbianism could easily become repressive precipitations of desire unless they were used to promote fluidity and multiplicity—transversal drifts across the social field (*AO* 350–351).

Transversality does not exclude the occasional crystallization of desire: "[M]olecular escapes and movements would be nothing if they did not return to the molar organizations to reshuffle their segments, their binary distributions of sexes, classes, and parties."[43] At the same time, the limitless libidinal flight has its dangers. It carries within itself the possibility of pure abolition in the form of a passion for war, self-destruction, and death whose clearest historical incarnation is fascism.[44] The liberating potential of sexuality lies then in the combination of potentially endless mobility and occasional arrests; in the way in which its lines of flight and investments may be used to rethink society, ethics, and politics in ever more open-ended, pluralistic directions. Or, to borrow momentarily from Guy Hocquenghem, a thinker influenced by Deleuze, sexuality is conceptually and politically productive if we follow "the descending line of desire as far as it will go" and create, along the way, "non-limitative, horizontal relations."[45] This is exactly what defines queerness: an extraordinarily productive libido that refuses to confine itself to an interiorized sexuality or to distinct subjectivities, and brings into play ample sectors of the social field, along with their vast panoply of props, gadgets, and accoutrements.

Such sexuality unfolds along the horizontal axis of planar relations. Its dominant trope is adjacency—what Eve K. Sedgwick has called *beside*. Unlike the prepositions "beneath," "behind," or "beyond," which suggest transcendence or teleology, "beside" designates the looser, additive work of desire on a field of immanence. It involves vicinity and tactile immediacy rather than the detachment of vision and demands "ecological or systems approaches" capable of communicating in detail the "intensive and defining relationality" of sexual and social encounters.[46] Sex then will then not be necessarily about buttressing imaginary wholes and struggling for a phantasmatic completeness, but about forms of enfoldment and connectivity that often bring the material into play.

From this perspective, the objéctum sexuals that act out their love and desire for objects, monuments, buildings, and architectural features are not replacing the human or (even more crudely) trying to annex an unattainable lost phallus. Their sexuality, Amber Jamilla Musser suggests, bypasses genitality and reduces sex to its most basic figure: the exchange of sensation and energy between surfaces.[47] Jennifer Terry sees in one of its most frequent avatars, monument love, a form of public sex—a "perverse nationalism" that literalizes the state's injunction to love objects of patriotic reverence by desiring them physically and wanting to rub against them.[48] Similarly, fetish substances do not restore corporeal wholeness or screen off the threat of castration but bring the body into formerly uncharted proximities. Leather, claims Pat Califia, is "atavistic, preindustrial, and romantic," and links up with the animal world—"the werewolf and the outlaw dressed in the skins of predators." And latex brings on "the futuristic, technological, science fictional" and "metahuman": "with a gas mask or goggles, someone in a latex suit becomes an insect or an alien."[49] Both leather and latex offer lines of escape from the human form and generate different "besidenesses" in which affect is scattered across a sentient continuum that no longer segregates human from thing. Mel Y. Chen has powerfully described a different modality of besideness, prompted not by fetish attachments but by Chen's susceptibility to toxicity. In themselves paragons of "nextness," since they are inextricably embedded in the body, toxins confine Chen to the couch and domestic environment for prolonged periods, prompting a style of closeness "that does not differentiate, is not dependent on a heartbeat": "In such a toxic period, anyone or anything that I manage to feel any kind of connection with, whether it's my cat or a chair of a friend or a plant or a stranger or my partner, I think they are, and remember they are, all the same ontological thing."[50] Far from disabling, Chen's toxicity is a generative condition; it heightens their affective range and allows them to engage "the queer inanimate socialities that exist beyond the fetish, beyond the animate, beyond the pure clash of human body sex."[51]

The Politics of Material

Privileging this para-human domain in sexuality might seem a politically evasive maneuver. It might appear as an attempt to avoid dealing with the complexities of trauma, vulnerability, and loss, all of which are deeply scored

16 EXPERIMENTAL FILM AND QUEER MATERIALITY

into the flesh, or with such messy marks of "the human" as race, ethnicity, gender, sexuality, and citizenship precisely when they have finally managed to command considerable attention in academia and beyond. Many of the main political battles in recent history have been fought around these issues, which remain hotly contested today. In fact, some of the most trenchant intellectual queer work in recent years has taken the form of queer of color critiques around these still highly sensitive areas.[52] The focus on materiality in this book should not be taken to imply that subjectivity, "the human," and their effects ought to be no longer a concern—far from it. For one, scholars such as Mel Y. Chen, Zakkiyah Iman Jackson, and Uri McMillan, among others, have shown how the variable adjudication of humanness has played—and continues to play—a fundamental role in the racial and cognitive hierarchies used to justify colonial violence and the forms of cultural and ethnic supremacy that serve as its alibis.[53] Ethnic, sexual, social, and colonial others have routinely been collapsed with various modes of animality and thingness. In response, these others have also critiqued and deposed prevailing conceptions of the human formulated from an ethnocentric perspective. And they have used their presumed proximity to animality and thingness as an epistemic launchpad for inventive worldings, epistemologies, and styles of being and relating. In fact, the films to be studied in the following pages do exactly that: rather than protest the relegation of queerness to a realm beyond the human, they occupy that margin to redraw the conceptual maps that made such relegation possible in the first instance and to reinvent, in the process, sexuality, togetherness, and collectivity. From a different perspective, precisely because the marks of the human and its embattled attribution remain as operative as ever, it is easy to forget that the politics of identity, nation, race, rights, and belonging rise from—and lean on—molecular investments and formations that often have a material character: images, fashions, objects, and gestures through which we channel our identifications and aspirations.

This is all the truer for queers. Historically suppressed, queerness lacks protected spaces, institutional seats, and formal archives. It has historically traveled discreetly, as José Muñoz has pointed out, under cover of fleeting contact and short-lived practices and gestures, and has lodged in ephemera, which form an alternative archive of queer existence.[54] The archive of the ephemeral prompts "alternative forms of textuality and narrativity," such as memory, which, in opposition to history, entails contingent, fragmentary reminiscence and performance, not only in the artistic space of the gallery

INTRODUCTION. SEXUALITY ON THE OUTSIDE   17

but also in the presentational mode of the dance floor, the bar, the party, the cruising site, the street. Ephemeral queer acts do not yield "epistemological foundations" or solid evidence of the kind favored by traditional history but "traces, glimmers, residues, and specks of things."[55] Things indeed, since, as Muñoz maintains, ephemera may not be "solid" but they are "material": they involve the body; temporary spaces; perishable, discarded, ruined, damaged, or purportedly risky substances, such as drugs; and images and objects suffused with affect that work as placeholders of emotion. Because of their very evanescence, queer acts take hold of whatever lies at hand, which is mostly the stuff of the everyday.

The stuff of the everyday is also the fulcrum of the political. Through stuff affect becomes visible, sharable, collective, and public. As Sara Ahmed and Ann Cvetkovich have stressed with different emphases, affect and emotion are not merely personal mental states, but social and political formations. Affective life, writes Cvetkovich, is "an index of public cultures and social systems," and emotional experience is always inevitably social.[56] Affects and emotions energize public cultures that have the potential of transforming commonality and nursing new ways of living and doing. But neither emotional nor social experience unfold in a void; they rise from, and are conveyed by, material mediators and might remain unidentifiable without them, or at least deprived of the significant leverage these mediators provide. Affect becomes recognizable in the archives it generates—archives of feelings that, as Cvetkovich shows, are also sites of public culture, communal convergence, shared attachments and aspirations, and political transformation.

Politics is only possible on the immanent, molecular level of concrete practice and materiality. One does not engage structures, identities, "power," or global agents head on; one starts at a particular time and place with whatever is at hand: staging a sit-in or a zap action, occupying a space, spreading a confrontational chant or a message, making noise, stripping in front of a camera or a cop, or submitting to a dangerous but exciting liaison. One always builds from the bottom up. "Action," writes Latour, "is only possible in a territory that has been opened up, flattened down, and cut to size; in a place where formats, structures, globalization, and totalities circulate inside tiny conduits, and where for each of their applications they need to rely on masses of hidden potentialities. If this is not possible, then there is no politics."[57]

There is no politics either if we only resort to discursively conveyed ideas and convictions. Politics is not only ideational content and articulated message but acting in complex ecologies where language and media representations, but also bodies, things, and various substances and materials, enter variable relations in human/nonhuman assemblages. It is incarnated in ways of doing, talking, dressing, acting, and wearing one's hair; in a language or an image repertoire; in the attachment to particular landscapes and concrete experiences. Susan Bordo and Kobina Mercer, among others, have analyzed black hairstyles as an often undertheorized material means for staging and signifying "blackness." Hairstyles convey vying views of race and community; have different histories, genealogies, and social resonances; and bring into play concrete locations and practices of care—from the semipublic space of the hair salon to the intimate gatherings where Bordo and other mothers of black children trade tips and develop a sense of connection around the care of their children's hair.[58] For her part, Susanne Bost has incisively shown that sickness and the material entanglement in the medical apparatus prompted Gloria Anzaldúa and Cherríe Moraga to remap their Chicanisma. Anzaldúa's diabetes, which forced her into a routine of medical checks, blood tests, needles, and chemicals, and Moraga's intimacy with the incubator and life-monitoring devices that kept her premature baby alive, led them to reroute their identities beyond the self-containment of the skin and traditional communal bonds. Wounds, body openings, incisions, feeding tubes, and connections, rather than "universalizing identities," rerouted their conceptions of self and their politics: "[T]he theoretical impulse of *mestiza* consciousness—synthesizing bloods and juggling differences—becomes concrete, imperative, and immediate with syringes and blood sugar levels."[59] These examples show that abstract constructs such as ethnicity, community, subjectivity, and identity are always divisible into momentary conjunctions of locations, materials, and sensory inputs in a given then-and-there. Without such concrete instantiations, these constructs dissolve into disembodied, foggy generalities. Or they retrench into the defensive policing of group boundaries. After all, identity categories and conceptions of the self retroactively bind scattered practices and objects into unifying wholes and grant isolated intensities a vector of meaning. Abstract categories lift into the realm of the general ("being" black, queer, or Spanish) the proliferating particularity that constitutes—in Latour's term, "gathers"—the social field.

Turning toward the material, then, is not avoiding politics—sexual or otherwise—but changing its scale; pulling it down from the lofty strata it frequently inhabits to a level where it may actually be seen and touched. Such downscaling shows, for Oskar Negt and Alexander Kluge, "the materialist instinct of the proletariat"—a term that might be understood, outside

INTRODUCTION. SEXUALITY ON THE OUTSIDE 19

the classical Marxist frame, as synonymous with "subalterns" of any kind. In Negt and Kluge's words: "Radicalism in analysis and struggle can only be intensified downward. It is a bourgeois reflex to process it upward, toward ideas, platforms, and authorities. The only reliable means of penetrating this veil is the 'materialist instinct' of the masses. In fact, this instinct acts as the emergency brake that brings the entire train to a halt, as is proven in the case of all counter-revolutions."[60]

Besides faithfulness to the mechanics of political engagement, there is an ethical wager in the heightened attention to material aggregates. Philosophers such as Theodor Adorno have pointed out that the oppression of human (and nonhuman) collectivities rests on the inherent violence of reason. Reason, Adorno claims, abstracts cognition from a tangle of sensation and matter; these make cognition possible but, at the same time, also obfuscate it, and must therefore be repressed as the dross that threatens the purity of the concept. Reason's oppositional stance toward sensorial and material otherness becomes, in turn, the model for relating to other human groups: "If a man looks upon thingness as radical evil, if he would like to dynamize all entity into pure actuality, he tends to be hostile to others, to the alien thing that has lent its name to alienation, and not in vain."[61] Reconciliation with otherness could come about through a "love of things" that respects their difference "beyond the heterogeneous and beyond that which is one's own."[62]

The difference of things "beyond that which is one's own" resides in part in their dynamism and creativity, qualities that were erased in the traditional ontologies that separated sovereign humans from inert matter but that recent thought has sought to restore. Inspired in Nils Bohr's Quantum Field Theory, Karen Barad posits matter as endlessly agentive and generative as human nature and regards the distinction between human and nonhuman as contingent and accidental, a question of the "differential boundaries" and "intra-active agential cuts" that constantly reconfigure phenomena. Phenomena are the basic constituents of existence: assemblages of actions, actants, and materials, whose tight interpenetration and indeterminacy precludes the existence of inter-actions between them, a term that assumes independently existing relata. Difference and change result instead from temporary ontological cuts, which she calls "intra-actions": "the ongoing reconfiguring of locally determinate causal structures with determinate boundaries, properties, meanings, and patterns of marks on bodies."[63] In the dynamism of matter, intelligibility is not an exclusively human prerogative but the result of "differential articulations and differential responsiveness/engagement" (823) and knowledge, in turn, is "part of the world making itself intelligible to another part" (829). For Barad, being and knowing are mutually implicated. And so are, in Vicki Kirby's view, being and processes of encryption and decoding: writing, reading, and recording are present in molecular biology, neural net behavior, geology, and weather. Nature and matter are, as she puts it, "articulate, communicative, and . . . intentional"; they read, write, record, archive, and retrieve information, and are crisscrossed by "a cacophony of conversations" and a web of mutualities.[64]

Taking the agency and unpredictability of the material realm into account shifts the scale of democracy. The unit of analysis for democratic theory can no longer be human collectives, as Jane Bennett claims, but assemblages of human and nonhuman actants, all of whom demand responsiveness and attention: "[S]urely the scope of democratization can be broadened to acknowledge nonhumans . . . in something like the ways in which we have come to hear the political voices of other humans formerly on the outs."[65] In addition, the attention to the nonhuman ought to bounce back onto a renewed regard for those humans whose attachment to heterogenous matter is often regarded, by standard criteria of rationality and ableism, as deviant, backward, or pathological. Mel Y. Chen proposes that respecting the heterogeneity of the material is of a piece with respecting politically suppressed "indigenous" cosmologies for whom nonhuman life is anything but static; neurodiverse people (within the autism spectrum, for example) whose primary relations are with nonhuman animals and objects; and queers keen on delving into non- and post-human affect.[66] And as democracy broadens, so does the scope of ethics, whose range of concern surpasses the animate. "Ethics," points out Barad, "is about taking account of the entangled materializations of which we are a part, including new configurations, new subjectivities, new possibilities— even the smallest cuts matter."[67] The allure of a new ethics, and of the new possibilities it opens, may be a further reason why queer thinkers and artists have historically sought to amplify the frequencies of the material world in various modes and media, from the textural excesses of camp, to pop art's delight in surface and color, to different modalities of noise, to the varied textural and objectual enmeshments present in experimental film. When a truly flattened social field seems unavailable, it can be envisioned in the parallel world of art. Except that what results is no longer "art" in any traditional sense but a conceptual laboratory and a playroom for the rehearsal of future life.

INTRODUCTION. SEXUALITY ON THE OUTSIDE   21

From this point on, the book continues with a reconsideration of experimental film in the postwar years. While the standard criticism of 1940s and 1950s avant-garde cinema stresses its subjectivism and mythical resonances, I will highlight instead its material investments. Chapter 2 tracks an alternative materialist streak in the postwar films of Harry Smith, Marie Menken, Ken Jacobs, Ron Rice, Sarah Kathryn Arledge, and Jim Davis, among others. Directly opposed to the functionality and transparency of postwar material culture, their films focus instead on the cluttered, useless, ambiguous, and quirky. In their work, ruins, junk, magical objects, dated *fin-de-siécle* images and designs, dime-store trifles, daily things, synthetic plastics and resins, and serially produced mechanical parts become part of trans-human and trans-material ensembles endowed with a queer animacy.

The middle chapters will focus on the 1960s and 1970s, the high years of underground film, a period characterized by the availability of synthetics such as plastics and mood-changing pharmaceuticals, such as amphetamine. Chapter 3 is devoted to the role of amphetamine in Warhol's Factory films. Widely consumed in the postwar years, the drug propitiated an absorbing immersion into matter and materiality that Warhol's films, and others made in their orbit, reflect. The chapter will study the social history of amphetamine, its reception in the art and literature of the time, the perceptual changes induced by the substance, the modes of eroticism and community it facilitated, and the ways in which it influenced the temporality and style of Warhol's films.

Chapter 4 will analyze the 1960s films of Mike and George Kuchar as exponents of "the plastic life." Plastics were ubiquitous by mid-century, endowed with an aura of functionality and newness. In the Kuchars' films, they range from the ornamental to the absurd to the degraded, excremental, and trashy. In their melodramatic and cartoonishly oversexed plots, plastic gadgets, synthetic fabrics, toys, knick-knacks, and figurines supplement, replace, or alter human bodies and create fantastic environments, that, while poised in counterpoint to normality, are still conjured out of the most ordinary of materials.

Made from a variety of plastic polymers, glitter pervades 1960s and 1970s underground performance and film. Chapter 5 reconstructs its elusive history, from its invention in the mid-1930s to its growing popularity in the mid-1960s. Glitter was initially used as a cheap ornament in underground performance and film and surfaced overground through fashion and popular music—glam rock, also called "glitter rock." The popularity of glitter responded to a contemporary fascination with sheen and sparkle, the immersive, and the ephemeral, interests that also drove light-based art, multimedia events, and discotheque design. In underground film and performance, glitter was featured in the production of bodies and interiors of uncertain outline and surface, whose glimmer prevented straightforward apprehension and triggered queer affect. This chapter will explore glitter's varied configurations in 1960s and 1970s performance—from Freddy Herko and John Vaccaro to The Cockettes—and film—from Jack Smith and Katharina Sieverding to Carles Comas and the members of the French *cinema corporel* school, such as Stéphane Marti and Teo Hernández.

Glitter produces its effects by means of distributed reflective particles, and ties in with a contemporary shift from the line to the dotted field as basic means of representation. Chapter 6 will explore this shift, which was apparent, for example, in the Ben-Day dots and half-tone photographic grain used in op and pop art, in the modeling of information patterns in cybernetics, and in the abundant film grain that swarmed in experimental screens, the ostensible theme of the chapter. Grain's pervasiveness in experimental film from the early 1960s forward was due to the widespread use of highly sensitive small-gauge film stocks, which yielded thickly textured images. Film grain is formally similar to the dotted textures of glitter and Ben-Day dots and, as this chapter will demonstrate, structurally cognate to the binary coding of information formalized by Claude Shannon in the postwar years. But while the binary coding of cybernetics was put at the service of formalizing information and increasing the control over natural and social processes, filmmakers used grain to convey the anarchic animation of queer bodies and desires and the liveliness of the material world. Extending the argument into subsequent forms of queer cinema, Chapter 7 explores granularity in AIDS activist film of the eighties and early nineties and in contemporary processed film of the early 2000s and beyond, when celluloid remains a relatively residual medium in a media ecology dominated by the digital image. In these formations, grain connotes different forms of precarity and fragility: embattled bodies and queer memory in AIDS-related film and the "poor" artisanal image in hand-processed celluloid. Yet vulnerability and precarity also inspire reparative impulses and unprecedented styles of corporeality, relationality, fantasy, and resistance which are likewise conveyed through the swarming instability of grain.

Depending on one's optic, grain may be seen as either noise or signal—formless background or intelligible form. The last chapter, Chapter 8, will tackle the association of visual and aural noise with queer embodiment and sociality. It will explore the three main avenues for the introduction of noise into experimental music and film from mid-century forward: the incorporation of new scales and timbral vocabularies, often borrowed from non-Western musical traditions; synthesized electronic sound; and magnetic tape. All of them had a considerable impact on queer filmmakers between mid-century and the present, from Sidney Peterson and James Broughton to Lionel Soukaz, Abigail Child, and (Ashley) Hans Scheirl. Like grain, noise casts an unformalizable shadow on the image. It connects experimental film with a parallel tradition of sound experimentation and prompts us to take into account the trans-medial connections of queer visual culture. Matter without a code, noise escapes the grids of intelligibility and the double articulation of language. It is the outer limit of culture (an annihilating vibration on the edge) *and* its enabling material, since culture is noise formalized into sense.[68] Ever-present but under-regarded, noise remains a marginal component in cultural analysis. It seems fitting that a book intent on amplifying the buzz of matter, which conventional theories of culture and sexuality have frequently overlooked, would end up with a consideration of it.

2

Ruins, Magical Objects, Litter, Synthetics

The Queer Materials of Postwar Avant-Garde Film

Kenneth Anger's *Fireworks* (1947) is, by widely accepted consensus, the inaugural moment of postwar queer experimental film. Made when Anger was only seventeen—twenty by other accounts—it is a characteristically artisanal work made with a group of friends and casual performers.[1] It has long been discussed as gay psychodrama, a trance, and a surreal rendering of sexual initiation. A work of introspection and subjective exploration, it is also about the way sexuality is routed through surfaces, textures, and objects. The desire of the protagonist, the motor of the narrative, is relayed through a combination of votive and trivial things: an African statuette rising from his crotch, erotic photographs, a cigarette, a flaming torch, a spent matchbook inscribed "US Navy," and a Roman candle that sparkles between a sailor's legs. His sexual initiation, which takes the form of a beating by a group of sailors, is a drama of soft, fragile flesh devastated by metal; of fluids that run under blows, as blood and milk trickle down the young man's face and chest. The most visceral scene in the film mingles the organic and the mechanical: the young man's chest is cut open with a piece of glass and his entrails are moved aside to show a pressure gauge or a meter ticking inside his body. The setting is a dark alley littered with old newspapers and unidentifiable discards, which could themselves be metaphors for the trashing of the protagonist, torn up and cast off like so much waste. In the aftermath of the beating, trash transmutes into light. A straight edit places the protagonist back in his room. Unscathed, he solemnly carries a tinseled Christmas tree whose sparkle rhymes with the phallic Roman candle that burns at the close of the previous scene, the fire on the hearth, and the halo that radiates from a man lying in bed next to him in a frame that resembles one of the opening shots and brings the film full circle.

The action strings together different objectual orders—transcendent and mundane; organic and mechanical; solid and liquid; exalted and

---

Experimental Film and Queer Materiality. Juan A. Suárez, Oxford University Press. © Oxford University Press 2024.
DOI: 10.1093/oso/9780197566992.003.0002

discarded—and constantly shifts between them, blurring their differences. Flesh embraces the mechanical; the transcendent (the burning torch signifying desire and destruction) speaks through the trivial (a matchbook, a cigarette); and litter and blood yield to the gleaming objects that evoke erotic fulfilment in the film's final scenes. In moving across these opposites, the film largely bypasses contemporary material culture. Filmed in Los Angeles in the postwar years, nothing betrays this provenance, with the possible exception of the protagonist's jeans and loafers—standard teenage wear at the time—and the night shot of highway traffic alluding to an increasingly car-centered city. The action unfolds in a vague contemporaneity and occasionally harks back to earlier representational regimes. The painted backdrop in the bar scene recalls the décor of early cinema or of rudimentary stage shows. The magical symbols in the protagonist's room invoke pre- or para-modern belief systems. And the corporeal fluids and steaming entrails reveal a timeless organic pulse beneath human action. *Fireworks's* sexuality runs alongside the deviant materiality of objects and substances that channel the film's heterodox desires and, in their disorder, ambiguity, datedness, and quirkiness, run counter to the dominant material culture of the suburban middle-class America of the time.

Criticism has seldom dealt with the intricate materiality of Anger's film—or of postwar experimental film, for that matter. Most commentators have read the cinematic strand represented by *Fireworks* as a cinema of the spirit: of sexual and social outsiders projecting their alienation on the screen and of cine-poets seeking to transfigure the everyday through invocations of myth and ritual. *Fireworks* is part of a trend spearheaded by Maya Deren in the early forties—with *Meshes of the Afternoon* (1943), *At Land* (1944), and *A Study in Choreography for Camera* (1945)—and seconded by young artists like Anger himself, Curtis Harrington, and Gregory Markopoulos in Los Angeles; James Broughton and Sidney Peterson in San Francisco; and by the New York-based "Gryphon Group," which included Willard Maas, Marie Menken, and a fluctuating roster of associates. Their loosely narrative films prolonged and updated in different ways the legacies of interwar surrealism. Contemporaneous with them but working in a different aesthetic were Harry Smith, who made visual abstractions and animated collages; Sara Kathryn Arledge, primarily a painter with a sporadic film career who pioneered the dance film; and Jim Davis, who produced largely abstract films. More distant epigones are Ken Jacobs, Ron Rice, and Jack Smith; their first titles from the late fifties were made in part under the influence of the early postwar underground, but they are also direct representatives of contemporaneous beat aesthetics.

Writing in the late 1940s, historian and filmmaker Lewis Jacobs described postwar experimental film as a cinema of "personal statements" and subjectivism, and German philosopher Siegfried Kracauer, exiled in New York since the war years, summarized it as an attempt to film "the subconscious."[2] In line with these early assessments, P. Adams Sitney, author of what remains the authoritative account of this trend, has demonstrated the centrality of the "trance film" in the postwar American avant-garde: first person narratives of "inward exploration" and "self-realization" often acted by the filmmakers themselves and featuring a "quest for sexual identity."[3] For Richard Dyer this quest was concurrent with the "newly assertive gay identities" being articulated at the time by homophile groups in Los Angeles, San Francisco, and New York. At the same time, Dyer cautions that these films did not offer straightforward identity models.[4] Predating the affirmative identity-based rhetoric of gay liberation by several decades, they depict less homosexual than non-straight desires, energies, and affects, a perspective that reflects the way most of these filmmakers conceived (their) sexuality as a fluid potential rather than a fixed personal trait.

Inner exploration and sexual quest frequently overlapped in these films with what Sitney called "mythopoesis": "the making of a new myth or the reinterpretation of an old one."[5] Anger's *Inauguration of the Pleasure Dome* (1954), Willard Maas and Ben Moore's *Narcissus* (1956), Maya Deren's *Ritual in Transfigured Time* (1948) or Gregory Markopoulos's trilogy *De la sang, de la volupté et de la mort* (1947–1949) are some examples of this trend. Mythopoetic impulses were allied in much of this work to the depiction of sexual heterodoxy. As Parker Tyler noted in 1958: "Very young experimentalists . . . are aware of the fact that in the simplest forms of human behavior, such as the deathless theme of adolescent sex, lie hidden some of the most indispensably meaningful patterns of legend, ritual and myth."[6] Whether an art of psychological exploration, of mythic rewriting, or both, the postwar avant-garde remained for critics a cinema of transcendence that hankered for a realm beyond the immediate and sought to access it, among other means, through nonnormative sexuality.

These transcendent aspirations, and the heterodox sexuality that fueled them, were embedded in the materials and objects of everyday life, which was both logical and counterintuitive. The new material culture of the postwar years, which emerged largely from the application of war technologies to the design of the domestic environment, was distant from the high modernist concerns of most filmmakers.[7] But as an unescapable horizon and a linchpin of normality, it was also a front to be critically engaged and infiltrated with dissident desires. Back in the United States after a decade living in Europe, Henry Miller rebuked the insidious materialism of the times in his satirical travelogue *The Air-Conditioned Nightmare* (1945): "Our world is a world of things . . . cluttered with useless objects which men and women, in order to be exploited and degraded, are taught to regard as useful."[8] Earlier that same year, *Life* magazine had started a series of articles on the American home. The first installment of the series, devoted to new storage systems, reported that an average American family owned around 10,000 objects, an amount that had the potential to disrupt ordinary house management.[9]

Object accumulation increased after the war. It was both an engine of economic recovery and part of a collective attempt to redesign the everyday. The end of World War II inaugurated what some have described as the largest shopping spree in the history of the United States. After the Armistice, the industrial apparatus redirected its efforts to satisfy a growing civilian demand that was fueled by rising prosperity. New lines of goods introduced into daily life versatile materials that had been first tested in the war—plywood, new plastics and resins, and steel and aluminum alloys. They were used in furniture, appliances, and common objects that merged the severity of machine-age modernism with traditional textures, colors, and finishes and blended, in this way, rationalism and emotional appeal. The combination characterized the work of the most successful postwar designers, such as George Nelson, Eero Saarinen, and Charles and Ray Eames, all of whom adapted the premises of modernist object culture to the popular taste. Like their Bauhaus precursors in the twenties, postwar American designers aspired to doing more than just putting new products in the market. They believed that their work had the ability to modify the attitudes and habits of their customers, foster transparency and coherence, and reorder a world cast by the war into chaotic disarray. In the words of historian Jeffrey Meikle, they hoped to provide "playful backgrounds for uncluttered postwar lives" or, in those of Justus Nieland, "happiness by design."[10]

Uncluttered lives and a reconstructed social world demanded a compliant material horizon of readable, manageable things, functionality, and transparency. Allied with the pull toward consumerism, the postwar design ethos cast aside unproductive, ambiguous, or impractical objects and materials. And yet clutter, useless junk, dated designs, and traditional materials

28 EXPERIMENTAL FILM AND QUEER MATERIALITY

retained their appeal, especially for subjects and communities who did not find themselves at ease in the new America. Eve Kosofsky Sedgwick's defense of the queer appeal of objects and experiences whose meaning seemed "mysterious, excessive, or oblique in relation to the codes most readily available to us" makes most sense when contextualized against what Henry Miller labeled "futilitarian" postwar material culture.[11] Precisely in reaction against this standard, queer experimental filmmakers embedded their fantasies in aberrant, eccentric, irrational, and unaccountable objects and materials, such as the magical props in Kenneth Anger's and Harry Smith's films or the stuttering trifles that populate Marie Menken's. Others, such as Willard Maas, James Broughton, Ken Jacobs, and Ron Rice explored the queer potential of dated and dysfunctional matter, such as ruins, rubble, and junk. And Fernand Léger, Sarah Kathryn Arledge, and Jim Davis gleefully perverted functional and industrially manufactured materials, such as chrome surfaces, plastics, and synthetics by aligning them with wayward sexualities and desires. Cumulatively, the work of these filmmakers offers a dissident guide to the postwar everyday. It articulates a queer-materialist genealogy in avantgarde cinema—where "materialist" does not refer to the basic constituents of the film image, as it did in Peter Gidal's definition of "structural-materialist" film in the 1970s, but to the stuff of common life. After all, the critical refusal that animated queer experimental film did not always take the high road of visions, interiority, and myth. It also took the low paths that wound around the odd discards, humble substances, rubble, and irrational objects that were some of modernity's unspoken material backgrounds.

Ruins

Ruins became integral components of American cities in the postwar years.[12] The combined effect of suburban expansion and urban renovation, which picked up pace after the end of World War II, left in its wake proverbial wastelands in the form of razed lots and rubble mounds. As city-dwellers abandoned metropolitan centers for the expanding suburban sprawl on the outskirts, urban cores steadily lost population and services, fell into disuse, and often ended up prey to slum clearance programs. The relocation of light industry to the city outskirts reinforced this tendency, siphoning off resources from centers to urban peripheries and vacating industrial structures. New York City is a well-studied example. The move of port services from

QUEER MATERIALS OF POSTWAR AVANT-GARDE FILM   29

metropolitan New York to New Jersey, the gradual dismantling of light industry, and the boom of the Levittowns springing up on Long Island and
Staten Island emptied out ample sections of Manhattan and Brooklyn,
which, from the mid-fifties forward, were increasingly targeted by urban re-
newal. Entire blocks were cleared to build high-rise public housing or to provide services and amenities, such as parks and playgrounds. In addition, the
increased mobility required by what historian Kenneth Jackson called the
new "beltway life" prompted further demolition to make way for highways
and expanded thoroughfares.[13] Marshall Berman has famously described the
devastation caused by the Cross-Bronx Expressway in the South Bronx as
part of "a new order" that sought to unify the nation—the modern world,
in fact—into a unified traffic network.[14] Only strenuous organizational effort and community activism—in which urban theorist Jane Jacobs played
a leading role—prevented Manhattan from experiencing a similar fate in
the early sixties.[15] This was a generalized trend. The highway network in the
Los Angeles area expanded vastly in the forties and early fifties, razing down
established neighborhoods. Kenneth Anger's family house on Holly Drive,
North Hollywood, was torn down in the early fifties to clear the ground for
the construction of the Hollywood Freeway.[16] Gregory Markopoulos's film
The Dead Ones (1949), set in Los Angeles, offers a passing glimpse of the road
works in a burial scene that takes place by an overpass under construction.

The burial scene in Markopoulos's film suggests a parallel between the
death of one of the film's protagonists, a member of an ill-fated love triangle,
and the liquidation of the traditional, walkable city. Postwar experimental
film evinced an elegiac attachment to the compact city of modernity and
made ample use of its ruins. These last were sites of fantasy and play and provided frequently spectacular settings for films. Part of the attraction of ruins
was their textural complexity, layered temporality, and unregulated use—
qualities that stood in counterpoint to the formal simplicity, lack of historical
depth, and controlled nature of the suburban sprawl.[17]

Ruins feature indeed as intricately spectacular backdrops in Maas's
Narcissus (1955), a recreation of the classical myth in modern-day costume
set in some of the demolished neighborhoods bordering on New York's
East River. Narcissus is an urban scavenger who lives in a shack in a derelict
neighborhood and roams the city in search for precious castoffs of value only
to himself. The mountains of debris that Narcissus traverses in his outings are
easily the most striking images in the film. Equally astonishing are the rubble
formations in Jack Smith's *Scotch Tape* (1962). It was filmed in the ruins of

what was once the San Juan Hill neighborhood, destroyed in the mid-fifties to clear the ground for Lincoln Center. Broken concrete, piled brick, and bent steel form a landscape of mind-boggling intricacy. Jacobs, Jerry Sims, and Reese Haire—this last in exotic drag—frolic in the wreckage, replicating with their bodies the impossible arabesques of the twisted girders around them. In the soundtrack, a light Brazilian tune in the version of pianist Eddy Duchin heightens the playfulness of the scene and the exoticism of the dancers and the environment.

Filmmakers were not alone in their interest in the formal complexity of debris. Ruins held considerable appeal for contemporary photographers such as Russell Lee and Morris Engel, who had started their careers as documentary photographers during the Depression, and Chester Kessler, a friend of Kenneth Anger who was the cameraman in *Fireworks* and was later active in the San Francisco beat scene. They all sought to capture the rich textures and unprecedented forms generated by wrecking balls and demolition teams: the untutored expressiveness of chance. Ruins could be seen as a sort of involuntary Abstract Expressionism whose gesturality resulted from random destruction rather than from psychological projection. It was an art of the world, undirected and free, and perhaps because of this, it held a particular attraction for artists connected with the improvisatory aesthetic of the beats, such as Kessler or Ron Rice, to be discussed soon.

Formally complex, ruins are also temporally layered. They show the persistence of the past in the present and bring to mind one of the compositional principles of modern poetry, which scavenged the literary archive for clues that might illuminate the present and orient the future—"These fragments I have shored against my ruins," reads one of the closing lines in T. S. Eliot's *The Waste Land* (1922), a line that offers a rationale to the patchwork of quotations that closes the poem. Against nineteenth-century notions of linear progress and evolution, much of modernist poetry defended, as Pound put it, that "all ages are contemporaneous" and history was less a forward march than a tortuously layered palimpsest.[18] One of the functions of art was to dig through the layers to rescue what remained relevant for the present. "Ghosts move about me/patched with histories," Pound wrote in an early draft of the first *Cantos*.[19] The *Cantos*, the monumental work that occupied him for nearly six decades, was a fragmentary conversation with these ghosts. The protagonist of Maas's *Image in the Snow* (1948) converses with ghosts in his own way. Some of them are biographical, appear to him in dreams, and embody repressed sexual impulses that conflict with his search for the ideal—an ideal that often takes the form of semi-naked muscular men. Other ghosts have a more collective character and materialize as ruins. He saunters in abandoned warehouse areas on the Brooklyn waterfront and lingers among demolished buildings. In his only affectionate gesture throughout the film, he caresses and presses his cheek against the remains of a huge classical head, part of a building's ornamentation. The ornament's elegance is a memory of a beauty that has been expelled from his immediate environment and can only be found in fragments among the rubble. Maas's characters, like Narcissus and the protagonist of *Image*, do not only inhabit ruins but are themselves ruins. They embody forsaken economies of longing and guilt, and are emblems of liquidation and eviction, dislodged from contemporary society and its gender arrangements, which they elude in their loneliness and isolation (Figure 2.1).

Perhaps the main attraction of ruins for queer filmmakers resided in the freedom and possibility they offered. Urbanist Kevin Lynch pointed out in his classic study of waste that ruined places "escape the weight of power": "They are liberated zones. They release us from the necessity of calculated communication and behavior."[20] This is certainly the case in James Broughton's films, where ruins are settings for absurdity, childish disruptiveness, and

Figure 2.1 Willard Maas, *Image in the Snow*, 1948. Frame enlargement.

amiable eroticism (Figure 2.2). His collaboration with Sidney Peterson, *The Potted Psalm* (1946) was filmed in part at a cemetery that was being torn down to make way for a shopping mall. Broken tombstones and funerary statuary appear oddly juxtaposed and a blond woman—perhaps a man in drag, by some accounts—runs as if in a panic through the broken landscape.[21] *Mother's Day* (1948) contrasts the Victorian interiors dominated by a frivolous, indifferent mother and a stern father, with the derelict lots and torn-down buildings where children (played by adults) scribble obscenities on the walls, fight, throw tantrums, and mimic sex with their stuffed animals. In *Four in the Afternoon* (1950) "Game Little Gladys" envisions her ten future husbands perched on the truncated columns of what looks like an eroded former structure—it is actually the pillars of a new building—and two harlequinesque figures romance each other in a humorous dance around the Palace of Fine Arts, on the grounds of the 1915 Panama-Pacific International Exposition, which were in disrepair and boarded up at the time. *The Pleasure Garden* (1953), made during Broughton's years of exile in the United Kingdom, was filmed in the site of the 1851 World Exhibition,

Figure 2.2 James Broughton and Sidney Peterson, *The Potted Psalm*, 1946. Frame enlargement.

which once held London's Crystal Palace and had been fenced off and locked to the public since 1937, when the structure caught fire and the glass dome collapsed.[22] In the "dilapidated splendor" of this setting, which suggested to Broughton "nothing less than the debris of Western civilization," a string of characters who have fallen under the influence of a plump, cheerful fairy in gauzy dress shed their inhibitions, while a squad of cartoonish Puritans seek to contain the sensuality. Among the pleasure-seekers are two lithe young men who wrestle in skimpy briefs and romp *à-trois* with a young woman behind the bushes.

The central scenes of Ron Rice's *The Flower Thief* (1960), filmed in San Francisco in 1959, also take place in a vacated industrial structure—an abandoned powerhouse—that is turned into a setting for play and fantasy by the protagonist of the film (played by Taylor Mead) and his friends.[23] Mead plays with leftover machinery and mechanical parts. He and his friends chase each other, light sparklers, start fires, break furniture, and put on pantomimes. One of these is a denunciation of the prison system, edited to a poetic musing about the "light years" human beings have been kept in captivity throughout history; another is a reenactment of the crucifixion that culminates in a spoof of the planting of the flag in Iwo Jima. In another scene, Mead mock-fights with a portly, dark-haired woman dressed in high heels and a bathing suit; they later sit down with great composure to have tea among shattered concrete while, in the soundtrack, Mead reads a parody of the tea party in *Alice in Wonderland*. The playfulness that the ruins inspire affects sexuality as well. Mead's friends hide in the factory's lockers to make out and two of them—a heterosexual couple—end up taking a shower together. In the meantime, Mead's affect is directed toward the nonhuman: a kitten and a teddy bear that he hugs tenderly and subjects to a thorough scrubbing with a toilet brush. It is only outside the ruins that he recasts his affections in a human register. Mead cruises a leather-jacketed youth at a penny arcade, and they end up going out together for a walk that culminates with Mead melting into the ocean in a series of dissolves. Ruins are not only the main setting of *The Flower Thief*, but also the film's structuring principle. With its improvised, fragmentary action, flowing camera work—which often yields strikingly beautiful frames—its use of available lighting, and constant non sequiturs, *The Flower Thief* seems less a deliberate artifact than loosely edited cinematic debris.

Junk

Junk and litter are the small change of the ruin: lacking the solidity of structural components and ornaments, they are more ephemeral and negligible, yet occupy a similar position in the ecology of value. Like ruins, they are the obverse of productivity and wealth, and they also became a considerable problem for urban management at mid-century. Garbage resulted from stepped-up consumption and from the improved hygienic standards that made dirt more evident than it had been before. After all, as a long line of thinkers about dirt and impurity have pointed out, from George Bataille and Mary Douglas to Kevin Lynch, Michael Thompson, and John Scanlan, garbage is a relative concept, subject to constant negotiation and change.[24] It is a direct emanation of social order. Social systems determine what is allowed within their precincts and what threatens their integrity and must therefore be cast out as dirt. "Where there is dirt, there is system," famously wrote Douglas.[25] And consequently, the stricter the system, the higher the dirt pile. In the postwar years, the alignment of spaces, bodies, and commodities in the production of a transparent, manageable sociality went hand in hand with the production of considerable waste. This included not only the rubble generated by slum clearance or the discards of a consumer apparatus in high gear, but also human debris: the ghostly figures that populated Allen Ginsberg's *Howl* (1955), the "best minds" of his generation, "cast on the pavement . . . who poverty and tatters and hollow-eyed and high."[26] Castoffs reveal the ruthlessness of the systems that create them and thus offer a critical perspective on them. But in addition, junk is also generative: just like ruins, trash heaps are spaces of freedom and invention, where the strictures that determine life within the system no longer hold, and the repressed may return.

Imbued with the spirit of play and critique, experimental filmmakers incorporated trash into their *mise-en-scene* and turned found discards into building blocks for their work. Jack Smith, for example, claimed that his ideas came exclusively from "old things and fantasies," "moldy things," and "unwanted objects."[27] These are the raw materials for the films he and Ken Jacobs made from the mid-fifties to the early sixties, when they had a calamitous falling-out that put an end to their collaboration. Their partnership resulted in titles such as Jacobs's *Little Stabs at Happiness* (1959–62), *Blonde Cobra* (1959–63, based on footage by Bob Fleischner), and the six-hour *Star-Spangled to Death* (1958–2004).[28] All of them feature Smith's performative abilities, Jacobs's extraordinarily precise visual style, and their uncanny sensibility for finding import and value in discards. These films are, to paraphrase Jacobs's description of *Blonde Cobra*, glimpses of the "exploding life" of several sensitive characters living in impoverished conditions and furnishing their destitution with the debris of the culture—thirties and forties Hollywood films that they recreate through threadbare parodies, magazine and newspapers cutouts, and literal trash.

The setting for their parodies and trash compositions are dilapidated or marginal spaces. *Blonde Cobra* was filmed in the derelict apartment of Smith and Jacobs's friend and collaborator Jerry Sims, and *Little Stabs at Happiness* and *Star-Spangled to Death* were filmed in various Lower East Side locations, in the yard and on the roof of an apartment building on West 75th Street where Jacobs worked as a janitor, and in various demolition sites on Manhattan's West Side—some look quite similar to the setting of *Scotch Tape* (1963), which is in fact a spin-off of *Star-Spangled to Death*. In these locations, garbage accumulates. It is a chaotic tangle in the demolition sites, but it is carefully culled and laid out in the yard and in Sims's apartment. Smith and Jacobs's use of trash is roughly contemporary with Robert Rauschenberg's, who, perhaps unknown to them, had started to make his "combines" just a few years earlier. Midway between painting and sculpture, Rauschenberg's combines integrated painted flat surfaces and found objects—from images and small-scale litter to stuffed animals (a goat in *Monogram*, 1959; an eagle in *Canyon*, 1959) and a partly burned mattress covered with bedding and set vertically on the wall (*Bed*, 1955). The "combines" were seismic ruptures of the conventional boundaries of the artwork at the time, but in them refuse was gathered in self-contained, relatively unified compositions. In Jacobs and Smith's films, however, garbage is an undifferentiated backdrop without clear focal points, where objects are distinct, in so far as they have become disconnected from their original milieus, but also blend into each other, losing their individuality to become sheer trash.[29] In this regard, Jacobs's and Smith's trashy backdrops are closer to—and foreshadow—the uniform grime of Claes Oldenburg or Jim Dine's junk environments of the late fifties or Arman's *poubelles*—Plexiglas containers filled with nondescript waste.

Rauschenberg's combines, Oldenburg's and Dine's environments, and Arman's *poubelles* were more artistic than existential statements, while Jacobs and Smith's embrace of trash was a survival tactic—an attempt to create a niche for themselves in a hostile world. It was a world that denied their artistry, their sensibility, their political radicalism (stronger in Jacobs), and (in Smith's case) their queerness. One of the main theses of *Star-Spangled* is that only among rejects—matter that no longer mattered—could one make a life non-complicit with the dominant consumerist-militaristic-genocidal compact underpinning the demented normality of the era. The film underlines the distance between life in the garbage, as it were, and the world of the normal by juxtaposing the enchanted, if poverty-stricken, existence of yard and rooftop dwellers to fragments of patriotic songs, instructional and political propaganda films, stilted radio and television broadcasts (including the entirety of Nixon's "Checkers Speech"), and oppressively racist documentaries and cartoons. Captured in brief, constantly mobile shots, the spontaneous play of the outcasts turns destitute materials into bits of imaginative décor. Plastic sheets draped over railings suggest mysterious chambers and secluded recesses, and they intriguingly diffuse the actions performed behind them, acting as fog. Small mirror balls glisten like jewels against cracked concrete, and a broken doll, in a brief animated segment, dances on the railings that enclose the yard where they stage their fantasies—a space that, as Jonathan Rosenbaum has noted, might be a playpen as much as a prison.[30] The film's performers deck themselves out with refuse, which they convert into elaborate costumes with exotic resonances. Smith, of course, excels at this: his headpieces incorporate old fabric, broken toys, ripped baskets, and assorted brick-a-brack, and he often wraps his body in a transparent plastic sheet that trails behind him and envelops his movements in a silvery halo.

Parker Tyler noted that much of the playacting in *Little Stabs* and *Blonde Cobra* is "infantile-neurotic."[31] So is it in *Star-Spangled to Death*, which is the originating matrix for the later titles. Smith and Sims are quite childish in their spastic mugging, their alternation between elation and sullenness, and their frequent befuddlement. They also play with children, who are frequent companions in their antics: children romp around in the courtyard, follow Smith around the street, and are liberated by him in a humorous street performance captioned "Jack frees the Slaves." Playing in the trash and childhood are often related. A life on the margins is a life liberated from adult regulations, such as the interdiction against dirt, and a return to infantile pleasures, such as a good tumble in the trash. Childhood play, wrote Theodor Adorno, deprives things of their "mediated usefulness" and takes them on their own terms, erasing the distinction between the functional and the useless, tool and refuse, living commodity and junk.[32] Playing with garbage is playing with detritus, and therefore akin to playing with feces. It enacts a regression to a stage before proper toilet training which, Sigmund Freud claimed, is also a training in the distinction between the proper and the improper and in the parsing out of one's pleasures, signified in the alternation between (fecal) retention and ejection.[33] The performers in *Star-Spangled to Death* do not hold anything back. As they cavort in the rubbish-strewn yard and in abandoned buildings, they shed all inhibition and lie among the garbage, confused with it, and indulge in orgies of destruction, ripping tiles off a wall or smashing junked appliances. They also refuse to abide by clear-cut gender distinctions, as if the undifferentiation of junk erased corporeal marks of identity. Smith in particular is prone to cross the gender divide and appears, by turns, as a manic dowager in headkerchiefs and under layers of bulky coats, as a somber Brunhilda with thick blonde braids, or as a skimpily dressed sinuous houri.

Rubbish, childishness, and gender anarchy are also interwoven in Ron Rice's *The Queen of Sheba Meets the Atom Man* (1963), a film that premiered shortly before the filmmaker's premature death from pneumonia while living destitute on the beaches of Veracruz. The film starts in a gigantic paper dump that blends into Taylor Mead's humble pad, which is supremely untidy: liberally littered with books, old newspapers and magazines, and assorted domestic castoffs. Mead gets up from bed, joyously smears his hands with Vaseline, which he then washes off, extracts a handful of white powder from a container labeled "heroin," and pretends to smoke it, laughing through this evocation of beat clichés. The sexual lubricant, the drug taking, and the trashed interior mark a junked existence outside the circuits of utility and respectability. After weaving its way through New York chasing its two protagonists—Mead and Winnifred Bryant, a portly black lady who often appears naked—the film repeatedly returns to trashy interiors where characters dance, play, and lie about, often with, and on top of, each other and surrounded by rubbish. They themselves are depicted like rubbish. Their tumbles in company are less sexual probes than aimless gropes. They are not guided by the goal-oriented genital economy of tension and discharge, but by the desire to commingle in and with junk in confused heaps, in all-over haptic contact with each other and with the discards that surround them. These scenes affirm a sexuality of trash; they vindicate the pleasures derived, to recall Mary Douglas's words, from "matter out of place" and from the radical impropriety of a world where bodies and things may crop up anywhere in any old way.

Stuttering Matter

Marie Menken's films also delight in radical impropriety and anarchic material play. Her work pries open and rearranges bodies and objects—humble materials such as pebbles, plants, beads, water, sand, and thread—through the camera's ability to surpass what Walter Benjamin called "natural optics" and to collate the real in surprising alignments. Long neglected and under-recognized during the 1940s and 1950s, and timidly celebrated during the 1960s by Stan Brakhage and Jonas Mekas, both of whom were decisively influenced by her highly mobile, impressionistic camera style, Menken was rediscovered in the 2000s under several guises: as a fundamental figure in the Emersonian tradition of American experimental film (Sitney); as a conceptualist attentive to the changing status of the art object and to cross-media dialogue (Ragona); as an astute explorer of the unacknowledged realities of modern labor (Guo); and as an exponent of a style of "queer materiality" that runs through postwar experimental cinema (Suárez).[34] It is this last perception that I want to amplify here, as these other critics'—certainly groundbreaking—explorations tend to elide the affect-laden character of Menken's work and to divorce her style and stance from a peculiar sexuality detoured through matter and things rather than through conventional corporeal form.

Menken's material explorations rely on a fragmentary visual perception that eschews global perspectives and concentrates instead on isolated particulars. In an interview with P. Adams Sitney, she dated her beginnings as a filmmaker to her fascination with shape and movement independent of story or sense: "The twittering of leaves when I was bored in class as a child, and the delights of moving my feet in silhouette against the lights of the window when I was being punished and sent to my room in 'solitary' led me to believe in private and personal dramas."[35] This way of finding dramatic import in minute incidentals already informs her first credited film, *Visual Variations on Noguchi* (1947), conceived as visual background to Merce Cunningham's ballet *The Seasons* (1947), with music by John Cage and sets by Japanese-American sculptor Isamu Noguchi.[36] The film captures Noguchi's work in moving close-ups that convey their textures, gentle curves, and the shadows they project, underscoring throughout their intriguing thingness rather than their artistic status. A comparable interest in detail characterizes as well *Arabesque for Kenneth Anger* (1958–61), *Glimpse of the Garden* (1957), and *Bagatelle for Willard Maas* (1961). Rather than offer holistic views of landscapes (the garden of friends Dwight Ripley and Rupert

Barneby in *Glimpse*) or architectural sites (the Alhambra in *Arabesque* and Versailles in *Bagatelle*), they dwell on extreme close-ups of rocks, flowers, puddles, tiles, ornamental details, and highlight surface and the reflections of light (Figure 2.3).

Other films fragment motion and events rather than objects or places. *Go! Go! Go!* (1963), *Excursion* (1968), *Andy Warhol* (1965), and *Wrestling* (1967) use single framing and time lapse photography to dissolve different kinds of movement into percussive gesture. In them, motion stops being directional, instrumental, and goal-oriented to become a vibratory intensity without apparent purpose or aim. It matters less that cars and city dwellers in *Go! Go! Go!* move toward something than that they shake in endless agitation true to the title's insistence. The Manhattan skyline, the waterfront, clouds, and the boats in the harbor all tremble together in *Excursion*, a time-lapse record of a cruise around the island on a Circle Line ferry. And in a similar manner, *Andy Warhol* (1965) turns Warhol and Gerard Malanga's silk-screening at the Factory into a spastic dance without apparent resolution. This sensation is amplified by the repetitive nature of their actions—they are shown producing multiples like the Brillo boxes—and by the emphasis the film places on the working process rather than on the result. Even the leisurely

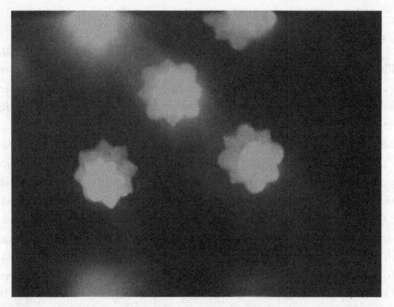

Figure 2.3 Marie Menken, *Arabesque for Kenneth Anger*, 1958–61. Frame enlargement.

40 EXPERIMENTAL FILM AND QUEER MATERIALITY

moments in the film—Warhol reading the newspaper or sitting on a chair—are rendered dizzyingly jittery by the rapid succession of extremely brief takes—most often single-frame—taken from slightly varying angles. Toward the end of the film, motion seems to take over entirely: Warhol and Malanga's movements are conveyed through darker and closer shots that have the effect of dissolving their bodies into flickering abstractions. *Wrestling* collates fragments of wrestling matches filmed off the television monitor a few frames at time and without any regard for their integrity, development, or outcome. The vertical rolling lines that signal the phase difference between television and film, the flat greyness of the picture, and the thick granularity—standard resolution of TV monitors at the time was 525 lines—smudge the contours of the wrestlers, while the speeded-up motion gives their blurry exertions the jerkiness of silent film physical comedy.

Other films elicit a similar motility from the inanimate by means of stop motion. "The Egg"—an episode in *Notebook* (1961)—*Dwightiana* (1957), and *Watts with Eggs* (1967) present extraordinary choreographies of glitter, glass and plastic beads, earrings, brooches, pencils, string, pebbles, and Robert Watts's chrome eggs. Their interaction oscillates between a graceful balletic rapport and an amusing animosity that makes these things and materials vie with each other for command of the field. In "Paper Cuts," different shapes move gracefully across the screen until they are invaded by a spread of glitter, but they rally together to push the intruding substance off the frame and continue gently gliding and winding around each other. Glitter gets the upper hand in "The Egg"; it starts by displacing the eponymous object at the outset and then proceeds to cover a print of several skeletons over which a glass ball also hovers. In *Dwightiana*, two spider-like earrings—or brooches?—swirl around a shiny granular substance that they end up rounding up and sweeping off court; then they peevishly chase each other, face off, and suddenly contract into two tiny specks of aluminum foil, as if imploding from sheer malice. Later on, two strands of shiny black and gold yarn slide together amorously and then tangle in a scuffle that ends with the disappearance of the black thread, seemingly swallowed by its golden paramour turned rival. The possibility of eliciting this nerviness in things is what drew Menken to film: "In painting I never liked the staid static, always looked for what could change with source of light and stance, using glitters, glass beads, luminous paint, so the camera was a natural for me to try."[37] The result of her camera work, however, was not just the kind of formal play that this quotation suggests, but an affect-laden perception of matter.

The feel of Menken's work emanates in part from the nature of her materials—the vivacious sparkle of glitter, the sheen of glass and plastic—and in part from her surgical use of the camera. In an insightful assessment, Brakhage located Menken's singularity in the way she focused her efforts less on wholistic projected images than on the strip of celluloid, susceptible of multiple division (in frame-by-frame shooting and editing), combination, and manipulation (scratching, hand-coloring). Her example led him, in his own words, "away from being screen-centered (surrounded, in considerations, by auditorium audience, public event, publicity, fame, etc.) to being film-strip centered (or centered in the 'reality' of the working process, even to the extent of being just as concerned that the strips of film cohere as strips, and as variable moving images thru an editor, and as even individual frames and as material for possibly projecting backward or reversed, as I was with the projector-cast image at 24-frames per second)."[38] Brakhage's words apply as much to his own work as to Menken's. Menken rejected the organic image (the one that most resembles, in Brakhage's words, "ordinary visual perception")[39] in favor of the artificially stitched one. With it, she revealed intricate formations indiscernible to the unaided eye. In addition, by stopping the camera every frame, or every few frames, she disassembled motion to reassemble it again in gradual increments, creating a specifically cinematic kinetics with no correlate in the world. The result highlighted the mediation of the recording apparatus and endowed the objects and processes portrayed with a stuttering material presence. This is a peculiar use of montage whose primary point is not to establish conceptual connections (in Eisenstein's style) or to taxonomize quotidian reality (like Vertov), but to endow simple gestures and movements with an insistent, pulsing materiality.

Brakhage was one of the few commentators to see a sexual component in Menken's vibrant intensity. He described her first film, *Visual Variations on Noguchi*, as "a sex dance" among Noguchi's pieces: "never was photographed wood so pornographic."[40] This sexual quality had nothing to do with the phallic shapes of the wood, but rested entirely on its visual rhythm: on what Brakhage called "the internal envisionment [sic] of sexuality in the mind." Menken's flowing takes and editing intended "not to simulate . . . first person singularity of any kind, but to be that vibration that the whole nervous system is, and ordinarily is, and in ecstasy can be, to make a form of such."[41] While Brakhage locates the sexiness of Menken's work in an intra-corporeal reaction to external stimulus, Parker Tyler situates it in her capture of external reality. Her work, he claimed, like that of other filmmakers such as

Brakhage, captures "an underground, quixotic *sexual* rhythm" in the world.[42] Tyler's not-too-subtle example is *Hurry! Hurry!* (1957), which superimposes found footage of racing spermatozoids over shots of an orange gas flame. The twitching advance of the microorganisms and the lurid glow of the flame transmit a nervous vitality. Their energy is doomed to extinction, however. *Hurry! Hurry!* is an unusually elegiac film about futility, since, as Menken herself put it, the sperms all die while looking for an egg, an end suggested by the explosions in the soundtrack. "It's a great tragedy," she said, a statement that some have read as a melancholy reflection about her own miscarriage.[43]

Beyond this particular example, however, what Tyler described as "quixotic sexual rhythm" drives most of Menken's work. This rhythm transforms directional motion into pulse and animates objects and substances, producing a generalized visual stutter. In addition to being a mode of vocal articulation, stuttering is, for Gilles Deleuze, a style of enunciation that reshapes language itself. He finds this style in a lineage of idiosyncratic writers that includes von Kleist, Melville, Kafka, Biely, and Beckett—creators who subject language to "constant disequilibrium and bifurcation." They treat language less as a stable system where each term is a constant in relation to other constants, than as a "a series of differential positions or points of view on a specifiable dynamism." Referents oscillate as language slips and gropes around them: "the indefinite article *a* covers the entire zone of variation included in a movement of particularization, and the definite article *the* covers the entire zone generated by the movement of generalization. It is a stuttering, with every position of *a* or *the* constituting a zone of vibration. Language trembles from head to toe."[44] This quiver, he continues, allows enunciation to imply more than it says and to contain unanticipated possibilities. It also introduces desire into the system, opening linguistic terms to wayward use and unexpected conjunction. Stuttering queers language, charging it with the corporeal intensity generated by the (metaphorical) stumbling, tottering, and repositioning that are the cost of unprecedented enunciation. This is exactly the kind of intensity that that drives Menken's work: it takes the world apart, allows its fragments to jiggle and vibrate momentarily together, detach again, and continue their merry march in search of further connections. If, as Freud once proposed, sexuality is at bottom the intensification of sensation, Menken sexualizes the surfaces and materials of the world by endowing them with a heightened sentience. "There is love and it is everywhere," she once said.[45] It takes the form of a vibratory eroticism that the camera is uniquely equipped to register.

Magic(k) Objects

Harry Smith's fifties films—*Film no. 11* (1956–57), *Film no. 12* (1956–57), and *Film no. 13* (1958–62), usually referred to as *Heaven and Earth Magic*— are driven by a similar stuttering intensity. While in Menken this intensity rises from the animacy of the material world, enhanced through the mediation of cinematic technology, in Smith it emanates from magic. The adult child of Rosacrucians and friends of Aleister Crowley, Smith had grown up surrounded by arcane lore, but his magical interests were also alive in postwar artistic cultures under the influence of surrealism.[46] While since its beginnings surrealism had occasionally drifted, as Walter Benjamin put it, into "the humid backroom of spiritualism,"[47] by the time the surrealists went into exile in New York, escaping the Nazi occupation of France, their mythographic interests had brought them into closer contact with magic. The main surrealist reviews in those years, *VVV* (1942–44) and *View* (1941–47), both published in New York, contained essays by Breton, Benjamin Peret, and Kurt Seligmann, among others, on the Tarot, alchemy, and various aspects of the occult. The influence of surrealism was compounded with a homegrown devotion to the "accursed sciences"—Breton's term—that was particularly prevalent among queer Californian artists, among them Kenneth Anger, Robert Duncan, Marjorie Cameron, as well several figures in Wallace Berman's circle. Smith was not in Berman's direct orbit, but he was connected to Anger and Duncan, and his beginnings as a filmmaker took place in San Francisco in an atmosphere that was sympathetic to the occult. The attraction of magic for queer artists lay in its secretive character, its promise of transcendence, its implicit rejection of the utilitarian everyday, and its traditional openness toward sexual dissidence, an openness that, for countercultural historian Arthur Evans, accounts for the virulence of its persecution and for its long-standing queer appeal.[48] Magic also involved a defamiliarization of object culture, as it infused the material world with supra-human energies and potentials that overlay their habitual functionality and use.

After establishing his reputation with a string of abstract films during the forties and early fifties, Smith turned in mid-decade to the production of collage films. The raw materials of these films are illustrations from late nineteenth-century novels, newspapers, biology and anatomy books, technical manuals, and mail order catalogs combined with magic and arcane iconography. Smith described them as expositions spiritual systems such as

44 EXPERIMENTAL FILM AND QUEER MATERIALITY

"Buddhism and the Kabbalah" or of arcane practices such as alchemy.[49] But they can also be seen as intensely sexual, since they encode the pursuit of spiritual enlightenment through bodies that chase each other and their elusive objects of desire through the anarchic materiality of a world in constant flux. And they offer, in addition, a magical perception of the material culture of the last decades of the nineteenth century.

Heaven and Earth Magic is the longest and most articulate of these films. It is dominated by the actions of human or humanoid figures that interact with each other and with machines, animals, eggs, vegetables, architectonic spaces, and objects (bags, hammers, couches, hats, syringes)—all of them represented by cut-outs of late nineteenth-century engravings. The main actants in the film are a series of Victorian ladies and gentlemen (these last only seen in effigy), a skeleton, several mechanical creatures that seem made up of spoon-like parts, and a spastic little man who is the driving force of the film. These creatures work intricate jerry-rigged mechanisms or wield guns and enema bulbs whose white liquid transforms what it touches. The figures float freely in a black space that occasionally mutates into a confined setting: an empty space framed by a head—sometimes two—in profile, ornate elevator cars, and a mysterious domed interior briefly seen at the end.[50] Within these spaces, inconstancy is the only constant. Moving continuously, nesting in recessed cubes and traversed by rays of light and pulsing circles, the elements of the film enter dynamic arrangements that speedily form and dissolve. The quick pace and episodic structure evoke a mystic vaudeville, in which figures and motifs take their turn on the stage and exit to leave room for the following number.

Smith has hinted at different keys for understanding his film: mysticism (the Kabbalah), science (Carl Stoermer's studies of magnetic fields in the upper layers of the atmosphere and Wilder Penfield's studies of the cortical zone of the brain), and biographical testimony (Daniel Paul Schreber's memoir of his mental illness). Critics have pursued in particular *Heaven and Earth Magic*'s connection to Schreber's memoir, a connection clinched by Smith's claim that part of the film depicts Schreber's delusions and that he cut out the central "character" in the film (the hyperactive little man) from *Ärtzliche Zimmergymnastik* (1857), the gymnastics manual written by Schreber's father, doctor, and pedagogue Daniel Gottlob Moritz Schreber.[51] An additional key that has had surprisingly little play is surrealism, a key that takes us back to magic and that forces us to consider in addition the film's sexual politics and its handling of objects.

Smith himself brought up surrealism's connection to *Heaven and Earth Magic* in conversation with P. Adams Sitney. During production, he claims, he slept next to his animation stand in order to incorporate into the film the suggestions transmitted by his dreams. "I tried as much as possible to make the whole thing automatic. . . . [A]ll that stuff comes from the Surrealists— that business of folding a piece of paper: One person·draws the head and then folds it over, and somebody else draws the body. What do they call it? The Exquisite Corpse." For Smith, these surrealist procedures do not reveal chance but a divine hand behind the works: "Somebody later, perhaps Burroughs, realized that something was directing it [the automatism], that it wasn't arbitrary, and that there was some kind of what you might call God."[52] The unconscious is the first name that the surrealists gave to the underlying order revealed by chance. Magic could be another: some of its versions proffer a syntax of the world and of the latencies that populate it.

The materials Smith chose to explore this automatism—cut-outs of late nineteenth-century popular publications—are themselves characteristically surrealist. As Benjamin famously wrote, Surrealism "was the first to perceive the revolutionary energies that appear in the 'outmoded,' in the first iron constructions, the first factory buildings, the earliest photos, the objects that have begun to be extinct, grand pianos, the dresses of five years ago, fashionable restaurants when the vogue has begun to ebb from them."[53] Having fallen out of circulation and habit, outmoded objects produce cognitive disorientation and reveal latencies and possibilities that remained unnoticed when they were current. In pursuit of these experiences, the surrealists haunted the old-fashioned Parisian arcades—the *Passage de l'Opera*, extensively described in Louis Aragon's *Le Paysan de Paris* (1926)—and flea markets where discards accumulated. And their writings and photographs championed *démodé* art nouveau against slick machine age designs. In line with these retro tastes, Breton praised "the splendid illustrations" of pulp novels and children's books from the early years of the century—*Rocambole*, *Fantômas*, *Costal the Indian*—for their "plethora of . . . disconcerting conjectures": "Many of these pictures, full of an agitation all the more extraordinary for its cause being unknown to us—and the case is the same as with diagrams from, say, some technical work, provided we know nothing of it—give the illusion of veritable *slits* in time, space, customs, and even belief, wherein there is not one element that is not finally a risk."[54] Breton wrote these words in his preface to Max Ernst's first collage book, *La femme 100 têtes* (1929), created out of cut-outs from popular novels of the second half of the nineteenth century and intending, indeed, to slit not only their physical surface. With their combination of sexuality, grotesquerie, and violence, Ernst's collage books make visible some of the traumatic kernels of bourgeois life at the time—namely, sexuality, colonial violence, industrial exploitation, and the destructive potential of science.[55] *La femme*, for example, places semi-naked men and women and monstrous and incongruous creatures (part human, part animal) in placid bourgeois interiors, factories, workshops, farm fields, and public spaces, where life proceeds unruffled by the presence of these disquieting portents.

Like Ernst's books, Smith's *Heaven and Earth Magic* explores the unconscious of a superseded stage of bourgeois culture. But while Ernst gives this unconscious a specific iconic embodiment—naked women, monsters, animals—Smith foregrounds its structural aspects instead, singling out, in particular, a mechanical automatism that is at once modern and ancient; industrial and magical. In Smith's film, modernity circa 1880 is a prodigious mechanism of divisible processes and interconnected parts; the product of technological innovation, it also keeps in circulation magical energies and iconography. If the unconscious of modernity is the machine, the machine's unconscious—the unconscious of the modern unconscious—is, in turn, magic.

Smith once described his film as "a sortilege of parts."[56] It is machine-like in its exhaustive permutations of a relatively limited number of elements: "All the permutations possible were built up."[57] Its combinatorial character also recalls the intricate interconnectedness of the magical correspondence tables, such as the ones in Aleister Crowley's *Liber 777*, where a relatively small number of items, such as planets, numbers, mythological characters, or substances, combine to produce a vast number of effects.[58] The tables demonstrate Crowley's maxim about the composite character of the world: "a continuous phenomenon" whose parts link up in ways only intelligible to initiates.[59] The idea is present in other mystic systems. The Kabbalah, for example, one of Smith's self-avowed inspirations, is an attempt to formalize the connections between the fragments that make up the universe. In his introduction to Christian Knorr von Rosenroth's *Kabbala Denudata*, a text that, according to Smith, contains some keys to the film, late nineteenth-century occultist S. L. MacGregor Mathers underlines the combinatorial quality of the different modalities of Kabbalistic hermeneutics. What Mathers calls the "literal Kabbalah" elicits a plurality of hidden significations from the permutation of letters and the ascription of numerical values to them. The "doctrinal"

Kabbalah derives an entire cosmogony from the permutation of the twenty-two letters of the Hebrew alphabet and from numbers one to ten. And the so-called tree of life explains the world's polymorphous variety through the interaction of the ten Sephirot—the principles that mediate divine powers. In Gershom Scholem's words, "The number 10 [the ten Sephirot] provided the framework for the growth of a seemingly endless multiplicity of lights and processes."[60] In all cases, a limited number of elements—the letters of the alphabet, numbers, the Sephirot—are the cogs of a vast machinery whose constantly moving parts encode the divine plan behind the visible and help to interpret it.[61]

Endowed with limited parts but potentially limitless connectivity, the machine is the material incarnation of the Kabbalah's—and other magic systems'—combinatorial dynamism. In *Heaven and Earth Magic*, hygrometers, pipelines, valves, clocks, and assortments of cogs, camshafts, and tools float aimlessly about, whirl, turn, link up momentarily, and implode. Out of their collapse rise other mechanical entities that start, in turn, a new cycle that is often a variation of the previous one. The human figures in the film also evince a mechanical quality. The pervasive little man (sometimes called the "homunculus") that triggers off much of the film's activity moves with stiff automatism and concludes his actions with a brief signature dance that recalls a wind-up toy. A bewhiskered respectable head (the effigy of nineteenth-century religious studies scholar and philologist Max Müller, translator of many of the sacred texts of Buddhism and Hinduism), swallows many of the film's objects and characters with machine-like regularity, while his eyes flash destructive light beams. After being swallowed, some of these figures travel down in an elevator car that ends up slushing in a liquid environment, in what may be a mechanical rendition of the digestive apparatus. The "heroine" of the film often falls apart like an ill-fitting ensemble, grows telescopic limbs or, deprived of a lower body, is reduced to a bust perched on a stand. She is injected, assembled, and disassembled by the little man, who delights in removing and replacing her arms, torso, head, and clothes as if she were a composite.

Perhaps because of their machine-like quality, the little man and "the heroine" lack a clear gender identity. They are integrated into multiply articulated ensembles that are governed less by gender difference than by gender indifference; everything in them sprouts appendixes, links up with other machines, folds in, and invaginates. The little man drives the action during much of the film, but he is also driven by it. While he is more self-contained and indivisible than most of his friable peerage, his stability in shape does not entail a stability in function. In his role as master of ceremonies, he is temporarily replaced by other entities, such as a skeleton, an undefinable figure made up of loosely attached organs, and "the heroine" herself. Melons and eggs open up and swallow him, and he is crunched up by Müller's teeth and gulped down. Intimately involved with the rest of the film's components, the "homunculus" and the "heroine" are engaged in a dance that is never binary, nor limited to themselves, nor simply corporeal, but expansively material and mechanical.

In this regard, the film may be read as a version of what Michel Carrouges called a "bachelor machine": a combination of bodies and machines that scripted sexuality through mechanical protocols and mechanics through sex.[62] The name comes from Marcel Duchamp's sculpture *Grand Verre*, or *The Bride Stripped Bare by her Bachelors, Even* (1911–1923), which Carrouges took as prototype of the bachelor machine. Duchamp's piece consists of two conjoined glass plates on which the artist painted organic and mechanical parts that interlock through helixes, cables, flanges, wheels, and insect-like appendages. Useless and delirious, bachelor machines are kindred to fairground attractions, which mobilize technology to produce sensorial stimulation. Carrouges notes their prevalence in turn-of-the-century literature, both in the high modernism of Alfred Jarry, Raymond Roussel, or Franz Kafka and in the popular fiction of Jules Verne, H. G. Wells, or Edgar R. Burroughs. With their purposeless intricacy, the bachelor machines are the playful double of goal-oriented industrial technology. And with their quirky, potentially endless conjunctions, they embody the anarchic libidinal spillage that the bourgeois family sought to contain. Rather than reproductive, socialized sex and recognizable gender, the bachelor machines offer instead what Gilles Deleuze and Félix Guattari called proliferating "intensities": a libido without stable shape or definite aim channeled through variable circuits.[63]

The energy that feeds these circuits is not merely libidinal. It also reveals a magical undertow in the objects and mechanisms of late capitalism. Part of the wonder of industrial technology resided in its ability to command natural forces and in its seemingly fantastic powers. The fantastic power of technology was transmitted, as if by contagion, to the mechanically manufactured goods, which were endowed, in turn, with otherworldly potency. In his classic analysis, Karl Marx noted the "queer" liveliness and "metaphysical subtleties" of commodities, whose value and meaning appeared to emanate from their intrinsic nature but were in fact determined by their market value and by the capital and labor invested in their production. Producers faced in commodities the results of their own activity in inverted form: "their own social action [their work] takes the form of the action of objects, which rule the producers instead of being ruled by them."[64] Marx described this inversion as a form of "fetishism." Like talismanic objects, commodities appeared to be endowed with an autonomous efficacy that, while appearing natural, was in fact manufactured and socially sanctioned. The Marxist critique of the commodity seeks to reverse this perception—to show that the apparent second nature of capitalism is in fact contingent and historical, and therefore no nature at all. The (commodity) fetish is a mere object whose users have convened to treat it as a force.

Hardly a Marxist, Smith did not attempt to denaturalize the commodity and restore its historicity, but to animate it still further, collapsing it even more with the natural world.[65] Rather than reduce the commodity's fetishistic qualities, he heightened them by turning the pieces of the material world into cyphers for the supernatural forces that commodity circulation and use constantly, if hazily, conjure. The mobility and elaborate connections of objects and creatures in *Heaven and Earth Magic* reveal the ability of everything to act on everything else through causal chains that bypass known physical laws and ordinary logic and may only be explained through alternate forms of causality that have often been called magic. Magic, pointed out Marcel Mauss in his classic study, is action at a distance, characterized by incommensurability between means and goals and by discontinuity between cause and effect: "this is the realm of the occult and of the spirits, a world of ideas which imbues ritual movements and gestures with a special kind of effectiveness, quite different from their mechanical effectiveness."[66] This efficacy is what he called "*mana*": "power per excellence, the general effectiveness of things." He compared it "to our notion of mechanical force," except it was brought about by non-mechanical means such as ritual and invocation.[67] The landscape of consumer culture and modern machinery could be imbued with mana in the same way that it was already pervaded with the mechanical and electrical energy that kept it in constant motion. The material culture of late capitalism was a gigantic combinatorial apparatus whose haphazard coincidences produced accidental conjurations and summons. Under the circulation of commodities and the chugging away of machinery ran, as an undertone, a stream of incantations whose nature and effect were only perceptible to the initiated.

Magic, however, was not always a hidden undercurrent in the world of objects and mechanisms; it could also be found in their midst. The Sears,

50   EXPERIMENTAL FILM AND QUEER MATERIALITY

Roebuck and Co. catalogs from around 1900 peddled modern technology *and* ancient lore. Alongside clothing, agricultural machinery, drugs, clocks, and a dizzying array of gadgets, the company sold books on "Hypnotism, Palmistry, Physiognomy, Astrology."[68] Especially popular were *Egyptian Secrets; or the Black and White Art for Man and Beast*, and *The Sixth and Seventh Books of Moses*. Apocryphally attributed to Albertus Magnus, the medieval philosopher and saint, *Egyptian Secrets* was a collection of folk remedies and magic formulae to fend off misfortune, disease, and ill will. *The Sixth and Seventh Books of Moses* was an abstruse eighteenth-century German tract attributed to Moses himself, with sections on cosmology, "the magic of the Israelites," conjures, and tables that linked different spirits to the four elements and to the planets. Widely read at the end of the nineteenth century, both titles had numerous editions and were kept in print well into the twentieth century by De Laurence, Scott, and Co., a Chicago publisher specializing in the occult. Several thematic motifs link Smith's film and these texts. Egyptian mummies appear at the opening and closing of *Heaven and Earth Magic*; they are metonymies for the ancient civilization that supposedly nurtured Moses's magic wisdom and have been regarded as the mythic source of much subsequent esoterica. In both books, just as in Smith's film, animals—particularly domestic and farm animals—have a significant presence, whether as property to be preserved from disease and psychic attack or as the guises in which the spirits manifest themselves. Two of these guises—oxen and dogs—recur through the film, as do ravens—which in *The Sixth and Seventh Books* are featured as allies in some invocations—and celestial bodies, visible behind the elevator cabins. Whether these parallels were intended or not, the numinous quality of these motifs and their atemporal character, when compared with more clearly datable late nineteenth-century objects and figures, point to a different order of time and belief. Through them, *Heaven and Earth Magic* reveals the plural, discontinuous temporalities of modernity and the ability of industrial material culture and modern objects to harbor anti-modern belief systems.

Queering the New

While Menken used objects and substances without clear temporal markers, Jacobs, Jack Smith, and Ron Rice reclaimed the outdated and cast-off, and Harry Smith combined the magical and the industrial; still others exploited the queer potential of the brazenly new. This was the case with painter and pioneer of experimental film Fernand Léger, who fled to New York from occupied France during World War II, and with painters-turned-filmmakers Sarah Kathryn Arledge and Jim Davis.

Léger's short *The Girl with the Prefabricated Heart* was part of the omnibus work *Films that Money Can't Buy* (1947), produced by Hans Richter but also containing segments by Man Ray, Marcel Duchamp, Max Ernst, and Alexander Calder, and Richter himself. Cleverly assembled and edited to Jean Latouche's song of the same name, Léger's sequence pokes fun at the technocratic fantasy of total control over the material world. It uses smartly attired mannequins to narrate a failed love story between two artificial creatures painstakingly designed for each other. One is a goddess "poured from a mold," with nylon hair, plastic arms, "chromium nerves," "platinum brain chastely encased in cellophane," and a prefabricated heart. Her paramour is a "mail-order male . . . sent by the gods directly from Yale." The match seems ideal at first, but her mechanical heart panics at his physical attentions—"You are so impetuous!" She ends up fleeing from his arms to ride instead with her Amazon sisters at sunset, "Isolde without a Tristan," while her suitor "dissolved into tears and disintegrated." The runaway bride rises from the world of modern synthetics, designed for an optimal erotic fit and ruled by gender dualism and strict heterosexism, but even plastics and chromium may rebel, and she ends up escaping into what Adrienne Rich would have called a mythic lesbian continuum that promises more flexible arrangements.[69] The Amazon escapee had a real-life correlative in Latouche's wife, Teodora, who was a lesbian and eventually left him.[70] The mismatch that the film narrates also reverberates in the soundtrack. Latouche's song is performed by Libby Holman (who was bisexual and had been the lover of several gay men) and by her frequent singing partner, black singer Josh White. Theirs was another (nearly) impossible partnership whose biracial character defied prevailing postwar segregationism and severely limited their radio play and the geographical reach of their tours.[71]

Jim Davis and Sarah Kathryn Arledge uphold the queer appeal of the modern inorganic more openly than Léger, who still idealizes the mythic neverland of the Amazons against the programmed boredom of the nylon-cellophane world. Initially trained as painters, Davis and Arledge followed a familiar pattern among postwar filmmakers, as both took up the camera in order to extend into time and motion the formal explorations they had been carrying out on canvas. Davis ended up devoting most of his creative energies

52 EXPERIMENTAL FILM AND QUEER MATERIALITY

to film; Arledge remained primarily attached to her two-dimensional art but continued making films throughout her life. In fact, her later titles, cinematic records of her paintings accompanied by sound effects, seem to attempt a synthesis between her two main media.

Arledge's first films consisted in recordings of Apache dances—the topic of some early figurative paintings as well.[72] Her first substantial effort, which also turned out to be her best-known, *Introspection* (1946), was started in 1941, while she was an art teacher at a Pasadena school. It was interrupted, when some of her performers were drafted to serve in the war, and eventually finished in 1946.[73] The temporal gap is not noticeable in the film, which is cohesively shot and edited. Described at times as "the first experimental dance film," *Introspection* presents heads, hands, limbs, torsos, and whole bodies carrying out fairly inexpressive, minimal movements, anticipating a style of dance that was still several decades in the future. The dancers are partly blacked out and filmed against a dark background in such a way that body parts—at times entire bodies—appear to soar free of gravity. The dancers are also reflected on a domed surface—an automobile's hubcap—whose curvature minimizes their torsos and heads and augments the proportions of hands and arms, which appear to revolve around an invisible axis. Skillful superimpositions make these shapes unfold from inside each other and create visual echoes and relays. (The optical printing was partly made by filmmaker John Whitney, a Pasadena neighbor and friend).[74] While the film introduces itself as "fragments of dancer imagery," frequent visual rhymes unify the whole. The ethereal nature and meditative pace of the dancers' movements have an oneiric quality. The effect was entirely deliberate (see Figure 2.4). The film's working title was in fact *Phantasmagoria*, but Arledge changed it after the release of Disney's *Fantasia* (1940) to avoid suggesting a connection between the two. Titled *Dance Film*, it premiered at the San Francisco Art in Cinema series on April 11, 1947 in the program "Trickery and Surrealism," alongside Méliès's *A Trip to the Moon* (1902), René Clair's *Paris qui dort* (1924), Watson and Webber's *Fall of the House of Usher* (1928), and "two French surrealist animations."[75] Further contributing to its unreality is the indefinite gender of the dancers: while they were biological males, their flesh-colored tights and makeup attenuate anatomical features, turning them into slightly otherworldly epicenes.

Introspection's unreality and corporeal vagueness rise in part from the distorting reflections on a Chrysler's hubcap, used, Arledge claimed, for its smoothness, as it was one of the few hubcaps that was not imprinted with the

Figure 2.4 Sara Kathryn Arledge, *Introspection*, 1946. Frame enlargement.

manufacturer's insignia.[76] Even though the hubcap is not identifiable as such in the film—it merely appears as a curved reflecting surface—its use links the dreamy, organic, and timeless, to the automotive and contemporary, making the latter a vehicle of the former. The rotating hands and arms mirrored on the hubcap enhance its roundness and refer to its ordinary circular motion, but they transpose this motion from the register of functionality and speed to that of contemplation and dance—that is, to the reflective and the aesthetic. Circularity also evokes the film's cyclical character—it is built upon subtle repetitions—and apparent impregnability to the outside—except, that is, for the mundane hubcap that pulls the film from Lester Horton's darkened dance studio, where it was filmed, to a topical convergence of bodies, buildings, and machinery. Chrysler car parts had entered the vocabulary of art deco in the ornamentation of the company's famous corporate tower in Manhattan, finished in 1930. Designed by William van Alen, the Chrysler Building combined granite and steel, was topped by a metallic needle and eagle-shaped gargoyles, and featured hood ornaments on the corners of the setbacks and friezes made of bumpers and hubcaps. Fenders and hubcaps clinched the building's identification with the company and underlined the

54   EXPERIMENTAL FILM AND QUEER MATERIALITY

association, by then commonplace, between modern architecture and machinery, while expunging corporeal presence and anthropomorphic shape. Arledge's film moves in the opposite direction; in it, the technological does not deny the human, but transforms it into the humanoid. While recognizable as belonging to people in motion, the reflections on the hubcap hover undecidedly between whole body and body part, human and thing, gesture and mass, organic and inert—oscillations that are also present in Arledge's painting.

In Arledge's subsequent film, *What is a Man?* (1956) cars play a significant part. Emblems of dispirited material comfort, they are also tinged with sexual anxiety. The pre-credit sequence edits together classic pictorial nudes (Cranach the Elder's paintings of Adam and Eve), an Edenically naked couple, and anatomical charts, and is capped by a shot of night traffic and a dissonant car horn. In a later scene, Somebody Elsie, the film's protagonist, buys a car and asks the vendor what to do next: "Brrr, brrr . . . which way?" "Face your reality," he says, and suggests that she visits "a medicine man." During her medical examination, the shadow of a steering wheel is projected on the back wall, as if the automobile loomed large in her discomfort. "I cling to the schizophringes of art and reality," she confesses, to which the doctor recommends—in the film's Joycean cant—"a sighcryatryst." And a tryst it is. At the end of the film, she has a rendezvous with Beowulf—her male counterpart—at a Motel that is synoptically represented by the static shot of a neon sign against which off-screen dialogue between the film's two protagonists unfolds. A classic setting for furtive sex, the motel does not contribute erotic fulfilment but further unease, caused in part by a threatening quality in contemporary technology: "What is that lovely apt to rape us?" Somebody Elsie puns off screen. The film withholds the answer, and the menacing apparatus that is "apt to rape us"—whether the automobile or, in vaster outline, the machinery of contemporary civilization, remains unseen and unspecified.[77]

Like Arledge, Jim Davis also used modern synthetics to articulate elusive bodies aligned with heterodox desires. Trained as a painter in the late 1920s, he evolved, in the words of his only exegete, Robert Haller, through "Cubist and American phases" and started, in the early 1940s, to make translucent plastic sculptures, bringing into art a material that had been used almost exclusively in manufacture.[78] (Naum Gabo's nylon thread and acrylic glass sculptures were among the few artistic uses of the new material). Plastic sculptures gave three-dimensional shape to the exploration of color that Davis had been carrying out in his paintings; they were attempts to reproduce, as he put it, "the dynamic element in nature," which traditional painting could not capture.[79] His film *Path of Motion* (1950), a visual synopsis of his painting career, shows the increasing dynamism of his brushstrokes and his evolution from the rendering of mass and outline to the calligraphic notation—in Futurist style—of vectors of force and lines of motion. The plastic sculptures were a further step in this trajectory. Suspended, lit, and rotated, they decomposed and refracted light in ever-changing ways, showing the multiplicity that lurked in light and the movement that was latent in apparently static shapes. By extension, they demonstrated the complexity of the everyday world, a complexity that he probed in figurative films, such as *The Sea* (1950) or *Variations on a Theme* (1957)—dealing with water currents, turbulence, and entropy—and that he conceived as aesthetic counterparts of scientific documentaries: "[T]he closest analogies to my abstract reflections are to be found in scientific films (growth of cells, development of crystals, explosions on the sun, hidden depths of the sea, etc.)," he once wrote to Frank Stauffacher.[80]

Davis gave performances of refracted light at institutions such as the Museum of Modern Art, the San Francisco Museum of Art, and Los Angeles County Museum, among others, as well as in the intimacy of his Princeton studio, and garnered in the process an impressive roster of supporters that included Frank Lloyd Wright, László Moholy-Nagy, Alfred Barr, Martha Graham, Richard Neutra, and Buckminster Fuller. Stauffacher, director of "Art in Cinema," was another of his devotees. Davis had started making films of the light reflections cast by his sculptures in 1946, and shortly afterward, in 1947, he sent Harry Smith, Stauffacher's assistant at the time, some of his early films for consideration. Smith and Stauffacher were evidently impressed. Davis was first featured in "Art in Cinema" in February of 1949 in the program "Contemporary Experimental Films of Importance" alongside work by James Broughton, Sidney Peterson, Dorsey Alexander, and Harry Smith himself. He was repeatedly programmed through the life of the series, an exposure that probably accounts for his reputation among abstract Californian filmmakers of the time, such as Curtis Opliger.[81]

Davis's engagement with the cinema and with plastics began to occupy him at a time of crucial personal and artistic change. While in his public writing he justified this engagement on formal and conceptual grounds, his private journals reveal also a personal investment. The adoption of modern technology and materials and the interest in moving, rather than fixed, color

56 EXPERIMENTAL FILM AND QUEER MATERIALITY

and shape, were timed to his growing detachment from his strict Puritanical background: "I not only abandoned the traditional tools of art for new and more progressive ones, but I also gave up trying to frustrate my own individual way of thinking and living by the obsolete precepts of my Calvinistic–Presbyterian upbringing."[82] The refracted light films may have been his way of channeling a sexuality that he did not feel comfortable expressing through other means.[83] "Personally, I have found that in my abstract films many people will be shocked by them as 'too sexy.' And perhaps at times they very well may be my unconscious revelations of otherwise suppressed sexual urges."[84] In the same journal entry where he ponders his "too sexy" work, he discusses the orgasmic rhythm of Wagner's music and the fact that the music's abstraction renders its sexiness both powerful and pervasive. Abstraction, he continues, allows artists to transmit contents that might not be openly expressed in a repressive environment: it "can express freely, and in *full, all* of the infinite variety of human experience and feelings, whether acceptable, or rejected as evil, by standard rules."[85]

"Evil by standard rules" may have been the naked bodies that lurk among the wispy gleams and color washes of his 1950s and 1960s films. These combine light refracted through plastics and close-ups of shapes reflected on metalized acetate—think Willard Maas's *Geography of the Body* (1943) in a hall of distorting mirrors. In *Thru the Looking Glass* (1953) arms, hands, feet, and a face are briefly seen but quickly melt again into swirling iridescence. The film is dominated by flesh and skin tones occasionally streaked with the blue and red of the garments that the performers peel off. *Energies* (1957) and *Death and Transfiguration* (1961) place corporeal reflections alongside abstract light patterns, suggesting continuity, even identity, between corporeal and luminous abstractions. Light abstractions dominate the beginning and end of the films, bracketing—perhaps containing—the corporeal, which is allowed to emerge only shyly and as long as it is detached from actuality and recognizability (Figure 2.5).

It is tempting to read these films as closet acts—as works that both allude to Davis's desires while simultaneously concealing them. He confessed that he destroyed much of his work out of fear: "I am afraid of revealing too clearly those things in myself that are 'taboo' in our social, legal, religious, etc. order." He wrote this in August of 1966, the summer when Andy Warhol was filming *The Chelsea Girls*, which premiered to moderate mainstream success in the fall. Davis was cautious even as the counterculture was in full swing and the sexual liberation movement was about to burst. But there are

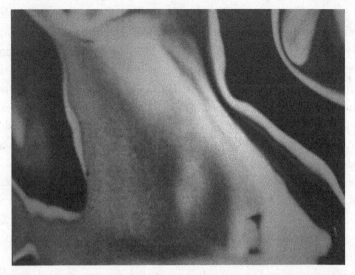

Figure 2.5 Jim Davis, *Thru the Looking Glass*, 1953. Frame enlargement.

other parts of his filmography where it seems that he allowed his desires to emerge. While Davis was crafting his abstractions, he was also busy making film portraits of Princeton University athletes in titles such as *Crew-Cut* (a portrait of Princeton's rowing team), *C. von Wrangell in Single Scull*, or *Princeton Sports*, all from 1951.[86] No doubt, they distract from Davis's formalist concerns, which is perhaps why they are not included in the DVD compilations of his work. It is easy to see how athletes encapsulated his interest with form pregnant with dynamism, along with his fascination with he described in his diaries as "the handsome youthful male in the nude—the most beautiful of all animals."[87] I doubt that there is much nudity in these films. But if he could openly make films of athletes, and not destroy them, it is hard to imagine what may have been so worrisome about the abstractions or in what way they revealed him.

Fear, concealment, revelation, and discretion all belong in the rhetoric of the closet. But did Davis need a closet? As single man, a dandified *artiste* and painting instructor who liked to make films of student athletes, one wonders how closeted Davis may have been in Princeton in the fifties and sixties. Abstraction for him may have been not only a strategy of subterfuge and disguise, but of amplification and exploration. Davis kept making abstractions when it was no longer strictly necessary. Perhaps he sticks to this mode precisely because it is risky and edgy but also subtle and haunting, like

58   EXPERIMENTAL FILM AND QUEER MATERIALITY

the orgasmic movement of Wagner's music. Abstraction relieved Davis from the imperative to explain himself or his films. "The more you use words, the more you are far from the truth. I don't understand poetry. I want to dance."[88] For many artists operating in a queer spectrum, abstraction was a tool of refusal—the refusal to make oneself clear and to explain oneself. Queer abstraction resists, as Lex Lancaster puts it, "the demand that we must always 'show up' in ways that are expected," and rejects, in David Getsy's words, "the cultural marking of the human body."[89] Davis was in good company in this regard. Jonathan D. Katz has shown that queer mid-century artists, such as Agnes Martin and John Cage, used abstraction as a means of projecting a sexuality without labels and identifiable contours. In this way they avoided homophobic censorship, which suppressed explicit sexual representation, and projected an eroticism that bypassed available categories and expanded beyond the restricting confines of the human body.[90]

Davis's exploration of motion and dynamic form was predicated, as he put it, on "the release from anthropomorphic compulsion"—a sort of posthuman perception before the posthuman was in vogue. This perception directed his gaze to the intricacies of light and color in complete independence of narrative frames or psychological grounding. His films are themselves the products of materials in interaction: light against plastics captured on film. They escape his own volition. As Cage did, who was also intent on eliminating personality from music, Davis set up a frame where motion, light, color, and optics could unfold at their own pace, slightly modulated by the human hand. While the human often rests on the stability of what we call personality and individuality, light and color are ever mutable and uncontainable, constantly sliding beyond their own limits. They also allow for nonhuman styles of relationality, which do not run on the familiar tracks of possession, mutuality, and reciprocation but on diffraction and distorting reflection. They stage *bad* relationships—the only ones Davis confessed he was ever capable of.[91] The subjects and objects placed in front of silver mylar sheets do not receive their image back, but lose it irremediably. Light decomposes as it traverses Plexiglas structures and mutates without purpose or resolution. Film only captures a fleeting moment in potentially endless metamorphoses.

The assemblages that produce Davis's films are heterogeneous mixtures of hard and soft, unholy alliances of light (timeless, spiritual) and plastics (topical, crassly material); they spiritualize the material but also materialize the spiritual by anchoring it on everyday industrial materials: Plexiglas, acetate, mylar, Lumarith (used in the manufacture of lamp shades).[92] At the height of Davis's engagement with plastic, this material was becoming a central support in a new information economy. Acetate and, especially, mylar, a new polyester widely commercialized since the early 1950s, were quickly becoming the base for technical blueprints, film, and the magnetic tape that stored audio recordings and computer programs. Ironically, Davis's plastics have a counter-informational function. They dilute shapes and vanishing lines. Rather than legible data and definite form, they yield blurred outlines, immersive enfoldment, and corporeal noise. On the material infrastructure of order and control, Davis's films inscribed corporealities that eluded the dominant protocols of gender and sexual legibility in those years and allowed queer bodies and relations to show up where they were least expected.

* * *

The discrepant materiality of postwar experimental film ranged widely from ruins and discards to refracting polymers and synthetic bodies, and from haunted machinery to stuttering everyday objects. This deliberately archaic, obfuscating horizon stands in vivid contrast to the material culture of the postwar years, which was dominated by functional, legible objects and transparent spaces—flashy appliances in tidy suburban sprawls. While the objecthood of experimental film was mutable, enfolding, and resisted detached observation and optical control, standard commodities, by contrast, were mere instruments: as housework aids, status signs, sources of entertainment, or all of these at once, they were expected to operate predictably and efficiently. When they were showcased as art objects, as in the Museum of Modern Art's "Good Design" exhibitions, held between 1950 and 1955, they were to be enjoyed for their formal qualities and observed at a distance.[93] By contrast, the deviant materials of experimental film undercut critical detachment and routed human (and para-human) sentience through constellations where it was not easy to separate human(oid) and material vicissitude. In this way, they made matter alive with queer possibility and channeled corporeal and affective formations that were suppressed or sidelined in hegemonic material culture.

As they lean toward the ornamental, excessive, and unstable, the material assemblages that populate postwar experimental film diverge from mid-century modern design. Color spills over outline and structure, motion destabilizes composition, and layered intricacy hinders unobstructed visibility. Experimental filmmakers were not alone in making their rupture with the modern. Other relatively marginal taste communities distanced

60 EXPERIMENTAL FILM AND QUEER MATERIALITY

themselves from hegemonic modern design. Historian Shelley Nickles has shown that working class consumers, for example, rejected what they perceived as the bureaucratic coldness and boredom of the modern in order to assert their class identity.[94] Having gained access to high-end goods thanks to their increased acquisitive power, they demanded what Nickles named a "more is better" aesthetic of embellishment, bulk, color, and shine. These features were abhorrent to establishment taste arbiters because they diluted the goals of high design and connoted femininity—an association that went back at least to Adolf Loos's conflation, in the early twentieth century, of ornamentation, criminality, primitivism, and women.[95] For working class consumers, and especially for the women among them, more substantial and ornate goods—cars, furniture, appliances—signified solidity and success. "More-is-better" also telegraphed the rejection of an alien taste imposed by the cultural elites and the desire to maintain working-class distinctiveness in a society that claimed to have done away with class difference. From this perspective, Nickles concludes, consumption was as much about acquiring goods as about "creating society" and "establishing new social bonds and distinctions."[96] Experimental filmmakers used material dissidence in a similar fashion. The unorthodox object culture they created signaled a willed distance from the contemporary mainstream and sheltered an alternative world that welcomed discrepant aesthetes, queers, occultists, anarchists, and various stripes of dissenters.

The dissident material practice of experimental filmmakers dovetails with the work of a bicoastal group of younger artists that started to produce their main work in the fifties and have often been associated with beat culture. Some of these are California artists such as sculptors Bruce Conner and George Herms, collagists Jess (Collins) and Wallace Berman, and filmmaker Larry Jordan.[97] Their counterparts on the East Coast, were artists such as Jim Dine, Allan Kaprow, and Claes Oldenburg, who pioneered assemblages, environments, and happenings. Like the experimental filmmakers surveyed in this chapter, they worked on rejects—sometimes on literal trash—resorted to older image repertoires, and kept alive the surrealist investment in incongruous objects and degraded materials. More than a mere artistic statement, their dissident object practice sought to communicate a different way of life and a sense of the possibilities untapped by an oppressive mainstream fixated on novelty and efficiency and mistrustful of social and cultural otherness.

Aligned with this body of work, postwar experimental film seems less an asynchronous development or an unplaceable rarity than the forerunner of a new sensibility toward the vernacular materiality that would characterize much of the art and film of the following decade, and to which we turn in the following chapters.

3

Amphetamine and Queer Materiality in Andy Warhol's Factory Films

As we saw in the Chapter 2, objects, ruins, substances, and commodities serve as external catalysts and allegorical stand-ins for alternative bodies and desires. By contrast, drugs work directly on the body from the inside, merging inextricably with it. They manufacture mood and sensation and supplement corporeal capacities with minute precision, revealing the dependence of the consciousness-perception apparatus on a material baseline of chemical compounds acting on the physiology of the brain. Drug use is, of course, ancestral; in traditional cultures it is tied to visionary and mystic experience and to communal ritual, associations that narcotics have never shaken off entirely. However, by the middle of the twentieth century, drugs had become largely desacralized, standardized, and integrated into the routines of modern living. Around them grew a massive pharmacological industry, biomedical protocols, and widespread untutored use, to the extent that, as Paul B. Preciado notes, "modern subjectivity amounts to the management of self-intoxication in a noxious chemical environment."[1] A central goal of self-intoxication has always been corporeal well-being and the pursuit of pleasure, but drug-taking also contains a critical refusal. For William Burroughs, for example, drugs permitted their users to resist the standardization of sensation and affect imposed by the mainstream media and to tune minds and bodies into alternative frequencies.[2] For other thinkers, such as John Barker, drugs are a threshold to a temporality, a physicality, and a sensorium outside the rhythms of paid labor and capitalist production and were therefore potentially liberatory in the tightly regimented environment of the postwar years.[3] And for Jack Halberstam, they contribute to a queer temporality, as they blur conventional narrative lifelines and prompt an existence based on intensive bursts and immediate gratification rather than on the careful management of time and energy to produce stability, longevity, and profit.[4]

Experimental Film and Queer Materiality. Juan A. Suárez, Oxford University Press. © Oxford University Press 2024.
DOI: 10.1093/oso/9780197566992.003.0003

Amphetamine contributed to the pursuit of pleasure and dissent but was also integrated into the routines of work and consumption. Sold in different forms over the counter until the late 1960s, when its unmonitored use was proscribed, it was taken for health and for enhanced work performance, but also—most often—for kicks, sex, thrills, and artistic inspiration. Despite its pervasiveness, it left relatively discrete traces in the cultural archive, and, consequently, it has been seldom studied, unlike opiates—aides to visionary rapture from Coleridge to Baudelaire to Burroughs—or LSD—which fueled the 1960s and 1970s psychedelia. Along with Beat literature, Andy Warhol's Factory is one of the sites where one can best track amphetamine's effects on art, community, corporeality, and affect—particularly, as we will see, on queer affect.

However, critics and historians have traditionally made little of Warhol's insistence, throughout his sixties memoirs, that "[t]he big social thrust behind the Factory from '64 to '67 was amphetamine," and that much that went on at the Factory, artistically or otherwise, had some connection with the drug.[5] For example: why did Warhol's assistant Billy Name line the Factory in silver? Silver was modern, connoted the space age and the classical Hollywood silver screen, muses Warhol, but, in the end, it must have been also "an amphetamine thing—everything always went back to that" (*P* 65). Amphetamine certainly fueled the energy and creativity of the two main groups that peopled the mid-1960s Factory—the "fags on speed" who gathered at the San Remo, a Village coffee shop, and the college-educated Harvard/Cambridge set (*P* 64). The former were peripherally involved in the creative ferment of downtown New York: in experimental poetry, dance, performance, and off-off-Broadway theater. The latter were bright scions of upper and upper-middle class families who became enmeshed in the life of the Factory between early 1965 and late 1966. Both groups left behind an ephemeral, largely performative, body of work consisting in amphetamine-driven patter and comedic routines, "trip books," environments (the silver Factory itself), and lighting designs.[6] It was art in a minor mode, made without any thought of solidity or permanence, to be consumed on the run and, at best, live on in memory. And this would have been its fate if it had not been for Warhol's films and recordings, which have, in this regard, an important documentary function. If Warhol lent visibility to these unconventional artists and performers, they in turn confirmed him in the possibilities of creativity under speed, which he had been exploring on his own before he enlisted them into his projects and world.

64 EXPERIMENTAL FILM AND QUEER MATERIALITY

The main San Remo "fags on speed" were Billy Linich—later Billy Name—Ondine, and Fred Herko.[7] Linich had lit some Judson Church dance shows and collaborated with Diane di Prima and Leroi Jones's mimeographed art review *The Floating Bear*. He was Warhol's some-time boyfriend and long-term assistant, and a fundamental shaper of the look and atmosphere of the "silver Factory" on West 47th Street, near the United Nations. Another of the San Remo personalities was Ondine (nickname of Robert Olivo), a street wit and hanger-on who wrote the column "Ondine's Advice to the Shopworn" for *The Sinking Bear*—the parodic reply to *The Floating Bear*. Ondine became one of the central performers in the mid-decade Factory films and had a brief theatrical career in the late 1960s acting in plays by John Vaccaro (*Conquest of the Universe*), Ronald Tavel (*Vinyl*, first produced as a Factory film), and Soren Agenoux (*Chas. Dickens' Christmas Carol*).[8] For his part, Herko was a prodigious, if ephemeral, talent in Judson Church dance. He quit his piano studies at Juilliard to enter the American Ballet Theater school at the comparatively late age of nineteen and became shortly afterward a choreographer and dancer in the downtown scene until his speed use started to erode his abilities. A close friend of Linich, with whom he shared an apartment for a while, Herko made a Warhol screen test and appears in *Kiss* (1963–64), in two versions of *Haircut* (no. 1 and no. 2, 1963), in *Jill and Freddy Dancing* (1963), purportedly in *Dance Movie* (aka *Rollerskates* 1963), a lost film that apparently showed him skating through different areas of New York while striking dance positions, and in several unpreserved six hundred-foot rolls containing close-ups, posing, and some skating.[9]

Linked to them by drugs and friendship, rather than artistic leanings, were "Rotten Rita" (Kenneth Knapp), the Duchess (Brigid Berlin), and Binghamton Birdie. Rita appears throughout Warhol's *a, a novel* (1968), essentially a transcript of 24 hours of speed-driven conversations recorded on magnetic tape over a period of two years, and Binghamton Birdie is fleetingly seen in *Couch* (1964) and cast in a screen test, but neither he nor Rita were an integral part of the Factory world. Berlin, however, furnished one of the most impacting performances in *The Chelsea Girls* (1966), starred in several 1967 films (*Bike Boy* and several reels of ****, the 24-hour program of December 1967), and remained in Warhol's orbit until the end of his life. The daughter of a prominent Manhattan family, she had been on diet pills since her teens, as her mother tried to curtail her unladylike appetite and chunky figure. Berlin plays herself as a brash drug retailer in an episode of *The Chelsea Girls* during which she shoots methedrine right through her jeans and gives her partner in the scene, Ingrid Superstar, a poke.

Some of the San Remo fags called themselves The Amphetamine Rapture Group, a group cemented by their cult of the drug and of opera (particularly of Maria Callas). Warhol often called them The Mole People for their furtiveness and night habits and "A-Men" for the amphetamine they took and the Catholic background many of them shared (Figure 3.1). More peripheral to the Factory, but also participants in the San Remo/downtown art scene were eccentric gallerist Dorothy Podber (known for showing up at the Factory and shooting a bullet through a stack of Warhol's Marilyns), artist Ray Johnson, and playwright Soren Agenoux. All three were considerable speed freaks. This was not the case with Ronald Tavel, another "San Remo fag" who was the Factory resident scenarist from late 1964 to late 1966.

The other "feeder of personalities and ideas" into the Factory, "the Harvard/Cambridge crowd," was also steeped in amphetamine. Edie Sedgwick's drug use has been widely and morbidly recorded, yet other figures in her set were also turned on to pep pills, even if they were less spectacular consumers. Danny Fields, the son of a Manhattan doctor, claimed that by the time he chanced on the Factory he had already been on amphetamine his "whole life"; since adolescence he had been in the habit of helping himself from the bowl of diet pills his parents kept on the dining room table.[10] And filmmaker and innovative light designer Danny Williams, a former Harvard student who was also Warhol's boyfriend for a while, was on extended speed

Figure 3.1 Andy Warhol, *The Chelsea Girls*, 1966. 16mm film, black-and-white and color, sound, 204 minutes in double screen © The Andy Warhol Museum, Pittsburgh, PA, a museum of Carnegie Institute. All rights reserved. Film still courtesy The Andy Warhol Museum.

66 EXPERIMENTAL FILM AND QUEER MATERIALITY

runs by the time of his disappearance in August of 1966, probably drowned in the sea near his family's home in Massachusetts.[11]

A-men and Harvard alumni frequently converge in the Warhol corpus in 1965 and 1966. *a, a novel*—where "a" stands in part for amphetamine—is one of these occasions. In the first of the tape-recording sessions that make up the book, which took place in July of 1965, Warhol, Sedgwick, Chuck Wein, Ondine, and Billy Name, among others, hang out, gossip, drop in on various friends, and end up at Rotten Rita's, where they telephone the recently hospitalized Brigid Berlin. Another occasion for the coming together of both groups is the film *Afternoon* (1965), part of the intended Edie Sedgwick saga and shot around the time of *a*'s first recording session with a similar cast of characters. Like in *a*, Ondine is the life of the party. Around him Sedgwick, Arthur Loeb, Donald Lyons, and Dorothy Dean—a black woman on the *New Yorker* staff who was close to the San Remo crowd[12]—gab, sing, tease each other, and take speed, which seems to cheer them all up halfway through the film and is the likely cause for Ondine's superlative irritation toward Loeb near the end, when he rough-handles and yells at him in response to his snobbery and lame banter. The film runs out as Ondine advises Dorothy on the right dosage for the speed he has just supplied her with.

The way amphetamine cuts across these worlds—from debutants and upper-class college students to working-class bohemians—indicates the spread of the drug at the time. While it had been widely commercialized since the early 1930s in the United States, its use peaked approximately during the Factory years. A 1962 survey by the Federal Drug Administration estimated a bulk production of eight billion standard ten-milligram tablets of amphetamine salts for that year, with a market value of approximately $48 million dollars.[13] According to another FDA estimate, production had risen to ten billion tablets at the end of the decade, when one in twenty American adults were using amphetamine by prescription.[14] These figures are only approximations, since several manufacturers refused to collaborate in the survey, and it was virtually impossible to keep tabs on the underground market, fed by the illegal laboratories that sprang up from the late 1950s onward.[15]

By the late 1960s, when the Factory relocated from 47th Street to Union Square, amphetamine was on its way out, its street reputation ruined by mounting evidence of its damaging side effects after prolonged use—violence and volatility, extraordinary addictiveness, and psychotic outbreaks. The Bay Area-based 1969 campaign "Speed Kills," to which numerous countercultural personalities such as Allen Ginsberg, The Grateful Dead, and Frank Zappa contributed, drew attention to its dangers. The campaign was launched by the Free Clinic of Haight-Ashbury, in San Francisco, which housed "The Amphetamine Research Project," funded by the National Institute of Mental Health.[16] Operating at one of the epicenters of the counterculture, the Free Clinic had garnered ample proof of amphetamine's dark side.[17] Still, until that point, it had remained a much sought-after medical remedy and recreational psychotropic. It was popular among family doctors for the treatment of despondency and excess body weight and was also widely consumed by underworld denizens, college students, and workers on grueling schedules— in sum, by anyone out for kicks or subject to boredom, despair, or exhaustion, which easily makes up a large segment of the population.

Warhol himself took it. Early in 1963, he drew a prescription for Obetrol (a 20-milligram mixture of methamphetamine, dextroamphetamine, and Benzedrine) after he saw his picture in a magazine and decided that he looked "really fat."[18] By his own confession, he took a fourth of a pill every day, "but even that much was enough to give you that wired, happy go-go-go feeling in your stomach that made you want to work-work-work" (*P* 33). He whimsically speculated that a reason for the popularity of speed at the time may have been "the new fashions": "everyone wanted to stay thin and stay up late to show off their new looks at all the new clubs" (*P* 69). Whatever the reason for its consumption, amphetamine was shifting society into a different tempo. "I could never finally figure out if more things happened in the 1960s because there was more awake time for them to happen in (since so many people were on amphetamine), or if people started taking amphetamine because there were so many things to do that they needed more awake time to do them in" (*P* 33). He only slept between three and four hours a night from 1965 to 1967. It was then, when sleep was becoming a thing of the past, that he conceived his first film, *Sleep*, made with his recently acquired 16mm Bolex in July of 1963.

I would contend that not just the motivation to make *Sleep* or to "work-work-work" but also the actual form and pace of the film, and indeed of many films, recordings, graphics, music, and multimedia shows that came out of the Factory in the mid-1960s are indebted to amphetamine. Amphetamine—drugs at large—has long been part of Factory folklore, but until recently critics and historians have had trouble incorporating the social use of the drug into their readings of Warhol's films and art. To a large extent, this may have been a legitimizing strategy: an attempt to detach the

68 EXPERIMENTAL FILM AND QUEER MATERIALITY

artwork from the Factory's scandalous aura, which emanated precisely from its association with the queer and drug subcultures of the time, and to shift discussion to the "purer" realm of aesthetics. However, Factory productions cannot be reduced to aesthetics, nor can they be seen exclusively as sociological symptoms without courting extreme simplification; eliminating all reference to drugs volatilizes a significant factor in their making, but attributing them to the influence of drug-shaped perception runs the risk of reviving a version of nineteenth-century positivism—reducing a complex cultural artifact to the effect of a chemical on the physiology of the brain. The challenge then is to ground the work in its material circumstances without conflating it with them; to show how a certain type of subcultural practice intersected with a parallel aesthetic project, and how a symbiotic rapport between the two generated an unprecedented body of work whose significance we are still trying to plumb.

Among the critics who tried to give drugs their due in Warhol's work are Parker Tyler and, decades after him, Michel Angelo Tata and Chelsea Weathers. Tyler distinguished between two distinct, supplementary temporalities in the Factory films: a time of boredom and uneventful contemplation ("dragtime") that could also be read as an entranced receptiveness to the everyday simulating, or arising from, narcotized perception ("drugtime").[19] For his part, Tata has described Warhol's "narcovoyeurism" and has related his fascination with drug consumption to his interest in glamour, marginality, and death.[20] And Weathers, replaying in part one of Tyler's motifs, has attributed to amphetamine the distended temporality of Warhol's films and the brittle, paranoid affect of some Factory productions—particularly the multimedia show *Exploding Plastic Inevitable*.[21]

Of these three critics, only Weathers focuses on amphetamine. Tyler does not differentiate between hallucinogens, which play a small part in Warhol's world, and stimulants, and Tata is more interested in a general rhetoric of drugs than in specificities of use and effect and covers indistinctly the amphetamine of the 1960s, the "cocaine blizzards" of the disco years, and the heroin use of friend and collaborator Jean-Michel Basquiat in the 1980s.[22] Both Tata and Weathers have an external perspective on the phenomenon; they have more to say about drugs as context and subject matter than as form generators or textual catalysts. Only Tyler engages Warhol's textuality head-on, reading his film aesthetic from the optic provided by substance use: "Dragtime/Drugtime is itself a split plastic 'personality,'" torn between an "sober, everyday reality" and the "magical durée inducible in watchers by marijuana and other drugs." "[T]he primitive Warhol films might function as dialectic antithesis, demonstrating how what is excruciatingly tiresome and commonplace cries out for the right conversion formula in the witness—not the intermediate witness, the camera, but the final witness, the audience."[23] But, as Tyler also points out, quick to argue against himself, this is a conversion that the films themselves perform by virtue of their hypnotic temporality and their sustained attention to the ordinary: "The anti-heroic film marathons he calls *Sleep, Eat, Haircut, Kiss*, and *Empire* can be conceived by dedicated audiences as if they were drugtime—that is, as inexplicable wonders of eventfulness."

Following Tyler's suggestion, I would propose that it was not the commonplace that called for the redemptive lift of the drug, but the drug that made the commonplace quite uncommon and lent Warhol and his collaborators a heightened receptivity toward that "excruciating" everydayness that this critic casts in temporal terms (drag*time*) because of the exorbitant duration of Warhol's films, but could also be discussed from other perspectives as well. What Tyler conceptualizes as "dragtime" encompasses more than time. The term recalls the use of "drag" in beat lingo—the deadening combination of material comfort, boredom, and spiritual vacuity that, according to William Burroughs, fostered drug use as means of escape: "But there is no drag like U.S. drag . . . And our [drug] habits build up with the drag."[24] And closer to the etymology of the word (from Old German, *dragan*: to pull, to draw heavily), and more apposite to Warhol's work, Tyler's "drag" references as well the density and blunt obduracy of the material world, qualities that are amply foregrounded in the 1960s Factory films as sources of new patterns and creative possibilities.

The films' material concerns, and the way these concerns stem from the perceptual reorientation brought about by amphetamine, will be the focus of this chapter. To a large extent, their peculiar handling of light, masses, textures, bodies, and sound are indebted to the "amphetamine thing"; after all, Warhol wrote, "everything always went back to that." These material concerns disclose a queer materiality. They open up unsuspected vibrations in the physical-objectual horizon captured by the camera, rendering it radically strange—or "queer"—and, in addition, they channel and embody the peculiar sexuality—the queerness—of Warhol's films.

My focus on queer materiality is akin to recent analyses that extend the queerness of Warhol's films from their ostensible representation of queer subjects—although there is plenty of that as well—to their temporality and to the marks of the labor that went into their production, shifting discussion from identity and representation to practice and performance. Both labor and temporality are indebted to the perceptual effects and the epistemics of amphetamine. Resulting from speed-induced tinkering, and often portraying the minute busyness produced by the drug, Warhol's films, for examples, are continuous with the "trip books," the intricate decorative patterning, and the verbal and gestural exuberance triggered off by amphetamine. Like these, they were autotelic and self-justified: a lot of work for little or no return, given their resistant qualities and, barring a few exceptions, their general lack of box office appeal. In this regard, they are examples of what Matthew Tinkcom described, applying Hannah Arendt's distinction, as non-alienated, creative "work" rather than regulated, profit-oriented "labor."[25] The films are largely based, Tinkcom maintains, on Warhol's transvaluation of mass culture's iconography through camp. Camp, which operates on the confluence of reception and production and identifies in the iconography of the commercial media ruptures where queer affect might lodge, is an avatar of this kind of work; it allows queer subjects—Warhol as a queer producer—to exist within the stringencies of labor and the alienated structure of the commodity.[26] Homay King sees in the extemporaneous, non-linear, durational, and interstitial activity that populates Warhol's films a form of queer temporality that defies the logics of narrative functionality and sequence associated with chrono-normative becoming, presumed to be ordered, purposeful, teleological, and productive.[27] King has associated the outlines of this temporality to Tyler's "drugtime." While in agreement with these readings, I would add that the upturning of labor and time that Tinkcom and King incisively describe were interwoven with the effects of amphetamine; they worked alongside, and indeed rested upon, not just an unspecified "drugtime" but, more concretely, the peculiar perception of the material that amphetaminized perception facilitates. This is a perception that brought about constant shifts between signal and noise, order and disorder, figure and ground; that rewarded the close tracking of the intricacies of matter; and that encouraged the cutaneous, non-genital eroticism that characterizes Warhol's films.

* * *

It is paradoxical that amphetamine might have prompted a closer relation with matter because excess matter—mucus, swollen respiratory tracts—was precisely what amphetamine was invented to eliminate. The drug had been first synthesized by Japanese and German scientists working independently in the 1880s and was rediscovered in 1929 by American chemist Gordon Alles, apparently unaware of these antecedents. Alles came across the compound while searching for a synthetic substitute for adrenalin, which had proven, since it was isolated in 1901, an effective decongestant, useful in the treatment of two common yet painful and resilient ailments: asthma and allergies. Adrenalin is a naturally occurring substance in the body, secreted by the adrenal glands, but it is costly and laborious to isolate. This gave Alles the motivation to find an artificial replacement; at the time of his discovery he was working at a Los Angeles clinic making anti-allergenic preparations. Early tests revealed that, in addition to clearing the respiratory tracts, amphetamine had other unexpected effects. It made one unusually alert, talkative, and active, eliminated sleep and appetite, and generated a sense of well-being that lasted for hours.[28]

This soon became known to the thousands who used the first amphetamine product in the market—the Benzedrine Inhaler, launched by Smith, Klein & French as a head cold remedy in 1934. The inhaler contained a hefty dose of volatile amphetamine base that, used properly, cleared the sinuses by contracting inflamed capillaries. Yet it was also possible to obtain a cheap, euphoric high by extracting the amphetamine-soaked paper inside the inhaler and swallowing it. Breaking inhalers and swallowing their contents quickly became a popular party ritual in the urban demimonde.[29] By 1947, however, the violence and psychosis caused by Benzedrine "jags" had become a national health alarm, and Benzedrine inhalers would eventually be banned by the Federal Drug Administration in 1959.[30]

Wayward street use anticipated the second legitimate use for the drug: mood elevator. After Alles patented amphetamine in 1932 and contracted its exploitation with the pharmaceutical firm Smith, Klein & French, early trials focused on the effect of the drug on sleep and mood. The prominent Boston psychiatrist Abraham Myerson, an authority on depression, tested it on his patients and reported excellent results among mild depressives, while also noting that it caused unwanted agitation in the profoundly depressed, chronically anxious, and schizophrenic. Myerson's endorsement allowed SK&F to launch Benzedrine Sulfate salts for the treatment of narcolepsy, Parkinson's disease, and melancholic prostration in 1937.[31] In 1946, SK&F gave amphetamine a further boost through two new products: Dexedrine and Dexomyl. Dexedrine, the brand name for dextroamphetamine, was a right-hand isomer of adrenaline that gave a stronger high with fewer jitters than Benzedrine or methamphetamine; it was primarily marketed as a diet pill designed to rein

72   EXPERIMENTAL FILM AND QUEER MATERIALITY

in appetite and improve the anxious-depressive state that leads to overeating. Developed and marketed simultaneously with Dexedrine was Dexomyl, a mixture of dextroamphetamine and the barbiturate amobarbital that became the most popular anti-depressant in the postwar years. Surveys revealed that the main consumers of these products were middle-class suburban women afflicted by that "problem that has no name," as Betty Friedan put it in her epochal *The Feminine Mystique* (1963): the malaise caused by a lifetime of relegation and self-effacement in an attempt to fill out the roles of wife and mother.[32] All these applications of amphetamine sought to eliminate literal or metaphorical matter and bodily inertias—clogging inflammation and mucus in the sinuses, the gravitational pull of sleep in the narcoleptic, the excess body mass of the overweight, or the metaphorical heaviness of the depressive. Not by chance the street name of amphetamine was "speed," coined, it seems, by Korean War veterans caught up in the acceleration of combat and of the drug.[33]

And yet, the elixir of uplift and take-off prompted a return to matter. Its functioning recalled the material bases of subjectivity. Advertised as the first drug capable of modifying mood, it permitted the manufacture of happiness and motivation by chemical means. With amphetamine, personality seemed no longer an immaterial entity molded through education and experience but a physiological mechanism manipulable by prescription. As Marshall McLuhan put it in a gloss of William Burroughs's work: "The human nervous system can be reprogrammed biologically as readily as any radio network can alter its fare."[34] In a way, drugs had managed this from time immemorial. What changed in the postwar years was that such mood engineering became widespread and institutionalized, endorsed by the medical establishment, facilitated by the pharmaceutical industry, and corroborated by prevailing standards of bodily figure, behavior, and performance—by the collective sanction of thinness, pep, and optimality.

Mood manufacture was part of an epochal shift, taking place at the time in first-world economies, from conventional industrial production (the production of goods) to the production of services and affects.[35] These last were purveyed, in addition to chemistry, by fashion, advertisement, and entertainment. It may not be a coincidence that the postwar years were, simultaneously, the years of the rise of amphetamine and television. Both were engaged in the material production of immaterial affect by means of mood modifiers that penetrated into the innermost recesses of bodies and homes. This was not lost on Warhol, who complained about radio and television trying to

AMPHETAMINE IN ANDY WARHOL'S FACTORY FILMS   73

"program everyone to feel so sad" after Kennedy's assassination (*P* 60). It seems logical that the inquiry into media images—social neurotransmitters implanting feeling and sensation on the collective body—that he carried out in his art would broaden out into the chemical manufacture of mood and perception. He may have had this possibility in mind, and not only the reproductive ability of the media, when he stated his desire "to be a machine"[36]: a storage-transmission device connected to the pharmaceutical and media networks.

In addition to recalling the physiochemical basis of mood and affect, amphetamine was a materializing drug for other reasons as well. Traditional psychotropics, such as alcohol, cannabis, opiates, yagé, peyote, or LSD—experienced, long before it was synthesized in 1938, through the inadvertent ingestion of the ergot fungus that grew on moldy rye—promoted a separation from the world by ushering into alternative sensorial coordinates. Amphetamine, on the other hand, when consumed for short periods of time in moderate doses, did not prompt a loss of the world but a deeper immersion into its rhythms, sounds, and striations. Joel Markman, an underground performer who starred in films by Ron Rice and Jack Smith in the early 1960s, put it as follows: "On amphetamine I drew very free letters and in the spaces between, the action and the flow of life was there, people dancing, making love, being together, and it came from the feeling, it was there in the rhythm, a crystallization."[37]

The reality-enhancing effect of amphetamine has its most articulate manifestation in Jack Kerouac's work.[38] Amphetamine—or, more precisely, Benzedrine, which fueled most of his writing—is probably behind the rhapsodic descriptions of minute nuances of mood and geography, character, and situation that fill *On the Road* and are, in a way, its subject. At a bus station in Cheyenne, Wyoming, the novel's protagonist, Sal Paradise, sits and stares entranced at the floor—a complex orography of stains and litter. Two other characters from *On the Road* (1957), Carlo (Allen Ginsberg) and Dean (Neil Cassady), take "bennies" to stay up all night and communicate "with absolute completeness everything on our minds," "digging everything" about each other while they are at it.[39] The words "digging" and "buzzing," as frequent as commas in the book, are coded ways to refer to Benzedrine elation. Under its effect, any subject tackled by the narrator of Kerouac's masterpiece, *Visions of Cody* (written in 1951 and 1952, published in 1972) exfoliates into a profusion of baroque detail.[40] A deli counter (7–8), a lit window on a tenement across the street (17), a woman's face at a cafeteria (31–33), or the floor of a pool hall, covered with cigarette butts and spit (65), reveal

74   EXPERIMENTAL FILM AND QUEER MATERIALITY

intricate configurations of color, mass, and texture, and become nodes for digressions, memories, and embryonic stories that succeed each other in a nervous, rhythmic flow. In part, the book—much of Kerouac's work—is an attempt to capture the flood of sublimely perceptible but largely unaccountable intimations dormant in quotidian, apparently insignificant landscapes and materials. Did amphetamine bring about this sensibility to the material dross of daily life or did it enhance a preexisting receptivity? Attention to the intricacies of what James Agee once called "the unimagined existence"[41] was a streak of modernist poetics found in authors innocent of speed— from William Carlos Williams to Agee himself to John Cage, to cite a few. However, what Kerouac called the "universal watchfulness"[42] of the amphetamine user certainly helped to follow the circumvolutions of matter and to record them with the kind of fervor demonstrated by Kerouac, who refused to let anything slip by unnoted.

Machines come in handy to this purpose. They inventory faithfully, within their preestablished thresholds of perception, the minutest contingencies of the real. In this way, they deliver that optical and aural unconscious that, as Walter Benjamin and Béla Balász pointed out in the 1930s, opens up to visual and sound technologies but remains hidden to the unaided eye and ear.[43] In addition, machine registration can keep up with the flight of thought under speed. Kerouac, again: "*do* need a recorder . . . then I could keep the most complete record in the world which in itself could be divided into twenty massive and pretty interesting volumes of tapes describing activities everywhere and excitements and thoughts."[44] Shortly after writing these lines, he purchased a tape recorder with the royalties of his first novel and used it to compose the central part of *Visions of Cody*, "Frisco: The Tape": purportedly a literal transcription of several amphetamine- and pot-driven exchanges between Jack and Cody—stand-ins for Kerouac and Cassady—that stretch over several nights and includes occasional walk-ins by friends and a party scene. The conversations review many of the events that were given fictional shape in *On the Road* as well as numerous anecdotes concerning Kerouac and his beat confrères in the late forties. In addition to having, for this reason, documentary value, "Frisco" is also an extremely self-conscious reflection about the relation between taping and writing. In the second recorded session, Jack and Cody talk about the first tape they had made and had later listened to, and compare the sound recording to a transcript by Jack. The chapter after "Frisco" is "Imitation of the Tape," which seeks to translate into a viable literary style the flow of speech caught by the machine.

With its close transcription of recorded speech, including false starts, hesitations, repetitions, and an extreme fragmentariness that frequently shades into nonsense, "Frisco: The Tape" is the immediate antecedent of *a, a novel. a* is often as self-conscious as Kerouac's text about the nature and effects of recording, but in it the literary transduction of the voice disappears and what remains is a naked rendition of taped talk—or rather an egregiously botched transcript full of misreportings and mistakes that Warhol never bothered to edit, given his fascination with serendipitous gaffes and chance. To tape the conversations that went into his book, Warhol also used a tape recorder. By the time he undertook sound recording, he was long familiar with mechanical reproduction. Early in his career as a gallery artist he abandoned painting in favor of stenciling and, later on, silk-screening, a process that implied several technological mediations: a photograph transferred to a screen and then used to produce multiple images. In July of 1963 he bought his first 16mm camera, a Bolex that could only fit 100-feet reels—three minutes of film—and was unequipped for sound registration, and in November of 1964, his first sound camera, an Auricon. In 1965 he started using video equipment on loan from the manufacturer Norelco but later settled on a Sony Portapak in the early 1970s. Writing in 1970, Jonas Mekas described Warhol's technophilia as an attempt "to record everything he saw; everything that happened around him."[45] For Mekas, this was an elegiac attempt to immortalize the fleeting moment, yet it may also be seen as an immersion in its often unattended intricate multiplicity—or what is the same, in its material unconscious.

Friedrich A. Kittler has pointed out that when artistic production is detoured through recording-transmission technologies, the result is no longer art in any traditional sense but media notation: "arbitrary selections from a noise that denies all selection."[46] Working with machines entails a heightened awareness of noise, as does working with—and on—drugs. Within their systemic and sensory constraints, automatic read–write protocols are nondiscriminatory. They register and emit sense and nonsense, information and the murmur of the world, with all its stochastic oscillation. Noise similarly floods the mind on speed—ask Kerouac. The high concentrations of dopamine and adrenaline in the brain caused by the drug puts the perception–consciousness apparatus in fast-forward, intensifying color, light, and movement and lowering aural and photosensitive thresholds;[47] peripheral vision increases and flicker becomes perceptible above the ordinary fusion rate of 40 flashes per second.[48] At the same

76　EXPERIMENTAL FILM AND QUEER MATERIALITY

time, the ability to discriminate between signal and noise diminishes, in part because noise becomes as entrancing as signal. The amphetamine user takes it all in and finds it all equally worthy, even portentous, if inexplicable. ("No possible way of avoiding enigmas," wrote Kerouac).[49] Subject to the onslaught of noise, the speedster becomes in turn a noise machine: a compulsive doodler or tinkerer, a nonstop talker or mad typist whose stories break off constantly or veer off in ever digressive paths.

* * *

Like Kerouac's writing, Warhol's films and *a, a novel* are junctions where noise never stops being produced, recorded, and relayed, emitted by subjects on speed and recorded-transmitted by mechanisms unable to filter out nonsense. They are low-fidelity environments. *a, a novel* is a tangle of broken sentences, non sequiturs, obscure puns, and overlapping exchanges where meaning is at best intermittent, submerged in an enveloping cacophonous massage. The films are similarly fuzzy. As Douglas Crimp has pointed out, it not easy to know where to look or what to look for; what to listen to, or how much one is supposed to hear or understand.[50] For some critics, such resistance to perceptual mastery throws spectators back on themselves, forcing them to confront their own sense-making strategies.[51] Yet the films' impregnability also thrusts spectators deeper into the realm of matter, that is, into the grain of the real, the actual hardware of experience, and the materiality of film. And in this process of material immersion, the films are intent on capturing not only the components in the world and the image that convey sense, but also—and very particularly—those that do not and purvey a massage on the senses. It all goes back, in a way, to amphetamine, to the peculiarities of machine registration, and to the hook-up between the two, linked in a feedback loop that amplifies the other's noise.

Noise is present above all in the way Warhol's films foreground the materiality of celluloid and the emulsion; the particularities of framing, camera movement, and lens optics; and the textural unconscious of mise-en-scene, body, and sound. The amplification of these material components of the apparatus and the profilmic contributes a continuum of buzz and crackle that blurs what many have taken to be the central concerns of the films—portraiture, documentation, observation, or parodic narrative—and turns Warhol's output into a sustained examination of noise, interrupted transmission, and entropy.

The early films—*Kiss, Sleep, Haircut, Eat, Empire, Blow Job* (1964), or *Henry Geldzahler* (1964), among others—present a tension between their conceptual clarity, as films, in Warhol's words, that it is better to hear and talk about than to see,[52] and the intricacy of their textures and internal movement, which makes actual description nearly impossible and turns them indeed into works that can *only* be experienced.[53] Their conceit points toward ultimate transparency: the registration of perfectly ordinary daily events—people kissing, a man eating, another sleeping, others getting haircuts or blow jobs, seven hours and twenty minutes of the Empire State Building, etc. And yet, their slowed-down speed, grain, duration, and the minute incidentals they capture blur their iconic straightforwardness and belie Warhol's own description of them as films about "just eating" or "just sleeping."[54]

Shot at 24 frames per second (fps), these early titles were intended to be screened at 16 fps, the standard silent speed in the 1960s, replaced, a few years later, by the slightly faster standard of 18 fps. This technological shift has made the original experience of these films nearly irretrievable by now.[55] At 16 fps, they had a slight flicker that amphetamine would have rendered more perceptible. The flicker may be regarded as a self-reflexive gesture; a means to underline the material basis of cinema as a stream of discontinuous images that only appear to be continuous due to a peculiarity of the retinal tissue. In addition, the subliminal pulse of flicker momentarily plunges the image into whiteout and negation. In this regard, the flicker that punctuates the early films is of a piece with the flares and perforations at the start and end of the reels, and with the dust and scratches on the leader, which Warhol always scrupulously kept. They serve as reminders of the materiality of celluloid and the vicissitudes of projection—the cause of the abrasions in the emulsion. But they also push the image into the noise from which it came and that also allowed its emergence. Noise, after all, indicates that the channel is open, ready for transmission.

Much like flicker, grain is a modality of visual noise. Grain is a constant in Warhol's early work. As a later chapter will explore more fully, it is a quiver that both composes and dissolves the image; the microscopic raw material that coalesces into form but whose oscillation also blurs masses and outlines. Grain is an inevitable consequence of the conditions of production of most of these films—the effect of low lighting on sensitive film stock (often Kodak Tri X). Yet its recurrence—the recurrence of these conditions as well—indicates a deliberate aesthetic choice. The grainy black and white image may have satisfied Warhol's fondness for a low-fi machine-made look, which he had been trying to achieve in some of his 1950s drawings by means of blotting paper and eraser stamps, and finally perfected through silk-screening. Silk-screening, discovered shortly before he started his filmmaking career, made him familiar with the way grain simultaneously composed and dissolved an image, filling out and attenuating its contour. The screens were perforated with minuscule dots that were covered with glue in those areas where paint was not supposed to seep through to the underlying canvass. Warhol relished the imperfections that the process generated: the flaws in register caused by the imperfect alignment of the screens and the bleed and whiteouts resulting from irregular seepage, clogging, or changes in the pressure of the squeegee—the sponge used to push the paint through. In silk-screening, paint and the surface of the canvass seemed to acquire a life of their own, independent of the maker's designs, and this life was often perceptible in fields of grain that recall the Ben Day dots of the periodical press—turned into a deliberate pop gesture in Roy Lichtenstein's work.

To an extent, the photographic grain in the early films takes on this quality; its molecular oscillations evoke a furtive life of matter. In some of the films, it becomes a central component, particularly in *Sleep*, a counterpoint to the amphetamine vigils,[56] and *Empire*, probably an offshoot of them. In both films, grain works as an undertow against the general stasis. In *Sleep*, it animates the sleeping body and the surrounding space, it heightens the abstraction of many of the frames, and, in Branden Joseph's view, it overlays the eroticism of the sleeping figure with "the death's instinct push toward a state of undifferentiated, inanimate matter."[57] In *Empire*, grain registers a transition from entropy to readable form. The film opens on a field of seething white and grey dots caused by extreme overexposure, since the lens aperture is set to night illumination. As the sun goes down and the light wanes, the particles slowly precipitate into an informative pattern: the outline of the Empire State and the city skyline. Halfway through the reel, the lights on the top of the building go up. When darkness finally sets in, the frame settles into its most durable image: a black field dominated by the lighted top of the skyscraper. Yet the fixity of this image, occasionally punctuated by bursts of grain and flairs caused by the film's sloppy push-processing, eventually shifts the image of the Empire from information back to the initial entropy.

Warhol has pointed out that prolonged exposure effected for him a voiding of meaning: "because the more you look at the same exact thing, the more the meaning goes away and the better and emptier you feel" (*P* 50). This voiding could be explained as complete redundancy: the restatement of the same yields no information, which is always a function of novelty. The more than six hours during which the frame remains fixed on the building's flood-lit top in a dark sky are completely uninformative—save for the periodic blinking of a light on top of the Metropolitan Life Insurance Tower and the three brief moments when the light in the room where the filming is taking place is turned on, and the shooting crew, Warhol included, is fleetingly reflected on the windows. Lack of information is another form of reversal to entropy, and entropy, in turn, another modality of noise. Formally, absolute redundancy is opposite to the cacophonous agitation of *a, a novel*, or the dusty wavering of grain in *Sleep* or in the first reel of *Empire*. Yet its informational value is the same: both maximal predictability and complete unpredictability yield results that approach zero in the binary logarithm that Claude E. Shannon designed to calculate the informational ratio of a communicative event.[58] Except that on speed, the entropic buzz of *Empire* might have been felt as signal instead and its duration would have been telescoped, and the minutest oscillations of grain in the dark or the periodical flash of the light on the Met Life Tower could have taken on climactic momentousness.

Along with these structural components of the image, the incidental occurrences that the camera picks up are another modality of noise, since they plunge the central events of the films into illegibility and undecidability. The succulent osculations of *Kiss* are occasionally blurred by an invading expanse of hair or a turn of the head that plunges the kissers into shadow; or they are rendered strange by the striking technique of some couples. (Gerard Malanga voraciously swallows Naomi Levine's entire chin, while two young men I have been unable to identify only peck demurely). *Eat* is especially prolific in peripheral incident. The title action is looped and edited out of order, with the opening reel returning toward the end of the film. The procedure undercuts the linearity of the event and draws attention away from the actual eating to its odd sequencing. In addition, there is much that distracts from the central activity. There is some interaction with a cat that the eater (artist Robert Indiana) picks up, holds toward the camera, nuzzles, and offers the mushroom to. (The cat refuses). At least twice Indiana seems to be smiling at someone off-screen. The rest of the time, he appears reasonably self-absorbed, slowly nibbling, dividing his attention between the window on his right, the interior of his studio on his left, and the mushroom in his hand, while he gently swivels and rocks in his chair. Despite the incidentals that stray from the film's ostensible topic, Indiana yields a more stable image than Henry Geldzahler in the eponymous ninety-minute portrait. Apparently

80 EXPERIMENTAL FILM AND QUEER MATERIALITY

left alone in front of the camera for most of the shoot, Geldzahler smokes a cigar, repeatedly puts on and takes off his sunglasses, drums his fingers, briefly mouths the words to a song, keeps pushing his hair behind his ears, pretends to sleep, and strikes subtly theatrical poses—interlaces his fingers on his chest and looks saintly, lies on his side Odalisque-style, stares quizzically into the lens . . . . Callie Angell has written that more than a portrait, *Henry Geldzahler* is a study in disintegration,[59] from composure to growing irritation and boredom in the absence of human interlocution. Yet I see in the film less a linear declension than a constant oscillation between expressiveness and blankness, between moments of lively human presence and others when the sitter's appearance cannot be easily deciphered, and body and face cease to function as conduits for personality and assert themselves as mere surface and matter, their softness and roundness rhyming with the curved embrace of the couch.[60]

Minute eventfulness also marks the similarly minimal *Blow Job*—also a portrait of sorts. The young man being serviced goes through a broad range of expression, from pleasure to pain, to absorption, to subtle sociability with the unseen spectators of the scene. As he constantly tilts his head up and down, faces forward, and (seldom) turns left, his expression changes, in part because of the shadows cast by a light above him. Roy Grundmann has seen in the up, down, and frontal positions of the head three registers of gay iconography (porn, James Dean-like rebel-juvenile, and Christ).[61] And Adriano Aprá has read in the same up and down motion a dialectic between spirit (when he looks up and his face is flooded with light) and mortal flesh (when he looks down and the shadows on his eye sockets and mouth create a skull-like shape).[62] For Douglas Crimp the constant movement of the young man's head and his ever-shifting expression thwart the possibility of "owning" this face as spectators and turning it into an object for us, foiling the voyeuristic lure proposed by the title.[63] While agreeing with the iconographic readings of Grundmann and Aprá, Crimp's more abstract view resonates with my own: at bottom, what may be crucial is not the precipitation of the face into readable figures but the constant transitions that keep it an errant sign and are a layer of noise over a seemingly transparent image.

The agitation of grain and the intermittence of flicker in the silent films has an equivalent, in many of the sound films, in the unmotivated framing and zooming that Warhol started to practice systematically in 1965. These resources highlight peripheral details in the mise-en-scene, neglect the ostensible subject being filmed, and work at cross-purposes with the performers.

We may think here of the way spastic zooming turns parts of *Since*, a recreation of the Kennedy assassination, into sheer optic vibration. In the "Hanoi Hannah" episodes of *The Chelsea Girls*, similar, if less frantic, shifts in focal length abstract us momentarily from the fractious scene and plunge us into extreme close-ups of Susan Bottomly's lush make-up, clothes, glossy hair, and gleaming sunglasses. A zoom out, accompanied with a slight pan, returns us to a wider frame that shows Bottomly sitting on the bed surrounded by some of her cohorts; on the left of the frame one can see the bathroom and the toilet seat inside, which adds an excremental insinuation to her stunning glamour.

Other times the camera roams across the set as if on a break from the tedious task of rendering a scene. In *Hedy* (1966), one of the earliest films to exploit this gesture, the frame often explores the length of a grimy, non-descript wall, or looks down to the floor—as *On the Road*'s Sal Paradise had done at a bus station—while the dramatic action continues off-screen. In the "Pope Ondine" sections of *The Chelsea Girls*, such stray framing plunges spectators into complete darkness, while the voices of the performers remain audible. Other times swish tilts and pans blur setting and performers—as in parts of *Lupe* (1966) and *Closet* (1966). Like the unmotivated zooming and roving frame, the swish pans create visual noise and impede smooth transmission. Yet the pervasiveness of these gestures suggests in fact that interruption and failure are indeed the goals of transmission, and that the ultimate purpose of the films is to invert the usual hierarchy between signal and noise; center and periphery; message and sensory massage. Such inversions were indeed dear to Warhol, for whom pop consisted in part of analogous reversals: "taking the outside and putting it on the inside and taking the inside and putting it on the outside."[64] In the films, in goes the noise; out, the readable signal.

The Velvet Underground and Nico (1966) is rich in such noise-signal reversals. It is a two-reel sound film of the Velvets and Nico rehearsing at the Factory while Ari, Nico's son, plays in their midst and, as the film progresses, becomes excited by the music, picks up a maraca and gleefully keeps the beat. Toward the end of the film, a policeman walks twice into the frame to lower the volume on the amplifier, probably in response to a noise complaint. Eventually the music is turned off and the Velvets, Warhol, and several Factory regulars stand around while the police complete their report. The aural and visual tracks proceed erratically in parallel throughout the film. The Velvets improvise an endless chord progression that sounds in part like a rambling fifty-minute intro to a song that is never delivered. The Velvets' improvisation may be interpreted as an aural counterpart of Warhol's minimalist films, in which stasis is accompanied by molecular agitation in the form of complex texture and minute incident. Or it could be read as a pop version of composer LaMonte Young's sustained tones, in which Velvet co-founder John Cale had participated. Except that instead of one single chord held for long stretches of time, the band explores a fairly static chord sequence that they manage to endow with considerable variation, in part through the overlay of idiosyncratic sonorities, as when Nico starts tapping the strings of a bass with a screwdriver or Cale stands up to pluck what looks like an ungainly home-made instrument. The rambling camera punctuates the relatively unfocused quality of the music and its constant drift into noise. It pans across the playing area; crawls up the wall behind the band; zooms in and out of the scene, landing abruptly on details of the performers' bodies, clothing, and instruments; or stares into an inexpressive middle ground where cables, chairs, body parts, and segments of instruments mingle. Toward the end, when the music stops and everyone momentarily moves off-screen, the camera remains fixed on the vacated rehearsal area, barely visible now because the aperture, momentarily adjusted to film a better lit section of the Factory, remains unchanged when the camera pans back to the darkness of the Velvets' corner. At this point, the Velvets' music has been displaced by ambient noise, and the camera remains stationary on the groups that form and dissolve in front of it. Yet until the interruption, the Velvets' sound hovered between noise and signal, while the visual track offered an idiosyn-cratically framed rehearsal and occasionally went out of focus, rendering un-readable movements and shapes, or briefly faded to black.

In what may be the most compelling reading of the Factory films to date, Douglas Crimp has read Warhol's peculiar framing and camera movement as indexes of the artist's radical non-relationality and delight in "mis-fitting together"—that is, not fitting together with others while remaining in their company *and* hanging out with kindred oddballs and outsiders.[65] It is cru-cial to think of these two senses of Warhol's phrase alongside each other. The literal lack of fit that somehow does not prevent togetherness—think of music and image in *The Velvet Underground and Nico*—serves to commu-nicate a profound regard for the singularity of the performers and scenes depicted, who are never reduced to mere objects for the spectators. In ad-dition, formal misfit—the roaming camera frequently at odds with the ac-tion; crazy zooming; elusive soundtrack—literalizes the centrifugal attention of the speed user, permanently pulled to the edges of the perceptual field. Amphetamine increased the sensitivity of peripheral vision and prompted an erratic attentiveness that tended to fixate on off-center detail, suddenly turned significant. (As Warhol put it: "intense concentration, but! only on minutiae.") It may have been this fascination—chemically induced or not—with the obdurate particular and the subterranean animation of matter, faces, and bodies that allowed Warhol's camera to register its subjects without reducing them to types. By virtue of these off-center details, performers remain somewhat opaque to the scrutiny of a "presumptive, knowing" subject.[66] One may locate here not only a Levinasian ethics of surrender in the face of inapprehensible otherness, as Crimp does, but also an ethics of amphetaminized perception—even an eroticism of amphetamine.

This is an admittedly lurid label for the erratic movement of sexuality in Warhol's films. They appear more focused on the preliminaries and adjacencies of the sexual act than on the act itself. Some exceptions, among the preserved films, are a few rolls of *Couch* with explicit sexual content and the lovemaking scene in *Blue Movie* (1969). Other than these, even films centrally concerned with sex, such as *Blow Job* and *Eating Too Fast* (1966), keep their titular action off screen, and the films made in 1967 and 1968 for the sexploitation market—*I, a Man*, *Bike Boy*, *Loves of Ondine*, and others—are more concerned with the byways and detours of desire than with explicit sexual scenes. They dwell on scenarios of failed or interrupted seduction, where proximity and talk do not lead to foreplay and where the abundant strobe-cuts are the formal correlative of break off and mismatch. For Tom Waugh, this avoidance of explicit sexuality is the tactic of the "cockteaser," motivated by Warhol's opportunistic desire to attract an audience without exposing himself to censorship.[67] Another reason, inscribed from the start in the Factory films, is that to Warhol the most interesting aspect of sex was not its purported goal—genital contact, let us say—but the circuitousness of eroticism. "Sex is so abstract," Warhol used to claim.[68] It is less a particular content or goal than an intensity that can become attached to practically anything—and under amphetamine, it often does.[69]

Due to the enormous variability of the sexual drive and of individual psychology, amphetamine has a broad range of effects on the libido. However, there is evidence to suggest that the main varieties of the drug consumed in the 1960s (Dexedrine, Benzedrine, and methamphetamine) promoted sexual indirectness. Studies made at the time showed that speed increased desire while delaying, even inhibiting, orgasm, and that it promoted "diffuse object relations" and intensified tactile sensation. For some users, the jumpy excitement triggered by amphetamine was actually equivalent to sex,

84   EXPERIMENTAL FILM AND QUEER MATERIALITY

especially for the mainliners who compared the flash of the drug to an "all over body orgasm," and eroticized the act and implements of shooting up.[70] In some cases, speed could mean sex without genital fixation: a cutaneous[71] intensity distributed over the body and spreading over adjoining spaces, props, and materials.

We could take Ondine's word for it. In an early section of *a, a novel*, he gently chides Warhol for wanting to gossip on his sexual exploits.

> Oh Drella, don't tell that story cause I'm . . . You have, you've got a walking heart on today huh. That's a little amphetamine and bang. I love. They used to tell me that amphetamine didn't do anything for you, they thought oh it's a wonderful drug, you don't, you don't get sexy. That's until you don't know about it and then you walk, and then it becomes a, you come and put the heart on.[72]

Becoming a walking "heart on"—hard-on—seems to point to conventional genitality, but the association is diffused by the fact that Warhol's speed-induced "heart on"—they have taken Obetrols together at the start of the taping session, which is also the beginning of the book—leads to a desire to dish and tape record. In turn, the aphrodisiac effect of speed on Ondine is manifest in his logorrhea, motility ("and then you walk"), and the ambiguity of "and then you come and put the heart on." Do you come and stay hard? Or is it that ordinary sex does not deflate speed-fed desire but merely sustains it? Or is "come" to be understood in a nonsexual way as "you happen to get" a "heart on," and that is that? In this case, excitement becomes an intransitive state that does not lead to sexual contact but to what Ondine does through the novel—talk and socialize intensely and desultorily. In fact, in *a*, Ondine breaks off his rumination on amphetamine with a totally unrelated question to Morrissey: "-Paul, Paul, are you from Brooklyn? (P) Where, Yonkers. (L) Yonkers? Yonkers? Yonkers. (*Loud music*) Yeah."[73] And the conversation trails off to *The Watchmaker*, set in Yonkers and starring Ruth Borden, on to the Patty Duke Show, to the possible use of the new video equipment to tape Ondine, and off further and further afield.

Warren Sonbert's first film, *Amphetamine* (1966), made in collaboration with Wendy Appel, further hints at the drug's diffuse erotics. Not a Factory title proper, it was made, however, in the spirit of in-group self-documentation of many Factory titles and on the outer edges of its social world. Sonbert shot his film at the apartment of Gerard Malanga's friend Debbie Caen—called

Debbie Drop-Out in *a, a novel* and *POPism*—and through Caen, he soon became friends with Malanga and René Ricard, who appear in Sonbert's subsequent films—*Where Did Our Love Go?* (1966) and *Hall of Mirrors* (1966).[74] *Amphetamine* is less about the drug itself than a collective portrait of a group of friends for whom speed-taking is a casual binding ritual. It divides its attention between loving depictions of his friends, the mechanics of shooting up, and the miscellaneous décor of the apartment, at once classy, trashy, and pop, with nineteenth-century portraits and movie posters on the walls and assorted litter everywhere. An early shot slowly tilts up the length of a handsome sitting youth, who, in the following takes, proceeds to rig up his syringe and shoot up in the company of another young fellow. Later frames pan across the table where they are sitting, strewn with empty bottles, cans, and undefinable discards, and show others in intimate conversation among eddies of cigarette smoke. Abstract takes (probably caused by the film slipping in the camera) shift the mood from amiable sociability to a reverie of blurred light and indistinct shapes, but the film soon returns to the original scene: two young men—not the speedsters at the outset—kiss and lie in bed, softly caressing each other. The songs in the soundtrack (the Supremes' hits "Where Did Our Love Go?," "Baby Love," and "I Hear a Symphony") suggest a narrative from despair to plenitude that contrasts with the sustained affability and hedonism in the images. The overall tone is of warm affection, not only toward the group, its habits, love affairs, and hangout but also toward the more abstract enjoyment of light and motion, and toward the driving rhythm of the pop songs. They all seem to exist on the same plane of equivalence as exchangeable, interrelated pleasures: "All relationships interconnect into a fantastic embroidery—no two people are complete," wrote Sonbert.[75]

The unfocused eroticism triggered by amphetamine is another modality of the microscopic animation that agitates and interrupts Warhol's frame, which I have been discussing under the rubric of noise. It is the noise of sexuality: extraneous material that both exceeds and falls short of conventional ideas of sex. Or it may also be sexuality as noise—an irregular vibration that spreads across bodies and things and cannot be easily focalized or pinned down. According to Warhol, this subliminal intensity (he also called it "a secret something")[76] made the "great stars": "[T]he ones who are doing something you can watch every second, even if it's just a movement inside their eye" (*P* 109). The secret of the star, and the source of their erotic allure, is a vibratory quality also found in amphetaminized perception: movement in place, pulsing intensity. It seems no accident that stardom and speed combined in many of the great performers of the silver Factory—Ondine, Berlin, Herko, and Sedgwick—or that there is a speedy tenor even in those who did not take the drug but acted as if they did—like Viva. But besides being communicated by actual performers, the quivering at the root of erotic magnetism transcended individuals and resided as well in trans-individual aggregates.

Haircut (No. 1), one of Warhol's earliest titles, is an example of this vibrant, unfocused, supra-individual eroticism. It is a silent film made up of six 100-feet rolls depicting a group scene in which Billy Linich cuts John Daley's hair while Freddy Herko sits just behind them and fiddles about, fills a pipe (with pot?), starts smoking, and divides his attention between a magazine and the barbering (Figure 3.2). Herko appears shirtless in the first reel, standing close to the lens, then turns round and strides, in a deliberate dancer's step toward the shadowy background. In subsequent reels he appears naked, wearing only a cowboy hat and well-worn ballet slippers. The only openly sexual overture is almost incidental, when Freddy Herko uncrosses his legs and casually shows his penis for a few seconds. The flash of the genitals is almost

Figure 3.2 Andy Warhol, *Haircut*, 1963. 16mm film, black-and-white, silent, 27 minutes at 16 frames per second © The Andy Warhol Museum, Pittsburgh, PA, a museum of Carnegie Institute. All rights reserved. Film still courtesy The Andy Warhol Museum.

an anticlimax, however. The true erotic transaction is in the intense triangle formed by Herko's slightly unsettling presence, Billy Linich's meticulous clipping, and John Daley's calm submission. (James Waring, the other participant in the film, casually hovers on the edges of the action and is only clearly visible in the last reel.) The intensity that pervades the scene prompted Amy Taubin to proclaim it "the hottest film ever made."[77] But it is a diffuse, pervasive "heat" without a single source or clear focus. The sexiness emanates from the indefinite homoerotic triangle; from the conjunction of visual and tactile stimuli (Herko's visually available body and Name's precise snipping, a sort of prolonged caress); and from the combination of unrelated affect-laden acts (stripping; snipping–caressing) that, put together, radiate their erotic charge onto each other.

Haircut (No. 1) is slightly atypical for its frontal exposure but, in other ways, it is nearly programmatic of the way sexuality is treated in most Factory films. Erotic intensity arises from gesture, pose, voice, and situation rather than from nudity, whether manifest or impending. The erotic quality of *Beauty # 2* (1965), for example, certainly owes much to the beautiful bodies of Edie Sedgwick and Gino Piserchio, stripped to their underwear and lounging together in bed for the duration of the film. But just as erotic is the touching mismatch of Sedgwick's animation and vulnerability with Piserchio's flatness, and the way they gang up to field Chuck Wein's annoying off-screen presence—an intrusive, insinuating voice that constantly interpellates the bed partners.

The second reel of *My Hustler* (1965) presents a comparable setting. In the confinement of a small bathroom, filmed with an unmoving camera, two young men shower and primp up interminably. One of them, an experienced hustler, flirts mercilessly with the younger one, an emergent colleague; the experienced one compliments the younger man's body, points to the complexity of the trade and the need for guidance, and eventually suggests they exchange hustler lore for sex, an insinuation that seems to fall on deaf ears. Like in *Beauty # 2*, much of the sexiness of the scene comes from the two handsome men, framed in medium shot, offered at length to our view. But just as sexy is the verbal fencing; the contrast between the cunning insinuations of one and the (feigned or real) unresponsiveness of the other. And equally exhilarating is the delicate, relentless choreography: the micro-movement in a severely restricted space, as they dry, shave, powder, moisturize, comb and recomb their hair, put cream on each other's backs, always intensely attentive to the slightest aspect of their grooming, abuzz with

88 EXPERIMENTAL FILM AND QUEER MATERIALITY

calm excitement. Here, as in most of Warhol's films, sensual intensity arises from gesture, pose, voice, and situation rather than from nudity or actual sex, whether manifest or impending. Erotic excitement surpasses genitality and, unattached to individuality, identity, or subjectivity, extends not just across the skin of actual organic bodies on screen, but also the skin of the world and of the film.

* * *

All that is pattern melts into noise: this could be the shorthand encapsulation of Warhol's 1960s film aesthetics *and* of the effect of amphetamine on the perceptual–cognitive apparatus. Beyond Warhol, the idea applies more broadly to an important swath of mid-century art. Warhol's noisy disruption of production-transmission protocols has much in common with William Burroughs and Brion Gysin's experiments with cut-ups, tape recordings, and stroboscopy (the hallucinogenic "dream machine"); with Nam June Paik's distortions of the television and video signal; with LaMonte Young's tone studies; with Cage's explorations of randomness and noise; and with some types of structural film—by Tony Conrad, Paul Sharits, Ken Jacobs, and Ernie Gehr, for example.[78] In an excellent account of 1960s and early 1970s art as part of the image ecology induced by television, David Joselit has seen in some of these experiments—including Warhol's multimedia show *Exploding Plastic Inevitable*—a viral aesthetic. They infiltrated mainstream technologies and media, but by scrambling the relations between figure and ground, they "interrupt[ed] the smooth reproduction of pattern in order to induce shake, quiver, and noise."[79] To do this they operated—as he puts it in relation to Paik—at the sub-objective level. Rather than propose a radically new image repertoire, they decomposed the available signifying systems down to their basic material units, which they reshuffled in new formations. Paik played with "protons and electrons" in the television scanning signal; Young with the microtonal shifts in a single sustained chord; Cage with randomness and disjunctive simultaneity; Burroughs and Gysin with basic syntactic segments, phonetic units, and strobe light; and structural filmmakers with the essential components of the cinema and the dynamics of retinal perception (the peculiarities of frame ratio, film speed, grain, montage, emulsion, and the persistence of vision). In many respects, these artists' analytical focus recalls other significant intellectual enterprises of the postwar period: cybernetics and incipient electronic computing, which translated biological phenomena and mathematical functions to informational integers formalized in binary logic, and the related discipline of structural linguistics, which reduced linguistic phenomena to limited sets of elements interrelated according to a finite number of rules. But while these disciplines were intent on communication and meaning, experimental art was drawn to disconnection and noise as possible repositories of difference in an organized environment.

Warhol too manipulated the elementary materials of filmmaking and explored the minute incidentals captured by the apparatus, but he had a slightly different angle of approach. While most of his contemporaries started from the exploration of their particular media and materials, Warhol added to these intra-artistic concerns the embodied experience of amphetamine. If, per McLuhan, the content of a medium is another medium, the content of the Factory films is in part amphetamine as medium—as image- and text-generator; purveyor of sensation and affect. This places the Factory films on the divide between art and (to cite Preciado) "self-administered toxicological script,"[80] and puts the body on the line. Not just the bodies on the screen—the usual subject of criticism—but also a lower corporeal substratum: the nervous system, the inhibiting action of amphetamine on monoamine oxidase, and the resulting accumulation of dopamine and adrenaline in the brain.

At the Factory, these brains on speed belonged to identifiably queer bodies—bodies that, as we have seen, interrupted the transmission of readable sexualities. There was indeed an affinity between queerness and speed at the Factory, perhaps because much in amphetamine's perceptual style has significant queer resonance. Amphetamine highlighted marginal details and "noise," in the same way that queerness flouts standard sexual vectors and gender divides and cultivates an off-center eroticism that includes the sex-appeal of the inorganic. Because of this, there is a direct connection between amphetamine, the formal qualities of the Factory films, and the willful marginality of their subjects—that is, between speed, on the one hand, and the films' formal and sexual "misfitting," on the other. And the conjunction of formal and sexual "misfitting" contains, in turn, an implicit bid for non-discriminatory affect, for unprejudiced ways of seeing and hearing that might lead to less exclusionary sociality.[81] In Warhol's words: "The world fascinates me. It's so nice, whatever it is. I approve of what everybody does."[82] Everybody and everything, since this lambent approval was not limited to the superstars, nor did it always operate in the name of identity or subjectivity. It was also, importantly, an affirmation of the queerness of matter; of

90 EXPERIMENTAL FILM AND QUEER MATERIALITY

matter as a locus of unassailable difference lodged in bodies, voices, spaces, situations, and things that were queered twice over. They were cast out by dominant systems of order and intelligibility, and they were animated by the strange intermittences of fuzz, grain, noise, and flare—by a queer vibration that amphetamine, like the Factory films, never ceased to amplify.

4

Crashing Bodies, Excrement, and Plastics

The Kuchar Brothers in the Sixties

It is odd that the queerness of George and Mike Kuchar's films has gone practically unremarked for so long, considering their visibility and the evident sexual charge of their work. Raised in the Bronx, the Kuchar twins started to make lurid parodies of Hollywood genre films and B pictures in 8mm in the mid-1950s, when they were still in their teens, and emerged in the avantgarde scene in 1963, when they were invited to show their work at Ken and Flo Jacobs' loft in downtown Manhattan. Their work, initially developed as amateurs innocent of experimental film, was immediately taken up by the contemporary underground, in part because it shared many traits with this movement: spontaneity, cut-rate production values, a critical and parodic engagement with popular culture, and an expansive, uninhibited depiction of corporeality and desire that we now call queer.[1] Unlike other filmmakers who remained circumscribed by the 1960s, the Kuchars have sustained longstanding careers, which, in the case of Mike Kuchar, still continue. (George passed away in 2011.) They have been steadily programmed, reviewed, and celebrated as important exponents of the 1960s underground and as forerunners of John Waters's trash aesthetic, of No-Wave film, of the "cinema of transgression," and of practically any low-fi, parodic approach to narrative film that has appeared since.[2]

As might be expected from their prominence, they have not lacked attention. Critics such as J. Hoberman, David James, Paul Arthur, Gene Youngblood, Chuck Kleinhans, Steve Reinke, and Scott MacDonald have produced valuable analyses of their films and have singled out the twins' fascination with the crass and low as the defining feature of their work.[3] Hoberman has noted their debt to the Hollywood of their childhood and the "tackball opulence" of their style; James and Arthur have discussed the way in which the Kuchars' style and themes deflate the pretensions of commercial filmmaking and the complacent seriousness of the underground; Kleinhans has underlined their role as forefathers of trash culture;

Experimental Film and Queer Materiality. Juan A. Suárez, Oxford University Press. © Oxford University Press 2024.
DOI: 10.1093/oso/9780197566992.003.0004

92   EXPERIMENTAL FILM AND QUEER MATERIALITY

MacDonald has described their mixture of cinematic know-how and low-grade production values and has studied George's interest in landscape; and Reinke and Youngblood have characterized the mock naive screen persona George projects in his video diaries as "alternately hungry, horny, or happy," in Youngblood's words.[4] However, none of these critics has connected the Kuchars' trashiness with the sexuality of their films. Gay critics Mike Finch and Raymond Murray have provided succinct surveys of George as a queer filmmaker, but they have been more descriptive than analytical and have not considered Mike—the more "out" of the two since the 1960s.[5]

The lack of queer critiques of the Kuchars is at once surprising and predictable. It is surprising because the twins' over-the-top campness, dishing of beefcake, occasional gay cruising scenes in their films, and, above all, their parodic handling of hetero- and homosexuality bespeaks the sociosexual unconventionality at the core of queerness. At the same time, the Kuchars' queerness may have been too quirky even for queer studies. Encased in comedy, their work may seem too giggly and trifling to merit scholarly interest; it is, in addition, gleefully indifferent to the vicissitudes of subjectivity, openly satirical of the confessional mode of much queer art and film, and completely unconcerned with the conceptions of gay identity and visibility that have impelled what has become known as identity politics. In fact, their most explicitly gay titles of the 1960s, Mike's *The Secret of Wendel Sampson* (1966), and George's *Eclipse of the Sun Virgin* (1967), mocked the postwar experimental films that took the tragic sadness of the closeted homosexual as their main subject. In these and many other titles, the Kuchars flouted gay-affirmative postures and overshot identity categories in favor of an expansive—often explosive—sensuality attached to the vivid surfaces of popular culture and material life.

Less inner affect than external jumble, the twins' peculiar queerness takes the form of an irreverent "materializing" drive, of a constant reduction of all idealistic concerns to the obduracy of matter in various guises: crass bodies, lowly substances, and excrement. Such materialist reduction is driven by a will to desecrate, and the main objects of the Kuchars' demotions are corporeality, desire, sexuality, and the object ecology of their formative years defined by the pervasiveness of plastics and synthetics, available in a panoply of colorful designs, that historians have labeled "populuxe" and "Tupperware modernity."[6] Bodies, sex, and plastic modernity are insistently brought into contact with excrement, at once their radical other and an earthy double to which they constantly revert. In this excremental tropism resides the Kuchars' peculiar queerness, doubly disreputable because it links disruptive sexuality with a low, defiling substance whose open display signals bodily and communal disorder. In this manner, the Kuchars' films force us to reconsider queerness through the attractions and repulsions of matter and materiality rather than through the usual routes of subjectivity and identity. Not only a register of psychic life and embodied desire, they show that queerness also involves a rapport with the things of the world—a rapport that renders matter sexual and oddly animate and, conversely, anchors sexuality in the surrounding material horizon.

On tracking such a non-anthropomorphic view of queerness through the Kuchars' corpus, this chapter, like the rest of this book, wants to contribute to what one could regard as a recent "new materialist" turn in queer critique. This includes recent work by Sara Ahmed on queer phenomenology, by Jennifer Terry on the objectúm sexuals subculture, by Scott Herring on the relation between deviant corporeality and the deviant "material use" of hoarders, and the "Queer Inhumanisms" special issue of GLQ edited by Dana Luciano and Mel Y. Chen.[7] In the realm of moving image studies, queer materialist analysis informs Karl Schoonover's writing on 1970s trash cinema and trashy stardom, Rosalind Galt's work on color in Derek Jarman's Super-8 films, Lucas Hilderbrand's analysis of deteriorated videotape, and Galt and Schoonover's characterization of global queer cinema.[8] Cumulatively, this body of work examines the (often unspoken) material horizons that subtend sexuality and its representations—be it the thingness of the body, particular objects, and substances or the renderings and distortions unique to various media—and shows that the range of the sexual exceeds interiority, individuality, and anthropomorphic embodiment to affix itself also to textures, surfaces, and things; indeed, it is in relation to this material interface that many of the political consequences of queerness arise.

While the Kuchars' materializing gestures run through their extensive careers, they appear with paradigmatic clarity in their 1960s films, which will be the focus of this chapter. This period includes many of their best-known and most expressive titles and anticipates, in many ways, their subsequent trajectories. Even though there are important reasons to consider the brothers separately, this chapter will study them together on the grounds of their shared origins and influences, their frequent collaboration, and their parallel articulation of a queer image embedded in the queerness of matter.

Speeding, Falling

The Kuchars' queer-materialist calling may derive in part from their earliest and most durable aesthetic education: the comic books and the Hollywood films that they sampled during their childhood and adolescence in the decaying movie palaces of the Bronx.[9] Both genres provided them with a vocabulary of emotional and stylistic extremes; the comics, in addition, purveyed fast-paced narratives and depictions of bodily aggression in an atmosphere of titillation and sexual ambiguity that eventually came to define their work.

By their own confession, the Kuchars particularly relished the most corporeal and stylistically excessive film genres: Douglas Sirk's melodramas, Alfred Zugsmith's B productions, and all manner of low-budget horror, action, and science fiction from which they borrowed liberally for their later work.[10] Their first films, made in 8mm, offered deranged versions of what were already emotionally and formally overwrought genres. Featuring titles such as *The Wet Destruction of the Atlantic Empire* (1954), *The Naked and the Nude* (1957), *The Thief and the Stripper* (1957), *A Tub Named Desire* (1960), *I was a Teenage Rumpot* (1960), *Pussy on a Hot Tin Roof* (1963) and *Tootsies in Autumn* (1963), these were rudimentary productions with crude lighting, makeup, and costumes, filmed in humdrum homes, in backyards, and on rooftops. They nevertheless displayed considerable ingenuity and moments of technical brilliance, such as simulating floods by means of cardboard models and inserting images of raging fires filmed off the television monitor. The plots are frequently undecipherable, despite the well-meant, often misspelled intertitles, and are invariably fast-moving, zestily acted, and rife with murderous rampage and sexual frenzy.

The pulp-ish quality of these narratives, their frantic action, spicy titling, and the hardboiled language of the title cards suggest the additional influence of the crime and horror comics that were immensely popular during the Kuchars' youth. Their childhood and early adolescence coincided with the golden era for these genres, whose popularity peaked in 1954 with an estimated monthly circulation of thirty million copies, accounting for a fifth of the total sales for all comics.[11] Magazines such as *Shock SuspenStories*, *Tales From the Crypt*, *Adventures into the Unknown*, and *The Vault of Horror* printed stories of murders, mutilations, dismemberments, and macabre supernatural visitations. The artwork uninhibitedly depicted half-decaying corpses, bleeding bodies, and all manner of gruesome atrocities that were

CRASHING BODIES, EXCREMENT, AND PLASTICS 95

most frequently perpetrated on women. Draftsman Johnny Craig's covers for *Crime SuspenStories*, published by the polemical company E. C. between November 1950 and March 1955, strike a characteristic note. One showed in lush detail the grimace in a hanged man's face (no. 20, 1954); another a young fellow shooting a bullet through his head at the precise moment when the top of his scalp explodes in a bloody gush (no. 17, 1953); while a third portrays a murderer, whose upper body and face remain unseen, holding in one hand the head of a decapitated woman and in the other a blood-dripping axe (no. 22, 1954). Covers by other artists feature men burying or strangling women or preparing to chop up a dead body in a trash container.[12] This virulence prompted a famous book-length denunciation by psychiatrist Fredric Wertham published in 1954 and ultimately put the comics under the scrutiny of a Senate sub-committee for their possible inducement to juvenile delinquency.

The Kuchars seem to have borrowed from the comics some of their characteristic materializing strategies, such as the fast pace and dense incident of their films, which privilege physicality over reflective consciousness, and their cartoonish physical cruelty. This last translates into a disregard for the integrity of bodies, treated in the comics and in the Kuchars' early films as disposable hunks of flesh frequently mishandled and knocked about—in the comics they were also torn apart with astonishing violence. Yet bodies in the comics were also there to be seen and fantasized about. Stock characters included tightly-dressed bosomy women ("whenever possible they protrude and obtrude," notes Wertham),[13] showing generous lengths of leg in the roles of gangsters' molls, mobsters, wanton seducers and, most frequently, hapless victims. Heroes are invariably muscular, and occasionally stripped down to their vests or bare chests to perform their feats, while the superheroes that populated a great number of action comics dressed in body socks that showed off their athletic shapes. For Dr Wertham, the stories promoted various forms of deviance, from the "psychological homosexuality" of the Batman series to a broad spectrum of sadomasochistic fantasies that included "erotic hanging" or sexual flogging and choking.[14] Sexual intimations did not emanate from the stories alone: comic book magazines included ads for mail-order weight-gaining nostrums and bodybuilding methods illustrated with pictures of bare-chested gymnasts that, Wertham warned, planted homoerotic suggestions in impressionable children or confirmed others in their "homosexual tendencies."[15] Additionally, the Senate investigation revealed that responding to ads in the comic magazines led to

96   EXPERIMENTAL FILM AND QUEER MATERIALITY

written solicitation for the purchase of "salacious" and "sexually stimulating materials."[16] This was hardly surprising, since publishers and wholesalers of comics usually delved into other corners of the print underground, such as "girlie" magazines, "pseudomedical sex books," "pseudo-science" (hypnotism manuals), and porn novelettes with titles such as *Wild Passion*, *Wanton by Night*, or *The Shame of Oscar Wild* [*sic*] that the committee found "nonmailable under postal obscenity law."[17] Hence not only the violence but also the sensuality simmering on the surface of the Kuchars' narratives may have stemmed partly from the comics, from both the stories themselves and from the slightly seedy aura that enveloped the medium.

The comics may have also provided an influential model for showcasing florid drama in a cheap, disposable medium. For their lack of cultural capital, they were like 8mm film—an inexpensive gauge exclusively destined for the home movie market into which the twins poured their inventiveness. The combination of high emotion and low technology remained a defining trait of the Kuchars' films of the 1960s and 1970s. In those years their palette broadened considerably. In addition to narratives, they made lyrical films with elusive scenarios (Mike's *Green Desire* [1965], *Cycles* [1967], *Variations* [1967]), artist's portraits (George's *Lady from Sands Point* [1967], *House of the White People* [1968], *Encyclopedia of the Blessed* [1968]), protonarrative vignettes with their particular take on everyday life in the Bronx (George's *Mosholu Holiday* [1967], *Leisure* [1966], *Knockturne* [1968]; Mike's *Tales of the Bronx* [1969]), or satires of art and experimental film (George's *Hold Me While I'm Naked* [1967], *Eclipse of the Sun Virgin*). Nevertheless, the parodic reworking of Hollywood genre films and B movies, crossed with the intensity of the comics and achieved with extremely spare technical means, remained a mainstay, as shown by George's *Corruption of the Damned* (1965) and *Color Me Shameless* (1967) or Mike's *Sins of the Fleshapoids* (1966) and *The Craven Sluck* (1967), all examples of a pulp–pop sensibility for which they are best known.

The Kuchars' fascination with commercial film and comic books was by no means exceptional in the underground; indeed one of its most vital strands developed in complex dialogue with classical studio films. The films of Jack Smith, Andy Warhol, Kenneth Anger, and José Rodríguez Soltero, for example, show a considerable fascination with star cults and movie glamour. They repurposed Hollywood icons, highlighting their gender unconventionality and queer affect, and occasionally indulged in demented remakes of classical plots. Smith and Ken Jacobs' *Blonde Cobra* was conceived as a desultory

CRASHING BODIES, EXCREMENT, AND PLASTICS   97

version of Von Sternberg's *Blonde Venus* (1932) and the Maria Montez vehicle *Cobra Woman* (1944), yet bears no evident relation to either; Rodríguez Soltero's *Lupe* (1967) is a biopic of "spitfire" Lupe Vélez; and Warhol's *Hedy* (1966) and *More Milk, Yvette* (1965) are homages to Hollywood stars Hedy Lamarr and Lana Turner.

At the same time, there are considerable differences between these underground remakes of Hollywood and the Kuchars' own. With the possible exception of Rodríguez Soltero's *Lupe*, which has a fairly nimble narrative, the underground's reworking of Hollywood usually neglected storytelling and highlighted static elements of the mise-en-scene or the stars' appearance—consider Mario Montez posing as Jean Harlow in Warhol's *Harlot* (1964), presented in an unvarying camera set-up for over sixty minutes, or Jack Smith's languid tableaus. Movement in these films takes place inside the individual shots rather than between them, and emanates from minute inflections in the performers' pose and gesture or from variations in light or framing. In this way most underground directors sought to slow down the action or to do away with it completely, to focus their attention on peculiarities of gesture, costume, or decor and to promote a more aestheticized, contemplative style of reception. It is, after all, in moments of spectacle "slightly askew to narrative functionality" where camp affect reworks conventional Hollywood iconography, as Matthew Tinkcom has pointed out.[18]

The Kuchars were, however, as interested in the iconic components of classical film and in formal detail as they were in plot development and in Hollywood's kinetic style of storytelling, which they speeded up further under the influence of the comics' condensed narratives. They favored fast action and thus remained faithful to a crucial ingredient of cinematic pleasure—the quick unfolding of events in time. Some critics have pointed out that, from beginning to end, every scene in their narrative films seems a climax. As George put it: "Usually you go to a theater and there are . . . three moments in the picture where it's intense . . . I don't believe in that. I believe the motion picture should be intense . . . constant turbulence from beginning to end."[19]

Sexuality and desire are the main suppliers of narrative turbulence and emotional intensity in the Kuchars' narratives—a sexuality that is anything but normative or containable and can therefore be described as queer. Their characters are driven by unsightly desires that refuse restraint and have potentially explosive effects on normality, or what passes for it in their films. At times these urges are homosexual hankerings (*The Secret of Wendel Samson*

98   EXPERIMENTAL FILM AND QUEER MATERIALITY

and *Eclipse of the Sun Virgin*), while at others they are demented 'hetero-sexual' passions pursued with suicidal insistence: robots that stop at nothing in order to consummate their love (*Sins of the Fleshapoids*), a bored house-wife who falls for a two-timing rake (*The Craven Sluck*), a young man hell-bent on revenge after his sweetheart leaves him for someone else (*Corruption of the Damned*)), or a sinister artist maniacally obsessed with his female models and neighbors (*Color Me Shameless*).

At the mercy of their trashy drives, the Kuchars' characters are open-ended and profligate. Invariably needy and easily unhinged, they are possessed by gargantuan passions that prompt them to clash with other equally needy characters, usually with catastrophically comic results. The Kuchars' world is one of inversions where the decorum of mass culture—built on denial and repression—and the psychological seriousness of the underground are turned upside down. If, in the famous Frankfurt School formulation, mass culture is "psychoanalysis in reverse," since it encodes wayward unconscious affect into acceptable public representations,[20] the Kuchars are determined on reversing this path. In conventional plots and pop clichés, and in quo-tidian scenarios of boredom and normality, they discover sexuality not as a cipher for internal motivation and individual psychology but as obstreperous embodiment and erratic melee. Counter to mainstream popular culture's emphasis on love and romance, the Kuchars emphasize sexually driven pas-sion, and, rather than cultivate the introspective and lyrical modes of much underground film, they dwell on runaway plot and external incident. It is not the etherealities of the visionary spirit that take center stage in their work but sexual compulsion and the weight of the body, an entity that stumbles and falls, seldom in control of itself. In sex, the body loses its individuality and self-containment, spills over, enters and is entered by other bodies, and comes to terms with its organic base—with being mere matter. By losing its balance, it knocks against and becomes part of its surroundings, turning into a castaway piece of junk (Figure 4.1). Knocking and falling are indeed fre-quent motifs in their films; they turn the body into a thing, highlighting its heft and obduracy and attenuating its sentient, cognitive capabilities.

George's *Corruption of the Damned* and Mike's *Tales of the Bronx* are good examples of their dynamic storytelling, of the urgent passions that drive their plots, and of their depiction of eroticism as corporeal incident and material jumble rather than inner affect. Mike's *Tales* could be defined as a multi-protagonist avant-garde comedy. In an elliptical manner, it follows the par-allel storylines of various residents in an apartment building, all of whom

Figure 4.1 Mike Kuchar, *The Craven Sluck*, 1967. Frame enlargement.

appear prey to a highly kinetic eroticism: a blond, middle-aged woman writhes alone in bed, seemingly consumed by unfulfilled desire while she watches television; a brunette in an evening gown pedals frantically on a static bicycle; a young fashion plate embarks on a casual tryst with a passer-by who follows her into her apartment; and a more sedate young fellow cruises a Tarzan-like blond youth sitting on a tree branch in a park wearing nothing but a loincloth. (The Tarzan motif recurs in one of Mike's covers for the short-lived comic magazine *Gay Heart Throbs* in the early 1980s.) Even the dog of the passer-by (George's mongrel Bocko, frequent star in the Kuchar films), left to his own devices during the tryst, succumbs to the general sexual hysteria and tries to hump a child in an alley, while the child, whose features have been erased by scratching the emulsion on the celluloid, struggles to escape. Not only kinetic, these erotic styles are variously heterodox, as characters libidinally commingle with things (a bicycle, a turned-on television set), long for those of their own sex, or are engaged by nonhumans.

Comparable to *Tales* for its manic motility and slapstick, *Corruption of the Damned*, George's first solitary effort after the brothers ceased codirecting, is a hotchpotch of generic motifs filmed in black and white. Zapping through the cinematic imaginary of his adolescence at breakneck speed, it strings together allusions to the juvenile delinquent picture, the family melodrama, the social problem film (there is an obscure labor dispute), the blue movie, and the horror picture. (There is, in addition, a brief homage to Yoko Ono's performance *Cut Piece*, which had been performed at Carnegie Recital Hall the year of the film). The film starts out with a betrayal (John's girlfriend Cora has run away with Paul) and narrates John's attempts to get Cora back and to get back at Cora with the help of his brother Marvin. The plot involves a psychic *séance* in a lonely house in the woods, a car crash, a suicide, several seduction scenes, an assault on a suburban home perpetrated by a gaggle of leather-clad youths, a wildcat strike, and a nudie picture shoot in which Cora and Paul—held against their will by John's aunt Anna—are forced to act for the camera. In the concluding sequences, Cora and Paul, along with the clandestine porn operation, are blown to bits by an accidental explosion of TNT, and John tries to rescue Anna from certain death as her boss and lover is about to saw her head off in a scene that harks back to the goriest comics. While Paul and Anna's lover slug it out, seer Lucille Lamont, who had surprisingly reappeared just outside the building, and Anna settle some account of their own by wrestling in a mound of shredded paper and tearing each other's clothes off.

The rendition of emotion as sheer motility does not result only from the speedy succession of events; every episode of *Corruption of the Damned* is mired in corporeal obstruction and awkwardness. The opening of the film strikes the dominant note. Shots of John and Marvin driving a car on a suburban street are juxtaposed with a high-angle frame of their mother's bunioned feet laboriously stepping on a scale that scores well over two hundred pounds. It is as if the horizontal sliding of the car were stalled by the heavy tread of a body tied to the earth. Gravity imposes itself throughout, bringing characters regularly to the ground, perhaps no one as often as Anna: she stumbles and falls when she receives John at the factory, after cutting short an afternoon tryst; is pushed down the stairs by Cora's father; and repeatedly topples over during her fight with Lamont. In turn, suburban housewife Conny seems as unsteady when she fends off the young thugs in her house as when she romances Marvin in the park at the very end of the film. Their encounter takes place after she faints, and Marvin obligingly drags her away by her feet—her blond mane trails on the ground behind her—and helps her come to.

These Kucharian falls are quite different from those found in other moments of film history. French philosopher Jacques Rancière has read the

CRASHING BODIES, EXCREMENT, AND PLASTICS   101

falls and jumps into the void in Roberto Rossellini's classic postwar films as allegories of a radical embrace of freedom against impossible odds; and numerous critics and historians have regarded the pratfalls and tumbles typical of silent comedy as symbols of the instability and unwieldiness of a mechanized modernity often indifferent to human demands.[21] In the Kuchars' work, by contrast, falling is neither an existential wager nor a mechanical reflex caused by a topsy-turvy world; it results from being in thrall to the demands of desire. Characters drop under the weight of overpowering passions, seldom verbalized but exuberantly acted out in chases, fisticuffs, by fetishistically rubbing (and rubbing against) other characters' feet, or by writhing on the grass of a cemetery in tight embrace: "Stop! We are laying [sic] on my grandmother," Cora warns Paul in a moment of amorous abandonment in *Corruption of the Damned*.

Excremental Aesthetics

The Kuchars' materialization of the body and sexual passion also takes other forms, in particular, that of a fascination with the excremental; after all, as Dominique Laporte points out in her canonical study, excrement is the apotheosis of matter—matter impregnable to idea, symbol, or spirit.[22] Once idealized and spiritualized, it becomes something else: compost, fertilizer or, in the metaphorical chain that Freud famously described, it is sublimated into gifts, the phallus, or money.[23]

Waste is never sublimated in the Kuchars; rather, it tends to function as a desublimating principle, a universal solvent that brings every act and aspiration down to sheer filth. In their calculatedly scandalous rhetoric, they made the excremental their calling card throughout the 1960s, frequently comparing filmmaking to an organic process akin to the production of body waste. In his first published statement in *Film Culture*, George confided that his creative process involved sleepless nights when he was affected by increased heart rate and vertiginous brainstorming: "I'm like a fleshy teletype machine.... My mind turns into a sponge and every lost electrical brain wave that humanity has ever sent forth, seems to convert on my skull." After protracted enervation, he would finally fall asleep to awaken "fresh, vibrant, but constipated with the urge to release a lump of cinematic material."[24] Mike seemed to agree with George's view: his *Sins* put an end to a severe case of filmic constipation that had dragged on for months.[25] The metaphor recurs in their memoirs, *Reflections from a Cinematic Cesspool*, where the oscillation between rest and work, blockage and creativity, is rendered in terms of intestinal retention and release. Film is then a residue that must be flushed out of the system in a way that is hygienic for the filmmaker yet noxious to the environment. Still, cinematic waste might also be fertile to others: "Just as the Egyptians revered the little beetle that pushed a ball of dung . . . so should we, as filmmakers and teachers, revere the crap peddled by our contemporaries. From that foul-smelling garbage a foundation can be laid."[26] Elsewhere in their memoirs, George wrote: "My inspirations have mainly been the profuse droppings of others who rendered the tormented souls haunting the covers of sleazy paperback books (the type my dad always read)."[27] If, for contemporary filmmaker and performance artist, Jack Smith, art was a junkyard of moldy discards,[28] for the twins it was a huge *pissoir*, and art consumption and influence were forms of coprophagic bottom-feeding. In this regard, the frequent references to defecation in their work (e.g. treacherous turds underfoot, unflushed deposits in the toilet bowl) might be read, in 1970s *Screen* language, as self-reflexive moments in which the films foreground their ontology and conditions of production.

One of the ways in which excrement "performs" in the Kuchars' films is as a reminder of the unavoidable prose of the body. When it pops up or out, excrement undercuts romantic love and idealized sex, eliciting a laugh at their pretensions; it is therefore one more materializing factor, aligned with other modes of corporeal and physical foregrounding such as speed and pratfalls. An unflushed stool in the toilet bowl signals to the female protagonist of *Pagan Rhapsody* (1970) that the liaison she is about to enter, with a stilted aristocrat who wants to cast her in the role of his dead wife in a play he is producing, may not lead to endless rapture. And this is indeed the case; the aristocrat's passion for the young actress soon cools down, their romance turns into routine, and, tired of spending much of her time alone, she ends up hosting sex parties for her younger beatnik friends behind her beau's back while he is away. Her tribulations end when she slips on the vomit of a young playwright in the aristocrat's employ and fatally bangs her head against the toilet seat. In Mike's *The Craven Sluck*, it is precisely at the height of the central romantic encounter that the dog of the female protagonist squats to make a bowel movement—unsurprisingly, a bad omen, since this romance too will turn out badly.

Eclipse of the Sun Virgin is particularly insistent on debunking romance by counterpointing it to anality and to the idiotic materiality of the flesh.

CRASHING BODIES, EXCREMENT, AND PLASTICS   103

Both homage and satire of the postwar homoerotic films of Anger, Willard Maas, and Gregory Markopoulos, it is dedicated, in George's words, "to the Behemoths of yesteryears that perished in Siberia long ago."[29] Early on, a blue-tinted sequence of a running stream edited to baroque harpsichord accompaniment reminiscent of Anger's *Eaux d'Artifice* (1953) culminates in a shot of a cave full of stagnant water and buzzing flies. The implication is that Anger's lyrical squirts, sprays, and aqueous reflections on sculpted stone are, at bottom, thin sublimations of golden showers and scat. Later in the film, a fractious telephone conversation between two lovers is punctuated by belches and farts: the lower body echoes the upper body, and upset stomach and intestines provide gross physical translations of the lovers' disdainful grimaces and sneers. In a kindred form of desublimation, the protagonist's erotic fixation on the neck of an adolescent he encounters—or imagines he encounters—in a public toilet (once again, excrement lurks in the vicinity) is reprised, at the end of the film, in his fascination with a medical film about the surgical extraction of a tumor in exactly the same spot. The fetish turns into a cankerous growth but somehow retains its allure, since the protagonist invites a friend to a screening of the film in his bedroom, apparently with intention of seducing him. As the scalpel slices into the flesh, the friends, ensconced in bed, smile at each other with naughty complicity.

Wayward passion and bodily functions are not the only causes of disruption in the Kuchars' world. Much like characters' desires and bodily urges, the unstoppable powers of hurricanes, heavy storms, earthquakes, and volcanic eruptions, along with aliens and occult forces, are apt to strike unannounced with devastating result. The fascination with these destructive forces may be attributed to the twins' residual Catholicism, a melodramatic ideology that envisions life as constantly menaced by temptation and evil; and it could also contain a reference to the social atmosphere of their formative years, when everyday existence appeared under various threats—communist infiltration, atomic apocalypse, all-out war—which were amply represented in some of the Kuchars' favorite pop genres, from science fiction and horror films to the superhero comics.[30] At the same time, natural disasters and excretion are closely linked in the tradition of grotesque humor famously studied by Russian critic Mikhail Bakhtin, a tradition that was the mainstay of European popular culture from Antiquity to the Renaissance, and of which the Kuchars, like the postwar crime and horror comics, are distant avatars. Bakhtin showed that in grotesque humor, natural catastrophes were often depicted as hyperbolic versions of corporeal excretions: floods and hurricanes as flows of urine streaming from the sky; earthquakes and eruptions as earthly flatulence and vomit. Conversely, corporeal functions were domestic versions of the periodical devastations of nature. In Bakhtin's words: "It was in the material acts and eliminations of the body—eating, drinking, defecations, sexual life—that man [sic] found and retraced within himself the earth, sea, air, fire, and the cosmic matter and its manifestations, and was thus able to assimilate them."[31] Transposed into bowel spasms and sexual drives, Bakhtin speculated, "cosmic upheavals" became humanized, less fearsome than humorous.

Egregious examples of the conflation of the cosmic and the physiological are found in George's weather diaries, in which hurricanes and flood rains are counterpointed to George's anal, digestive, and sexual vicissitudes. In *Weather Diary # 1* (1986), for example, his voiceover compares a night storm to "a wet dream" as a giant puddle is shown on the screen; another day, "severe storms" gather outside his motel room as massed clouds in a moody sky *and* inside his body as "gastric distress" and wrecking flatulence. Earlier films are also punctuated with similar parallels. In George's *Pussy on a Hot Tin Roof*, the burning sexual desires of three call girls (who happen to be sisters) and their clients end up causing a massive conflagration as, in the abandon of a raunchy party, one of them drops a burning cigarette that sets their house and eventually their entire neighborhood ablaze. In Mike's *Death Quest of the Ju-Ju Cult* (1976)[32] an erupting volcano echoes the overbrimming passions of the film's prehistoric protagonists, involved in an unhappy love triangle. And an earthquake disrupts a dance party in George's *The Sunshine Sisters* (1972), as if the earth itself had caught the excitement of the partygoers. In all these examples, invisible lines of empathy connect excitable bodies and geological disturbances as they are turned into each other's material counterparts.

Excrement is not only thematized in visual allusions and fecal scenarios, it also smears the Kuchars' filmic syntax, an extremely condensed editing style that elides transitions and establishing shots and, with the exception of an occasional landscape in long shot, relies mostly on medium shots and close-ups. Tight framing brings spectators up against performers and their milieu, and withdraws distance, gradation, and perspective. A prime example might be what some critics have regarded as George's trademark shot, first used, as far as I have been able to ascertain, in *Hold Me While I'm Naked*: a low-angle, extreme close-up of his face filmed by holding the camera right in front of him. Usually taken with a wide-angle lens, it swells George's chin and lips and slightly distorts his features, augmenting the fleshiness of his face and suggesting oppressive nearness. A similarly invasive proximity characterizes *Pagan Rhapsody, Eclipse of the Sun Virgin,* and substantial segments of *The Devil's Cleavage* (1975), among others, which are all filmed largely in medium close-up. The effect of such tight framing is a tactile involvement with the action, against which the spectator, plunged into its midst, seemingly chafes. But in such proximity, one may also read an attempt to recreate, through visual means, a commonality of flesh and odor that remains the suppressed underside of knowledge, beauty, and community in modernity.

Laporte has pointed out that the first official measures in mass hygiene, enforced in France during the Renaissance, had as their purpose the privatization of excrement and its withdrawal from public view. Hygiene also brought about the marginalization of smell, which since the Renaissance came to occupy the lowest rung in the scale of the senses. Laporte recalls that for a number of Enlightenment thinkers such as Étienne de Condillac or Immanuel Kant, smell was the sense furthest removed from knowledge or beauty, two categories dominated by sight and predicated upon the analytical separation of the subject from the objects of contemplation.[33] Freud also noted that "civilized" sexuality was marked by the dominance of vision and by a concomitant demotion of smell that he attributed to the erect posture of humans. As primates evolved from four- to two-legged animals, genital and excretory organs were no longer within easy reach of the face, and smell lost its formerly essential role in eroticism, becoming instead the uncomfortable reminder of an earlier evolutionary stage that modern societies strove to repress.[34] Sight replaced smell as the driving source of sexual stimulation, reinforcing its already privileged position in science and aesthetics.

Seen from this perspective, the Kuchars' penchant for narrowing down the visual field and rubbing the spectator's nose in the action enacts a return of the repressed—smell and therefore body waste—and this return is communicated by means of visual proximity. Nearness is an apt synesthesia for the penetrative embrace of odor. Caused by the invasion of the body by foreign particulate matter, odor entails the annulment of distance between subject and object, self and other, upon which sight is predicated. Close-ups of feet sinking into soft brown lumps or slipping on vomit at climactic moments of *Knockturne* and *Pagan Rhapsody;* the nearness of bodies dancing, eating, loitering, or cavorting in *Leisure, Eclipse of the Sun Virgin,* or *Moshulu Holiday;* the unappetizing borscht presented at close range at the end of *Hold Me While I'm Naked:* in their propinquity, all of these images suggest a redolence inevitably missing from the cinematic image and largely

106 EXPERIMENTAL FILM AND QUEER MATERIALITY

alien to modern visuality.[35] These recreations of smell by means of sight fuse the highest and lowest of the senses, rendering the latter by means of the former. They also seek to interpellate audiences olfactorily as well as visually by plunging them into the films' pungent ambience, and in doing so, they pull spectators into the orbit of the films' crass materiality. The body pervaded by smell, like the one constantly tumbling about or racked by excremental urges, is a body reduced to sensation and merged into its environment. In this way, the Kuchars' olfactory aesthetic combines characters, materials, environments, and audiences into an ill-matched sentient aggregate.

Troubling Tupperware Modernity

In a more situated manner, the pungency of waste was also the counter-part for the blandness of the postwar material culture that prided itself on cleanness, comfort, and detachment—the perfect foil for the Kuchars' embrace of the unclean, paroxysmic, and olfactory. Theirs was the first generation to grow up entirely surrounded by plastics, or more specifically "thermoplastics," a mid-1940s variety of this material that was cheaper, less durable and less stable than earlier varieties such as bakelite and celluloid, and whose production had increased exponentially during the war.[36] Plastic is insistently featured in their films in the formica surfaces, vinyl linoleum, polyester faux-furs, leatherette outfits and upholstery, polysterene kitchen decor and toys, Naugahyde furniture, Melamine tumblers and dishes, and a long synthetic etcetera. It is the material backdrop of their fictional world as it was the actual backdrop of daily life during their formative years, and it is also a further materializing element that, alongside excrement and recalcitrant embodiment, brings bodies and sexuality down to the level of crass objecthood.

Plastic introduces a topical element in the Kuchars' films, which register the smooth surfaces of Tupperware modernity even as it smears them with body waste and tears them apart with the infusion of volcanic passions that seem out of place in such staid milieux (Figure 4.2). Plastic was the defining, if often overlooked, raw material of the postwar years, used indiscriminately in high and low design: in Saarinen's tulip chairs and the Smithsons' "House of the Future" as well as Tupper Corporation kitchenware, low-grade trinkets, and roadside architecture. The vernacular rococo venerated by post-modern architects depended heavily on vinyl and formica for its flights of

Figure 4.2 Mike Kuchar, *The Secret of Wendel Samson*, 1966. Frame enlargement.

fancy, as did many of the comforts of postwar America, supplied in the shape of accessible, hygienic, user-friendly furniture and housewares. These came in a motley assortment of styles—colonial revival, "prairie," Scandinavian modern, "space-age" . . .—that Thomas Hine has grouped under the term "populuxe."[37]

To its advocates and enthusiastic consumers, plastic signified pragmatism and novelty; it heralded the affordable ease that had come to supersede Depression-era hardship and wartime rationing and radiated cleanliness and asepsis. Critical observers, however, scorned plastic's superficiality, cheapness, and spuriousness. In their eyes it was an emblem of the overabundance of developed societies and the meretricious character of their products—the reasons why Norman Mailer denounced contemporary America as a plastic nightmare.[38] Yet even though it had eminently suburban, conformist connotations, which Mailer frequently expounded upon, it was also the raw material of much dissident subcultural life. Surfing, skateboarding, and car-customizing, for example, depended on the availability of polyester, synthetic resins and enamels, and fiberglass. The instruments that made the rock revolution possible were partly made of plastic, and so were the casings of sound recorders, video recorders and film cameras, and the mylar magnetic tapes and celluloid film stock that disseminated new musical and visual styles.

In the Kuchars' films, plastics straddle the divide between consumerist conformity and dissidence, only this last comes less from the uses to which plastics are put than from a discrepant quality in the material. Plastics were the sign of the times, immediately visible in the absurd trinkets and useless but expressive props that dot their interiors. They are often foregrounded in inserts that show their whimsical design. Perhaps because of their imaginative, if not always tasteful, configuration, these objects have a strange instability and appear endowed with a life of their own. They are vehicles for a sort of dime-store surrealism that punctures the surface of the humdrum everyday. In George's *Eclipse of the Sun Virgin*, a mother and her doted-upon son play a schmaltzy version of Chopin together on harmonium and piano; without missing a beat, she puts out her cigarette on a plastic ashtray from which, at the touch of a button, a skeletal hand emerges to scoop in the butt. In a similar vein, George's *Knockturne*, comparable in some ways to *Tales of the Bronx* for following in parallel several neighbors in an apartment building, is peopled with humanoid plastic dolls that cross the line between the animate and the inanimate. A giant Mr Peanut, animated by means of frame shooting, moves across the landing unnoticed; a pink-haired, synthetic yellow doll is pulled out of a suitcase by a young woman (filmmaker Joyce Wieland), dumped in a bath, and later unceremoniously cast out of the window; and the eyeless head of a rubber doll is chewed on and dragged around by a dog. The doll's lacerated head first appears in a disorienting close-up that disrupts the succession of long and medium shots dominating the film up to that point, but is quickly recontextualized by a wider frame as a broken toy at the mercy of the dog. A subhuman liveliness agitates these seemingly banal things. A kindred agitation of everyday objects not made of plastic is present in other corners of the Kuchars' world. Toward the end of George's *Color Me Shameless*, the shoes and pieces of female underwear that the film's fetishistic protagonist has collected and stored in a kitchen drawer break out of their confinement and perform a brief choreography. And in George's *Leisure* a cloth doll slips out of an old woman's grasp to scoot across her body.

Apart from channeling a subterranean life of objects, plastics often bridged the gap between organic bodies and inorganic matter. Even though plastic was the opposite of organic corporeality, and feared and despised

CRASHING BODIES, EXCREMENT, AND PLASTICS 109

for this reason, it was also capable of adopting organic shapes, and had a sexual dimension that critics and artists of the time—the Kuchars were no exception—were quick to pick up on. For British architect and theorist Reyner Banham, plastic was capable of replicating the smoothness and pliancy of human flesh; it promised the "triumph of software"—supple, responsive structures—over "hardware"—the rigid constructions and designs that had been the sole interest of traditional architecture.[39] French sculptor Alexandre Bonnier, creator of brightly colored and slightly disquieting polyp-like shapes, concurred, noting that while some plastics are reminiscent of death, others are directly linked to the flesh and pervaded with erotic promise: "soft polystyrene, produced by the meter . . . has exactly the warmth and consistency of a woman's flesh, bulbous inflatable membranes and seats so reminiscent of the fetal sac and from which are made the life-size, adult dolls sold in sex-shops."[40] British pop artist Richard Hamilton regarded plastic as the harbinger of a new sexuality that blended the organic and inorganic, humans, and commodities. Ubiquitous, discreet, and slick, this new sexuality was channeled through ads, fashions, and appliances: "Sex is everywhere, symbolized in the glamour of mass-produced luxury—the interplay of fleshy plastic and smooth, fleshier metal."[41] The new plastic sexuality was also a new sexual plasticity. Warhol noted that "dildos and all kinds of vibrators" made out of PVC and silicone had taken over people's sex lives by the end of the 1960s.[42] No one needed to make do without a penis, and castration could become a thing of the past. At the same time, artificial fibers, synthetic wigs, silicone implants, and plastic accessories permitted unprecedented gender malleability, as the lively drag queen scene of the time amply demonstrated.[43]

Plastic sex was cheap, artificial, and unnatural and brought bodies into intimate communion with the inorganic. The Kuchars' films further expounded these qualities. There is a revealing moment in George's *Hold Me While I'm Naked* when, about to be abandoned by his main star who is "tired of being naked in almost every scene," the protagonist film director lies in bed with a plastic doll whose lips he daubs with lipstick. The doll is a substitute for the actresses he cannot possess visually, much less carnally; it is a sign of his frustration and disconnection, but also suggests the exchangeability of flesh and inert matter, and hints that, at some level, sex may just be a question of friction between surfaces, regardless of type. In *Eclipse of the Sun Virgin* plastic evokes less the translatability of flesh into matter than a sort of incommunicability that thwarts erotic fusion. On two occasions, the protagonist boy and girl, unable to spark up their relationship due to the boy's homoerotic longings, converge in a bucolic setting and stare at each other through a plastic curtain that covers the entrance to a shed. Astir in the breeze, the translucent sheet trashes the pastoral ambience, hinders the view, and suggests the impossibility of their union. The idea is confirmed when in these very scenes, to the strains of an unctuous love song in the background, both characters puncture their fingers on a rose stem and draw "blood," which is evidently red pigment crudely poured on their fingertips.

There is no trace of nostalgia for a lost organic world in these scenes. On the contrary, they contain a bemused celebration of the deflationary power of plastic. An example is a brief scene in *Eclipse* intended as a jab at the lofty mythic concerns of postwar homoerotic cinema. After oscillating between a girlfriend he cannot desire and—real or fantasized—fleeting encounters with men in public toilets, the film's protagonist seems ready to embrace his gay-ness. Apparently naked, he shoves aside the garish plastic fruit that covers a mirror placed on the ground and gazes enraptured at his reflection; the image suggests he has reached some sort of self-recognition and self-acceptance, except that his silly grin, the artificial colors, and the garish plastic bananas and apples signal biting irony at the gay cliché. The scene brings to mind Willard Maas and Ben Moore's *Narcissus* (1956), a film in which a similarly closeted protagonist rejects various erotic advances and uses a mirror to pass into a parallel dream-world, where he takes refuge in moments of suf-fering. (The motif reworks Jean Cocteau's similar use of mirrors in *Orphée* (1950).) *Eclipse* replaces the moody black and white, tortured introspection and dreaminess of Maas and Moore's title with a bemused immersion into synthetic surface and color, an immersion that marks in the film the shift from repression to action. The mirror in *Eclipse* does not lead to an alterna-tive transcendent universe but into the corporeal demands of the film's pro-tagonist, whose homoerotic fantasies become progressively more lurid as the film advances.

In some ways, Mike's *Sins of the Fleshapoids* is programmatic of the twins' love of the cheap in film, sex, and materials. It is an homage to B and Z cinema—to low-grade science fiction, Italian Roman epics, and homoerotic physique films—and a celebration of synthetic disposability, which turns out to be the site of the authentic and permanent. *Sins* is set "one million years from now," as the tremulous voiceover states, in interiors that mix an ancient Greek quality with multicolored beads, faux furs, and "gadgetry of the plastic persuasion."[44] Prominent among these gadgets are the "synthetic"

CRASHING BODIES, EXCREMENT, AND PLASTICS   111

fleshapoids, at once heroes and moral center of gravity of the film—if that is not too onerous a concept in Kucharland. Manufactured by humans to facilitate a life of endless leisure and dissipation, the fleshapoids develop self-consciousness and emotions and eventually rebel against their heartless owners. While the cruel prince of humans, queenly Gianbino (played by George Kuchar), his wife, and her muscular lover (shown to advantage in several beefcake shots) form a triangle of greed and deceit, two of their fleshapoid servants, united as a couple, pour tenderness and good feelings on each other. Eventually they rebel, eliminate their human masters, and consummate their love by letting an orgasmic current fly between their outstretched fingers—an effect achieved by scratching the emulsion on the celluloid. The outcome of the passionate encounter is a plastic baby robot that toddles from between the legs of the lady fleshapoid in a dramatic birth scene and completes the inorganic organic family. "Where the humans failed to find love, the robots succeeded," exults the off-screen chronicler. The triumph of the metal-and-plastic humanoids and of their unnatural desires is perfectly consonant with the Kuchars' materializing drive, with their insistent vindication of the pull of the flesh, their reduction of narrative to sexuality and of sexuality to bodies that crash and excrete, and with their fascination with the odd animation of lowly matter.

Not just organic and sexy, plastic was frequently excremental in the 1960s, and the emergence of the baby fleshapoid between its mother's legs is as much an act of defecation as it is a birth. In fact, the two are intrinsically linked in the carnivalesque and psychoanalytic imaginaries. Bakhtin shows that folk culture viewed organic waste as a fertilizing principle that enriches the earth and prolongs the life cycle as much as birth does;[45] and Freud posited the analogy between giving birth and giving the world the gift of one's feces. The homology was particularly operative in the sexual theories of children, who tend to equate babies, gifts, and excrement as detachable elements that leave the body to go off into the environment; in addition, babies and excrement seemed to emerge from the same general region.[46] Plastic adopted fecal shapes in Lynda Benglis's poured latex sculptures and Oldenburg's vinyl soft objects of the 1960s, while plastic (as) detritus featured prominently in the work of late 1950s and early 1960s French *nouveau rèalistes*, who were occasionally aligned with pop art at the time (for example, in the 1962 show "The New Realists" at the Sidney Janis Gallery in New York). Some examples are Arman's *poubelles* and accumulations and Gérard Deschamps' assemblages of shower curtains, oiled tablecloths, and worn brooms, mashed

112 EXPERIMENTAL FILM AND QUEER MATERIALITY

and tangled as if retrieved from a rubbish tip.[47] The implicit suggestion in these works may have been that in its profusion and disposability, plastic was the detritus of the overfed western societies, a non-decomposing residue that by the end of the 1960s would be denounced as a major ecological hazard. Such a view implicitly rebutted an idea frequently held by design critics of the period, that due to plastic's immense suppleness and throwaway quality, it represented the triumph of image and idea over actual material, which became volatilized under texture and concept.[48] Yet contemporary artists also showed that plastic had a way of returning precisely as unassimilable matter or excreta. The Kuchars must be counted among these artists; yet in their films, plastic not only returns as corporeal discharge but is also smeared with it. In this way, they questioned Tupperware modernity's aspiration to total hygiene and its concomitant denial of the messiness of bodies and their natural functions.

Heterologies and the Queer Underground

The Kuchars were not alone in their excremental leanings. A rich fecal streak in early-to-mid 1960s experimental culture contained a critique of corporeal conformity and material sameness. Claes Oldenburg's 1961 manifesto "Environments, situations, spaces" famously defended an art that "embroiders itself with everyday crap," "spits and drips," "sheds hair," "is eaten, like a piece of pie, or is abandoned with great contempt, like a piece of shit"; and further on, the manifesto extolled "the majestic art of dog turds, rising like cathedrals."[49] The bathroom fixtures in Jim Dine's environment "The House" (Judson Church Gallery, 1960; Sidney Janis, 1963) invoked private bodily functions. Kaprow's environment-happening *Eat* (1963), staged at a cave in the Bronx that had formerly served as a storage space for the Ebling Brewery, resembled both a uterus and a digestive tract and thus brought together reproduction and digestion; and Carolee Schneemann's watercolor illustration "Guerrilla Gut Room," printed in her 1966 artist book *Parts of a Body House*, showed human figures creeping inside an intestinal tract.[50] Across the Atlantic, Italian artist Piero Manzoni, often regarded as a "new realist," produced a series of cans labeled "Merda d'artista" (artist's shit) in 1961. In a different medium, Eleanor Drexel's musical *Home Movies* (1964), a Judson Poets' Theater production, openly refers to flatulence and excretion, as does the title of Charles Ludlam and Bill Vehr's *Turds in Hell* (1967),

CRASHING BODIES, EXCREMENT, AND PLASTICS 113

which was less scatological than rambunctiously pansexual. Fluxus artists Nam June Paik, Emmett Williams, Yoshi Wada, George Maciunas and Dieter Roth jointly dabbled in various excretory and lavatorial noises that were to be included in a radio project dated 1962.[51] Fluxus, recalled George Maciunas in the collective's manifesto, comes from "flux": "a flowing or fluid discharge from the bowels or other part of the body."[52] Included in a Fluxfilm Program in 1966 was a well-known celebration of the bottom: Yoko Ono's short *No. 4* (1966), remade later the same year as a feature-length project with the title *No. 4 (Bottoms).*[53] Both showed close-ups of buttocks in oscillating motion filmed as their owners walked on a treadmill. It is unlikely that Ono may have known of a film based on a similar idea: Andy Warhol's *Taylor Mead's Ass* (1963), a sixty-six minute close-up of the titular performer's backside, which completely fills the screen, during which Mead squeezes, fondles, and scratches his buttocks, swings his hips, shimmies, thrusts, and gyrates, as if performing a dance and striking insinuating poses. He continues by placing a number of objects between his cheeks, from money to photographs of stars, to magazines and books (*Anna Karenina, A Moveable Feast*), turning his rear into an inexhaustible cornucopia.

Artists and critics have ventured various interpretations of this fecal spread. For Kaprow. the excremental vocation of 1960s art evinced an interest in metamorphosis and mutability, the only constants in an essentially inconstant world, while for Schneemann it was part of an attempt to regain the body, buried under a hygienic civility that detached people, especially women, from their sentient organic foundation.[54] Following Oldenburg's and Kaprow's clues, Miles Orvell has read the artistic exploitation of waste as an attempt to locate authenticity in culturally unclaimed material.[55] And Sally Banes saw in the digestive, "effervescent body" of the early 1960s avant-garde a frontal rejection of bourgeois gentility and an unprecedented openness toward new corporeal and, by extension, social realities.[56] Apart from the striving for authenticity suggested by Orvell, these interpretations easily fit the Kuchars' oeuvre, in which excrementality is metamorphic, unruly, and expressive of a muted corporeality.

At the same time, delving into waste may be seen as an exercise in what Georges Bataille called "heterology." Heterology was the conceptual version of "excretion," or the production of heterogeneity. Heterogeneity was produced by generating, or coming into contact with, forms of radical otherness, as happened in sex, defecation, death, and the experience of the sacred; all of them marked for Bataille the limits of the thinkable and thus entailed

114   EXPERIMENTAL FILM AND QUEER MATERIALITY

moments of social and discursive crisis. Opposing the representation of the world as a homogeneous whole, heterology liberated "the heterogeneous excremental element" by considering realities, experiences, and materials that had been "the abortion and the shame of human thought."[57] Heterology was accompanied by laughter, which was "the only imaginable and definitively terminal result of philosophical speculation."[58] When thought faltered, as happened in the encounter with unassimilable otherness, laughter burst out. A visceral corporeal response irreducible to language, laughter could be regarded as another modality of excretion. In Bataille's view, heterology forced philosophy to confront its limits and pointed beyond them to a realm of generative energies routinely repressed by modern rationality. These energies arose from crass corporeality and catastrophic nature and were the only ones capable of fueling radical change in a deadening modernity: "Without a profound complicity with natural forces such as violent death, gushing blood, sudden catastrophes and the horrible cries that accompany them, terrifying ruptures of what seemed to be immutable, the fall into stinking filth of what had been elevated, without a sadistic understanding of an incontestably thundering and torrential nature, there could be no revolutionaries, there could only be a revolting, utopian sentimentality."[59] Bataille's solemnity seems ill-suited to the Kuchars' farcicality, and yet his words outline with precision much of the twins' thematic scope: their sadism, catastrophic imagination, savage humor, and unsentimental affect. For all their buffoonery and high jinks, the Kuchars' films imagined a revolution in everyday life. Taking as their starting point the most immediate and proximate (bodies and their waste, the plastic consumables in their midst), they unleashed the rage of "thundering and torrential nature" on the inanity of postwar culture, bringing its pieties down to "stinking filth."

Reveling in filth also has an important queer resonance.[60] The vindication of refuse was not only at the service of Bataille's vaguely defined "revolutionaries" but also of a contemporary queer underground. Filth amplified a queer vibration in sexuality and the body, and it seems no coincidence that many artists who worked with junk and excreta were queer—Warhol, Smith, Rauschenberg, Ludlam, the Kuchars, and Schneemann, who balked at conventional heterosexual femininity. It is as if their "deviance," to invoke the sociological parlance of the time, had found in literal and figurative excrement an appropriate object correlative. After all, shit is, by definition, what has no place in the social body and must be flushed out of sight, as queerness often was at the time by means of censorship, police raids, and bar

CRASHING BODIES, EXCREMENT, AND PLASTICS   115

closings. With shit at their center, art and queerness resisted normative recuperation and asserted their radical otherness.

But making queerness equivalent to this supreme form of otherness also contains a deliberate regression. Excremental play harks back to that regime of pleasure in which the anal cavity and bowel movements provided the earliest focus of enjoyment. This regime holds sway before the onset of language, gender distinction and individuation, but is pushed aside by normative sexual maturation, when genitality supersedes orality and anality, and sexual pleasure becomes relocated in the reproductive organs, socialized and coded in terms of gender difference.[61] Left behind in this process are the unproductive and essentially genderless joys of the ass and its offshoots. Yet these pleasures are not necessarily lost; a repository of unruly somatic memories, they occasionally return in art, fantasy, or daily behavior to haunt "normality." As this essay has tried to show, they make a grand comeback in the Kuchars' films, where they animate their queer materialism and crass materiality, their olfactory proclivities, their physical roughness, and their canny disruption of the pristine surfaces and aseptic aspirations of plastic modernity.

5

Glitter and Queer Embodiment in 1960s and 1970s Experimental Film and Performance

If there were an inherently queer substance, glitter might be it. From underground sixties performance to seventies glam rock and gay disco, from the relatively clandestine drag circuits of the postwar years to Ru Paul's TV show, Drag Race, and from private indulgence to public statement—as in glitter-bombing conservative politicians opposed to LGTBQ rights—glitter is scattered far and wide across queer culture. It has long been closely identified with androgyny, drag, and, more generally, with the kind of corporeal and sexual waywardness that we have been calling *queer* for quite some time. Writing about glam rock, for example, Todd Haynes has stated that "the shock of glitter was the shock of the feminine" in masculinist rock culture and confesses that Bowie's face on the cover of the album *Aladdin Sane* (1973), crossed by the famous gold dust lightning design, "cast an eerie pall over the certitude of my looming sexual identity."[1] Exploring a different corner of pop culture, Loran Marsan traces Cher's fondness for wigs, glitter, and shiny fabrics, to the aesthetics of drag and camp. And Michele White's incisive study of women's self-fashioning in contemporary social media stresses the association between glitter and "male femininity" and claims that, because of its link to gay culture and cross-dressing, glitter queers women regardless of their actual sexual orientation.[2]

The co-extensiveness of glitter and queerdom has led artist Gordon Hall to name "the glitter problem" the tendency to discuss queer art on the basis of its representational and biographical, rather than structural, traits: "Often, artwork is described as queer when it depicts LGBT subjects or figures, is produced by a self-identified LGBT person, or references gay culture through recognizable motifs, references, or aesthetics. I call this the glitter problem."[3] Against such reductiveness, Hall advocates a more structural understanding of queer textuality, whereby alternative bodies, genders, and

Experimental Film and Queer Materiality. Juan A. Suárez, Oxford University Press. © Oxford University Press 2024.
DOI: 10.1093/oso/9780197566992.003.0005

styles of sociability may be elicited from the abstract, non-anthropomorphic forms of minimalist sculpture, for example. In Hall's use, glitter stands for a too literal queerness—a queerness that sticks too close to the representational content on a textual surface, a bit like the shiny material itself: once it is on the skin, it is difficult to rub off.

I do not necessarily disagree with Hall. In many ways, it *is* a problem to discuss queer art *only* on the basis of its representational values, and *only* in so far as it shows explicit queer bodies and behaviors or emanates from purportedly queer creators. This book, in fact, is a reaction to the same plight that Hall decries. But it is intriguing that Hall calls this "the glitter problem," assuming between glitter and queerness a correlation whose origin, evolution, and meanings have never really been thought through. Just what is it about glitter that makes it so queer? Is it an intrinsic property of the substance itself? Or is it the associations it has accrued over time and the company it has kept? That is, is glitter metaphorically or metonymically queer? Does it stand for queerness, or has it just stuck around—on—it long enough? Or both? How did glitter come to signify, to reprise Haynes' assessment of glam, "that identities and sexualities are not stable things but quivery and costumed"?[4]

This chapter traces the convoluted relation between glitter and queerness both historically and theoretically, tapping in the process into one of those archives of ephemera where, as José Muñoz has pointed out, queer cultures, devoid of institutional recognition or support, characteristically articulate dissent, strategies of worldmaking, and futurity.[5] Glitter has long signified the possibility of corporeal transformation and, along with it, the reconfiguration of gender and of attached regimes of visuality, intelligibility, and relationality. Starting as a relatively underutilized industrial material in the thirties and continuing as a dime-store trifle in the forties and fifties, glitter became a frequent stylistic gesture in sixties' queer underground theater and performance and surfaced overground in the early seventies through the mainstream success of such glam rock acts as Marc Bolan, David Bowie, and Roxy Music, among others. At the time, the use of glitter in underground art converged with a contemporaneous cult of shine and gloss that shaped fashion, gallery art, and discotheque design— but also had ties to the drug culture. Signifying different things in different milieus, glitter was in the sixties and early seventies a marker of spectacular femininity, an index of modernity, a recall of jazz-age female fashions, a means of reflecting and radiating light, and an aid to narcotic enjoyment.

And for its ability to spectacularize the body and blur gender distinctions, it was also the indispensable prop in the drag queen kit. The meanings and uses that glitter accrued in art and fashion, over- and underground, were reprised but also nuanced and modified in late sixties and seventies queer experimental films both in America and Europe. Filmmakers such as Jack Smith and Steven Arnold in the United States; Katharine Sieverding in Western Germany; Stéphane Martí and Teo Hernández in France; and Carles Comas in Spain sprinkled with glitter their erotic and visual utopias and their varied refusals of sexual and gender norms. Throughout these examples, glitter promoted a peculiar style of representation based on diffuse color and light rather than on distinct shape, and on distributed dots rather than on lines or continuous color fields. This kind of discontinuous representation is characteristic of mid-century art and visual culture. Chapter 6 will chart glitter's emergence taking as a referent the use of film grain in queer experimental film.

Glitter and the Luminous Sixties

Glitter is pulverized plastic—usually mylar—covered with coloring and layered with various reflecting materials, many of which are aluminum oxides. Its invention is attributed to Henry Ruschman, a machinist from Bernardsville, New Jersey, who in 1934 devised an appliance to cut plastic sheets into very small particles that he called "slivers."[6] Commercialized as cheap, ornamental material, it led a largely undocumented life for decades. In a humorous profile of the substance, journalist Caity Weaver has recently expounded its enigmatic origins and the secrecy that surrounds its exact composition and manufacture. She uncovered what is probably its first appearance in print: a *New York Times* article from December 20, 1942, that recommended its use as a substitute for the Christmas candles and lights that had to be extinguished after dark due to wartime dim-out regulations.[7] Among the means of creating shiny seasonal effects without giving away one's location to potential enemy bombers, the article recommends silver paper and cellophane cut-outs, clusters of baubles, frosted windows, and a tin pitcher filled with Christmas greens whose tips might be covered with "mica or dime-store 'glitter'" for "additional scintillation."[8] Shortly after the war, glitter began to make discreet inroads into women's fashions. Fifties' women's eyewear, for example, dominated by the traditional harlequin—or cat eye—shape, sported new textures and finishes, such as opalescent colors, glitter laminates, gilding, and metal studs and rhinestones.[9]

Glitter's first significant surge in popularity dates from the early sixties, when cosmetic companies such as Revlon, Estée Lauder, Elizabeth Arden, and Helena Rubinstein launched glittery powders, lipsticks, and eye shadows.[10] A fashion report in *The New York Times* at the end of 1963 noted the new varieties of shiny make-up available for the season's outings: Revlon's gold and silver lamé face powder, Estée Lauder's "Golden Diamond" tones, and Arden's gold and silver eyeshadow. During 1964, Helena Rubinstein launched new glossy lines in a variety of products, from nail polish to hair coloring. Other companies followed suit: Cotex's marketed glitter lipsticks in four flavors—including cola—for the young, and the more upmarket brand Charles of the Ritz brought out "transluminant" lipstick for the young at heart.[11] A *New York Times* summary of the year's fashions declared that 1964 had been the year "when women were all eyes," with eyelashes "piled on and . . . glitter on their eyelids."[12] Indeed, the December 1, 1964 cover of *Vogue* featured a model with heavy sequin and glitter eye make-up by Arden, "part of a growing rage for ornamental eyes, fantastic, imaginative." And the "Beauty Bulletin" section of the January 1, 1965 issue predicted, rightly as it turned out, the continuing popularity of the look; it was illustrated with another model with glittered eyelids, again by Arden.[13] Perhaps sensing something in the air, Ruschman, the inventor of glitter, had just filed patents for his plastic pulverizer in 1961, when he also founded Meadowbrooks Inventions, Inc., the first industrial manufacturer of the material and still today one of its main providers, worldwide. His main competitor, Glitterex, also based in New Jersey, was started in 1963.

Glitter did not stay only on the eyes or face. It was also used in stockings (by Alix Grés, Geoffrey Beene, Rudi Gernreich), suede evening coats (by Givenchy), and shoes. It was part of a broad fascination with luminous textures and effects that ran through fashion, discotheque design, and art and that produced some of the most distinctive looks of the decade. The same fashion reviews that spotted the sparkle of glitter in make-up and accessories also noted the increasing use of glimmering fabrics in day and informal evening wear. Historically, shiny fabrics, beads, and spangles had been the prerogative of the court—European sumptuary laws limited their use by plebians until the early nineteenth century—or of formal evening women's wear. Glimmering textiles had also been characteristic of twenties' flapper dresses, which accompanied the hedonistic dance culture of the time, and reemerged in the sixties impelled by a combination of futurism, the use of unprecedented industrial and synthetic materials in fashion, and new techniques in costume assemblage. "By 1967," writes fashion historian Joel Lobental, "*le dernier cri* was sounded by anything short, sleek, and phosphorescent."[14]

Shiny clothing broke into daywear in the "space age" fashions pioneered by French designers in the mid-sixties.[15] André Courrèges used silver-tinted fabrics and silver-dyed leather in his "Moon Girl" look of 1964. In 1964 and 1966, Pierre Cardin combined wool with vinyl and metal appliqués in women's dresses and coats for his "*cosmocorps*" and "*cosmonauts*" collections. And from 1966 forward, Paco Rabanne made clothes out of aluminum knits, coat of mail, and geometric pieces of leather, metal, or hard plastic that were held together with metal rings, wire, and glue; and he accessorized them with plastic helmets, visors, and chunky jewelry that were quickly imitated by other designers.[16]

Futuristic fashions, along with their luminosity and their use of innovative materials, were eagerly taken up by American designers in the mid-sixties, from established figures, such as Rudi Gernreich and John Kloss, to a younger crop of art school graduates, such as Sylvia de Gay, Betsey Johnson, Joel Schumacher, and Deanne Littell, to name a few. Following in part the example of the French, they employed a broad variety of plastics and industrial materials. Gernreich and Kloss made vinyl dresses with op-art patterns; Sylvia de Gay popularized silver-toned fabrics; Johnston made clothes out of cellophane, tinsel, vinyl, aluminum foil, and the metallic sheets out of which sequins were stamped; and Littell used Day-Glo and night-reflectant synthetics. Yet the most strikingly futuristic costumes of the time incorporated their own lighting. Joan Tiger Morse designed a dress with miniature bulbs that she sold at her boutique Teenie Weenie on Madison Avenue. And Diana Dew, an electronic engineer and occasional musician, sold through Parafernalia, the most *avant* boutique of its day, electric pants and dresses with lights powered by a cobalt battery and with a potentiometer that allowed the wearer to regulate the intensity of the light and its flashing frequency.[17]

Much as it evoked the space age and the future, sheen also harked back to the past. Ever the sharp fashion commentator, Andy Warhol noticed the ambiguity: "silver was the future, it was spacy—the astronauts wore silver suits .... And silver was also the past—the Silver Screen—Hollywood actresses photographed in silver sets."[18] He was not the only one to perceive the echoes of earlier decades in contemporary styles. The shiny fabrics gaining popularity around 1964 were, in the words of a reviewer, "a throwback to the 1930s era of Carole Lombard and Greta Garbo," even though they may have seemed "very new."[19] Wrapped in satin and "glistening hammered silk (a favorite of the 1930s)," the "spirit of '65" revived that of '35 or even of '25.[20] Fashion critic Patricia Peterson, writing in September of 1965, reported that the young crowd had initially discovered the clothes of the twenties and thirties "in old trunks and thrift shops," but now the market had responded to the demand with a "flood of flippant hem dresses for flappers with limited funds."[21] In her view, the silver glitter of earlier times lent its "special aura of razzle and dazzle" to contemporary clothes.[22] Fashion reviewers fell short of elaborating the connections, but they are not difficult to discern. Like the twenties, the mid-sixties were a time of prosperity, optimism, melting taboos, and blurring social distinctions. Glimmer on faces and clothes signified hedonism, the aspiration to social mobility, and the democratic spread of elite styles among the less affluent and the young. It further revealed the desire to glamorize oneself and surroundings, turning the self into a work of art and everyday life into a constant performance.

At the same time, glitter and the cult of sheen and gloss in which it was inserted helped to loosen gender from its conventional moorings and to turn it into a category that was up for grabs and could be linked to various corporeal configurations. Attached as they were to women's fashions, glimmer and shine promoted a highly cosmetic femininity that had nothing of the natural about it. Electric, synthetic, and patched up, it was a portable womanhood that was put on and performed rather than simply "owned" as an organic extension of anatomy. This was gender as something that one does rather than something that one is—to paraphrase Jack Halberstam.[23] From this perspective, the vogue of glitter stands as an early, perhaps unwitting, episode in a growing denaturalization of gender and its associated dynamics that unfolded through the decade and has continued into the present.

The main settings for such transfigurations were dance clubs and discothèques, which pioneered free unisex dancing styles and whose lighting schemes set off the glimmer of shiny make-up and clothes. Watching his multimedia show The Exploding Plastic Inevitable at New York's Dom, in Saint Marks Place, in April of 1966, Warhol noted the audience's refulgence: "The kids . . . looked really great, glittering and reflecting in vinyl, suede, and feathers, in skirts and boots and bright-colored mesh tights, and patent leather shoes, and silver and gold hip-riding miniskirts, and the Paco Rabanne thin plastic look with the linked plastic disks in the dresses."[24] His film *The Velvet Underground in Boston* captures the violent chiaroscuro of the Exploding light show and the metallic gleams in the clothing and jewelry of the audience. As is well known, the Exploding Plastic Inevitable was an early multimedia show that combined The Velvet Underground performing on stage accompanied by Factory regulars dancing and an onslaught of visual stimuli: Warhol's films, slides, stroboscopic lights, and moving spotlights in front of which Warhol and his collaborators held colored gels and stencils. Warhol's Dom shows have often been cited as the antecedent for a new kind of dance club: more frantic, rock-oriented, and visually complex than its more sedate antecedents. Yet rather than a matter of direct influence, it may have been coincidence that shortly after Warhol's spectacle opened at the Dom, new multimedia dance environments began to sprout up around New York City and elsewhere. Cheetah, the first of the new clubs, opened in April of 1966 just as The Exploding Plastic Inevitable premiered at the Dom. Cheetah had a dance-floor, a screening room for underground films, a lounge with color televisions, and a boutique.[25] Similar clubs in New York were The Electric Circus—which started at the Dom a few months after Warhol's tenure expired—Arthur, Salvation, and Cerebrum.[26] The trend took root in other parts of the country and in Europe. Chicago was home to Le Bison, Los Angeles to The Trip, and San Francisco had its own tradition of multimedia environments, such as the Trips Festival and Family Dog's and Chet Helms's parties at Longshoremen's Hall and Fillmore West. In Europe, *discothèques* often became spaces for architectural experimentation and cross-media collaboration. Saint Tropez's Voom Voom Club (1966), in the South of France, is a paramount example—a "*luminodynamique*" environment designed by architect Paul Bertrand and light artist Nicholas Schöffer. These new dance environments made ample use of transparent and reflective materials, multicolored plastics, and aluminum surfaces. Spotlights, strobes, and projected images turned light into the main architectural feature of the new clubs. The Voom Voom, for example, featured Schöffer's light-sensitive moving structures and a prism with reflecting steel walls and bulbs that flashed and changed hue to the beat of the music.[27]

The new lighting regimes of the mid-sixties, from fashion to clubs, were harbingers of, and aids to, the drugs of the era, from the psychedelic stimulants to the ever-present amphetamines. A pocket lighting technology, glitter went with either; it was as cherished by acid-ingesting hippie drag queens as by speed freaks—often overlapping constituencies. Warhol associated it with uppers. He attributed the rage for shiny surfaces to the widespread use of amphetamine, especially among the young and the marginal. Amphetamine promoted an intense concentration on minute detail and microscopic eventfulness; and glittery textures, with their irregular twinkle, provided both. Whenever he found a profusion of reflecting glass, sequins, or glass beads in someone's apartment, Warhol figured that amphetamine could not be far away: "Every A-head's apartment always had broken mirrors, smoky, chipped, fractured, whatever—just like the Factory did."[28]

Warhol and Voom Voom architect Nicholas Schöffer are pivotal figures linking fashion, clubbing, and art. The art world was not immune to the charm of sparkle. Shine crops up in a diverse range of sixties' art. In two essays of 1967 devoted respectively to "Luminism" and "Kineticism," critic and curator Willoughby Sharp eulogized the artistic use of light: "The art of light and movement is the only new art of our time." Light and movement are, for Sharp, the materials of the electric age—an era of movement and rapid mutation, of flow and becoming, whose most apposite artworks were not traditional art objects (the detached, inert paintings and sculptures of yore) but dynamic environments and situations:

> We now demand greater participation in situations and events. . . . Today painting and static sculpture are no longer wholly satisfying. We need an art of greater energy. We need an art of total environment. . . . The art of light and movement is dynamic, environmental, and inclusive. . . . The old art was an object. The new art is a system. . . . The art of light and movement is non-figurative. It does not aim to tell a story. It does not want to be decorative. It cannot be durable, since its parts quickly become obsolete. In its most advanced state, it is immaterial or disposable.[29]

His examples of kinetic-luminous art ranged encyclopedically: from the Bauhaus (Naum Gabo and Moholy-Nagy) to early minimalists Julio Le Parc and Lucio Fontana, to Dan Flavin's neon sculptures, and on to contemporary light-centered events by Otto Piene and Heinz Mack's Group Zero, by the *Group de Recherche d'Art Visuel*, by Voom Voom co-creator Nicholas Schöffer, and by American video collective USCO, which ran various multimedia light shows. Wide-ranging and generous as Sharp's survey was, it did not mention Warhol's Exploding Plastic Inevitable, nor the psychedelic Trips Festivals and multimedia celebrations in San Francisco, nor the equally psychedelic "sculpture with light" by Jackie Cassen and Rudi Stern that had just preceded Warhol's act at the Dom. All of these may have been too druggy

124   EXPERIMENTAL FILM AND QUEER MATERIALITY

and pop, too distant from the more conventional art channels and spaces on which Sharp had trained his radar.

"We Even Pooped Glitter": Underground Performance

Being an art critic, Sharp did not mention another realm where not just glimmer and shine but actual glitter—the material—was ever present: queer underground theater and performance. Glitter-drenched queer performance was driven by many of the same impulses and ideas that Sharp identified in, as he put it, "the only new art of our time." Dynamic, participatory, and process- rather than product-oriented, underground queer theater created environments and relations rather than conventional art objects; it generated "systems," in the cybernetic sense popular at the time: sets of elements in interaction, rather than well-wrought "plays" and tightly scripted events.[30] The glitter that adorned these performances enhanced provisionality and ephemerality; constantly changing with the light, it was variable and atmospheric, and bound disparate elements into a transient whole. Its contingent, environmental quality made it especially suitable to arts of improvised gesture and fleeting motion. And its mutability made it an appropriate embellishment for the discrepant bodies and sexualities that populated this scene and that abjured fixity or conventionality of any sort.

Freddy Herko, a New York-based experimental dancer, choreographer, and a co-founder of the seminal Judson Dance Theater, was a pioneer in the use of glitter in underground performance. A Warhol acquaintance and the subject of some of his early films, Herko used glitter in a number of early 1960s choreographies. In one of them, a female performer stood in a point of light surrounded by complete darkness, and she accompanied a crescendo of organ music by throwing about her increasing amounts of glitter until she turned into a shimmering cloud by the end of the piece.[31] After Herko's death, his friend Stanley Amos inherited the glitter and occasionally held "Glitter Festivals" in his own apartment: guests would drop acid or take speed and, as Warhol put it, would "shower sparkles in the air" until the place was covered in them.[32]

Warhol found Herko exceptional: his use of "cheap, sleazy elements" such as glitter was unusual at the time "because of the cliché aspect."[33] Yet given glitter's currency in up-market fashion, it is difficult to understand why Herko was unusual or why Warhol found glitter "cheap" and "sleazy." In

GLITTER AND QUEER EMBODIMENT   125

any case, Herko was not an isolated example: quite a few artists were happy to use glitter, especially fringe performers and creators whose marginality led them to identify more easily with disparaged samples of contemporary material culture. At the Caffé Cino, a coffeehouse and performance venue in New York's Greenwich Village that spearheaded the early sixties off-off Broadway theater, queerness and glitter mingled freely. The Cino was decorated as "a magical grotto" with crunched-up silver foil, fairy lights, glitter angels, glitter dust on the floor on show nights, and, according to a reviewer, enough ornaments to decorate "a forest of psychedelic Christmas trees."[34] For some, the twinkly atmosphere was cozy and inviting, while others found its campiness intrusive and complained that it affected the mood of the plays performed there. Playwright Jean-Claude van Itallie—one of Herko's friends—found it "too full of sequins, fishnets, and a generally swishy loudness," and therefore not a proper setting for his work,[35] while others such as Lanford Wilson, H. M. Koutoukas, and Soren Agenoux, found the Cino's atmosphere perfectly congenial.

Outside the Cino, glimmer and swishiness went hand in hand in numerous underground productions throughout what Stefan Brecht, the best chronicler of the sixties and seventies queer stage, called New York's "queer theater." Glitter abounded in Charles Ludlam's early shows, especially in his messier, less structured productions of the late 1960s, shortly after he broke up with John Vaccaro in 1966 to start The Ridiculous Theatrical Company. In plays such as *When Queens Collide* (originally titled *The Conquest of the Universe*), *Turds in Hell* (co-written with Bill Vehr), and *The Grand Tarot*, glitter is liberally scattered on faces, bodies, and clothing. Its luminous chaos added to the delirious quality of the mise-en-scene, the excess of the performances, and the heady atmosphere, saturated with incense and marihuana smoke. Glitter was used alongside ingeniously cheap effects, such as trans performer Mario Montez shimmying behind sheets of plastic splashed with buckets of water to simulate an underwater dance.[36] In a similar spirit, the performers of Jackie Curtis's *Vain Victory* (1971), a parody of Hollywood musicals starring Factory-associated drag queens Mario Montez, Candy Darling, and Curtis herself,[37] sported glitter on their faces and bodies. Curtis, who played a male rock idol, had his face and chest streaked with it, and Eric Emerson, another Warhol superstar in the cast, sang a number with his entire body smeared in Vaseline and glitter and wearing only leather chaps.[38] The effect had been tried already in Curtis's previous play, *Heaven Grand in Amber Orbit* (1970), with drag performer Holly Woodlawn, who would star in several Factory

126   EXPERIMENTAL FILM AND QUEER MATERIALITY

films in the seventies, slathered in petroleum jelly and sprinkled with silver glitter to play one of the Moon Reindeer Girls.[39]

A lesser known act in this tradition was The Hot Peaches, founded in 1972 by Jimmy Centola (also called Camicia), a follower of Charles Ludlam and John Vaccaro. Tired of constantly changing venues for his shows, Centola rented a space—the Peach Pitts—in New York's Chelsea neighborhood and proceeded to cover the stage in beads and glitter. Just like all the other theater troupes, The Hot Peaches were chronically bankrupt and tried to achieve flashy effects at minimal cost. Like Ludlam and Curtis's performers, they bought their clothes in thrift stores or scavenged them from the garbage in Soho or the Fashion District, areas which still housed a declining clothing industry: "The costumes . . . rarely fit, but then we did not bother with that as long as they sparkled with beads and rhinestones."[40] Larry Ree and his dancers of The Original Trockadero of Gloxinia Ballet Company also sparkled fiercely. Ree had danced in Ludlam and Curtis's plays before starting an all-male troupe of unevenly trained performers with decidedly un-balletic physiques who danced classic female ballet parts in tutus and *pointe* shoes with a mixture of camp humor and affecting poignancy.[41] Some of Peter Hujar's photographs capture Ree backstage in twinkling make-up, sequined bodices, and rhinestone-encrusted tiaras.

Hot Peach Jim Centola drew his main inspiration from The Cockettes, a San Francisco troupe whose brief (and calamitous) theatrical run in New York in the fall of 1971 spurred him into jump-starting his own theatrical career. The Cockettes, perhaps the most famous of the queer theater companies, started their trajectory almost by chance on New Year's Eve of 1969 at the Palace Theater in San Francisco's North Beach neighborhood.[42] They were largely the creation of George Harris III. Raised in Florida and New York by parents who dabbled in the theater, Harris had acted in several off-off Broadway productions at La Mama and the Judson Poets' Theater, notably in Ronald Tavel's *Gorilla Queen* (1967). A few months after his appearance in Tavel's play, Harris became the poster child of the peace movement when he was captured by photographer Bernie Boston putting a flower in the barrel of a National Guard's gun during an anti-war march on the Pentagon. A friend and sometime lover of Allen Ginsberg, Harris drove to San Francisco with Ginsberg's partner Peter Orlovsky.[43] In San Francisco, Harris, renamed Hibiscus, conceived an open-ended, improvised theater that he started practicing in the street and later transferred to the stage of The Palace. The Cockettes's shows consisted initially in dancing expressively to pop songs, both new and old. A troupe member described their first show as a "high-stepping can-can free-for-all that brought audiences to near dementia."[44] Whatever it was, it was enough to grant the group an indefinite residence at the theater.

A considerable part of The Cockettes's impact emanated from their costumes and make-up. They wore vintage female clothing with corsets, boas, flowing scarves; baroque headgear and sequined cocktail dresses from the thirties; evening gowns of shiny fabrics, silk, and lace; and elaborately flounced skirts and shirts, which they found easily in thrift stores around San Francisco.[45] Their sartorial panache was not limited to appropriating past styles. Alexandra Jacopetti and Julia Bryan-Wilson have noted The Cockettes's dexterity as designers and customizers. In her classic study of handmade hippie fashions, Jacopetti pointed out that "the Glitter Boys" excelled in "the use of common elements like patchwork pieces and old doilies. It's all joined with a fantastic ability to achieve an effect, rivaling the scary of [sic] shamans of past times for sheer outrageous impact."[46] And she went on to single out the skill of Cockettes members Scrumbley—one of the troupe's main songwriters—and Pristine Condition, and of their occasional collaborator Billy Bowers, who went on to become a noted designer—he was reviewed in *L'Uomo Vogue* in March, 1973—and to dress The Rolling Stones, Alice Cooper, and, perhaps most appropriately, The New York Dolls.[47] Naturally, glitter was an integral part of The Cockettes's effect and a trademark of their style. It covered their costumes, bodies, and hair. Hibiscus and fellow Cockette Martin Worman were virtuosos of sequin and glitter make-up, but the substance did not stay only on their faces. "You lived in glitter and you ate glitter—the whole thing was glitter," said Sylvester, a group member who went on to become a well-known disco diva in the seventies. "We . . . even pooped glitter," concurred Cockette Pam Tent.[48]

Trash, Spirituality, and the Dark Side of Camp

An unstable signifier, glitter meant differently in different underground contexts. A technology of gender indistinctness, it contributed to the anarchic corporeality of underground performance; it turned all bodies into spectacle, endowing them with the "to-be-looked-at-ness" that, as Laura Mulvey famously pointed out, is the traditional feminine pole in the classical economy of the gaze. In addition, cheap and easily available, glitter signified

128 EXPERIMENTAL FILM AND QUEER MATERIALITY

poverty, but its gaudy gleam also evoked the ability to rise above it and transfigure the ordinary, transmitting a spiritual aspiration that infused some of underground manifestations. And in a more dystopian register, glitter was also aligned with a dark side of camp that reveled in violence, illness, disease, and decay.

Glitter was an instant means to transform hand-me-downs and street finds, covering them with a glamorous glow. In his biography of Charles Ludlam, David Kaufman recalls the Ludlam troupe's skill at creating "an expensive look": "With an emphasis on glitter, sequins, baubles, bangles, and beads, they turned shoestrings into gold laces."[49] Mario Montez was particularly adept at spotting promising garments and altering them spectacularly. A one-person costume department, he decisively influenced the look of Ludlam's early shows, whose outfits were often credited to Montez Creations. Montez may have learned some of his skills from Jack Smith—or vice versa, since they lived together for a time in the early sixties and had an intense, fruitful collaboration.[50] Smith was similarly practiced at redeeming (literal) trash through sheen. Stefan Brecht and Jonas Mekas have described the assemblages of street refuse that he composed to serve as backdrops for his performances of the late sixties and early seventies. With titles such as *Withdrawal from Orchid Lagoon, Claptailism of Palmola Christmas Spectacle*, and *Gas Stations of the Cross Religious Spectacle*, these performances were hypnotically paced and unfolded against thickly disposed objects scavenged from the streets and made to sparkle with carefully placed lights, beads, tinsel, and glitter: "The hard-core refuse up there sits quietly glittering . . . The heap glitters melodiously . . . It is clearly exotic, a landscape of desire."[51] These landscapes were built in his loft in Greene Street, in New York's Soho district, at once a performance space, movie studio, and living quarters. After he was evicted from Greene Street, Smith moved his studio to Mercer Street, where he worked for some time on an adaptation of Shakespeare's *Hamlet*. The show required twenty pounds of white glitter; some of it would be tinted blue to evoke an underwater atmosphere—the action took place at sea bottom— and some would be tinted grey and applied to the character of Plaudius (a composite of Polonius + Claudius), who was "also an octopus" to be played by Stefan Brecht.[52]

The use of glitter to glamorize discards and leftovers is analogous to the revaluation of classical Hollywood cinema by underground performers, particularly genres of low cultural capital such as B films, serials, Depression-era musicals, and assorted Hollywood exotica. These were what Jack Smith called "secret flix." Associated to childhood memories of cinematic pleasure, they were cliché-ridden yet energetic, visually striking, and populated with performers whose idiosyncratic acting styles turned them into camp icons, as was the case with Maria Montez.[53] They were major inspirations for queer playwrights and performers in the sixties. Plays like Ludlam's *Grand Hotel* and Curtis's *Glamour, Glory, and Gold* and *Heaven Grand in Amber Orbit* were largely based on the indiscriminate mixture of mass culture motifs.[54] They belonged to what *New York Times* critic Rosalyn Regelson described as "that special genre created by the Playhouse of the Ridiculous—the nonplay that is a pastiche of lines from Aeschylus, 1930s movies, grand opera, TV commercials, and comic books, in no apparent order."[55] In a way, glitter was the material embodiment of queer theater's generous responsiveness toward the debris of the entertainment industry. It showed the desire not to let anything go to waste. After all, rightly combined or positioned, anything could be a vehicle of camp expressiveness in the same way that (almost) anything could be transmuted and redeemed with a sprinkling of glitter.

More transcendentally, glitter's luminosity evoked a spiritual aspiration that has at times lurked in the heart of camp, where it has long remained unattended.[56] While many of The Cockettes were merely interested in putting on a show—and charging for their labors—others saw their theater as a sacramental experience and a means of spiritual transformation. Hibiscus belonged to the latter camp. He conceived his brand of street theater while living in San Francisco's Sutter Street commune, also known as the Kaliflower commune for the name of the periodical they edited and distributed for free—a newsletter that published news, notices, and offers for goods and services for Bay-Area hippies, psychedelic enthusiasts, and all manner of urban communards. Kaliflower had been started by Irving Rosenthal, a writer, photographer, and editor, and a friend of Ginsberg and Jack Smith. At the heart of the commune's creed was the rejection of money and the attempt to base all transactions on barter and gifts. The Cockettes's shows were initially conceived as spontaneous gifts to the community. They were also meant as transformative experiences that intended to foster creativity and self-expression: acts of radical freedom that opened the gates to new forms of perception and relation and were, in this regard, aligned with the troupe's fluid sexuality and their use of drugs. Their performances did work in this way, to judge from their influence and from the members that entered the troupe and embraced its lifestyle after seeing the shows.

130 EXPERIMENTAL FILM AND QUEER MATERIALITY

Costume and make-up were aids in this process: they helped to redraw the self and the body's appearance and to channel transcendent energies. It was a belief held in other corners of the San Francisco counter-culture. Jacopetti regarded herself and the folk designers she showcased in her writing as "modern-day shamans"; they pursued psychic enlightenment through their textiles, as evinced by the mythological motifs they frequently embroidered or appliquéd in their work. In a similar vein, Cockette Fayette Hauser described the troupe's clothing as "an eclectic mystical collage" with colors, jewelry, and accessories coming together "as a sufi flame."[57] Sheen—in fabrics, sequins, jewelry, and, of course, glitter—was a unifying element in these collages, a visual cement that held the look together; it also brought in a range of symbolic associations connected with light: purity, truthfulness, transparency, and a drive for the absolute—impulses that traversed much of hippie culture.[58] Hibiscus had originally conceived his theatrical group as The Angels of Light, a name that was replaced by the witty moniker that made them famous, but that he recovered after splitting from The Cockettes when the troupe started to become more professional and to charge admission to their shows.

As a redeemer of poor materials and a vehicle of spiritual aspiration, glitter is transformative and vehicular. Its unstable flicker underlines an excess and mobility in whatever it touches, revealing immanent power in material and lack of containment in bodies. Under its touch, trash—literal or cultural—is more than just discarded matter but an occasion for rapture and emotion; and costumes, bodies, and sex are conduits for transcendental yearnings. Transcendence in queer underground performance entailed the desire to lose the human form and enter a vibrational field where subjects, objects, and material lost their contours and dwelled on a common plane of intensity, with bodies set aflame through fabrics, jewelry, make-up, and glitter—scattered inside and out, in the interior organs and on the skin, ingested and excreted, proper and alien. Recalling Gilles Deleuze's distinction, the transcendental here is not the transcendent of traditional religion and metaphysics—a position above the messiness of the world and the flesh—but the immersion in "a pure stream of a-subjective consciousness," in an endless differential becoming that can also be seen as a sexual innervation without subjects or objects, organs, or direction, where bodies are contingent and fluid and commune with the world.[59]

Besides affectionate recycling and sensuous transcendence, glitter also had less utopian connotations. It occasionally expressed aggression, malice,

GLITTER AND QUEER EMBODIMENT   131

and decay in works informed by what artist Mike Kelley called a "black" version of camp.[60] This was a kind of camp that, while still reveling in gender-bending, sexual dissidence, and stylistic excess, celebrated the ugly, abject, decadent, and cruel. These characteristics are an integral part of camp aesthetics, as Ingrid Hotz-Davies, Georg Vogt, and Franzeska Bergmann have recently claimed, but have usually been downplayed in favor of camp's lighter side—its humor and wit.[61] Kelley's main examples of black camp were John Waters, Frank Zappa's The Mothers of Invention and the Los Angeles Freak Scene that grew around them, and Kenneth Anger's *Hollywood Babylon*, "a dark and degraded sub-history of Hollywood glamour."[62] And while Kelley only mentioned him in passing, the dark side of camp was nowhere as evident as in John Vaccaro's glitter-ridden productions and, to a lesser extent, in Lindsay Kemp.

A founder, along with Ronald Tavel, of the so-called "theater of the ridiculous," Vaccaro was one of the most original and influential stage directors in the New York avant-garde between the mid-1960s and the early 1980s. Glitter was one of his trademarks, to the extent that he claimed (wrongly) to have pioneered its use in underground theater.[63] He used it by the bucket in his shows: it covered the stage and the performers and at times it floated through the air, enveloping the action in a shimmery vibration. It was part of Vaccaro's predilection for highly saturated, disorienting atmospheres that a contemporary reviewer compared to "an animated Bosch painting with perpetual sexual motion."[64]

Vaccaro used glitter mostly as makeup. The sexy ghouls that beset the protagonist in *Cock Strong* (1969), by "Alien Comic" Tom Murrin, had glitter on their lips and around their eyes, and the characters of Kenneth Bernard's *Moke-Eater* (1972), also a Vaccaro production, wore, according to Stefan Brecht, "simple facial masks, broadly ringed mouths and eyes, strong reds and blacks, glitter."[65] Brecht described Vaccaro's makeup as "a suspension of the faces, as in memories of the defunct." It contributed to the director's penchant for hyperbole and broad acting and attenuated psychological depth. Vaccaro typically sidelined psychological characterization at the expense of visuality and motion, and chose plays that privileged emphatic action over verbal or conceptual subtlety—such as the works of Kenneth Bernard, with whom Vaccaro collaborated steadily between 1968 and 1978.[66] Tony Zanetta, an actor who worked with Vaccaro in the seventies, recalled that performers "didn't have roles; didn't have lines; they had energy."[67] Characters were less personalities than simple drives locked into repetitive action and grotesque violence. The six Bernard plays Vaccaro directed, for example, feature rapes, beheadings, suggestions of cannibalism, eviscerations, hangings, and lethal orgies in which sexual frenzy leads to murder. In them, glitter was both incongruous and appropriate. Its festive character sat uncomfortably with the bleakness of the action, while its way of drawing attention to surface heightened the cartoonish flatness of characters and plot. When asked about his use of the substance, Vaccaro oscillated between dismissive and analytical. On the one hand, it was "a way of presentation; nothing more," and he stressed his distance from directors and performers—Ludlam or Curtis—who used it to "glorify" drag queens and homosexuality. On the other hand, glitter stood for "the gaudiness of America": "I used it because it was shoving America back into American faces. It was the gaudiness of Time's Square. You know, take away the lights and what do you have in Time's Square? Nothing."[68] It seems that Vaccaro's audiences did not feel confronted with their own vulgarity, however, but immersed in a volatile situation that was part dream, part fairy tale, and part speed rush in a madhouse.

Independently from Vaccaro, British mime Lindsay Kemp also practiced a dark brand of camp in which glitter and shine punctuate violence. A television film of his show *Pierrot in Turquoise (The Looking Glass Murders)* (1967) featured Jack Birkett ("The Incredible Orlando") as Harlequin with blotches of glitter around his eyes, Lindsay as Pierrot in a pearl-studded doublet, and Annie Stainer as Columbine in a multilayered gauzy skirt and chemise. In the schematic plot, Pierrot kills Columbine in a jealous fit over her preference for Harlequin. The violence is sudden and implacable, unleashed in a fantastic setting sprinkled with old toys and manikins and presided by Cloud (played by David Bowie, who was briefly a company member), a one-person Greek chorus who sings the characters' fortunes atop a folding ladder.[69] In Celestino Coronado's film *The Lindsay Kemp Circus* (1973), Kemp wears a body sock with glitter accents on his nipples and crotch, and performs a solo dance on a bare stage to an audience of inexpressive sailors sitting at a café and absorbed primarily in each other. It is not him, however, but Birkett-Orlando who communicates a vague menace as he performs a song in demi drag (bald head and men's shirt with women's stockings and high heels) that shows off his powerful physique. Later shows like *Salomé* (1973) and especially *Flowers* (1970), inspired by the criminals and demimondaines of Jean Genet's *Our Lady of the Flowers*, develop most extensively Kemp's dark camp, with dark passions set in precious, overwrought atmospheres and actions wrapped in a haze of sequins, glitter, and confetti.[70]

GLITTER AND QUEER EMBODIMENT   133

In these examples of black camp, glitter's unsteady gleam accompanies a different kind of corporeal uncontainment. Rather than transvaluation and erotic transcendence, it communicates a garish animacy, an energy overspill that makes bodies strike out and impose their weight on others, curtailing their vibrancy and power and causing them to collapse and dissolve.

Glitter Films

Glitter was by no means as abundant in film as it was in underground performance, perhaps because its sheen is not always easy to capture on celluloid. Still, partly because of the influence of underground performance, queer experimental film began to be covered with a dusting of glitter from the late sixties onward. A quick canon of glitter films includes late underground titles by Jack Smith (*Reefers of Technicolor Island*, 1967, *No President*, 1967–70) and Steven Arnold (*Luminous Procuress*, 1972) and by European artists, such as Katharina Sieverding (*Life-Death*, 1969, 1972), Stéphane Marti (*La cité de neuf portes*, 1977), Teo Hernández (*Salomé*, 1976), and Carles Comas (*Fosca*, 1977). In their works, glitter remains a technology for transforming and reshaping the body and retains its dual allegiance to the two different strands of camp mentioned above. While in Smith's and Carles Comas's films glitter appears in amiably playful contexts, and in Arnold it evokes spiritual transformation, in Sieverding, Marti, and Hernández it ornaments darker scenarios of aggression and corporeal and psychic undoing.

In Jack Smith's *Reefers of Technicolor Island/Jungle Island* (1967) and *No President* (1967–70) glitter heightens the exoticism and otherworldliness of the performers and of the baroque tableaux they inhabit. Both films were first screened publicly in Smith's program *Horror and Fantasy at Midnight*, initially shown at New York's New Cinema Playhouse in November of 1967, later reprised at Tambellini's Gate in early 1968, and again in March of 1969, this last time retitled *The Kidnapping and Auctioning of Wendell Willkie by the Love Bandit*.[71] These programs combined footage by Smith together with fragments of documentaries and old Hollywood films shown to an accompaniment of taped music. The footage was eventually edited into films such as *Reefers* and *No President*—this last incorporated some of the found fragments that Smith used in his shows. Even though the programs for these shows listed specific titles—*Scrubwoman of Atlantis*, *Ratdroppings of Uranus*, *Marshgas of Flatulandia* . . . —it is difficult to know whether Smith thought of

134 EXPERIMENTAL FILM AND QUEER MATERIALITY

his footage as a collection of individual works or as combinable material to be reshuffled at will, since the length and order of the sequences kept changing with each iteration.

Glitter appears in these films on the faces of the performers and on some of the props. It seems to have loomed large in Smith's mind, as he advertised it emphatically. The publicity for *Horror and Fantasy* at Tambellini's Gate in January 1968 touted the participation of Irving Rosenthal—founder of the Kaliflower commune—"author of the Flamboyante [sic] new esoteric novel SHEEPER and 1st actor to appear on the American screen in glitter makeup."[72] While glitter was an incidental ingredient, hardly deserving such fanfare, it contributed to the films' atmosphere and visual style. *Reefers* was one of the titles listed in *Horror and Fantasy*, and it has survived as a relatively self-contained piece. Filmed in lush color, it stars Mario Montez heavily made up with blue eyeshadow and glittered eyelids, decked out with jewelry and flower garlands, and dressed in a Hawaiian skirt. He sits among flowers in what looks like a roof garden and, at other moments, among the carefully laid out debris that filled Smith's loft and served as the backdrop for his shows. Mario's stillness and scintillating adornment turn him into one more element in the shimmering décor, an identification underscored by superimpositions that merge his face and body with the objects around him. The sheen also enhances his exoticism. It chimes with the *Moana*-like intimations of Montez's costume and the atmosphere of the closing scenes. A young man with dark eye makeup and flowers on his head swims in a pool, knife in hand, as if he were a pearl diver, and later smokes a joint next to Mario. In the last frame of the film, they gaze enraptured at a clear evening sky, the picture of contentment, filmed in a tight medium close-up (see Figure 5.1). The flowers, the vines on the young man's head, the chiaroscuro of the interior scenes, and the South Sea intimations yield a tropicalist scenario dressed by Caravaggio, a scenario whose dreamy unreality is underscored by the twinkle of glitter that pervades the film.

No President offers a series of tableaux filmed in black and white and performed by a number of Smith regulars—Mario Montez, Jerry Sims, and Irving Rosenthal—and by acquaintances rallied for the occasion—Susanna de Maria and Tally Brown, among others. They are costumed in an eclectic array of styles that runs from fin-de-siècle tulles and gowns to Arabian djellabas to forties' evening dresses to loincloths to nothing at all. In their variegated outfits, they pose in frontal arrangements with minimal action; by turns, watchful, seductive, and threatening, they hover around each

Figure 5.1 Jack Smith, *Jungle Island*, 1967. Film Still. © Jack Smith Archive. Courtesy of Gladstone Gallery

other and occasionally tangle in a languorous orgy. The glitter on their faces is noticeable but discreet, since its sparkle is swallowed by the glare of the floodlight that illuminates the scene. Glitter adds to the eccentricity of the performers and the oddness of the tableaux, and lifts both out of the ordinary, locating them in a fully imaginary space—a visual utopia. It is also central to the cinema's hypnotic allure. Since, as Smith once wrote, "[a] bad film is one that doesn't flicker and move and shift through lights and shadows," a good one, conversely, would need the sparkle of glitter to sustain the optical enchantment.

The sparkling surfaces of Steven Arnold's *Luminous Procuress* (1972) also transport viewers and the film's protagonists—not to an exotic nowhere land but to a transcendent realm where "luminosity" portends a different plane of consciousness. A combination of grand camp and trippy mysticism, the film rose from the San Francisco drag–hippie scene to which The Cockettes also belonged. Arnold was closely connected to the troupe, some of whose members appear in the film. It was he who gave The Cockettes the chance to perform at the Palace Theater late in 1969 in the Nocturnal Dream Shows,

136   EXPERIMENTAL FILM AND QUEER MATERIALITY

the midnight programs that he curated.[73] The Nocturnal Dream Shows were usually devoted to film—to Arnold's inventive combination of rarities, cult fare, classics, and avant-garde—but they also included theatrical and multimedia events, such as the pantomimes and fashion shows of Arnold's friend Kaisik Wong, a San Francisco designer, or the performances of The Cockettes.[74]

Arnold was born in Oakland, and studied painting and photography at the San Francisco Art Institute, where he also became interested in film.[75] As a student, he made the witty *The Liberation of Mannique Mechanique* (1967) and *Messages, Messages* (1968). *Messages, Messages,* Arnold's M. A. project, made in collaboration with Michael Wiese, depicts the pilgrimage of a young man through an oneiric, slightly unnerving space populated by creatures to whom he relates uneasily, as in a struggle to maintain his autonomy and personal boundaries. The film ends with the protagonist facing off a cantankerous-looking creature with a face painted in solid white. When they appear about to meld into one, an impression conveyed by the alternation between gradually tighter close-ups of each, the camera pulls back to restore the protagonist to his own space, confirming his independence but also his isolation. *Mannique Mechanique* is a similar parable of emergence and self-affirmation. A bald young woman, wearing pancake makeup and exquisite shimmery gowns, is rescued from a menacing inorganic world—the hostile masks massing about her—by the caresses of a second woman who appears to be her lover—played by beat poet ruth weiss—and by a group of lethargically amorous youths—Pandora, artist and frequent Arnold collaborator, is one of them. In the end, it all seems to have been a dream; she is woken up by the embrace of her female lover—repeated in three variant takes—and in the last sequence of the film, she lies in bed, in her natural hair and unmade face smiling in pensive contentment. With its baroque intricacy and polysexual range, *Mannique Mechanique* is strongly evocative of Smith's work. Much of the action is captured in high angle takes with the performers lying and writhing on the ground, as is also the case in *Flaming Creatures*, and it is often filmed through gauze, baubles, glass cases, feathers, and a small forest of burning candles.[76] Shine envelops humans and nonhuman substances alike, objectifying the former while endowing the inert with an enticing liveliness. It also increases the equivocal allure of the dream and disappears once the protagonist comes to.

Luminous Procuress prolongs the interest of these early works in dreamlike spaces as settings for psychic and corporeal metamorphosis. While the film

GLITTER AND QUEER EMBODIMENT 137

defies coherent retelling—Arnold was a self-avowed surrealist who eventually befriended Salvador Dalí and travelled to Figueras to sit at the feet of the master—it can be summarized as the chemically induced transit of two young men into some sort of spiritual enlightenment that involves shedding their individuality and corporeal outline. In their journey, they confront enigmas and grotesques, enjoy polymorphous sex, take part in a banquet that turns into a joyous dance, with many Cockettes among the celebrants, and end up face to face with a deity encased in a glass cabinet. Entering the deity's space might be the surrender that the protagonist of *Messages, Messages* resisted. But while in the earlier films, submission entailed annihilating engulfment, in *Luminous*, it is a pleasant transition to a different plane of being.

The guide in this underground passage and the procuress of the title, played by Pandora, is luminous indeed. She is encased in resplendent clothing—designed by Stephen Runyon—her cheeks and eyelids are covered with glitter, her eyes are outlined with sequins, and her hair sparkles in the dark. As in all other examples we have discussed so far, glitter is also here part of a larger ecology of light—of a shine continuum in which other characters also participate; an atmosphere into which they dip and that contains and dissolves them in a pervasive glow. A recurring female figure—ruth weiss once more—wears a head cover and shirt made up of mirror squares; a silvery mummy awakes in its sarcophagus; and the jubilant banquet is presided over by a naked woman and man with their bodies painted, respectively, in silver and gold. In all these examples, luminosity heightens corporeal sensuality while also signaling supersession into a plane of incandescence beyond sex, gender, place, history, and time. In the final moments of the film, the deity in the glass urn wears a metallic turban with flashing lights, but it quickly mutates into a brightly lit head floating in a dark void and flanked by the young seekers who are similarly bathed in a white glow that brings them together, blurs their outline, and suggests their divine engulfment.

While in *Luminous Procuress* glitter radiates upward, dissolving the flesh into a vibrant glow, in the other titles I will discuss here it points downward, into the body's density and intricacy, and into the passions it harbors. This is the case with Carles Comas's *Fosca* (1977). *Fosca*'s setting is radically different from *Luminous Procuress*'s: not hippie San Francisco but post-Franco Spain. It was made during a time of transition toward democracy and newly regained freedom but also of fascist resistance against these emancipatory impulses. Carles Comas, its director, was active in the lively Barcelona countercultural scene of the mid-seventies, in which rock, underground comics, anarchist

138   EXPERIMENTAL FILM AND QUEER MATERIALITY

communalism, and experimental film and video flourished, often fueled by the energies of the incipient feminist and sexual liberation fronts. He was particularly active in the collective Barcelona Super 8, devoted to the promotion of small gauge cinema in experimental modes. As film historian Alberto Berzosa has shown, queer filmmaking was prominent among these modes, whether in the form of amateur documentaries of Barcelona's queer life or of irreverent, sexually explicit satires of commercial films.[77] Comas's first film, *Show de otoño* [Autumn Show] (1976) belongs to the first kind: it records a parodic fashion show whose models are drag queens and queer performers; visible among them is Ocaña, an emblematic artist of the period, known for his painting and for staging spontaneous street performances in elaborate retro drag.[78]

Fosca celebrates the first carnival held in the city in nearly four decades. The celebration had been banned under Franco due to its pagan character, but was revived quickly after his death. Part document, part poetic recreation, the film follows a group of friends during a carnival night. They exit a subway station, gather at an apartment to put on costumes and makeup, walk the streets, and dance at an open-air party and at a disco. The title—meaning "darkness" in Catalan—alludes to the nocturnal pleasures it depicts and to the dimness of the film, which is shot in Super-8 in very poorly lit settings. At the disco, for example, the frame remains mostly black, only pierced by the flash of strobe lights and the glow of a mirror ball, and in the interior scenes the figures are often barely readable in the grainy dusk. At the same time, darkness sets off the luster of shiny fabrics and of glitter on cheeks and apparel.

Glitter is particularly foregrounded throughout. The film's title is composed with this material, and a small pile of it is shown at the very end—the fairy dust settles after the party is over (see Figure 5.2). Glitter is also quite abundant in a scene that splits the film in two and disrupts its unity as the record of an outing, while opening it up to a broader network of queer dissidence. A fast-moving montage of images, culled from magazines, shows leather boys and drag queens exuberantly dressed and made up. Most are anonymous or may have enjoyed some topical relevance and are difficult to identify today. Among those identifiable in the barrage are several performers from the underground stage, such as Hibiscus, Holly Woodlawn, Candy Darling, and Taylor Mead. Cumulatively, these effigies offer a queer pantheon that stands in continuity with the costumed celebrants in the film. The suggestion that the Barcelona denizens are part of a global community of

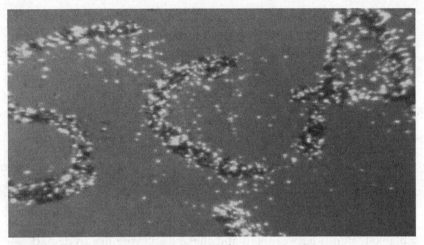

Figure 5.2 Carles Comas, *Fosca*, 1976. Frame enlargement. Courtesy of Filmoteca de Catalunya and Marcel Cifré

sexual dissenters, and a fabulous-looking one at that, may have felt quite comforting in the Spain of the time. While sexual minorities were increasingly vocal and visible—the first gay and lesbian demonstration in the country took place also in Barcelona only a few months after the film was shot—open homosexuality was still punishable by law—the *Ley de peligrosidad social* of 1970—and was often met with violence. The montage suggests that local and risky as their pleasures may seem, the carnival revelers in *Fosca* are at the vanguard of a new understanding of sex and gender that had been spreading wide across the world for over a decade. Glitter is a mark of this connection. It streaks the faces of the young men and women in the film as it does the figures in the magazine cutouts, tying them all into a queer international that was also a glitter international.

Katharina Sieverding's *Life-Death* (1969–72) is part of this queer/glitter continuum, which it recreates in interior rather than public spaces and in individual rather than collective terms. She made the film shortly upon graduating from the Kunstakademie Düsseldorf, where she studied under Joseph Beuys, at a time when she still hesitated between moving images and still photography, which eventually became her main medium. *Life-Death* tests on film the kind of portraiture that she was beginning to practice at the time.[79] Its four distinct sequences show close-ups and medium shots of nightclub performer Othello, artist Stephan Runge, Sieverding's friend

140 EXPERIMENTAL FILM AND QUEER MATERIALITY

Holger Bambusch, and Sieverding herself. These sequences are bracketed by unrelated takes: a string of red lights in the dark, a fire in an open field, a long-haired young man walking among peacocks in a public garden—Peacock Island, in Berlin's Tiergarten—and a humdrum skyline of flat rooftops with television antennas.

Each of the portrait scenes has a different style and gestural vocabulary. Othello appears in cheerful conversation with friends in a dimly lit apartment, stands in front of the camera in a black leather coat, and at the end of his section, lies down on the floor. Runge lies down inert and inexpressive, as the camera pans laterally along his body and captures his face in a close-up, and later stands up to take off his red kaftan. Sieverding smiles enigmatically with her face partly covered by a blanket, stands between sun and shade displaying her trademark androgynous appearance, and later on sits on an armchair and eats honey from a jar. Bambusch reclines in bed and appears to sleep as daffodils rest on his shoulder. The visual style also changes throughout: Othello is filmed in grainy black and white and muted color, Runge in sharp focus and vivid hues, Sieverding in soft focus and tones that are slightly bleached at times, and Bambusch in a reddish light that might derive from defective exposure or processing.

While color and light change from one sequence to the next, framings, interior settings, and some props recur, tightening up the disparate segments into a fairly compact design. Othello and Runge appear to lie on the same furry rug. Othello's headband, ornamented with a peacock feather, rhymes with the actual peacocks in the garden sequence. And half-hidden under a blanket, Sieverding plays with the leaf of a plant that later appears by her side. Runge and Sieverding hold a hand mirror, and so does the young man disporting among the peacocks. And shimmer crosses the film from end to end, from the red lightbulbs at the outset to the whiteouts at the end. In between, glitter adorns Othello's eyelids and cheeks; a golden vest sparkles under Runge's kaftan; Sieverding's silver makeup glimmers in the sun; and white frames, flares, and leakage—caused by defective registration or development—punctuate the image track throughout. While the film's subjects remain relatively still, light wavers and flickers on and around them. In fact, the contrast between the stillness of the bodies and the dynamism of light may be one of the possible meanings of the film's title, *Life-Death*. Light is the animating principle that counters the inertia of the flesh, which tends to slide to the ground and shift into immobility and inexpressiveness—although some brief moments in Othello's and Sieverding's sequences briefly belie this tendency.

Life-Death's bodies are androgynous in attire or in the way the camera addresses them. While the males are framed as spectacles, a position that conventional film reserves for feminine or feminized bodies, the one woman in the group refuses to be spectacularized, covering her body under a blanket, and adopts some marks of masculinity in pose and demeanor. For its androgyny, the film foreshadows Sieverding's series "Transformer" (1972–73), which was included in Jean-Claude Amman's landmark show "Transformer: Aspekte der Travestie," held at the Kunstmuseum Luzern in 1974.[80] Sieverding's "Transformer" was a slide projection of over a hundred black and white slides of her face and that of her partner, Klaus Mettig. In the course of projection, their features blend into each other and their identities and genders become subtly blurred. In an insightful, well-documented reading, Colin Lang has linked the film and the photographic series to the vogue of glam rock, a connection confirmed both by the title of the series—it alludes to Lou Reed's 1972 album of the same name—and by the photographs' visual style, which echoes the color scheme and composition of Mike Rock's photograph of Reed on the album cover.[81] Lang has read the film and the series as symptoms of the post-1968 disenchantment with activism and communal action. The events of 1968 rippled through Düsseldorf's Kunstakademie in the form of a student rebellion, spearheaded by Joseph Beuys, that led to the temporary closure of the school but not to the desired transformation of its structure and curriculum. Sieverding was involved in the events and documented them in the style of journalistic reportage in one of her first photographic series. The work she produced after the rebellion shows a different orientation. Featuring decontextualized faces—in the photographic series "Maton"—and interiors—in *Life-Death*—it suggests, Lang continues, a withdrawal into the self, privacy and interiority, and a concern with the cultivation of personal style in isolation from the outer world.

While Lang's reading is persuasive, it is possible, at the same time, to understand Sieverding's transition differently, less as a withdrawal than as a change of scenery and a shift in scale: from macro- to micropolitics; from public to private; and from contesting institutional strictures and state organization, to retooling the understanding and self-presentation of the body, gender, and sexuality at an intimate level. This turned out to be a different politics: a politics of difference that involved aesthetic strategies rather than the gestures of conventional activism. Sieverding's particular aesthetic kept its distance from the euphoric expressiveness of much underground performance and, in a more subdued register, stressed unreadability and defied the imperative to verbalize and explain that often accompanies political action. Opaque and decontextualized, the bodies in *Life-Death* refuse to tell their stories or reveal their secrets, and anticipate, in this regard, the blankness of her well-known self-portraits. These are bodies conceived as surfaces and screens rather than as narrative agents or thresholds to an inner self. Sheen and sparkle highlight their exteriority—turn them, in fact, into mere exterior: surfaces to be watched rather than messages to be decoded. They are gem-like accretions, impregnable and obdurate, alive mostly in their scintillating vibrancy—a vibrancy that may be contemplated but not comprehended, that exists outside identities and sexual preferences and affirms only an irreducible thingness answerable to no one.[82]

If in Arnold glitter transmits the evanescence of light and in Sieverding it heightens surface and objecthood, in the seventies work of Teo Hernández and Stéphane Marti, it merges with, and stands for, bodily fluids and, by metonymic extension, with the desires that make these fluids run. Hernández and Marti belong to a trend in the French experimental film of the seventies that French critic Dominique Noguez labeled in 1977 "*l'école du corps*,"[83] whose main representatives were, in addition to Hernández and Marti, Lionel Soukaz, Jacques Haubois (Jakobois), Michel Nedjar, and the artistic couple formed by Maria Klonaris and Katerina Thomadaki. They had been preceded in French experimental cinema by Pierre Clementi and Jean-Pierre Bouyxou, who were making quite "corporeal" films in the late sixties, and more distantly by Jean Genet, whose sole film, the intensely homoerotic *Un Chant d'amour* (1950), remained banned in France until the early seventies. The term *école du corps* deliberately evoked *l'art corporel* of Gina Pane and Michel Journiac, artists who, since the beginning of the decade, had been working on and with their body, subjecting it to stressful or painful situations that purported to make visible the unacknowledged violence of social regulations.[84] While the cinematic school of the body was less about putting the body under duress than about contemplating it in sexual or intimate scenarios, the two trends occasionally converged. The Collectif Jeune Cinéma, the main experimental film outlet in France at the time, programmed videotapes of actions by Pane or Journiac alongside films by Nedjar, and Marti documented several of Journiac's performances of the seventies and devoted one of his titles to his career (*Michel, La magistére du corps*, 1998).[85]

The filmmakers of the school of the body shared a taste for baroque settings; an interest in performance—dancing, posing, miming, dressing up; a sharp sense of color; and the use of post-synchronized soundtracks made of heterogeneous musical mixes. And they tended to work in Super-8, whose lightness and portability permitted, wrote Noguez, "an intimate dialogue with the body and face," and whose characteristic lack of depth conflated performers and their objectual backdrop, suggesting an equivalence between humans and their material surrounds.[86] During the seventies and early eighties, these filmmakers shared circuits and distributors (like the Collectif Jeune Cinema) and were shown together in festivals (Hyères, Toulon, or *Cinéma en marge*) and experimental film venues (the Musée National d'Art Moderne or the Cinema Club St. Charles, Noguez's film programs at the University of Paris-I). And in typical underground fashion, they often collaborated with each other. Katarina Thomadaki acted in some of Hernández's titles and Hernández, Jakobois, Nedjar, and Gaël Badaud—a latecomer to the "school"—acted in each other's work and banded together in the group MétroBarbèsRochechou Art, named after the subway stop of their Paris neighborhood. Under this rubric, they made two films together, shared equipment, and performed for each other's cameras, while simultaneously pursuing their separate trajectories.[87]

Stéphane Marti was not part of the Barbès Rochechou Art group, even if his work was often shown and discussed alongside theirs. He started making films in the mid-seventies, after graduating from the School of Fine Arts at University of Paris-I, where he had studied under André Almuró, Journiac, and Noguez.[88] Marti's work scrutinized mostly male bodies using a visual vocabulary that combined references to sadomasochism, glam and punk styles, and classical myth—through classical statuary and evocations of Dionysian excess. His films are concerned with the duality of the flesh and desire. Bodies sparkle invitingly, but they also tear, bleed, and convulse, and desire is a Dionysian force of pleasure and destruction. This duality is coded by color and material: glitter communicates sexual allure, while red and white paint convey respectively the vulnerability of wounded flesh and the possibility of transcending it through a state of serene completeness that is always provisional and susceptible to new assault.

Marti's third film, *La cité des neuf portes* (1977)—a metaphor for the human body and its orifices—encapsulates this dialectic of desire and its imbrication in material. Like Sieverding's *Life-Death*, it is a film of interiors (a *chambre film*, in Raphaël Bassan's term) in which several young men, women,

144 EXPERIMENTAL FILM AND QUEER MATERIALITY

and drag queens hang around leisurely, put on make-up, paint their nails, take off their clothes, dance, and seduce each other. Brief takes glide close to their faces and bodies and the editing blurs them all in a continuum of skin covered with jewelry, make-up, paint, and glitter. A third of the way through, the mood shifts from listless contentment to agitation. The adolescents of the opening sequences are replaced by slightly older youths who dance, embrace each other, and end up collapsing on the floor racked by spasms, while the camera shakes sympathetically. Blood (red paint) trickles from open wounds at the base of their neck down their sequin-covered chests and smears bodies and clothes. In the third section, Dionysian ecstasy and bleeding flesh yield to jubilant dancing and shortly afterward again to placid lounging. Blood is replaced by thick white paint that the celebrants pour on each other and might be a metaphor for seminal emission (joyous sexuality), but also evokes the whiteness of a classical stucco bust that appears in the agonic second section and recurs periodically through the rest of the film as the reminder of a wholeness and serenity that film occasionally strives for but just as frequently disrupts. The film concludes with another vignette of contentment—two young men playfully chase each other in a colonnade. The soundtrack, by sound artist and filmmaker Bernd DePrez, Marti's frequent collaborator at the time, accompanies the changing mood of the images with an eclectic mix that ranges from peppy to frantic to tragic to elegiac, and combines spurts of Brazilian drumming, opera (Verdi and Mussorgski), disco (Donna Summer and Thelma Huston), and excerpts of Lou Reed's album *Berlin* (1973).

Marti's subsequent films remain consistent with this iconography. In *Allegoria* (1979), *Ora Pro Nobis* (1979), and *Diasparagmos* (1980), glitter telegraphs appeal; red, blue, and black pigment on the performers' bodies evoke bleeding flesh and ravaging pleasures; and white paint is soothing and reparative. The two male protagonists of *Allegoria*, encased in jumpsuits, their faces crossed by lines of glitter, rub against each other and strip in a bathtub, drip color on themselves, and, modulating from sensuous to savage, interrupt their caresses to tear a fish apart with their teeth—all filmed impressionistically in quick, gestural takes. At the end, in a Seine embankment, one of the bathers stabs the other, who crumples in agony; an immediately juxtaposed alternate scene has these same characters in the same setting smiling and whispering flirtatiously into each other's ear. Cruelty and violence, then, are not the outer limits of pleasure, but its inner lining. In these ambiguous scenarios of love and destruction, glitter communicates the appeal of the flesh but also its vulnerability to the disruptions of desire.

GLITTER AND QUEER EMBODIMENT 145

Teo Hernández's *Salomé* (1976) also enlists glitter in the depiction of destructive passion. A central title in Noguez's *école du corps*, *Salomé* cemented Hernández's stature in French experimental film. Hernández was born in Ciudad Hidalgo, Mexico, in 1939, and studied architecture in Mexico City. After a brief stay in San Francisco, he settled down in Paris in 1967, where he remained until his death in 1992.[89] His beginnings as a filmmaker, however, took place in sojourns outside this city. While visiting friends in London, he made his first finished film, *14 Bina Gardens* (1968), and in Tangiers, once a Spanish colonial outpost on the Moroccan coast where he spent a few months in 1969, he made his best early titles: *Estrellas del ayer* (1969) and *Images du bord de la mer* (1969).[90] He made two more films in Tangiers the following year (*Juanito* and *Michel lá bas*, this last with Michel Nedjar, a life-long friend and collaborator), and later in the year, he filmed *Pause* (1970) in Copenhagen, a light postcard of Hernández's friends at the central court of the Carlsberg Glypotek. The title was premonitory. After completing these films, Hernández took a five-year trip around the world with Nedjar. *Salomé* marked his return to filmmaking and the restart of what would remain an uninterrupted, prolific career.

Salomé is an extremely loose recreation of the Biblical episode centered on the eponymous character. It volatilizes the narrative components of the story to focus instead on details of color, light, and gesture. The story is stripped to its bare ingredients: to its four protagonists and to several crucial moments that are placed out of sequence, repeated with slight variations, and rendered so elliptically as to be barely recognizable. Salomé gestures seductively at the Baptist and dances tangled up in colored gauze; Herod stands hieratically in interlocution with Herodias and Salomé; Salomé and Herodias remove veils off the Baptist's head—a roundabout depiction of his execution?—and the characters pass around a Mexican ceramic skull and various spheres that might stand for the saint's severed head.

The identification of these motifs, however, is not essential to the experience of the film, which Hernández conceived as an independent artistic artifact built on the dynamism of "light, color, and projection speed": "[The film] proposes a perceptual experience: that is, refusing the use of external elements of analysis (psychological, moral, social, etc.) to justify its functioning, it creates its own body, discernible only through the transformation of the gaze of the spectator and the engagement of [their] perception."[91] Especially important to this engagement was the tempo of the image. Shot at standard sound speed, *Salomé* was screened at 18, 12, 9, and 6 frames per

146 EXPERIMENTAL FILM AND QUEER MATERIALITY

second, with Hernández changing the projection speed on the spot, turning each screening into an unrepeatable performance.[92] The shifts in speed produced a hypnotic retardation of actions and gestures, which often give the impression of being filmed under water. Even without the diminished speed, the actions portrayed are quite lethargic, and, except for the moments identified above, largely devoid of narrative consequence: hands dig through yards of fabric or hold bracelets and necklaces; characters smoke, stare at each other and at the camera, and put on and take off veils and garments with great deliberation. Slowness was central to Hernández in those years. Against the forward drive of commercial narrative cinema, which according to him, streamlined responses and curtailed the spectator's ability to dream, the slow-paced, inconsequential action in *Salomé* and other titles from the same period was an inducement to imaginative drift.[93]

Even though Hernández did not claim as much, shine and sparkle contribute to the entrancement. While the human actors in Salomé languish, their clothes, headdress, jewels, and props glimmer vividly. Their gleam is enhanced by the black backdrop and dim lighting. Despite Hernández rejection of external referents and his defense of the film as a self-enclosed perceptual experience, it is possible to read sheen allegorically as a way to project the blazing passions that animate the story and have been the main reason for its long cultural life. As in other examples of dark camp, gleaming surfaces and glitter are aligned with moments that convey the entanglement of sexuality and violence. One of the segments when Salomé seductively approaches the Baptist segues into shots of a pair of incandescent hands covered in gold sequins rummaging through beads and glitter (see Figure 5.3). Herodias fills a cup with gold glitter as a gift to Herod, who proceeds to grant the execution. And after one of the scenes that evokes the beheading—Salomé blows out a candle and provokes a blackout—a spill of golden glitter trickles down the frame, as if the Baptist's flowing blood had mineralized (see Figure 5.4). In these examples, glitter makes passion visible and tangible. It occupies the frontier between the emotive and the material, the lively and the inert. A lifeless substance, it becomes a marker of anger, desire, and revenge—of bloodshed and life wasted—and acquires in the process a life of its own.

This chiasmic interchange between material and immaterial, animate and inanimate, makes the world of *Salomé* a world of inversion and undecidability, where things and bodies exchange attributes. It is a radically queer world. In the same way that liveliness transfers from the human to the inhuman and inert, power and control seep from its traditional embodiments—the

Figure 5.3 Teo Hernández, *Salomé*, 1976. Frame enlargement. Courtesy of Michel Nedjar.

Figure 5.4 Teo Hernández, *Salomé*, 1976. Frame enlargement. Courtesy of Michel Nedjar.

148 EXPERIMENTAL FILM AND QUEER MATERIALITY

king, the prophet touched by the divinity—to marginal characters, such as courtesans and their teenage daughters. These reversals may have made the story dear to queer creators in times of sexual upheaval. At different points in the 1970s, in the wake of the sexual revolution, Carmelo Bene, Lindsay Kemp, Pedro Almodóvar, and Werner Schroeter offered versions of the myth in their own particular styles. The singularity of Hernández's contribution to Salomé's queer afterlife lies in the way shine—and particularly glitter— anchors the depiction of a topsy-turvy world, where those pushed low down in the scale of being—women, things—may, for once, have the upper hand.

Shimmers, Tickles, Dots

In a recent study of trans cinema, Eliza Steinbock posits "the shimmering image" as the figure for the proliferating possibilities contained in trans corporeality and its filmic representation. With its intermittence and variability, shimmer, like glitter, escapes the kinds of binaries that have traditionally framed discussion of trans bodies—binaries such as truth and appearance, anatomy and gender identification, body and mind, truth and falseness, masculine and feminine. Shimmering directs attention instead to the manifold gradations possible between those poles.[94] For Steinbock, the term is synonymous with "change in its emergent, flickering form" and outlines an area of uncertainty and cognitive challenge akin to Roland Barthes's notion of "the neutral" and Sandy Stone's "posttranssexuality"—concepts or bodies that elude clear-cut binaries and resist definition.

While Steinbock does not give glitter—the material—much shrift, it is an apt embodiment of her conception of "shimmer." Hovering between artificial and natural, ordinary and extraordinary, material and spiritual, solid and evanescent, glitter wavers in meaning and queers—"transes"?—what it touches.[95] A mark of artificiality—made out of that most artificial of substances, plastic—it is often a second skin in intimate communion with the organic body and stands for its fluids—blood and semen—in Marti's and Hernández's films. Crassly material, it also conveys spiritual aspiration as in Hibiscus's shamanistic performances with The Angels of Light and in Arnold's *Luminous Procuress*. A mark of individual style, it has the political effect of channeling communities of sexual dissenters, as in Sieverding and Comas. It is cheap and easily available but lifts the ordinary into an exotic otherworldliness, as Smith does in his films. And neither particularly

GLITTER AND QUEER EMBODIMENT   149

masculine nor exclusively feminine, it seems to shift the bodies it touches into "transing"—a zone of indiscernibility that does not only affect gender but also gender's attachments and locations in the social field.

Glitter's indiscernibility, to retake a question raised at the outset of the chapter, rises largely from the company it has kept—from the variegated cultural life I have reviewed in this chapter—but also from its intrinsic qualities. To the binaries just cited, we could add a further one: glitter stands between solid and fluid. Glitter's particulate structure attenuates the solidity of the surfaces on which it lands, while its luminosity transposes them into uncertain expanses of shine and shadow that constantly change with ambient light. It sublimates mass and body into light. Under glitter, all that is solid melts into shine, as *Luminous Procuress* amply illustrates. But in an opposite pull, visible in Smith's work and in Sieverding's *Life-Death*, glitter also heightens surface in contradictory ways—as an indeterminate expanse punctured by multiple points of light *and* as a gem-like precipitate endowed with mineral solidity. While gems appeal to the eye rather than the touch and stand indifferent and unresponsive, glittery expanses, by contrast, foster a haptic visuality that renders the optical through the tactile and solicits touch as much as the gaze. The trope of glitter's hapticity is the tickle: the uneven cutaneous innervation rather than the steady grasp or the caress.

The tickled, glittery body lacks clear-cut boundaries; its outline is outstripped by the surface glow that radiates beyond it. The glittering body restages through the reflection of light the dialectic between color and line that, as Jacqueline Lichtenstein has shown, informs much of painting as well as philosophy's response to it.[96] In this dialectic, the line is a masculine principle, a phallic instance of control, containment, and intellection, while color—or, in this case, light—is a feminine force associated with surface, corporeality, and a sensual excess that escapes discursive containment. It is a dialectic that Rosalind Galt has insightfully reprised in her book *Pretty*, in which she vindicates categories such as color, the decorative, the oriental, the baroque, the sumptuous, and the composed.[97] These categories, Galt shows, are often vehicles for marginal expressiveness and, perhaps for that reason, often dismissed by critics and historians as frivolous, facile, tasteless, and conceptually slack. Glitter is one more avatar of the pretty for its deliberate superficiality, its exuberance, and its way of debunking, with its shivering luminescence, the controlling line and its strict contours.

And to add one more point, in addition to being the rebellion of light and color against the line, glitter is also the rise of the dot, or rather, the dotted field, against the line and the colored surface. The history of modernism and postmodern art has often been summarized as a duel of lines: the straight modern line versus the curves of late nineteenth-century ornamentalism; the less-is-more functionalist grid versus the postmodern waves and arabesques inspired by vernacular architecture and the downtown signscape. But much of what we associate with the mid-century crisis of modernism took the form of the rise of the dot against the line. The dot, or rather, the dotted field, replaces the continuity and directionality of the line as a model of temporality, a paradigm of knowledge, or a style of social praxis in fields ranging from cybernetics to physics to politics to art. Some of the shifts that characterized the evolution of these fields from the second half of the twentieth century forward may be described as acupuncture-like interventions in the social and cultural field rather than systemic make-overs: singular interventions, instead of forward movement and totalizing claims; fields of probability—points in a grid of coordinates—rather than absolute certainties; porous planes—silkscreens, Ben Day dots—rather than saturated surfaces; and finally, shimmery, glittery bodies rather than clear-cut, assignable ones: bodies pierced by points of light, organic and mineral, spiritual and corporeal, immaterial and vaporous but also cutaneous and ticklish, uncontainable, and gender-indifferent.

So, what remains, at this point of Gordon Hall's "glitter" problem? To recall: that was the problem of discussing queer art on the basis of its biographical filiation and representational contents rather than its structural attributes. While, as Hall claims, it is a problem to confine queer textuality to a relatively circumscribed number of artists, works, and reading protocols, this is not exactly a problem that glitter warrants. As I have tried to establish, glitter's queerness is not univocal and straightforward, but circuitous and ambiguous, polyvalent, and contextual. Glitter is queer not for its representational potential nor for its association with particular queer bodies, but precisely for the way in which it queers the idea of the body itself.

6

Film Grain, Discontinuous Representation, and the Queer Corporealities of Underground Cinema

Glitter's dissolution of surface and outline into sparkling intermittence has an analogue in film grain, perhaps the dominant texture in experimental film from the late 1950s forward. The pervasiveness of grain resulted from the proliferation of small gauge film at the time. 8mm and 16mm, the amateur alternatives to the professional standard of 35mm, had long been available, but their use grew considerably around mid-century, when the market was flooded with affordable cameras, projectors, and stocks thanks in part to massive production for military purposes during the war years.[1] By the mid-fifties, 16mm had become the preferred gauge for industrial, instructional, documentary, and news film, with many television programs shifting from 35mm to 16mm production, and 8mm was the widely available alternative for amateur and home moviemaking, to be supplemented in the mid-sixties with Super-8.[2] Manufacturers responded to the rising demand for small formats with a nuanced supply, which included the development of sensitive film: Kodak Tri-X and 4-X 16mm stocks, for example, were designed so that news cameras could work in interiors with available lighting. With them, it was easy to obtain images in almost any light, yet the occasional underside was a graininess that might compromise readability.

Evident grain connoted amateurism and was often regarded as an embarrassment. Manuals, photography magazines, and amateur film guides gave frequent advice on how to minimize it. Even as late as 2018, Kodak claimed on its web site that the main challenge to its "emulsion scientists" was "to increase film speed while maintaining image quality and keeping performance"—or sharpness.[3] Lenny Lipton's popular manual *Independent Filmmaking* (1972), an excellent source about the technical means available to experimental filmmakers in the sixties and early seventies, is often ambivalent about granularity. As the experimental filmmaker that he was, Lipton

Experimental Film and Queer Materiality. Juan A. Suárez, Oxford University Press. © Oxford University Press 2024.
DOI: 10.1093/oso/9780197566992.003.0006

152   EXPERIMENTAL FILM AND QUEER MATERIALITY

conceded grain's artistic potential, but he also tended to treat it as a defect that improved stocks sought to eliminate. In fact, his praise of particular stocks is often directly proportional to their sharpness and the fineness of their grain, and he gave frequent advice on how to attenuate grain through the appropriate combination of stocks, filters, and aperture adjustments. The point to be explained, then, is why so many filmmakers of the time chose to enhance rather than conceal grain; and, secondly, what grain added to the images they produced.

Jonas Mekas noted the rising interest in texture in his *Village Voice* column in the summer of 1965: "The texture and grain of the film is [sic] coming into its own through Brakhage's and Ken Jacobs' 8mm work." What prompted his reflection, however, was neither Brakhage nor Jacobs, but George Landow's *This Film Will Be Interrupted After 11 Minutes by a Commercial*—later retitled *Film in Which There Appear Edge Lettering, Sprocket Holes, Dust Particles, Etc.* (1966). It was a loop of well-worn leader with a China girl blinking at the camera. Originally printed in 8mm, it was blown up to 35mm, split length-wise, and reprinted on 16mm; the processing amplified the dirt, scratches, and grain of the original. Mekas continued: "In Landow's loop you can see and feel the film sprockets, the splices, and even the running of film through the projector—really, it is a particular characteristic of this new film form that it pulls you into a total film experience, all its aspects included."[4] While the commercial film image was slick and transparent and seldom drew attention to itself, the avant-garde beamed its unconventionality, among other ways, by foregrounding its optics and mechanics, surface accidents and roiling grain.

Despite its pervasiveness, grain has seldom been explored in itself.[5] It has been mentioned in passing in discussions of the structural cinema of the late sixties and seventies and of 8mm and of Super-8 filmmaking from the mid-sixties forward. In fact, Mekas's article is one of the earliest mentions of this trait in—yet to be so-named—structural cinema, a cinema that focused its attention on the basic components and functioning of the cinematic image and whose canon would end up including Landow's and some of Jacobs's work.[6] Structural filmmakers enhanced granularity through the rephotography of found film—Ken Jacobs's *Tom, Tom, the Piper's Son* (1969); Ernie Gehr's *Eureka* (1974)—through the use of fast film in dim lighting—Gehr's *Reberveration* (1969); Peter Gidal's *Clouds* (1969) and *Room Film 1973* (1973)—and through the exposure of the stock to light in order to create dotted fields devoid of representational content—Paul Sharits' *Axiomatic*

QUEER CORPOREALITIES OF UNDERGROUND CINEMA 153

Granularity (1973) and Gehr's *History* (1970). (Nathaniel Dorsky's *Pneuma* (1983) is another result of this last process, even though Dorsky has kept his distance from structural film).[7] In all these cases, grain was foregrounded as part of cinema's unheeded material substratum.[8] It made evident the basic material proviso of the cinematic image: that it was an aggregate of burnt molecules of silver halide suspended on the gelatin emulsion coating a strip of celluloid. Brakhage, hardly a representative of the cinema of structure, but a pioneer in the play with grain, had a structural epiphany when he saw his 8mm films blown up in projection: "you were viewing the actual chemical constituency that was making up the images as well as the images: they were imbedded [sic] in the very crystals that made for a yellow shape as distinct from a red shape and it was quite a spatial experience! If you blew them large enough you could almost see through the space the various dye levels."[9]

In 8mm and Super-8, granularity was less a matter of choice than of technological inevitability. As the exposed surface of the 8mm strip of celluloid was quite small—less than half that of 16mm film—its accidents appeared much larger in projection. Surface marks attenuated depth and deflated illusionism, and formed, in the words of Fred Camper, "a kind of almost-random scrim through which any representational image is inevitably seen."[10]

In addition to its structural import as harbinger of film's basic materiality, grain accrued affective and semantic associations that derived from its low-fidelity, small scale, artisanal quality, and association with intimacy. Granularity connoted gritty realism—documentary and news coverage. But it was also the look of intimacy, the minor, the familiar, and the immediate: an indoor realm that included corporeal closeness and, after the late 1960s, explicit sexuality, since pornography for home use circulated in small formats.[11] As a channel for the intimate and corporeal, grain characterizes a broad swath of queer cinema from the sixties to the present, a tradition that filmmaker Bradley Eros has poetically described as "Cinema le difference": "queer & binocular, transistor and stereo . . . *a universe in which the inverse is holy* . . . off-stage. *obscene* . . . exchanging forbidden rites and fluids."[12] Eros's statement notwithstanding, the queer attractions of granularity have seldom been noted, perhaps because, until relatively recently, queer criticism has tended to focus more on representational content than on nonreferential form and textural particulars.[13]

Film grain is a different kind of materiality from the one explored in previous chapters. Unlike rubble, junk, old-fashioned and magical objects, amphetamine, plastic, or glitter, grain does not preexist filmic representation.

It is a photographic effect that may attach to anything captured on celluloid. By drawing attention to its effect and significance in queer experimental cinema, I am bringing into contact two traditions that have seldom spoken to each other—the underground and structural-materialist film—and the two sensibilities usually associated with each: the corporeal-expressive impulse of the former and the formalist reflection of the latter.[14] This should not be a surprising convergence. Some types of queer film were a formative influence on the cinema of structure while, at the same time, structural concerns have played a larger role in queer film than has been recognized so far. The structural-material consciousness that P. Adams Sitney and Peter Gidal discerned in Warhol's minimal films of 1963 and 1964 and that Sitney also spotted in Gregory Markopoulos's *Galaxy* (1966) was not restricted to these titles alone. It fed into the sexual-corporeal politics of the underground and of subsequent forms of queer cinema, in which the exploration of the body and sexuality was tied to a (more or less tacit) reflection about the apparatus and its functioning in what we might call a queer structuralism.

Placed in a broader context, granularity puts queer experimental film in dialogue with a number of parallel artistic practices characterized by what could be named discontinuous representation: the replacement of wholistic gestalts by dotted composites—aggregates of minimal integers that, in combination, articulate larger patterns. Discontinuous representation looks back to nineteenth-century printing innovations (half-tone printing and Ben-Day dots) and sideways to digital sampling and signal modulation. These two processes were exhaustively studied in postwar information science and computer research (often combined under the label of cybernetics) as means to streamline and control information and to optimize its storage and transmission. At the same time, discontinuous representation was not the exclusive concern of communication engineers and mathematicians; it was also intuitively applied, with discrepant purposes, by artists working in photography, painting, and experimental film—including queer underground cinema. In fact, the sixties and seventies queer underground offers a good vantage point to track the spread and significance of discontinuous representation in art, not as a mechanism of control but as a form of inverted cybernetics that was used to channel unconventional bodies, sexualities, and communities. The chapter will track the emergence of discontinuous representation from late nineteenth-century half-tone printing techniques to the rise of cybernetics and further to its subsequent adoption by artists in a variety of fields, from pop art to performance to different kinds of moving-image experiments to queer underground cinema. A later chapter will explore the afterlives of granular images in queer experimental film from the eighties to the present in contexts determined by the devastation of AIDS and its aftermaths, by the reworking of earlier iconographic repertoires driven by queer cinephilia, and by attachment to the alternative corporealities that rise from processed low-fi celluloid in the era of the hi-fi digital image.

Dots, Pop Art, and Electronic Vision

Grain results from the oxidation of the silver halide molecules dissolved in the gelatin emulsion that covers the strip of celluloid when struck by light. The visual configuration of a grainy image depends on the size and density of these molecules, which yield a dotted likeness that renders the continuum of experience through aggregate points. A photographic effect, dot-based rendering was widely used, decades before the invention of the cinema, in halftone printing and Ben Day dots: industrial methods of image (re)production that are in some ways the immediate forbears of filmic grain.

Halftone printing used dot patterns to reproduce the seemingly continuous tones of photographic plates. It involved the rephotography of an original through a screen that translated the image into arrangements of dots of variable density. This copy was then turned into a printing plate from which further replicas would be generated.[15] As simplified renderings of the original, these replicas required less ink and were therefore cheaper to print and circulate than more faithful reproductions. Ben Day dots adapted the principle of halftone printing to the application of color. Attributed to Benjamin Henry Day, a Philadelphia illustrator and printer who first used them in 1879, it was a system of tinting that interspersed dots of different colors—usually cyan, magenta, yellow, and black—in various combinations to generate a variety of tonalities and shadings.[16] It was a factory-made *pointillism* that anticipated its fine art relative by a few years. In combination, halftone printing and Ben Day dots fostered the expansion of the illustrated press at the end of the nineteenth century and contributed to bringing about what poet and film theorist Vachel Lindsay named a "hieroglyphic" modernity, dominated by endlessly proliferating images rather than by writing.[17] Ironically, the techniques that made of modernity a visual civilization relied on the limitations of the human eye. Like the cinema, another technology that contributed to the modern reign of vision, halftone printing and Ben

Day dots were optical illusions: they tricked the eye into perceiving continuous color, mass, and line where there were in fact discontinuous dot patterns—fractal, porous, and intermittent. They combined industrial hard edge and poetic indistinction, rigor and fuzziness, dualities that also conditioned the perception and uses of film grain.

Fascinated with mass-production and media images, sixties pop art incorporated into painting the dotted halftone textures. Roy Lichtenstein was a pioneer in this regard. His early pop canvases inspired in advertisements and comic book panels replicated the printer's dots and mechanically rendered contours. He applied these finishes to classic topics, such as landscapes and still lives, and to versions of the great masters. His *Seascape* prints (1964–65) wittily reduced the infinite gradations of the ocean to a uniform spread of blue dots on a white background, and, in a further embrace of the synthetic, were screened onto laminated plastic. And his versions of Picasso, Cézanne, and Mondrian translated the characteristic gestures of these artists into an industrial vocabulary of flat colors, thick black lines, and standardized points.

Lichtenstein reduced images to their common lowest denominator: the varying configurations of the dot. Reduced in this fashion to their atomic components, images were no longer the exclusive result of embodied gesture and subjective interpretation but of a combination of data sampling and signal encoding. But one no longer needed an artist for that. Dot patterns could be easily programmed and automated, which is the reason why they were created in the first place. Not that this was a problem for Lichtenstein and other pop artists: their standardized character and industrial regularity were part of the appeal. "I want my painting to look exactly as if it had been programmed. I want to hide the work of my hand," said Lichtenstein in interview with John Coplans.[18] Warhol keenly concurred: "I want to be a machine."[19]

It was a logical aspiration: machines excelled at sampling perceptual data and recasting them in images that were fed back into the visual stream. If the antecedents of this procedure were the mechanical reproduction technologies of the late nineteenth century, its main contemporary version was television, which is often featured in pop art but whose basic functioning and characteristic texture are seldom discussed in relation to it. The pixelated televised image was an electronic version of the halftone print. It fragmented a visual continuum into discrete electronic signals that were broadcast and eventually decoded, at the receiver's end, on the dot matrix of the television screen: a raster of 525 horizontal lines that was read by the beam of electrons fired by a cathode gun—three guns in color sets—thirty times per second. Each of the dots on the television screen is a pixel—etymologically, picture element—a term that began to be used in the mid-sixties in relation to digitized computer displays based on an analogous sampling principle.[20] Television technology reverted to dots as the universal dissolvents of vision: everything could be rendered through them. In a form of delayed action—of psychoanalytic *Nachträglichkeit*, the name that Sigmund Freud gave to the reactivation of a former trauma by a later one—it may have been the pervasiveness of the television screen that made printer's dots a common interest among pop artists. Or differently put, the shock to the character and composition of the image provoked by the shaky pixilation of television may have clarified what was at stake from the start in the industrial reduction of image to machine-made patterns: endless reducibility and automation; the reduction of subjective and gestural traits—what traditional art history called a style—to standardized programmable protocols.[21]

Dots were not only the image's universal dissolvent. They were also its primary instigators. Television was based on much the same optical illusion as half-tone—the (mis)perception of a discontinuous rendering as if it were continuous. But not only television was based on this misperception. From the late fifties forward, Bela Julesz, an engineer at Bell Laboratories, used randomly generated dot stereograms in order to explore the human perception of shape and depth. Exposed to Julesz's cards and films, test subjects ascertained patterns and depth relations where none existed, conjured by the combined effect of stereoscopic vision and post-retinal processing. The world could be dissolved into patterns of dots as much as dot patterns could be hallucinated into a world.[22] Julesz's stereograms resemble television noise, especially the filmed versions—cinematograms—which he started to produce in the early sixties in order to extend his research into the perception of moving images.[23] The cinematograms are also reminiscent of several structural film experiments, such as Ernie Gehr's *History*. Gehr's film foregrounds grain not only as an elementary component of the cinematographic image, but as the precondition to any representational procedure. Consisting of twenty minutes of swarming black and grey dots, the blanket inclusiveness of its title suggests that histories, stories, and sense emerge out of this primordial magma. They are particular precipitations, different ways of connecting the dots in a field of potentially endless virtuality.

Cybernetics and Its Shadow

Television, like all electronic transmission, was based on frequency modulation: a form of sampling which broke down a continuous data stream into a finite number of discrete components in order to facilitate its storage and broadcast. Since the interwar years, sound engineers had pioneered the sampling and quantizing methods that permitted the emission of sound signals over telephone wires and the reduction of noise.[24] These advances became the blueprint for television broadcasting. They are further examples of the spread of a new regime of representation whose standard was not the exact reproduction of an original—a task that was, if not impossible, often exorbitantly inefficient—but the reduction of the original to structural patterns—an informational footprint—that permitted its recognition and manipulation.

Norbert Wiener's epochal *Cybernetics: Control and Communication in the Animal and the Machine* (1948) surveyed this new representational regime and spun out its consequences in various fields, from physics to communication to artificial intelligence to prosthetics. In his account, sampling-based representation displaced traditional mimetic approaches and ushered in a different temporality. While conventional mimesis operated on Newtonian time, irreversible and predictable, the new representational mode introduced a Bergsonian temporality: variable, reversible, and open-ended. In turn, exact quantification and prediction, the goal of Newtonian science, yielded to statistical mechanics and the calculation of "possible futures" on the basis of probabilistic distribution.[25] One of Wiener's most generative insights was that information theory could provide a model for such calculations. Understanding the functioning of a system was equivalent to calculating the possible variables of a message. The unknowability of a system was a factor of its vulnerability to noise, or unpatterned occurrence, while its knowability derived from the possibility of discerning its patterns, that is, from establishing a favorable signal-to-noise ratio. Both noise and signal-to-noise ratios could be calculated numerically following the premises of information theory as developed since the late thirties most notably by Claude Shannon, who was working as an engineer at Bell Laboratories at the time he published his revolutionary formulations in the late forties. All that was necessary was to quantify and process enough variables to gain a workable approximation. Or, in the language of communication engineers, all that was needed was the appropriate pulse code modulation (PCM) that permitted the encoding, transmission, and eventual decoding of an original message.[26]

Cybernetics, regarded as the science of information, translated mechanical, biological, and physiological processes into statistical frequencies. It reduced the world to pulses that could be measured in bits—the basic information integers calculable through logarithms to the basis of two. Reduced to this shared digital language, vastly disparate phenomena could be measured and assessed against a common scale. They could also be placed in communication, since all interactions could be modeled as messages.[27] On the basis of this translation, cybernetics formalized the transactions between machines, live organs, and bodies as messages that were governed by protocols of mapping and patterning; of information retrieval and matching.[28] Shannon famously proposed that the basic structure underlying these communicative protocols was the electrical switching system, a binary system that only knows two positions: on/off; closed/open.[29] In Wiener's paraphrase of Shannon, each discrete message that circulated through the system was "a series of yeses and noes distributed in time" and "single decisions between yes and no" were "the element of information."[30] This is the binary code on which digital culture is based; into which everything could be—has been— translated. The breakdown of processes into discrete communicative events and the formalization of these events through binary coding is analogous to the functioning of dot printing and film and photographic grain. All dissolve wholes into discrete individual components, and these either *are* or *are not* present, and when present, gradable through quantizable traits— numerically scaled thickness and hue—that could be formalized, in turn, through binary code.

Grain was a form of signal modulation, prevalent, as we have seen, in pop art's fascination with dot patterns and in experimental film from the early sixties forward. György Kepes, an influential postwar design theorist and a professor at MIT who was well versed in cybernetics, pointed out in the early sixties: "Possibly the key techniques of our civilization are instrumentation based on the transformation of patterns into the structural analogues through the modulation of signals."[31] Modulation is largely based on "structure": it is "structural correspondence" that allows us to find "a common denominator in all sensed experience," Kepes wrote, tacitly echoing Alan Turing's idea of a "universal machine" capable of translating any data stream into algorithmic form. "It is possible to convert sound to sight, space to time,

160 EXPERIMENTAL FILM AND QUEER MATERIALITY

light to form, and interchange phases and events, static and dynamic, sensible and conceptual."[32]

There was infinite potential in such transferability. Although Kepes did not put the matter so starkly, early cyberneticians posited an endlessly malleable world that could be reduced to mathematically calculated patterns and therefore known and controlled better than ever before, an idea embedded in the very etymology of the world cybernetics. Derived from the Greek word *xibernetés* or helms-person, its root is also in terms like "governor" or "government." Cybernetics, the reduction of the world to communication and control mechanisms, was from the start linked to governmentality, power, control, and sense. Its earliest impulse came from the use of predictive statistics in war technologies. In fact, the statistical problems derived from coordinating a human operator and an antiaircraft gun in order to predict the trajectory of an enemy airplane inspired Wiener's earliest cybernetic formulations and the idea of cybernetics itself.[33]

Without explicitly disavowing the idea of a controllable universe, Kepes underlined the relative instability that haunted modulation and algorithmic reduction. These processes revealed that the world was less an aggregate of static things than of highly variable information patterns. His book *The New Landscape of Art and Science*, where he expounded these theories, was largely an archive of such patterns, showing the structural correspondences between vegetable growth, geographical accidents pictured from the air, the contours of modern sculptures, and the motion of subatomic particles. Dynamic in their interrelations, pattens are "the meeting points of actions and processes."[34] The visual media, and in particular film and television, enhanced the awareness that the world is made of processes and that form itself is "a gathering of . . . dynamisms."[35] This idea was, for political theorist Karl Deutsch, one of the main contributions of Kepes's book: "Today we are learning in television to translate any outline of a static or slow changing thing, such as the edge of a mountain, or the edge of a human skull, or the lines of a human face, into a sequence of rapidly changing dots."[36] For both Deutsch and Kepes, such a fluid understanding of reality ought to prompt a reconfiguration of mental habits and the adoption of more flexible ways of thinking. At the same time, Kepes added, the dynamism that information science was discovering and trying to formalize in reality had long been envisioned by art.

Except that, in highlighting the world's dynamism, artists often worked against the tenets of information science and cybernetics. Several artists during the sixties engaged the gestures and basic ideas of cybernetics while disputing its claims to absolute control. In the avant-garde, the reduction of a global event—an image, a message—to dot patterns modeled on the binary working of electrical switches was not put to the service of sense but of *noise*. The granulation of the image did not seek to streamline the signal but to diffuse it, to prevent the possibility of diaphanous reception and to practice in this fashion a cybernetics of disorder.

Dissident Dots

A case in point would be the dissident use of dots and dotted surfaces by artists such as Yayoi Kusama, Yoko Ono, Bridget Riley, Andy Warhol, and Richard Hamilton. They are a heterogenous group dominated by (male) pop artists but also including representatives of op art—Riley—Fluxus conceptualism—Ono—and of the mixture of installation and performance practiced in the early sixties by Kusama, who has also been associated with pop and the contemporary "new realisms."[37] Yet despite their diversity, their work embodies some similarities in their attitudes toward the dot and its potentials.

Dots are parodic and gestural in Ono and in Kusama's early works. Ono drew them by hand using felt tip pens on small white squares that were part of her conceptual proposals, such as the rain of red flecks that accompanies one of her "Architecture pieces dedicated to a phantom architect": "Build a dotted line house. Let people imagine the missing parts (a) Let people forget the missing parts (b)."[38] As if in dialogue with Julesz card stereograms—which became well-known enough to deserve an homage by Dalí (*Cybernetic Odalisque*, 1978)—Ono prompted viewers to imagine an environment from dots. But while Julesz explored involuntary perception, Ono proposed a deliberate game of reversible imagination.

Kusama's first dot drawings and paintings are roughly contemporary with Ono's phantom architectures. They soon jumped from the flat surface of paper and canvas into the world. She painted polka dots on herself and others and scattered circular paper cut-outs on animals, plants and the environment in the performances that she made in the sixties during her extended stay in New York. (Jud Yalkut's film *Kusama's Self-Obliteration*, 1968, is an ebullient digest of these activities). In later installations and sculptures, the dots were produced mechanically rather than manually and covered flat-colored surfaces, such as rugged yellow pumpkins, vaguely tentacular appendixes, or curvaceous cavities halfway between pneumatic and organic. No matter how mechanical they might appear, Kusama's dots retain a link with the artist's subjectivity: obsessive and enveloping, they replicate the psychotic episodes she experienced since childhood, in which patterns multiplied around her, covering every available surface. This biographical reference, and the organic resonances of her installations and sculptures, also pose a limit to the dot as essential component of a controllable universe. In her work, dots cover the world but, far from reducing it to predictable patterns, they enhance its riotous materiality.

Riley's dotted canvases, for their part, were exempt of comparable personal reference. The product of painstaking handiwork, they evoked mechanical standards through painterly means, yet also introduced in her "periodic structures"—as they were named by a critic at the time—fractional irregularities and subtle modulations that evoked dizziness and disorientation. The dynamism of her dot-based structures was far from Kepes' utopianism. In the view of some critics, her work recalled the shakiness of the television signal and portended a similar invasion of the spectators' sensorium. For Thomas Hess, the influential editor of *Artnews* at the time of Riley's emergence in the early sixties, her work, like most of op art, had "the same quivering glare to the light, the same ping effects, the radar blips" that characterized "the appalling moiré patterns" of television.[39]

Andy Warhol and Richard Hamilton were also fascinated with the dissolution of the image into dots and with the potential for failure and semiotic derailment that this process entailed. While Lichtenstein assimilated industrial means of illustration into painting through manual means, giving them high-art endorsement, Warhol and Hamilton were interested in bringing painting into the realm of technologically mediated photography and illustration.[40] Warhol's "Death and Disaster" series and early star portraits—the Elvises, Marilyns, Lizes, and Jackies—were based on found press photographs, whose granularity was emphasized by silk-screening. In a manner analogous to halftone screens or Ben Day tinting plates, silkscreens allowed the paint to seep through unobturated pores in the fabric on which the design to be reproduced had previously been drawn. While silk-screening could render smooth tone and surface, Warhol preferred to accentuate the accidents that arose in the process: irregular coloring caused by uneven pressure, slips in registration, and smears and blots where the pores clogged, and the ink flowed erratically. By showing off the mistakes, his early silk-screened images emphasized their borrowed quality and the fact that they copied other copies. In Hal Foster's reading, these glitches also punctured the integrity and illusionism of the originals and encoded into surface texture the traumatic character of many of Warhol's images—testimonies of a culture steeped in death, transiency, and finitude.[41]

Hamilton, for his part, used grain as a fulcrum for an epistemology of the photograph and as a testing ground for the ability of painting to absorb new visual technologies.[42] Mid-sixties series such as *Whitley Bay* (1965), *Trafalgar Square* (1965–67) and *People* (1965–66) apply gouache and oil to canvases previously printed with photographic enlargements of details from found postcards. As the scale of the blow-ups grows, details lose legibility and end up becoming floating dots of tenuous referentiality. He illustrated this process in two popular formats. One is the multiples *To Mother* (1968), which consisted of a reproduction of the original postcard with an attached fold-out of eight progressive enlargements that grew increasingly abstract.[43] The second is Hamilton's brief cameo as an (unnamed) artist in Brian de Palma's film *Greetings* (1968), in which he casually explains the rationale of this particular piece to one of the film's characters while they share a bench in a New York park. "This is like the movie. Like *Blow-Up*," the character says. "So I am told," Hamilton replies, "but I did this eighteen months before." Hamilton does not appear again in *Greetings*, but his illustration of the relativity of photographic evidence impregnates de Palma's quirky comedy, in which characters muse on the unreliability of appearance and obsess on the Zapruder film and the visual testimony of the Kennedy assassination.

These works by Hamilton explore the border between reference and abstraction, a borderline that he situated at the heart of photography rather than in the procedures of painting, as was the usual modernist habit. The "moment of loss" when the referent disappears and the image modulates into an abstraction became the driving concern of the series.[44] That moment arises by probing into the minimal components that allow information to emerge: the dots and stains that translate the continuum of the world into reproducible images, but that may also dissolve images into unreadable surfaces. At the center of information, then, and as an essential component of its structure, lies noise. The grain of the photograph in these images by Hamilton is as much a structuring element as a vehicle for entropy—for the un-differentiation that dissolves patterns and turns images into dots, flecks, and unreadable blobs on a flat screen.

164   EXPERIMENTAL FILM AND QUEER MATERIALITY

Hamilton and Warhol were far from alone in their probing of the photographic dot. Filmmakers James and John Whitney, Stan Brakhage, and Carolee Schneemann—who was also a painter and performer—all acknowledged the structuring role of dots and dot-based patterns, bowing in this way to the insights of cybernetics and information theory. But they also generated discontinuous dot-based representations in contexts that bore little relation to the original concerns of information engineers—namely, in mysticism, psychophysical experimentation, and embodied perception.

Around 1950, James Whitney, who had been making abstract films with his brother John since the early forties—like the classic *Five Film Exercises* (1941–44)—started to produce animations of mandala-like shapes by using hand-drawn dot patterns. The first of these films was *Yantra* (1957), a term that designates patterns used in yogic meditation, to which Whitney was passionately attached. The film emerged at the crossroads of meditation and seriality. It started as the attempt to produce "a unity of structure" through repetition but eventually mutated into the striving to make "exterior imagery more closely related to the inner" and to mimic the experience of meditation, where forms congeal and dissolve in the mind. Both interests converged on the film's pulsing dot arrangements. For Whitney, the dotted image "gives a quality which in India is called the *Akasha*, or ether, a subtle element before creation like the *Breath of Brahma*, the substance that permeates the universe before it begins to break down into the more finite world."[45] Since the dot charts were extremely laborious to make by hand, he enlisted, for his later films, the computer programs that engineer and programmer Jack Citron had developed in collaboration with James's brother John for an early IBM graphic display console. The resulting film, *Lapis* (1966) is, like *Yantra*, another meditative piece where points in space quiver, congregate, and detach—in Gene Youngblood's words—with "implacable grace," generating multiple circular patterns and radiating structures to the drone of a tamboura.[46] If *Yantra* blended seriality and mysticism, *Lapis* added to the mix early digitized displays, which rendered, through electronic means, the atomized motility of Brahma's breath.

Dots were also the basic units of vision for Stan Brakhage, but he framed them in relation to the physiology of vision and to his own view of the cinema as an art of pure visuality unmediated by language or narrative. The primacy of granularity became evident, for him, in closed-eye vision, which is the result of pure optic feedback—the autotelic reaction of the optic nerves to the lack of light: "The primary thing that people see when they close their eyes is a whirling, grainy moving particles that . . . make shapes. I call them grains of sand. [Nineteenth-century German physiologist Herman von] Helmholtz called them flying gnats."[47] While Brakhage did not pursue further connections, these gnats or grains of sand may also be related to Julesz's "textons"—minimal stimuli that trigger perceptual processing in the cortex—and to Ralph Hartley's "elementary areas"—the squares into which an image could be divided for sampling and transmission, immediate antecedents of the pixel.[48] As people become socialized, Brakhage continues, the swirl of primal vision becomes stabilized into distinct forms through the agency of language. Language flattens the world into predetermined conceptual categories that deprive vision of its exfoliating multiplicity. In his films, Brakhage sought to revert the process and return viewers to a state of pristine, unmediated receptiveness, that is, to dissolve the phenomena unified by the effect of the word into the optical atoms out of which they were constituted. Enhancing granularity was one of the main ways to do so: "The film grain approximates the first stage of hypnagogic vision, which occurs at a pulse within the range of film's possibilities of projection."[49] In order to produce grainy fields, he processed his films with household chemicals, scratched and scoured them, and glued on them dust, polen, iron filings, and even moth wings and insects—as he did most famously in *Mothlight* (1963) and *The Garden of Earthly Delights* (1981).

The rationale for these experiments is largely the subject of his early collection of writings, *Metaphors on Vision* (1963). Familiar with some of the experiments at Bell Labs, especially through his friend and occasional collaborator, musician James Tenney, Brakhage acknowledges in one of the essays in the book the binary coding on which the digitization of information was based, but excoriates its habitual uses.[50] Camera-eye vision—meaning standard filmmaking—and "IBM" are "essentially restricted to 'yes-no,' 'stop-go,' 'on-off,' and instrumentally dedicated to communication of the simplest sort."[51] The atomization of vision and its dissolution into unbound minimal components, however, has the potential to transcend customary structures of perception and intelligibility: "Imagine a world alive with incomprehensible objects and shimmering with an endless variety of movement and endless gradations of color."[52] Such a world is not immediately composed of wholesale shapes, which betray the ballast of language on the senses, but of swirling particles and optical microevents conveying "the innards of what we once knew only as outline"; "the internal movement of each one object."[53] Rather than a spread of solid blue, the sky would appear as "flakes of God-gold of

166 EXPERIMENTAL FILM AND QUEER MATERIALITY

it falling as if down into my eyes" and the sea as inapprehensible multiple vibrancy. This inherent dynamism and uncontrollability of things was conveyed as well in sound poetry, in the poetry of Gertrude Stein or Chales Olson, or in the work of the Abstract Expressionists, "who are fashioning the symbol-cuneiform-hieroglyphic letters of future civilization" and toward whom Brakhage felt a strong sense of affinity.

If for Brakhage grain reverted to vision's neural baseline, for Carolee Schneeman, it brought back a kind of embodied perception reminiscent of her friend Yayoi Kosama's environments and performances, in which she occasionally participated. Schneemann's film *Kitch's Last Meal* (1976) contains a well-known monologue that she also incorporated, in truncated form, in her landmark performance *Interior Scroll* (1975, 1977). While in the film she recites it off-screen, asynchronously with the image, in the performance she read it out of a roll of paper that she extracted from her vagina while standing naked on a table. The monologue imagines an exchange between herself and a "structural filmmaker," "a happy man"—actually modeled on film critic Annette Michelson—who is dismissive of her work and appears to speak for a cabal of like-minded artists.

> He said we are fond of you
> you are charming.
> But don't ask us to look
> at your films.
> We cannot.
> There are certain films
> we cannot look at:
> the personal clutter
> the persistence of feelings
> the hand-touch sensibility
> the painterly mess
> the dense gestalt
> the primitive technique.

He advices:

> . . . you can do as I do
> take one clean process
> follow its strictest
> implications intellectually
> establish a system of
> permutations establish
> their visual set.[54]

QUEER CORPOREALITIES OF UNDERGROUND CINEMA   167

But his films do not lead Schneemann—or the persona in her monologue—
to high-minded abstractions, but immerse her in the concrete and corporeal.
She confesses:

> When I watch your
> films my mind wanders freely
> during the half hour of
> pulsing dots I dream of my lovers
> write a grocery list
> rummage in the trunk for a lost sweater.[55]

He protests her faulty intellection: "you are unable to appreciate the system
the grid / the numerical rational / procedure . . . the Pythagorean clues."

And yet, there is a lot of systematic procedure in Schneemann's work.
While she has often been read primarily as an artist focused on the sentient
body, explicit sexuality, and instinctual drives, an interpretation that she
herself has promoted, she was also profoundly aware of form and its effects
on perception. But her presentation of the body "without contrivance, fet-
ishization, displacement," has often obscured her sharp self-reflexivity.[56]
As she shrewdly observed: "The content can be used to trivialize the formal
complexity."[57] This complexity is evident in the careful plotting of her films,
commented by Ara Osterweil and Scott MacDonald, among others. They
are built, as Schneemann pointed out, on the cumulative effect of minimal integers of perception—the dot and its avatars. In her "Notebooks" of
1962, these integers are the marks of pigment on the painterly surface: "the
individualized mesh of individualized strokes, streaks, smudges, and marks,"
that convey subtle nuance in Velazquez or Monet or rhythmic motion in
Pollock.[58] In later work, the elementary unit of the image is photographic
grain. *Viet Flakes* (1966), which she premiered as part of her anti-Vietman
war performance *Snows* (1967), used extreme close-ups, created by placing
a magnifying glass in front of the lens, to dissolve press photographs of the
war into dotted tint patterns. Focus shifts and reframes turn what look like
"pointillistic black specks"—her words—into clusters of bombs dropped
from airplanes and into the horror-stricken faces of war victims. The soundtrack for the performance applied to music a similar oscillation between
signal and channel. James Tenney, Schneemann's husband at the time,
broke down musical pieces (by Bach, Mozart, The Beatles, Question Mark,
and the Mysterians) into fragments that became recognizable by effect of

168   EXPERIMENTAL FILM AND QUEER MATERIALITY

their scattered repetition.[59] And in interview with critic Scott MacDonald, Schneemann held that her diaristic film *Kitch's Last Meal*, a two-screen piece assembled from 8mm home movies shot during the mid-seventies, is less about "people (characters, personalization)" than about the visual patterns that emerge from its cadenced repetitions and grainy surface: "It is more as if the film is some constant motion of particles on which certain moments and pressure of material imprint themselves, and some of those imprints are persons, and some have more to do with elements in the landscape or changes of light."[60]

Hence, if Schneemann's mind wanders freely through the pulsing dots of structural film, it is not because of theoretical naiveté. It is just that her inquiries into process and structure do not lead only—as Peter Gidal advised—to the awareness of "film as film" but also to film as trace of the material, sentient body in the flow of experience. Much as permutational sets and Pythagorean implication matter, what matters *most* to Schneemann, as she put it in one of her latest essays, is "the drench, distractions, tensions, struggle of the daily art-life."[61] These are not alien contents arbitrarily overlaid on the grainy visuals. The dotted, pockmarked skin of her films conveys the pull and drag of workaday existence as well as its minute triumphs and illuminations.[62] Surface marks capture small accidents in her intimate environment, which become in this way permanently fixed on celluloid. Again in interview with MacDonald, she recalled that she edited her films in a dusty space, often invaded by insects and with her cat on her lap: "Every day another bunch of spiders had crawled under the table . . . I felt that all my images had to be available to the natural kinds of damages that would occur in my working situation."[63]

Damage and accident are to a large extent what *Kitch's Last Meal* is about. It is a poetic chronicle of a period of her life marked by the physical decline and eventual death of her cat, Kitch, her constant companion since the late fifties. In addition to documenting Kitch's last years, the film shows Schneemann writing, working on her art, meeting with friends, and sharing her life with her partner, filmmaker Anthony McCall, at her farm in upstate New York. During this period, her house is broken into, books are stolen, furniture is damaged—more clutter and mess. Much of the film is taken up with house chores: cooking, cleaning, tidying up, gardening, and feeding and caring for Kitch. These tasks revolve around "diet and digestion," with an emphasis on "die" in both words, she pointed out. They are metabolic processes that encapsulate the cycle of existence, the recurring rounds of emergence and dissolution that the boiling grain in the film, on which images rise and dissolve, also evokes.

Ono, Kusama, Riley, Warhol, Hamilton, Whitney, Brakhage, and Schneemann bring up the noisy underside of the new protocols of information modeling. Their exploration of the textural and informational capabilities of dots and discontinuous representation is indebted to the sampling, pulse code modulation, and digital reduction developed by postwar information technologies, which were intent on translating complex information bundles into computable units. Yet these artists put these possibilities to a far different use. In their work, granular rendering does not formalize information but produces oscillation, fluttering, and noise: sensual stimulation beyond sense, massage rather than message. Perhaps this is why film grain recurs so much in relation with queer bodies and sexualities that are caught in a dialectic of opacity and transparency, signal and noise, analogous to the one we have traced in this section. In this dialectic, grain is part of the vocabulary of what Jack Halberstam has called "the queer art of failure."[64] It visualizes the unpredictability and noise of the body and sexuality—that resistant kernel that we call *queerness*. Noise or failure, however, are not merely negative factors. Not yet recognizable as pattern, noise—like failure—is also generative; anthropologist Gregory Bateson, one of the pioneers in cybernetics, regarded it "the only possible source of *new* patterns," and, by extension, of new ways of thinking about and representing the body and its sexual and affective resonances.[65] Among these resonances are the uncontrollable vibrancy, vagueness, and permeability of queer bodies and sexualities. We can turn to some examples.

Grain and the Uncertain Corporealities of Underground Film

The graininess of Jack Smith's *Flaming Creatures* (1963) communicates temporal and corporeal indefiniteness. The film offers a disjointed series of tableaus in which people in retro drag flirt and dance together, embark on an orgy—a swirl of limbs and body parts—are killed in mid-joy by an earthquake, but rise again from the dead and shake off the dust to proceed with their frolics. The film's grain is the result of poverty and circumstance: of the outdated black and white Tri-X rolls that Smith apparently stole at a camera shop—they were reportedly in a bin near the door and therefore easy to

170 EXPERIMENTAL FILM AND QUEER MATERIALITY

purloin—and of the dim lighting on the set—the roof of the Windsor Theater, shadowed over by surrounding buildings during most of the shoot.[66]

Grain imparts on the film a dreaminess and ethereality that suits the ambiguity of the action and the unreality of the creatures that populate it. These creatures are ambiguously gendered beings whose rapport oscillates from dancing and collective smooching to (feigned) sexual assault immediately followed by further celebrating. The film's silvery hue rhymes with the retro quality of the iconography and the soundtrack: the performers impersonate thrift shop versions of classic movie glamour, and the musical cues, like the clothing styles, are largely memos from a bygone era—Franz Waxman's orchestral blasts, an Ernesto Lecuona bolero ("Siboney"), a turn-of-the century *pasodoble*, a Spanish *tonadilla*, and a tune from a Chinese film of the forties. In addition to being reminiscent of old Hollywood, the image has the tone of a faded photograph. Its graininess evokes the erosion caused by the passing of time, whose corrosive effect is compounded by sporadic overexposures and occasional lateral flares, probably caused by light leaking into the magazine, that white out portions of the frame. These surface accidents keep the image on the edge of dissolution, turning it into a precarious record of furtive desires that, because of their unlawful nature, are doomed to quick extinction, as in fact happened when the film was seized by city police in March of 1963 for its alleged violation of New York State obscenity laws. The uncertainty of the grainy, self-dissolving texture and the ambiguity of the action and of Smith's creatures mirror and abet each other. Overall, the film yields a tentative visuality that presents bodies and actions but also holds them at a remove, as they are seen but not totally known or knowable. This was, of course, central to Smith's aesthetic: he defended that film was a merely visual phenomenon—"a thing of lights and shadows"—not a discursive one, to be sensuously apprehended rather than critically dissected.[67] The rejection of discursive gloss reveals as well an anti-panoptic desire to thwart the attempts to categorize and explain bodies and sexualities that preferred to remain in flux, outside standard frames of intelligibility.

Film Creatures was already an underground classic, instantly canonized by its prosecution, when Warhol started to film his first significant title, *Sleep*, in early July of 1963.[68] *Sleep* is another example of the uncertain visuality associated with granular textures. It is a portrait of poet John Giorno asleep. Filmed at night with available light, it roils with grain, a quality accentuated by the rephotography of some of the takes. It is a fairly sexual film: Giorno's naked body is completely exposed and offers itself to unimpeded contemplation. But nakedness here does not necessarily mean availability; the fragmentary framing turns his body into an often unreadable abstraction in a field of dark grays. *Sleep* tries to possess visually—symbolically—a recalcitrant body that would not be "had" otherwise. While Warhol was sexually interested in Giorno, and they did enjoy an intermittent dalliance, they were not sexually compatible and Giorno preferred to remain a friend. As it makes the image more remote and complicates its visibility, graininess enhances the tension between desire and reality, availability and detachment. In the end, this body is not for Warhol nor for the film's spectators. It is a familiar trait in Warhol's films. As Douglas Crimp has said of the young man being fellated in *Blow Job* (1964), Giorno's body is not "for us," but remains opaque and unassailable in its particularity and uniqueness.[69] Affective complexity and respect for singularity, Crimp continues, are trademarks of Warhol's films as well as their queerest traits. It is a queerness that is reinforced by the boiling grain, whose chaotic churn suggests the difficulty of reading and defining the proximate, for the closer one gets to it, and the longer one observes, the fuzzier and blurrier its contours become, the more the image slides into abstraction, and the less it may be reduced, owned, or possessed.

Carolee Schneemann's *Fuses* (1967) is seldom discussed as a significant queer text, yet in many ways it is. It breaks the taboo on explicit sexual representation, breaches the divide between private and public, and depicts the complicated affects attendant on the sexual act—mostly joy, with occasional intimations of tension, vulnerability, and even pain. Perhaps most importantly, it is a direct attack against the gendered division of labor characteristic of Western artistic representation, in which women were routinely objects of the gaze but seldom its subjects. "I WAS PERMITTED TO BE AN IMAGE BUT NOT AN IMAGE-MAKER CREATING HER OWN IMAGE," Schneemann once wrote.[70] She filmed herself and her husband James Tenney having sex—although a few scenes were also shot by friends like filmmaker Stan Vanderbeek—and intercut explicit moments and close-ups of their genitals and other body parts with images of their house, their daily routines, the surrounding landscape, Schneemann bathing in the ocean, and Schneemann's cat Kitch, whom she called the main spectator of the action.[71] The image is hand-colored, scratched, and stamped with stenciled geometric shapes, and often contains several layers of superimposition and abundant grain.

172   EXPERIMENTAL FILM AND QUEER MATERIALITY

Fuses brings into cinema the explorations of the weight, density, and energy of the body that Schneemann had been carrying out at the time in painting and performance. In *Meat Joy*, for example, first performed four years before *Fuses* was completed, she and some collaborators rolled on the floor and on each other naked, splattered with paint, covered with dead chickens, fish, and garbage, and entangled in transparent plastics. By her own admission, *Fuses* sought to translate into images her perceptions during "the intimacy of lovemaking"—perceptions characterized by a mixture of density and transparency, of holding on to and losing one's body. One may see the density in the visual intricacy of the film, in the suggested weight and mass of bodies in the throes of passion, and even in the actual bulk that her camera original acquired as an ever-growing body. Since Schneemann did not have access to an optical printer, she taped layers of film together, making her working reel so thick that it would not run through the gate. Transparency, on the other hand, is communicated by the airy feel of scenes shot through, or against, windows and door frames, or by takes of Schneemann emerging from the ocean against a vast blue sky. Grain contributes further to this dialectic of corporeal density and transparency. It adds another coating to the images, increasing their thickness and material presence. But at the same time, as a porous, inconsistent surface, grain also threatens to volatilize the bodies in the film, acting in concert with the splashes of color and the black shapes that block their visibility.

The push-and-pull between density and transparency is analogous to the dialectic of blindness and vision that Ara Osterweil has located in the film's rendering of sexuality. This is in part a matter of distance: "Although certain hard-core images of the 'fuck' remain recognizable, the closer the camera gets to the erotic encounter, the less visible the specific machinations of sex become."[72] It is also a matter of Schneemann's conception of vision as "an aggregate of sensations" that involves tactility and spatial orientation as well. The close-ups of body parts, the abstraction, the visible splices and traces of hand-processing, and the film's layered intricacy convey a tactile, embodied vision. They also simulate the experience of sexuality as engulfment and (Osterweil's term) "immersive blindness": a surfeit of corporeal stimulus that the brain cannot process into an orderly configuration. Grain enhances the haptic quality of *Fuses* by embedding the image in a vibratory intermittence that transforms body mass into something like a tickle or a caress.

It is an un-gendered tickle, as the visual style of the film works to volatilize gender difference. While some scenes showcase a clear sexual dimorphism

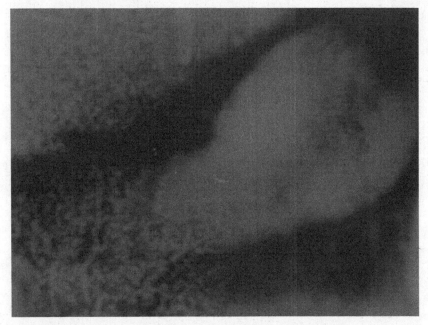

Figure 6.1 Carolee Schneemann, *Fuses*, 1967. Frame enlargement.

in the form of distinct active/passive, penetrator/penetrated roles, in others, erect or semi-turgid penises and caressed labia appear disconnected from the bodies where they belong, interspersed with abstractions or with takes of the filmmakers' environs, and made adjacent, through editing, to either Schneemann or Tenney, as if wandering indifferently between both (see Figure 6.1). The editing, as Schneemann has pointed out, deliberately dissolves the difference between male and female genitals by sliding from one to the other so that neither is fixed by a static, objectifying stare.[73] Thick textures, extreme close-ups, and foggy grain further obliterate the bodies' particulars. For much of its length, rather than recognizably gendered bodies, the film offers a vibrant, fleshy ensemble of uncertain limits and attributes. In fact, besides blurring the binary gender economy, the editing also volatilizes the boundaries between bodies and their environment. Far from confined to the couple, sexuality is pervasive and all-englobing, amply spread across the lovers' milieu. The lovers merge and interweave with their living spaces and surrounding nature as much as they do with each other. Schneemann recalled: "I montaged a burning bush joke—there's a close-up of my 'bush.' Then the clouds over a silhouetted bush—the sun setting behind

174 EXPERIMENTAL FILM AND QUEER MATERIALITY

the shrub."[74] The film's granularity is the medium that brings it all together in interconnected sentience.

Much less known than Smith, Warhol, or Schneemann, Tom Chomont emerged into the underground in the late-sixties, even though he had been making films since the beginning of the decade. He was a member of Gregory Markopoulos's circle—along with filmmakers José Rodríguez Soltero, Nathaniel Dorsky, Jerome Hiler, Robert Beavers, Andrew Meyer, and Warren Sonbert—and eventually followed Markopoulos and Beavers to Europe, where he lived with them for several years, leading a nomadic existence.[75] By the early eighties he returned to the United States and settled in New York. Chomont's work oscillates between the diaristic and the structural. Most of his titles recorded, in elliptical, poetic fashion, incidents of his life, acquaintances, and relationships—first on film and, after the early 1980s, on video, which eventually became his preferred medium. Part of his 1970s work consists in structural exercises in rhythm and form. The early films belong to the tradition of the trance film: they present dreams and twilight perceptions using complex color schemes and intricate hand-processed textures.

Grain is a constant in Chomont, from the early 8mm work to the 16mm films to the analog videos, where the correlate of film grain is pixels and variable scan-line density. In the work on celluloid, grain is enhanced by shifts between color positive and black-and-white negatives and by overlaying positive and negative, and, at times, differently tinted takes of the same image. This shows a structural awareness: a desire to explore the fundamentals of the image. But his investigation of form and materials also has mystical overtones. Through grain and texture he sought to reproduce on film the raw space and untouched portions in Cezanne's canvasses. But he also tried to communicate his belief in the embeddedness and plurality of the world and the self: of a reality inhabited by multiple, often mutually invisible realms and a subjectivity capable of hosting a variety of selves.[76]

The dance of grain gives form to the infinite divisibility of matter and selfhood. Film for Chomont, and for many other filmmakers of his generation, bridged the material and spiritual; it transcended the banality of the world, revealing the hidden energies that inhabited it and connecting it to supernatural principles. This supra-natural energy often emanates from the sexualized body, a body that is always other than itself, multiplied, exfoliating, haunted by impulses that push it beyond its habitual boundaries and make it lose its contours. This is the reason why bodies in his films are so often doubly, or

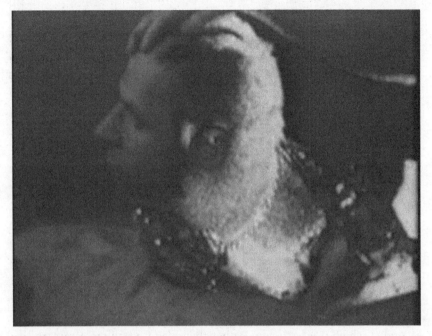

Figure 6.2 Tom Chomont, *Razor Head*, 1980. Frame enlargement.

triply inscribed, inhabited by slightly differing, layered versions of themselves (*Oblivion* 1969), crossed by lines of force and beams of light, filled with gaps (*Ophelia, Jabbok*), torn apart into a proliferation of floating parts (*Love Objects* 1971), or scattered into fields of grain (*Razor Head* 1980, see Figure 6.2).

By the early 1970s, when Chomont decamped for Europe after Markopoulos and Beavers, the example and rhetorical strategies of the American underground were spreading across the world, particularly across Europe and Latin America, where similar alternative film scenes emerged. One of the most active underground scenes sprang up in France in the early seventies around the filmmakers of the *école du corps* mentioned in Chapter 5. Teo Hernández and Michel Nedjar, who is primarily a painter and sculptor, are among the most remarkable exponents of this scene, authors of substantial output depicting their intimate environments, lives, and friendships in grainy Super-8. In their work, bodies oscillate between mass and motion; as soon as they assert their presence, they are turned, by means of camera movement and framing, into blurs of energized flesh and color. The title of Nedjar's *Gestuel* (1978) alludes to his gestural camera style, which

176   EXPERIMENTAL FILM AND QUEER MATERIALITY

dissolves the body of Gaël Badaud—also a filmmaker and a frequent presence in Nedjar's and Hernández's films—into smudges by means of abrupt hand-held motion. Filmed in a dim black-walled chamber, Badaud puts on and takes off a red tank top, swathes his arms in white gauze, wears a gas mask—while explosions and gun shots rack the soundtrack—and plays with a small hand mirror while the camera pans across and around him. The result is a grainy field disturbed by movement and washes of color that precipitate into shape on the few occasions when Badaud keeps still, or the camera momentarily comes to rest on him. Blackouts interrupt the brief takes and give the film a hiccupping rhythm. As Nedjar did not look through the viewfinder during the shoot, it was his body's intuitive motion rather than his eyesight that determined framing.

Gestuel had an important influence on Hernández, inspiring his *Corps aboli* (1978), and most of his subsequent filmmaking. *Corps aboli* is a stripped-down version of *Gestuel* with Badaud nude and with his head shaven in what looks like the same black-box setting of Nedjar's film. His motion is slower now—and further slowed down by screening speeds of 16 and 18 frames per second at which it was shown. Rather than play frontally to a camera that swirls across his body, both the camera, placed at a slightly high angle with regard to him, and Badaud himself wander in the semi-darkness, at times intersecting and other times missing each other in a somnambulistic hide-and-seek that often yields screens of black and grey dots. Halfway through, the film becomes dominated by close-ups of body parts that are often barely legible and filmed out of focus. While Hernández's work had explored, since the beginning, the interplay of camera and body, *Corps aboli* launched him into the exploration of bodies in motion captured through a camera that moves independently of them, a direction that culminated in numerous collaborations, in the last years of his life, with French choreographers Bernardo Montet and Catherine Diverrés.

While in Nedjar's and Hernández's films grain is allied to moving bodies and to a restless camera that hovers around them, in the work of Iván Zulueta, a Spanish underground filmmaker active mostly in the seventies, it is associated to corporeal stasis. What movement there is tends to be created on camera through frame-shooting, which grants objects and people a staccato dynamism similar to the one discussed in relation to Marie Menken's films in Chapter 2. Zulueta's films are inhabited by loners and dreamers who hang out in somber rooms bathed in the bluish glow of the television screen, gaze at themselves in the mirror, dress, undress, smoke, doze, talk on the phone, and wait, as does the glamorous female protagonist of *Leo es pardo* (1978) or the dandified male character in *Aquarium* (1975). The title of this last one adequately suggests that Zulueta's characters live as if enclosed in a terrarium or a fish-bowl, separated from the world by thick glass walls. In an uncommon spurt of curiosity toward the outside, the protagonist of *Aquarium* (1975) peeks into the street from his high-rise apartment to see police vans parked under his window; he grimaces with disgust and immediately pulls back inside, brusquely closing the shutters. Grain further enhances the sense of distance and withdrawal of these enigmatic creatures. Zulueta's signature use of time-lapse further suggests that around them life moves to a different clock. As they languish indoors, the sun rises and sets in fast motion, clouds scoot across the sky like rockets, and cigarettes speed-burn to extinction. In addition, things take on an unusual liveliness: closet doors and drawers open and close spasmodically, sinks fill up and drain out, objects migrate across the room, and the toilet bowl becomes glutted with a rising mountain of paper balls that materialize from nowhere. Grain further conveys the feeling of a reality furtively observed; of looking in uninvited as in surveillance footage. It also evokes narcosis, particularly in films such as *A-Mal-Gam-A* (1976), a gloomy figuration of heroin solipsism and narcissistic retreat.

* * *

Across these vastly different examples, grain indexes film's materiality. It pops cinematic illusionism, highlights that cinema is a surface effect—a two-dimensional projection—and brings to the fore the chemical substrate of the image. Yet, as I have been maintaining throughout, grain also conveys a different kind of materiality—the materiality of the body and sexuality. Grain's discontinuity and unevenness deflates not only the ideality of cinema but also sexuality's idealistic overtones: its presumed orientation toward wholeness, personalized quality, and narrative directionality. Grain underlines instead the molecular pulses that animate the sensual body and transform it into a scattering of stimuli on a sentient surface. It recreates desire as an overall elation rather than a genitally-located pleasure, and flattens the hierarchies that conventional sexuality establishes among body parts. In the films we have discussed, faces and genitals, usual foci of desire, are either elided or made equivalent with any other body part. In addition, as grain flattens depth and blurs the distinction between figure and ground, it blends the corporeal into its surrounding milieu, turning the body into a material pulsation and the environment into a sentient expanse.

178 EXPERIMENTAL FILM AND QUEER MATERIALITY

Exempt of genital telos or narrative frames, the grainy sexuality of the films discussed here unfolds as a static intensity rather than the pursuit of a goal, and provides an atmosphere rather than a narrative arc from foreplay to consummation. Warhol's *Sleep*, Nedjar's *Gestuel* or Hernandez's *Corps aboli* portray static situations or repeat a simple premise with slight variations and next to no development. In Chomont's *Razor Head* there is minimal progress as the head of a young man is gradually shaved, yet the emphasis of the film is not on completion, but on the sensuous tension of the scene, in which a man submits to the manipulations of another one who remains mostly off-screen. Such situational rather than goal-oriented sexuality owes as much to the conception of the body as sentient surface as to the temporality of grain. The intermittence of the dots, constantly in motion but constantly in place, accentuates repetitiveness and cyclicality. It overlays the actions portrayed with a second temporal order characterized by insistence and recurrence; this temporal order exerts a gravitational drag that stalls and delays what action there is, anchoring it on a sort of eternal present that is constantly repeated yet never quite the same.

In the dialectic between sameness and difference may reside part of the fascination with grain. Granular representation encapsulates a dialectic intrinsic to form between containment and spillage, figuration and dissolution. Grainy images arise from the attempt to rationalize image reproduction at the end of the nineteenth century and received further impulse from the protocols for the modeling and digitization of information developed by cybernetics during and after World War II. But as Kepes pointed out during cybernetics' heyday and subsequent artists—from Ono and Kusama to Warhol and Hamilton—were quick to perceive, grain also communicated the irreducible dynamism of form and the processual character of reality. In turn, sixties and seventies underground filmmakers channeled through it critical visualities, "effervescent" bodies—Sally Banes's term—and lively materiality.[77]

As they used grain to convey the sensuality of dissident bodies and the vibrancy of matter around them, underground filmmakers foregrounded the chemical substratum of cinematic illusionism without dispelling film's capacity for fascination and pleasure. Their use of grain questions the binary logic that underpinned the theory of structural-materialist cinema, usually discussed through dualities such as illusionism versus materialism, eclipsing versus foregrounding the apparatus, seduction versus critique, yielding to imaginary wholeness versus waking to the fragmenting imperative of the signifying chain. Grain in underground film works on both sides of these binaries and resists their dual schematism. It invites us to envision a queer materialism skilled at having it all—at being debunking *and* seductive, critical *and* pleasurable, capable of undermining conventional visuality in the very act of contemplating the irrepressible vitality of bodies and worlds that will not stay still and will forever refuse to behave.

7

The Afterlives of Film Grain

Precarious Bodies and Poor Images

The fascination with granularity extends well beyond 1960s and 1970s experimental film and reaches into the present. During this time, grain has led a peculiar afterlife hosted by a medium whose death began to be announced in the late eighties, as celluloid gradually ceased to be the dominant moving image technology, challenged—first by analog video and later by the rise of the digital image. The presumed demise of cinema, which turned out to be its pluralization across a variety of platforms, contexts, and devices, was not only brought about by the vogue of competing supports, but also by the phasing out of its traditional configuration as an eminently public, collective form of entertainment. Analog video and digital technologies propitiated the spread of home viewing and helped to make cinema also a domestic, individualized experience. Throughout the repositioning of cinema in a new visual environment, grain has remained on the horizon in works—including in digital video—that seek to replicate the artisanal look, organic feel, and nostalgic associations of celluloid texture. Much more trenchantly, grain is very much alive in experimental film, which remains concerned with the specificity of the medium and amply uses small-gauge formats and processes that heighten textural accidents and different forms of inscription on the celluloid surface, as Kim Knowles and Jonathan Walley have exhaustively theorized and documented.[1]

This chapter looks at the afterlives of the granular image in two different repertoires: AIDS-related film of the eighties and early nineties and queer experimental film (and, very occasionally, video) from the nineties to the present. The first of these repertoires is more compact in focus, chronological distribution, and roster of participants than the second—a sprawling, unwieldy field that this chapter will traverse selectively in an attempt to account for and structure the uses of grain in recent queer production. The meaning of film grain varies in each of these repertoires. If during the 1960s and 1970s, as we have pointed out in Chapter 6, the rough texture of queer underground

Experimental Film and Queer Materiality. Juan A. Suárez, Oxford University Press. © Oxford University Press 2024.
DOI: 10.1093/oso/9780197566992.003.0007

FILM GRAIN: PRECARIOUS BODIES, POOR IMAGES   181

film opposed the smooth finish and bland sexuality of Hollywood, from the mid-eighties forward, as celluloid grew marginal in the media ecology, grain came to signify different kinds of "pastness" and vulnerability. In a context determined by the devastation of AIDS and by activist responses to the pandemic, the grainy celluloid image acquired an elegiac tonality and connoted not only the fragility of queer bodies and pleasures and the precariousness of queer visual memory but also resilience in the face of crisis. In more recent decades, in an environment dominated by the digital image and its fixation with fidelity and transparency, grain is one of the traits of what Hito Steyerl called "the poor image."[2] It is the look of archival immersion, queer cinephilia, memory, and fantasy and the support of the abstract corporealities that rise from the manipulation and decay of the emulsion.

AIDS, Vulnerability, and the Reparative

AIDS film—as opposed to video—was a relative rarity and has been largely neglected by critics and historians. The AIDS crisis coincides with the commercialization of portable video cameras, and visual activism was most often channeled through this support. Video was cheaper than film, easier to shoot and edit, and extremely movable—especially after the appearance of the camcorder, Video 8, and Hi8 halfway through the decade. In addition, it did not require development, and even though projection equipment was not yet easily available, videotapes could be effectively shown to small groups on standard television monitors. Furthermore, the flat, pixelated video image seemed more urgent and biting than celluloid. Video bore the look of television, of immediacy and quickness, and offered instant reports of sit-ins, demonstrations, and zap actions. Celluloid, however, was technically demanding, retained a patina of artistry and lyricism, and was more connected to the history of earlier experimental film than to the struggles of the moment. In addition, video work was often collective, while celluloid work tended to be solitary, a quality that linked it further to a romantic aestheticism more suited to easier times than to the middle of a pandemic.

Still, quite a few artist-activists, such as Barbara Hammer, Jerry Tartaglia, Roger Jacoby, David Wojnarowicz, Lawrence Brose, and Jim Hubbard, used celluloid in ways that were both political and poetic, confrontational, and experimental. Their work, however, has been often bypassed by criticism of queer AIDS-related media by Alexandra Juhasz, Douglas Crimp, and Gregg

182 EXPERIMENTAL FILM AND QUEER MATERIALITY

Bordowitz, whose main interests lay in video,[3] and by the main narratives of the eighties film avant-garde by Tom Gunning, Paul Arthur, and Joan Hawkins.[4] Of varied backgrounds, aesthetics, and careers, these filmmakers cannot be easily englobed in one group, as they only shared some personal ties and the interest in visualizing AIDS. While they were all born in a little over a decade—Hammer and Jacoby were born in 1939 and 1945, respectively, and Tartaglia, Hubbard, Brose, and Wojnarowicz, in the early fifties—by the eighties, Hammer and Jacoby already had significant trajectories, while Tartaglia, Hubbard, Brose, and Wojnarowicz were starting theirs. They all worked under the shadow of the sixties underground, to which they were indebted, but their ways of assimilating it varied considerably among them. Tartaglia, Hubbard, Brose, and Jacoby made mostly lyrical shorts, even though Hubbard also made the feature-length diary film, *Homosexual Desire in Minnesota* (1981–85). Wojnarowicz was closer to the punk aesthetic of the "cinema of transgression" and collaborated with some of its practitioners, such as Richard Kern. And Hammer alternated at the time between abstract, optically driven work; short activist video pieces (*Snow Job*, 1986); and essay films, such as *Nitrate Kisses* (1991) and *History Lessons* (2000), meditations on queer history marked by the urgency of AIDS.

Despite this stylistic range, these filmmakers coincided in the graininess of their images. Granularity communicates in their work different forms of queer vulnerability: of queer bodies in the middle of an epidemic and of queer memory—the incomplete record of a past that has often been forcibly erased. Both types of vulnerability are signified by the obsolescence of cinema in the age of video—as a medium marked for eventual disappearance—and by the precarious chemistry of celluloid. Film's material support is, like the organic body, subject to deterioration and decay over time, a deterioration that increases with its use. As David Rodowick has noted, "the chemical substrate of film is perhaps the most impermanent and variable substance for the registration of images yet found in the history of art-making: what doesn't explode in flames (nitrate) will slowly dissolve (vinegar syndrome). . . . [T]he material basis of film is a chemically encoded process of entropy."[5] The impermanence of the celluloid image was also heightened by hand-processing, which became quite popular in the seventies, with filmmakers increasingly developing and printing their own films. They often did so in open disregard of industrial standards, with the purpose of generating visual effects that could not be achieved through orthodox developing and printing.[6] Hand-processing further revealed the fragility of film's chemistry and the

FILM GRAIN: PRECARIOUS BODIES, POOR IMAGES   183

susceptibility of the celluloid image to different kinds of erosion and manipulation. With its fragile body marked by obsolescence, vulnerability, and decay, film was a suitable medium to reflect on the fragility of queer life and its traces, all the more when this life was lived under the pressure of the homophobic backlash that accompanied the AIDS crisis since its emergence in the early 1980s.

In Barbara Hammer's most directly historical films, *Nitrate Kisses* (1992) and *History Lessons* (2000), grain signifies the fragility of a queer past that—to cite Walter Benjamin's well-known words—"flashes at a moment of danger" and must be rescued before it vanishes irretrievably.[7] Like the porous granularity of old films, the queer past is less a smooth continuum than a pitted field scarred by erasure and loss. The beginning of *Nitrate Kisses* combines Hammer's voiced-over reflections on the untraceability of much queer history with panoramic shots of dilapidated neighborhoods, full of vacant lots and burnt-out, boarded up homes filmed in grainy black and white. This sequence is followed by another metaphorically blasted site. Speaking off-screen over images of the Nebraska plains and early twentieth-century photographs of writer Willa Cather in men's clothing, Hammer recalls that the writer often dressed in male garb as a young woman, but turned to conventional female clothing and to a life of utter discretion halfway through college. Shortly before death, she burned her correspondence, destroying, along with it, the possibility of a more intimate knowledge of her life and, through its testimony, of a slice of queer experience. The gaps in the queer past and in the urban landscape are replicated in the molecular fragmentariness of the image's dancing dots—a way of inscribing fragility on the very skin of the film. In a later sequence, the camera wanders in the dappled shadow under a pier; nearby, a man combs the area with a metal detector, casually entering and leaving the frame. In the soundtrack, two German historians discuss the homophobia that has shaped the accounts of some Holocaust survivors who abhorred the presence of lesbians in the camps or deliberately omitted mentioning them. In search of erased traces, one moves in the shadows and sifts the sands of the past. The checkered shade, the grains of sand, and the film grain are emblems of discontinuity and incompleteness, tropes for a damaged collective memory. The only images grainier than these are the takes of young lesbian couples making love that are woven into the second half of the film. (See Figure 7.1) Leather-harnessed, tattooed, pierced, and with their hair spiked and partly shaven, they are the queer present, and perhaps an update of Hammer's own *Dyketactics* (1974), a lyrical, explicit

Figure 7.1 Barbara Hammer, *Nitrate Kisses*, 1992. Frame enlargement.

depiction of lesbian sex in the seventies. The extreme graininess of those sequences—captured in 8mm—recalls the frothy enjoyment that grain transmits in the underground films of the sixties but also hints at the precariousness of this enjoyment. The present, too, may be subject to erasure; it is not any safer from the homophobia bent on blotting out all traces of queer possibility.

While *Nitrate Kisses* focuses on loss, *History Lessons* centers on its recovery. It tries to construct a lesbian imaginary from the same artifacts used to closet it: lesbian scenes in 8mm porn film, educational films, early twentieth-century stereopticon erotic photographs, newsreel coverage of a women's convention presided over by Eleanor Roosevelt, and even an Edison film of a woman's execution by hanging—an allegory of the extreme violence meted out to the sexually heterodox. Some of the found footage is badly worn and scratched by use; deliberately added blots and stains underline its critical condition as remains perched on the verge of disappearance. Sound and images are played against each other, often humorously, to produce an oscillation between latent and manifest, past repression, and present recovery. In Eleanor Roosevelt's cheerful address to a council of terminally

FILM GRAIN: PRECARIOUS BODIES, POOR IMAGES   185

proper doyennes gathered in the early forties to discuss "the women's question," Hammer replaced the word "woman" with "lesbian," parachuting Roosevelt—rumored to have had female lovers—into contemporary queer politics. An 8mm porn film of two women making love is crosscut with the demure conversation of two teenage girls confessing their very special friendship to each other in a fifties television show; juxtaposed against the sexually explicit image, the bland show is turned from a site of loss, where lesbian desire was no sooner hinted at than quickly covered up, into one of recovery, where it may be more clearly ascertained. If, in *Nitrate Kisses*, graininess is an allegory for the gaps and the fragility of queer collective memory, in *History*, it stands for the ambiguity of a visual archive that allows us to conjecture a queer imaginary where none is extant. The dots of history can be joined in many different ways.

While Hammer reaches back to the early twentieth century and the postwar years in order to rescue a collective queer memory for the present, many of Jim Hubbard's films look at the present as if it were long gone. With its granular surface, silvery hue, and occasional bleached-out frames, *June 12, 1982* (1982) looks like a badly damaged reel of a demonstration long past, but the contemporary fashions and hairdos and the topical placards and banners indicate otherwise. The film conveys the present through the eyes of the future, turning a vibrant event into a memory trace. The change is brought about by the intrinsic capacity of photochemical media to fix and archive the contemporary moment. *June 12, 1982* also depicts this process in individual terms. What the film captures is not only an event—an anti-nuclear energy demonstration with substantial queer presence, as it turns out—but its dissolution into a multiplicity of passersby, most of them anonymous. They form a constellation of unrepeatable singularities—complex entanglements of corporeality, personality, and experience that Hubbard's film registers as they fleet by toward oblivion and finitude.

Several of Hubbard's other films are similarly situated at the crossroads of private and public, individual and collective, present and past. *Two Marches* (1991) juxtaposes footage of two gay and lesbian demonstrations held in Washington, DC: one in 1979, at the height of the sexual liberation movement, and a second one in 1987, amid the AIDS crisis. And *Elegy in the Streets* (1989) registers mid-1980s demonstrations, protests, and zap actions by the activist collective ACT-UP New York, of which Hubbard was a member at the time. Just like *June 12, 1982*, *Elegy*, and *Two Marches* are couched in an intensely textured grain—parts of *Two Marches* were filmed in

186 EXPERIMENTAL FILM AND QUEER MATERIALITY

Super 8—deliberately augmented through hand processing. Solarization and bleaching fade the image and bleed its contours, and impart on these films a ghostliness that makes them pivot between lyrical and documentary. Texture also heightens the film's subjective perspective, which is as much collective chronicle as Hubbard's personal recollections.

Both films pay homage to filmmaker Roger Jacoby, Hubbard's friend, boyfriend, and mentor, who had died from AIDS-related illnesses in 1985, shortly before these films were made. Jacoby recurs in both titles in brief shots that are tinted blue, printed in negative, heavily scratched, and shimmering with flares. *Elegy* also contains subtle homages to Jacoby's filmmaking: the frame is cracked and layered with the reticulated patterns that Jacoby created in his own works by immersing exposed film stock in baths of different temperatures. *Two Marches* opens with Jacoby and Hubbard embracing in the street, a personal prelude to a collective event; in the soundtrack, the duo "Parìgi, O Cara," from *La Traviata*, professes long-lasting love and hope in a future that turned out to be sadly unavailable both in the opera and in Jacoby's life. In *Elegy*, Jacoby appears in a garden, in nature, and engaged in various domestic routines. Flowers, as emblems of ephemerality, and a campy angel-like figure who bats his wings (two stretches of cloth) in slow motion underline the melancholia announced by the title.[8] The graininess in both films communicates domesticity—daily life caught on the run—and perishability. Yet for all the sorrowful overtones, grain also evokes the immediacy of guerrilla filmmaking, particularly in the scenes of a confrontation in front of the Capitol, in *Two Marches*, and in the confrontations with the police in *Elegy*. Roger Haller noted that, as if anticipating Douglas Crimp's famous essay, *Elegy* intertwines mourning and militancy, two impulses that were often regarded as antithetical at the time.[9] Protest helps to process loss, while mourning, recalibrated as a public rather than individual experience, fosters mobilization and collective action.

Neither mourning nor militance lack humor or sexiness. In *Elegy*, a man in fairy drag, which includes diminutive wings and a wand, skates gracefully through a demonstration. In a different scene, the angel shakes his floppy wings next to a naked man lying down with his genitals fully exposed to the camera; with casual posture—gently swinging foot, hand keeping the sun off his face—the man spoofs elegiac statuary and stands in humorous contrast to the angel's melancholy demeanor (see Figure 7.2). The skating fairy and the angel and his bemused companion are avatars of the ridiculous—a combination of exuberant campiness, anger, and humor that Gregg Bordowitz

Figure 7.2 Jim Hubbard, *Elegy in the Streets*, 1989. Frame enlargement. Courtesy of Jim Hubbard.

discussed as a queer structure of feeling in much AIDS protest and activist video.[10] But the recumbent nude may also be a reminder of pleasure. Even with a heavy heart, the angel still has his fun. In another scene, a naked Jacoby administers himself a shot in the bathroom, vulnerable but also sexy with his lithe body and boyish charm. The tonal instability of these scenes may be these films' most radical trait: their refusal to settle on any one mood and their willingness to remain in transit across anger, humor, loss, and sex. The dance of grain, along with scratches and flares, are formal correlatives for Hubbard's films fluid affect.[11]

If Hammer looks at the past from the perspective of the present, and Hubbard looks at the present as if it were already past, Jerry Tartaglia occupies a middle ground. He mobilizes images of the immediately pre-AIDS years as catalysts for political awareness. His films *A.I.D.S.C.R.E.A.M.* (1988) and *Ecce Homo* (1989) recycle seventies gay pornography—testimony of an arrested sexual revolution—in order to denounce the repression of sexuality provoked by AIDS. In *A.I.D.S.C.R.E.A.M.*, the title of the film in dramatic block letters slides horizontally across the screen interrupting the spectacle

188 EXPERIMENTAL FILM AND QUEER MATERIALITY

of sexual enjoyment while a voice in the soundtrack protests the desexualization of gay life prompted by the pandemia and the slanderous conflation of gayness and disease. Tinted and printed in negative, the excerpts of seventies porn look remote and evoke the dispossession of what was once a rich, fully owned sexual culture. In *Ecce Homo*, the evocation of AIDS is more roundabout. Making skillful use of the optical printer, the screen is split into four quadrants of changing size; at times they all play simultaneously while other times some quadrants are blank.[12] Toward the end, they fade to black one by one. All the excerpts that make up the film are densely scratched and grainy, and in some of them the emulsion has begun to turn orange. They reproduce fragments of Jean Genet's (once prosecuted) *Un Chant d'amour* (1950) alongside sequences of seventies hard-core gay porn and blank screens of different colors. The pornographic segments recall the empowering joys of sex while the fragments of *Un Chant d'amour*—a guard furtively peeps at prisoners masturbating in their cells and puts a gun in the mouth of one of them— allegorizes the phobic response to untrammeled pleasure. Throughout the film, a fragmented, incantatory monologue in Tartaglia's own voice mixes descriptions of Genet's film with reflections on the policing of desire, the memory of the Stonewall revolt, and the disruptive power of uninhibited "homosex," and ends in a call to arms: "Personal desire is power.... Collective desire is power. Reclaim our desire, reclaim our power." The Gregorian chant audible under the filmmaker's words suggests the complicity of organized religion—particularly the Catholic church—in the repression of sexuality, a collusion often targeted by activists.[13] Although there is no explicit mention of AIDS in the film, the juxtapositions between pleasure and control, free sexual activity and imprisonment, and the dual spectacle of the gay body as subject of pleasure and object of punishment evokes the shift from the sexual liberation of the 1970s to the criminalization of queer sexualities in the 1980s, when they were held responsible for the spread of AIDS. Grain here evokes pastness once again: a hard-won, recently lost sexual·utopia whose memory could be mobilized against a repressive present.

In both films celluloid—grainy, faded, tinted, damaged—harbors the revolutionary spark. Tartaglia's subsequent *Final Solutions* (1990) further cements this idea. Edited into the flow of shrill advertisements directly filmed off the television set, two self-portraits of the filmmaker in grainy celluloid present the unassimilable gay body. Tartaglia's voice in the soundtrack ruminates: "The final solution is management of all situations. Consume and be consumed. Tolerate, adapt, incorporate, manage the disease, manage

FILM GRAIN: PRECARIOUS BODIES, POOR IMAGES 189

the resistant underground." Against the gaudiness and vapidity of consumer goods, the filmmaker is the unmanageable image from the resistant underground. He appears, alternately, in his leather gear and lying naked in the grass in two blue-tinted scenes. His recalcitrance is also conveyed by the difference between the variable dance of grain in his sections and the managed regularity of the pixels of the television screen.

In addition to the vagaries and frailty of queer memory, grain also communicates a kind of corporeal vulnerability that was acutely felt in the time of AIDS and that was depicted in the films of Carl M. George, Lawrence Brose, and David Wojnarowicz. Most vulnerable were, of course, HIV-positive bodies. Carl M. George's *DHPG, Mon Amour* (1989) depicts in Super 8 the daily life of a gay couple, both HIV-positive, one of whose members uses DHPG (dihydroxyphenyl glycine) as an alternative to AZT in order to boost his immune system. The home footage of the partners shopping, cooking, watching television, and preparing and administering a DHPG solution through an intravenous feed is accompanied by their voice-over commentary on their life together and on the effects of the drug. The punctured, infused body in the film has an analogue in the grainy, pockmarked Super 8 capture, yet their combination does not convey damage and decline. Despite the progress of the disease—the DHPG user went blind during the production of the film—the film transmits resilience and feistiness. In the soundtrack, the partners encourage prospective viewers to be critical of standard treatments and to fight for alternatives, and in the closing sequence they smile at each other with complicity while they watch a video in their living room, an experience that, by the time the film was completed, was no longer possible as one of them had gone blind.

In George's film, damage is literal and inscribed on the filmed bodies and on the film body—on the dotted surface of the emulsion. In the works of Lawrence Brose and David Wojnarowicz, vulnerability is more indirectly communicated, but similarly enfolded in grain. Lawrence Brose's *An Individual Desires Solution* (1986) is an homage to a friend dying from AIDS. It is a peculiar portrait film that barely shows its subject. He plays piano, appears engaged in conversation—filmed in profile against a window—and sits in a dark interior, but, due to severe underexposure, he occasionally melts into a grainy blackness. The soundtrack combines brief piano phrases with ambient noise and a recording of his voice distorted through echo and flange. While the words themselves are unintelligible—they are provided in advance in the opening titles of the film—the emotion they transmit is unmistakable and ranges across tiredness, humor, irritation, and despair. The fraying of image and voice conveys indirectly a corporeal damage that is pervasively felt but not seen.

David Wojnarowicz's films are similarly indirect in their tackling of corporeal vulnerability. At times—as in his collaboration with Phil Zwickler, *Fear of Disclosure: Psycho-Social Implications of HIV Revelation* (1990)—he explores the vulnerability of an infected body; other times, he focuses on the bodies of the poor, the sick, and the ethnic and social minorities: all those, "born with the cross hairs of a rifle scope printed on our backs or skulls," ready-made targets of a society that despises difference.[14] *Fear of Disclosure* shows two go-go boys in gold lame shorts dancing, mock-wrestling, and embracing in a backlit studio rain to the sounds of techno. The image is slowed down and thickly textured, which accentuates the smoothness of the bodies and the excitement in their motion. In the soundtrack, a young man narrates how he is rejected by other gay men for his HIV-positive status. Under the veneer of gay hedonism and desirability, a fierce hierarchy pushes bodies with HIV to the margins of gay life. The health problems that AIDS entails are compounded with ostracism and rejection even from other gays, the dissolution of social ties, and a thinning sense of self. The image's granularity, echoed in the sparkling raindrops that wrap the go-go boys, conveys the corrosive effect of the disease, if not on the gilded club life, on infected bodies and on personal and communal bonds.

The allegorical quality of grain persists in Wojnarowicz's *Super 8* (1988) and in the two versions of *A Fire in My Belly* (1986–87), less finished works than collections of working footage that he showed during his lifetime. They abound in images of collision and disaster that threaten the integrity of the body. *Super 8* is structured as a rollercoaster ride filmed through a point-of-view shot. Images of the front of the rollercoaster cart hurtling forward are intermixed with explosions, a projectile impacting on a wall, images of the Guanajuato mummies, ants crawling over dollar bills and over a handgun display, the rotten carcass of an opossum, and coins falling on a bandaged hand. (Many of these motifs recur, with slight variations, in both versions of *A Fire in My Belly* and are reprised in Wojnarowicz's paintings.) Restful shots of jellyfish and of a Greek statue dispel only momentarily the pervasive hints of death and aggression.

Death equally pervades both versions of *A Fire in My Belly*. The first one, subtitled "a film in progress," is an impressionistic travelogue of Wojnarowicz's journey to Mexico in 1985.[15] The film starts with panoramic

FILM GRAIN: PRECARIOUS BODIES, POOR IMAGES   191

street views crosscut with headlines of crime reports and continues weaving together different thematic strands, all of which impinge on violence: a gruesome cockfight, bullfights seen on television, wrestling matches, children spitting fire on the streets, and a statue of the Aztec goddess Coatlicue, with her usual adornment of skulls and severed heads, filmed in a flashing light.[16] Ragged circus acts, colorful lottery cards, and empty colored screens provide brief respite from the tension. At the end, however, the map of Mexico, which also opens the film, combusts in a self-destructive paroxysm. But the violence that provokes this conflagration is organic and ritualistic; it is part of the cycle of life and tied to folk culture and popular resistance and therefore radically different from the one presented in the second version of the film. In this version, the violence emanates from technology (a steam locomotive, the spinning wheels of an old-fashioned mechanism), greed (coins fall on a dish full of blood and drop out of an injured hand), the police, and the desperate poverty that Wojnarowicz captures in the streets of Mexico, where legless men panhandle in moving traffic at risk of their own lives. Shots of the artist's lips sewn shut in protest against censorship add a further source of aggression: the political right's crusade to defund art found in violation of "community standards," which amounted, in fact, to the suppression of queer and feminist creativity. Against the well-oiled political machinery of the right and the cyclopean forces of finance, technology, and control—the "huge fat clockwork of civilization; the whole onward crush of the world as we know it"—Wojnarowicz's grainy Super 8 fragments offer precarious testimony, barely perceptible in the mainstream media churn.[17] Bearing witness to the machinery of death, they are themselves prone to self-implosion and disintegration.

Roger Jacoby and Michael Hoolboom modulate vulnerability through a slightly different register that could be termed, in Eve Kosofsky Sedgwick's terms, reparative rather than paranoid.[18] In contrast to the critical mode and the emphasis on finitude and disintegration of films by George, Brose, or Wojnarowicz, Jacoby and Hoolboom highlight the immunocompromised body's productivity and capacity for connection. Roger Jacoby's last finished film, *How to Be a Homosexual, Part II* (1982), captures the onset of early AIDS symptoms. Known for his adventurous hand processing, which produced rich, unstable coloring and unpredictable optical effects, Jacoby offers his body to the camera while showering and brushing his teeth, sitting on the toilet, inserting a tube into his anus, and curing skin lesions. Much of the film has a bleached look: "both over- and underexposed," writes

Ben Ogrodnik, "the film seems to have been processed in curdled milk."[19] Ogrodnik links Jacoby's damaged body to the surface accidents on the emulsion: both filmmaker and film appear to be dying in front of the spectator's eyes. The washed-out color and opaque screens hinder the visual consumption of his disease as a legible spectacle and counter the mainstream media's sensationalized treatment of people with AIDS.[20] At the same time there is more than death, disease, and critique to the film. Solarized and awash in shimmering blue, pink, and lilac, the early scenes are more poetic than mournful, while the insertion of the tube in Jacoby's rectum seems played for comedy, as the filmmaker, on all fours and filmed from behind, childishly kicks his legs as he eases the tube up his rectum. Disease does not entail complete interruption; life, art, and filmmaking do go on, if under more beleaguered circumstances, a point underlined in the shots of Jacoby's friend Jim Hubbard working on what looks like a mixture of home developing laboratory and editing facility.

Jacoby was diagnosed in the early eighties and died from AIDS-related complications in 1985, when he was barely forty. Hoolboom was diagnosed with AIDS in 1988, while still in his twenties, and benefitted from the retrovirals introduced in the mid-nineties that turned HIV infection from unappealable sentence to chronic condition. Some of Hoolboom's mid-nineties films revolve around living with a body that will not always behave, is haunted by death, and is often alien to itself. It is also a porous body open to difference and quirky affect and capable, for this reason, of unprecedented connections.

His compilation film *Panic Bodies* (1998), consisting of six independent shorts filmed in Super 8 and 16mm, is exemplary in this regard. The opening title in the series, *Positive*, is an autobiographical piece that recalls Hoolboom's diagnosis and the effects of his serostatus on his body and family relations. He recalls leaving home at an early age and hitchhiking across Canada in what, at the time, seemed an irreversible rupture. His immuno-compromised status brought him back years later and rekindled his relationship with his brother. Like Tartaglia's *Ecce Homo*, *Positive* makes ample use of the optical printer. With the screen split in four equal sections, a closeup of Hoolboom in the upper right hand provides the spoken commentary, while home movies and images of himself undergoing blood tests and medical examinations unfold right underneath. On the left quadrants, takes from nature documentaries, B movies, and a Michael Jackson video clip illustrate his monologue—often ironically—and offer abundant images of danger and

FILM GRAIN: PRECARIOUS BODIES, POOR IMAGES   193

catastrophe. As Hallas has pointed out, these images show how in a media-drenched society, the personal becomes inevitably mediated through the popular culture imaginary—and more concretely through the tradition of gay cinephilia, with its taste for intensely singular moments often found in films of negligible narrative or ideological import.[21] Popular images also provide an ironic contrast between the modesty of the personal recordings and the florid dramas and exuberant mise-en-scene of horror and disaster films, whose excess may provide cathartic release for individual suffering and pent-up anger.

Other films in the series are more indirect in handling the productive relationality of vulnerable—and vulnerated—bodies. Some stress transiency, while others mock the presumed unity of the body. *Eternity* combines the text of a letter from filmmaker Tom Chomont—a close friend of Hoolboom's, also HIV-positive—with images of water, microphotography of cells and veg-etable tissue, and high-contrast, underexposed takes of visitors at an amuse-ment park. Chomont's text narrates a near-death experience and his brother's recent passing, and reflects on the ephemerality of life and the need to ac-cept it. Drips and sloshes in the soundtrack evoke the fluidity that Chomont attributes to experience and the bodies of water that, in various mythological systems, separate the living from the dead. *Moucle's Island* edits together a blue movie from the forties featuring topless young women playing on a de-serted beach, a home movie of a fifties' children's party, and takes of Austrian filmmaker Moucle Blackout in the present. She rides a ferry, explores an abandoned house, masturbates, exposing her aging body to the camera, and appears to grasp the horizon with her hands while musing on the sustaining power of happy memories. *Passing On* captures an overexposed snowed landscape where ghostly human forms flit by, as if in transit to a different plane of existence.

Against the elegiac character of these segments, others, in a manner akin to Jacoby, find humor in mutating, uncontrollable bodies. In *A Boy's Story* a young man's penis detaches from his body and is lost; he later finds it—or one just like it—washed up on the shore and reinserts in its place. The young man's naked body is filmed in black and white and printed in superimposed, mirrored frames that yield a kaleidoscopic dance of flesh. And *1 + 1+1* shows a young couple probing each other's bodies with hammers and shears; put-ting on devil's masks, swimming hats, and goggles; and dressing in each other's clothes. At the end, they take off into space to the strains of Johann Strauss' "Blue Danube," an effect crudely simulated by crawling supine on the asphalt and waving their arms until they exit the frame. Throughout, the speeded-up motion evokes the pace of silent physical comedy. Many scenes show changing monochrome tints, as if the different layers of the emulsion were alternately stripped through chemical baths. There are frequent shifts between positive and negative and the constant visual noise of stains and scratches. The vulnerable body here is that of the film itself, whose abrasions and chemical erosions yield rich visual textures in surprising mutation. As in the rest of the series—and in Jacoby's *How to Be a Homosexual, Part II*—failure and vulnerability are fraught and stressful but not necessarily diminished conditions. They are also generative and restorative. Enfolded in grain, they enable other ways of connecting the dots that make up the world and point to alternative ways of living with disease and building new forms of political resistance around it.

Grain in the Digital Age: Memory, Fantasy, Abstraction

Beyond AIDS-related film, grain in the digital age connotes other kinds of vulnerability while also retaining a reparative character. The low-grade granular image implicitly contests the smoothness and crispness of digital representation and is an avatar of what Hito Steyerl has called the "poor image": the low-definition artifact that resists the imperative of sharpness and resolution driving mainstream visuality. In Steyerl's account, the poor image is a digital file, a pirated copy that has been "uploaded, downloaded, shared, reformatted and reedited." It is compressed to "travel more lightly" through non-commercial networks of hackers and fans who freely share their goods in the attempt to buck the market. The poor image sacrifices definition in favor of mobility and accessibility, losing "matter" in order to "gain speed": "It mocks the promises of digital technology. Not only is it often degraded to the point of being just a hurried blur, but one also even doubts whether it could be called an image at all. Only digital technology could produce such a dilapidated image in the first place."[22] One might add as well that, more than a decade after Steyerl penned these ideas, the "poor" digital image is largely a thing of the past, since broader bandwidth, faster processors, and improved compression software have phased out the connection between deterioration and the clandestine dissemination. Still, the "poor image" remains a useful tool to map the fate of celluloid in digital visuality.

The celluloid poor image does not pursue increased mobility in pirate networks. If it too ends up traveling through them in digital form, it is not for its market value, but precisely for its lack of it. Its loss of definition does not result from automatized format change and compression but from artisanal manipulation and artistic choice. Low definition in film results from the use of low-fi, often dated technology; from hand processing that heightens accidental marks on the emulsion and the vagaries of chemistry; and/or from the exploitation of what Tess Takahashi has insightfully named film's "expanded indexicality," which does not derive from photographic capture but from the way in which the celluloid surface may be directly imprinted by touch, the passage of time, or the natural elements—processes that do not yield iconic likenesses.[23] Despite these differences, digital and analog poor images share their marginality and resistance to mainstream visual economies. Whether immaterial or tangible, whether a YouTube stream or an 8mm hand-developed reel, the low-fi "poor image" offers an alternative to the grandiloquent visuality of mainstream media. These last are based on transparency and control; their focus and sharpness of outline bespeak, in Steyerl's view, power, economic value, technological prowess, and even phallic self-assertion: "Resolution is fetishized and its lack amount[s] to castration of the author."[24]

Granularity, by contrast, stands for the old, the odd, and the queer. For the old because grain is a remnant of a pretendedly superseded technology and therefore a marker of pastness. Even though it may be produced digitally, it is originally a celluloid texture and evokes an earlier media ecology. Graininess has a "dream memory quality," in the words of San Francisco super-8 collective silt.[25] It is a vehicle for the odd because its fogginess makes it the apt vehicle of dreams, fantasies, and the half-known life. Grain deposits a layer of dust on the image. A particulate sediment, dust, George Bataille wrote, enchants what it touches, fogs the clarity of reason, and makes way for the obsessive, mysterious, and ghostly, and so does grain's dusty texture.[26] Further, grain underlines the queer physicality of film. At a time when the dominant visual support consists in ungraspable coded electronic pulses, film has a body and a skin that can be handled and felt. "We do not work with 'images,'" claims filmmaker Pip Chodorov, "but with organic physical material that comes from the earth: salts, silvers, minerals."[27] This organic substratum makes film, for Kim Knowles, "a reassuring reflection of our own bodies."[28] Or perhaps not so reassuring. As we have seen in an earlier section, the bodies that rise from grainy celluloid are elusive and undeterminable and

196 EXPERIMENTAL FILM AND QUEER MATERIALITY

often escape optic and conceptual control. Even more undefinable are those bodies, common in recent experimental film and video, whose uncertain granular outline is compounded by erratic emulsion decay and unorthodox manual processing. If resolution is phallic—as per Steyerl—grainy shapes and blurred outlines abjure from the start the economies of completion and self-presence that pivot on the phallus and prefer to remain dispersed, distributed, and indefinable.

These three connotations of grain—memory, enchantment, corporeal anarchy—infuse the work of recent queer experimental filmmakers working in celluloid, video, or in hybrids of both. The sense of pastness and personal memory pervades William E. Jones's *No Product* (2012) series: brief montages of severely faded advertisement films from the seventies—to judge from the looks of the models—that the filmmaker has additionally scratched, bleached, and painted over, leaving the paint to dry up and crack. These films connote nostalgia for a nearly extinct technology and for the marks of an earlier time that adhere to the surface of the image: the fashions, hairstyles, and body types of the models beckon from a past that happens to coincide with the filmmaker's childhood. If the ruined advertisements revive childhood memories of watching television commercials in the privacy of the home, *Tearoom* (2008), also a found footage piece, features more adult, public pleasures. It is composed of surveillance films taken in 1962 by the police of Mansfield, Ohio, at a busy tearoom, where men converged during the daytime for anonymous sex. The thick grain and bluish tone give away the film's datedness, as do the clothes and styling of the bathroom goers. *Tearoom* recalls an era of furtive sex and fierce repression but also of significant passive resistance, given the surprising number and variety of men who venture into the facility in search of partners. And the compilation films *V. O.* (2006), *All-Male Mash-Up* (2006), and *Film Montages (For Peter Roehr)* (2006) edit fragments of porn films from the seventies, ranging from classics by Fred Halstead, Joe Gage, or Peter Berlin, to lesser known works. The fragments show the preliminaries and peripheries of sex: urban views caught on cruising rambles; glimpses of the worlds that these films traverse quickly in order to zero in on the sexual act. In *V. O.*, these peripheral moments are edited to excerpts of the soundtracks of post-war art films, a device that generates absurd dislocations and surprising counterpoints and that brings together two disparate film cultures seldom put in dialogue, but equally queer-identified: porn and arthouse fare. The excerpts that make up *All-Male Mash-Up* and *Film Montages* retain their own soundtrack. In *Film*

Montages, sound and image are looped in the percussive, hypnotic style of German artist and filmmaker Peter Roehr, a pop artist and filmmaker whose work Jones brings into a queer orbit by means of this homage.

These works are digital transfers of analog video versions of 35mm films or of 16mm films blown up to 35mm for commercial exhibition. The visible pixilation, flattening, color bleed, and glare resulting from this chain of conversions reproduce the visuality of analog home video, which is the medium in which these films were consumed, especially by those not old enough to experience them at porn theaters. A similar effect is conveyed by Nguyen Tan Hoang's video *K. I. P.* (2002), which edits scenes of porn films starring seventies porn star Kip Noll taped off a television screen on which one can see the reflection of a young man (Nguyen himself) watching the images. The tape is badly damaged by frequent use; the sex scenes, in particular, have become nearly illegible because repeated rewinding and replay have stretched and scratched the tape. It presents, Lucas Hilderbrand writes, "an archive of erotic consumption recorded (or, perhaps more appropriately, stripped) off the magnetic surface of the tapes themselves."[29] While the iconography of Jones's and Hoang's works brings back, as Jones himself has put it, "a lost world of eroticism and sociability" mostly associated with the seventies, years of sexual utopianism and experimentation, their visual texture recalls a later moment, from the early eighties forward, when individualized home viewing of porn became the norm, and the sexual cultures of previous years were severely curtailed by AIDS.[30] This lost world is revisited in the 2000s with a mixture of longing and melancholia that, for Elizabeth Freeman, is already evoked in the title of Nguyen's video: "a riff not only on Kip Noll's name but also on R. I. P., or 'Rest in Peace,' indicating both the desire to enliven the dead and the understanding that this is never wholly possible."[31] The textural complexity of Jones' and Hoang's videos give graphic shape to the combination of distance and attachment that, in Sigmund Freud's classic account, characterizes melancholia's unassimilated sense of loss. The object of melancholia here is the loss of a sexual collectivity that had to be let go of in the years of AIDS but that younger generations remain fascinated with for the sense of freedom and utopia it still radiates.

A similar fascination animates Liz Rosenfeld's *Untitled (Dyketactics Revisited)* (2006), a reworking of Barbara Hammer's classic *Dyketactics* (1974). Combining 16mm Kodachrome and video, Rosenfeld remakes the most collective moments of Hammer's film: women walking naked in the grass, bathing in a stream, lighting candles, and goofing around in nature.

198   EXPERIMENTAL FILM AND QUEER MATERIALITY

Rosenfeld imitates Hammer's superimpositions and fluid camera work and replicates several shots in the original. But she also keeps her distance from it. The setting is no longer pristine. The streams and verdant meadows of Northern California are replaced in Rosenfeld's film by the vacant lots, loading docks, and abandoned silos of a warehouse district; and the flowers of the seventies have become cartoonish daisies and cherries made out of plastic. The limpid electronic phrase of the original is also dirtied-up— whistled and mixed with the high-pitched hum produced by running a finger on the rim of a glass. And the thoroughly cis femininity of *Dyketactics* blooms in Rosenfeld's remake into a wider array of gender configurations with a significant trans presence. Yet the dreamy abandon of *Untitled*'s performers fully matches that of their counterparts in *Dyketactics*. As Gregg Youman has insightfully noted, Rosenfeld acknowledges that the utopianism of Hammer's original is no longer possible but cannot be easily discarded without casting off, at the same time, an important part of queer heritage.[32] The film relives the idealistic communalism of seventies lesbian culture through a contemporary queer optic. It betrays nostalgia for what was never lived but can still be revisited for the lessons it may hold for an embattled present and future. As in Jones and Nguyen, the film's granularity communicates this liminality: the simultaneous distance from and attachment to a utopia that can be neither embraced because it is not fully ours, nor entirely given up because of its dazzling promises, and is, for this reason, perceived through a patina of irony and desire.

A similar irony pervades Frédéric Moffet's video *Jean Genet in Chicago* (2006), a reconsideration of the events surrounding the 1968 Democratic National Convention from Jean Genet's perspective. Genet was commissioned by *Esquire* magazine, along with William Burroughs and Terry Southern, to report what was building up to be a tumultuous event.[33] Moffet's account combines found footage of the protests and the Convention with reenactments by actors wearing paper masks of Genet, Allen Ginsberg, William Burroughs, Bobby Seale, and several others—a device that explicitly pays homage to David Wojnarowicz's photo series *Rimbaud in New York* (1978–79). The soundtrack features mainly quotes from Genet's writings read in French, along with brief excerpts from Southern's own report and from a speech by Seale.[34] Sometimes, the quotations emanate from the on-screen actors; other times, they are delivered as off-screen commentary.

Moffet calls the work a "thief's video" in homage to the title of Genet's first book, *The Thief's Journal* (1949), and in recognition of his reliance on

FILM GRAIN: PRECARIOUS BODIES, POOR IMAGES 199

archival material, which is interspersed with contemporary reenactments filmed in digital video. The reenactments are filmed in black and white to match the archival images—only a few of them are in color—but the smooth surface of contemporary digital video contrasts with the gritty graininess of sixties' celluloid. The newsreel footage bears the weight of the past; it depicts the violent police repression of the peaceful demonstrations and the blandness of the convention, whose attendees impersonate the stodgy conservatism that crushed a youthful revolution. The reenactments in digital video have a lighter touch. They rearrange the past with a mixture of poignancy and humor, and open it to a queer reading that seeks to refashion the negative outcome of the riots. With this intention, Moffet gives the floor to Genet's arch campiness. While he was acutely sensitive to the political issues involved, Genet was also moved by the angelic beauty of the hippies and turned on by the athleticism and toughness of the brutal Chicago police. He noted that the ruthless minions of the establishment were also fodder for queer fantasizing and porn clichés—"often photographed and displayed in dirty books"—and he placed them into a circuit of looks and desires that they could not control and that undermined much of what they stood for. Through Genet, Moffet inserts into the events of August 1968—and into the countercultural imaginary at large—a queer presence that has seldom been acknowledged, in part due to the masculinist mystique of much New Left activism. It is a rereading that is made possible by the present awareness of the intricacies of queer history and by the versatility of digital video. The dense surface texture of sixties footage signals the inertia of received history while the slickness of video permits its redemption through subversive rearrangement. Once again, the past is revisited with irony. It cannot be assumed wholesale but cannot be entirely abandoned either and may still be mined for its revolutionary possibilities.

In addition to connoting pastness and memory, grain also conveys the revolutionary possibilities of fantasy as a mode where the rules of ordinary reality may be upended and remade. This is a defining trait of the work of British filmmaker Sarah Pucill, active since the early nineties. Influenced by Maya Deren and surrealism—one of her last films, *Confessions to the Mirror* (2016) is a tribute to Claude Cahun—Pucill's 16mm films explore an uncanny hominess where objects become animated, quotidian actions acquire a threatening pregnancy, and women interact, at times antagonistically, with the props of domesticity. Kitchens and dining tables, with their respective accoutrements, are turned from settings for ordinariness to catalysts

200 EXPERIMENTAL FILM AND QUEER MATERIALITY

for danger and imbalance under the influence of dark feminine agencies. In *Back Comb* (1995), a dining table is overgrown with wildly proliferating woman's hair. Teeming dark locks invade plates and glasses, snake under the white tablecloth, weave around cutlery, and knock down jars of milk and water in their inexorable advance. *You Be Mother* (1990) projects a photograph of the filmmaker's face against a still life of teapots, jars, cups, and saucers. As the face is caught on the objects that compose the scene, it is dislocated into an aggregate of distinct parts while the objects become grotesquely humanized: they grow eyes, nose, and mouth, they shake and tussle with each other and radiate a sullen menace. *Mirrored Measure* (1996) pays infinitesimal attention to the liquid in the glasses, jars, and bottles of an elegantly set table. Caught in extreme closeups, liquids dribble, tremble, bubble, swirl, and ebb into lips pursed around the rims of glasses. They communicate confined agitation, pent-up tension, and fragile balance and turn a refined tabletop into a stage for an imminent, unspecified disaster. *Swollen Enigma* (1998) moves from dining sets to dark kitchens and hallways in which a woman remembers—or hallucinates about—an absent lover: a dolled-up inexpressive woman who materializes around the house, hanging from the ceiling, lying blood-stained on the floor, or propped head down on an armchair. Impervious, the protagonist calmly washes dishes, twirls a lock round her fingers, plucks unseemly hairs with painful deliberation, and licks the chalices of flowers in a roundabout evocation of sex.[35] The graininess of these images accentuates their unreality. Reports from the half-known life, they convey the frustration and violence sedimented in women's traditional roles and spaces.

Spanish filmmaker David Domingo's Super 8 films also delve into uncanny domesticities. Mixing found footage, abstract shots, stop-motion animation, and live action, his work often takes place in fantastic home environments where the inanimate becomes animated, and fantasies saturate mental and existential space (see Figure 7.3). In *La mansión acelerada* (1997), *Desayunos y meriendas* (2002), and *Super 8* (1996), the furniture slides on floors and walls, shelves empty and refill again, plastic figurines and dime store toys flit across kitchen counters and tabletops, and drawers open and close of their own accord. In *El monstruo me come* (1999) a young man—Manolo Dos, a frequent performer in Domingo's work—is attacked by black plastic bags and ends up being swallowed up by a crevice in his bedroom wall. And in *Bea comunica* (1998) the protagonist is engulfed in an avalanche of paper balls that seemingly emerge from nowhere.

Figure 7.3 David Domingo, *La mansión acelerada*, 1998. Film still. Courtesy of David Domingo.

The demented physical world is densely populated with fantasies drawn from gay porn, superhero lore, Hollywood classics seen on TV, and films that premiered during Domingo's childhood and adolescence and were part of his sentimental and cinematic education. Fragments of *The Wizard of Oz*, Christopher Reeves' *Superman*, *Star Wars*, *The Blue Lagoon*, or *Ben Hur*, for example, recur in Domingo's universe. Disney is a particular favorite: *Snow White* appears in several titles—occasionally crosscut with gay porn—and the studio is paid homage in *Disney Attraction Highlights no. 1* (2009). The found fragments are often looped to highlight the absurdity of particular gestures or movements, rather than to preserve dramatic moments or instances of star charisma, and they are edited to frantic mambos, psychedelic rock, or dance tracks. Borrowed images are usually encountered in home viewing devices—often filmed off the television monitor, its pixilation further augmented by the graininess of Super 8. In addition, Domingo's films endlessly feature cassette tapes, videotapes, Super 8 cartridges, fragments of celluloid, and television sets. *Desayunos y meriendas* opens with a couple of young men inserting a video tape into a player, an action that frames much of what follows as the images contained in the tape and the young men's reactions to them. The pervasive home media contribute to suspending the outside world and turn domesticity into a stage for an incontrollable materiality and an endless stream of fantasies that mix childhood cinephilia and adult erotic longings, all enveloped in grain.

Jennifer Reeves and M. M. Serra's *Darling International* (1999) is also a cinephiliac object—a queer pastiche of film noir set in nocturnal New York City. Its vague narrative depicts a lesbian love triangle between an elegant, middle-aged executive—played by filmmaker M. M. Serra—and two younger women—played by Reeves herself and Sasha Berman. Reeves is a butch metal shop worker by day and masochistic femme by night, and Berman might be the Darling of the title, a foreign visitor who hopes, according to her breathy, accented confession at the start of the film, "to find something better" in her new environs. The film starts with Serra's dalliance with Reeves; they arrange their dates through Serra's secretary, who solicitously brushes her boss's hair before the latter steps out to meet her paramour. They are later joined by Berman for a heavy S&M session in which Reeves is tied and flogged. By the end of the film, Reeves and Berman seem to have become lovers, while Serra is kicked out of the triangle. The film seems to be structured as a flashback, with the narrative providing an explanation for Serra's puzzlement at the start of the film, when she muses about Reeves's disappearance.

The atmospheric black and white, the nocturnal atmosphere, the voice-overs—kept to a schematic minimum—and the narrative elusiveness are direct noir borrowings. At the same time, the film feminizes a predominantly masculine genre and places center stage the kind of sexual unorthodoxy that classic noir could only hint at and usually located in relationships between men.[36] The high-contrast granularity makes the film dreamy and unreal. It also facilitates the conversion of contemporary New York into a noir—or neo-noir—set in which it is possible to reimagine the genre and redress its biases and omissions, making it more hospitable to a contemporary queer sensibility.

Grain does not only de-realize spaces—domestic or public—but also the bodies that inhabit them. The films by Pucill, Domingo, and Reeves abound in bodies that spread beyond the contour of human form onto the stuff of daily life. They are extended through crumpled papers, burning cigarettes, kitchen crockery, and rumpled clothes piled in corners; they live out their fantasies on the screens of television monitors and store their memories in

FILM GRAIN: PRECARIOUS BODIES, POOR IMAGES   203

dime store toys, collectible cards, and pop memorabilia. Odd corporealities emerge as well from the metamorphoses and abstractions provoked by image degradation—glitched digital files, damaged videotape, or decaying celluloid. Celluloid, in particular, has been a privileged medium for the exploration of the reversion of pattern to entropy. This reversion culminates a trend that starts with the increasing presence of grainy bodies in experimental film since the early sixties—a trend that, as this chapter has sought to track, defamiliarizes the corporeal by dissolving it into the minimal components of the cinematic image while opening it up, at the same time, to queer formations of desire, relationality, memory, and fantasy.

Peggy Ahwesh's *The Color of Love* (1994) is an emblematic signpost in this trend. It is a deteriorated 8mm porn reel of two women making love next to a recumbent, mostly catatonic man. Found by Ahwesh in a bin that had been exposed to the elements for quite some time, the film is opulently ruined. The decomposition of the emulsion and the seepage of the dyes make bodies bleed and break into vaguely organic shapes that often cover the image under layers of abstraction. The choreography of sex unfolds intermittently, often disappearing into sprawling color splotches and fungus-like spreads that heighten the original grain of the film, which is all the more conspicuous for being liberated from its subservience to a representational design. No longer seen than gone again, the human bodies are now readable, now blotted out under another squirt of color, another pulsing blotch, a web of cracks or a swarm of quivering dots in a process that recalls, writes Steven Shapiro, various orders of ephemerality: the effervescent fleetingness of sex and the inevitable mortality of film (see Figure 7.4).[37] Along similar lines, Elena Gorfinkel reads the film in melancholic terms as an object lesson on transiency, historicity, and the elegiac (necrophiliac) quality of cinephilia, which often attaches to dated images whose time in the limelight has elapsed.[38]

At the same time, Ahwesh's film could also be read as a reflection on the ontology of the cinematic image. The susceptibility of celluloid to injury and abrasion is also the cinema's enabling condition. After all, what allows the film strip to capture images of the world is precisely the fact that the grains of silver halide suspended in the emulsion are burned by light and then pierced again, with cumulative damage, by the projector's beam during projection. Decay, then, may not be an endpoint in the evolution of celluloid but just a point in a gradual continuum: another process through which images emerge on the chemically treated strip. Deterioration may not be only coextensive with dissolution and failure, terms that assume the primacy of transparency

Figure 7.4 Peggy Ahwesh, *The Color of Love*, 1998. Film still. Courtesy of Peggy Ahwesh.

and goal-oriented visuality, but just another stage in the life of celluloid and another means of generating images—in the case of Ahwesh's film, images outside the conventional iconic repertoire of gender and sexuality. From this perspective, the bodies in *The Color of Love* not only dissolve and dissipate but also morph and multiply. Lush decomposition extends and transforms recognizable bodies, and draws around them graphs of desire and vectors of relation, touch, and entwinement that are not guided by the ideal of corporeal wholeness or by limiting gender morphologies.

The abstract erotics of the nonhuman form is abundantly featured in Jennifer Reeves's *Landfill 16* (2011, see Figure 7.5) and Luther Price's *Inkblot* series (2007–10)—works generated by subjecting found footage to various kinds of manipulation and decay. Reeves buried 16mm outtakes of her double-projection piece *When It Was Blue* in landfill and then painted them over, producing palpitating abstractions in which one can fleetingly discern clouds, flying planes, or insects. "This 'recycling,'" Reeves writes, "is a meditation on the demise of the beautiful 16mm medium and nature's losing battle to decompose the relics of our abandoned technologies."[39] The

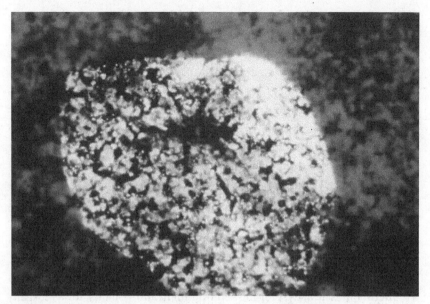

Figure 7.5 Jennifer Reeves, *Landfill 16*, 2011. Courtesy of Jennifer Reeves.

medium remains the bearer of entrancing images even after its presumed demise, and nature's destructiveness is also creative and generative, qualities borne out by the new skins that grow on decaying celluloid. Read against the context of Reeves's early work, which often dwells on male sexual abuse of women and its consequent emotional scars, *Landfill 16* is also a redemptive piece that figures a way out of the multiple violences endemic to sexual and affective intimacy, especially when they are conditioned by gender-coded power imbalances. The abstract skins and bodies of *Landfill 16* do not fit into known gender identities, vie for ascendancy, or cause harm. They momentarily occupy the visual field in succession without stabilizing into namable configurations, supremely equal and serene.

Luther Price's *Inkblot* films lend themselves to a similar reading. Predating *Landfill 16* by a few years, they are also the combined product of random deterioration and of a kind of artistic manipulation that Roberta Smith described as a "sculptural" approach to film.[40] Price scratched his footage with pins and razors; drew on it with permanent markers; glued to it glitter, hair, and sand; dipped it in bleach, acid, and olive oil; left it out in the sun; and buried it. The unrepeatable—often unduplicatable—pieces were often shown as camera originals that would barely run through the projector on account

206 EXPERIMENTAL FILM AND QUEER MATERIALITY

of their warping and swelling. These works dovetail with Price's interest in bodily damage, an interest prompted, by his own admission, by the random gunshot he suffered in the summer of 1985 in Nicaragua during the fights between the Sandinista government and the *contras*.[41]

Wounds and scars allegorize physical and psychological endurance as well as the art that emerges in the process of healing. Some of his early Super 8 films—*Green* (1988) and *Warm Broth* (1987–88), both signed as Tom Rhoads—revive opaque childhood memories that combine longing and hurt and feature toys, dolls, old-fashioned knick-knacks, Price in drag playing his mother doing household chores, and close-ups of broken and scraped skin. Art might be the scar tissue that covers emotional wounds as they heal or at least turn into livable memories. The process is literalized in *Inkblot*, whose abstract imagery is the product of direct attack on the film or grows from the injury wrought by water, sun, dirt, and deliberately inadequate storage. But, as in *The Color of Love* and *Landfill 16*, injury is not only synonymous with harm but is a catalyst for new embodiment and visuality, for a reorganization of vision and matter. "I feel like the camellia plant. I grow, and then I crumble. Super-8 really talks about this process. The process never ends. It is always rediscovering itself."[42] The transit from referentiality to abstraction, from recognizable image to patterns of damage and injury is not a move only toward finitude and dissolution but also toward generation and growth and toward bodies and shapes that point to future potencies and structures of sensation. There is no sadness or melancholia over the way in which shape reverts to abstractions, cracks, and of course, grain, a visual dust from which everything rises, but to which everything may also return in the end, only to rise again in yet unscripted arrangements.

* * *

The dialectic of creation and ruin, emergence, and dissolution runs through the use of grain explored in this chapter and ties together the two repertoires I have examined. In them, granularity embodies an atomism that cycles from form to dissolution and back again; it is the dance of minimal units that come into play in the constant self-constitution and diffusion of the world, bodies, and perceptual patterns. It signifies vulnerability and decline, the impermanence of form, but also the reparative impulses that allow the dots to cohere in new configurations. While this speaks of seemingly timeless cycles of loss, reparation, and return, it acquires concrete political lineaments in particular historical conditions, as in the AIDS epidemic or in an embattled present where queer bodies and sexualities are still targets of suppression and violence. In both cases, granularity is coextensive with fragility and impermanence but also with the possibility of sustaining queer memory and envisioning unimagined spaces, communities, and corporealities. Open and mutable, the dancing dots and the spaces between can be joined in different ways.

In the body of film surveyed in this chapter, grain works less as structural index than as formal allegory. Its anti-illusionistic function gives way to its allegorical import and political use. In a progressively diverse media environment where the cinematic image is just one of a range of possibilities for audiovisual consumption, where visual technologies are inescapable, and "life" is more often lived on screens than between them, film's illusionism ceases to be the urgent target it once was. We are by now fully awake to the materiality of the image and its technological mediation. What may matter most at present is the pragmatics of images and viewing supports—their affordances and effects on the social field. From this perspective, grain alerts less to the image's chemical substratum and the unnaturalness of representation than to the possibilities inherent in a marginal technology to generate alternative repertoires, foster resistant communities, preserve usable pasts, and conjure workable futures.

Finally, while I have treated grain allegorically, making it signify in queer contexts, there is another characteristic of it that I have only touched upon in passing: its intractability to sense. Grain is a gratuitous, proliferating layer whose effect is not really exhausted through these explorations, which have tried to capture, perhaps in vain, its alluring motility. In addition to everything that the last two chapters have suggested, grain is *noise*, an unformalizable accretion that debunks informational protocols and threatens to drown the communicable signal. For its destabilizing effect, noise is another kind of queer material. To its sonic incarnation, I turn in the following chapter.

8

Synthetic, Exotic, Magnetic

The Noise of Queer Experimental Film

Noise has been a constant throughout this book. It has been audible, to cite a few instances, in the clangs, bells, and train whistles of Harry Smith's *Heaven and Earth Magic*, in the percussive effects of Marie Menken's films, in the room tone and distortion that muddle Warhol's soundtracks, in the scratchy aural collages in the films of Ron Rice, the Kuchars, and David Domingo, or in the disintegrating echoes and synthetic sonorities of Laurence Brose, Roger Jacoby, Barbara Hammer, or Jennifer Reeves. These examples—and many more are possible—show that noise is in fact a steady ingredient in queer experimental film, if seldom taken into account.

Noise is also an index of materiality. Whether we think of it as irregular sonic vibration—traditionally opposed to regular musical tone—as interference that breaks up the signal, or as unwanted acoustic occurrence, noise recalls the material substratum that underlies sociality, communication, and sense. Noise makes evident that whatever else the world may be, it is a physical aggregate of interlocking objects and substances whose contact triggers airborne vibration. What Michel Chion describes as one of sound's primary functions on film—its working as a "materializing index," anchoring insubstantial images on the material world—remains operative in life off the screen.[1] But not all sound is noise. This last is a disruptive, opaque instantiation of the former. Noise is sound that perturbs, disorients, or fails to signify. It is queer for its capacity to deviate and derail meaning and to add a layer of strangeness to experience, but also, in a more constructive capacity, for invoking untested potentialities and unprecedented connections: in Luigi Russolo's words, for holding "innumerable surprises" and promising "a new and unsuspected pleasure of the senses."[2] Because of its conceptual and sensorial productivity, noise has long been a harbinger of deviant bodies and communities. If queerness has developed a considerable visual archive, it has also developed an aural archive in which noise features prominently.

Experimental Film and Queer Materiality. Juan A. Suárez, Oxford University Press. © Oxford University Press 2024.
DOI: 10.1093/oso/9780197566992.003.0008

SYNTHETIC, EXOTIC, MAGNETIC 209

Experimental film is a significant repository of this archive. From the start, film was hospitable to dissenting bodies and desires, and, after its reinvention as a sound medium in the twenties, it was also host to experiments in sound synthesis and unprecedented tonalities. The optical sound band could capture incidental sound that might be disjunct with the image—a possibility that was not fully explored until the forties—and could also be used for sonic synthesis. Drawing upon and scratching the optical track—as did Rudolph Pfenninger—and exposing it to various visual patterns—as did Arseni Avraamov and Oskar Fischinger—resulted in unprecedented acoustic universes.[3]

Queer sound and images met in experimental film particularly after World War II. From the mid-forties forward, the cinematic avant-garde took a decidedly queer turn just as musical languages expanded. Experiments with turntables, pickup cartridges, and electronic sound generation; the growing introduction of non-Western scales and alternative tuning and tonal systems; and the popularization of magnetic tape, which permitted an unprecedented agility in the manipulation of found sound, broadened the sonic palette, and many of the new sonorities found their way into film. In fact, filmmakers and visual artists, rather than conventional musicians, were often the first and most receptive audiences for these experiments. As a result of the synergies between avant-garde music and film, queer images on screen became matched to various types of noise, a convergence that will be the subject of this chapter.

This convergence will be explored here theoretically and historically. I will start by considering the conceptual connections between noise and queerness and will continue exploring the queer dimensions of the post–World War II musical avant-garde—in percussion, microtonality, and electronic instrumentation—and its resonances in experimental film—in Maya Deren, Sidney Peterson, Kenneth Anger, Marie Menken, and James Broughton, among others. These filmmakers tended to use commissioned soundtracks conceived wholistically in relation to the image. From the late fifties forward, however, queer filmmakers tended to favor audio collages of preexisting sound—and noise—afforded by magnetic tape and stimulated by a culture of recycling and repurposing in music but also in the visual arts and literature. Later sections will explore the queer sound mixes of the sixties underground—in Jack Smith, José Rodríguez Soltero, and Andy Warhol—and of later experimental film—by Lionel Soukaz, Abigail Child, and Hans/Ashley Scheirl—influenced by punk, disco, and queer subcultures that jelled

210 EXPERIMENTAL FILM AND QUEER MATERIALITY

around AIDS protests and made sophisticated use of audiovisual media. At the time, many of the acoustic experiments of the postwar years had become integrated into a broad array of music genres, from pop and dance styles to contemporary composer music, without necessarily losing their edge or queer evocativeness. The roughly six decades that we will be considering span a broad range of sonic idioms. While from the forties to the sixties experimental film was influenced by the theories and practice of postwar innovators such as John Cage, Lou Harrison, and Harry Partch, by new electronic instruments, the early use of magnetic tape, and the pop idiom of hit radio, from the seventies forward and up to the early decades of the present century, it found inspiration in punk and post-punk music, turntable experiments, scratch, and glitch.

Noise: The Sound of Others

Noise and queerness are products of the late industrial age. The modern study of sexuality consolidated, according to historians from Michel Foucault and Jeffrey Weeks to Paul Robinson and Jennifer Terry, in the fin-de-siècle, the time of the "invention" of homosexuality (according to Foucault) and heterosexuality (according to Jonathan Ned Katz) and of the proliferation of discourse about the sexual—for Foucault, "the noisiest of our preoccupations."[4] The backdrop of this discursive emergence was what some called "the age of noise," characterized by the sonorous assault led by the machinery of modern life.[5] Noise, like deviance, drew the attention of hygienists and social reformers. An inescapable consequence of technological advancement, noise was often regarded as barbaric, aggressive, and destructive. Since the late years of the nineteenth century, it was regarded as the root of a string of bodily and psychic ailments, such as weak nerves, distraction, and physical fatigue. Writing in the early 1880s, American neurologist George M. Beard singled the "unrhythmical, unmelodious, and therefore annoying, if not injurious" noise of contemporary machinery ("the appliances and accompaniments of civilization") as a prime cause for neurasthenia, one of the diseases of the time.[6] Environmental stress was also believed to be at the root of the nervous dissipation and degeneration that, many physiologists and psychiatrists agreed, led to sexual perversions.[7] Both noise and sexual perversion posited a threat to the wholeness of the social body and they ought to be managed and, if possible, eradicated. This enterprise was destined to fail, however, since noise and runaway sexuality were consubstantial to the life of the modern West. Industrial power and technological development resulted in a vast increase in the intensity and variety of noises. And urbanization, social mobility, and the dissolution of the traditional social fabric facilitated a plurality of desires that ran afoul of convention. Around these desires emerged in large urban centers what British sexologist Havelock Ellis described as "a distinctly organized" homosexual world with its own vocabulary, customs, and institutions, from cafés and churches to "streets where, at night, every fifth man is an invert."[8]

Queerness and noise were difficult to conjure not only because of their pervasiveness, but also because of their slipperiness. They designate less fixed, assignable traits, than movable positions occupied by what hegemonic sexual and aural regimes have regarded as unwanted and unassimilated. Since the rise of queer theory, "queerness" has designated the shifting contours of that vast continent lying beyond heteronormative acceptability. In an early moment of queer critique, this lability was situated in relation to sexual definition and practice but was later located in a broader social arena that comprised the crisscrossing of unaligned bodies and desires with race, nationality, the state, migrancy, (post)coloniality, and even with cognitive fundamentals such as time and space. In this multitude of contexts, "queer," wrote Eve Sedgwick, "never can only denote; nor even can it only connote." Its strength derives less from conceptual tightness than from its performative effectiveness through "acts of experimental self-perception and filiation."[9] For other writers, queer designates "a zone of possibilities" and a utopian aspiration.[10] In any case, it is to a great extent an empty signifier,[11] a placeholder for what slips through the available conceptual grids that try to "know," and therefore fix and control, bodies and desires in their passage through the social field.

Noise has a similarly open character, in part, as Paul Hegarty points out, because it has often been negatively defined as "unwanted, other . . . not music, not valid, not a message or a meaning."[12] This negativity recalls the original use of queer as an insult for sexual others—similarly not wanted, not valid, not meaningful . . . . The contours and meanings of noise change through time, since what counts as aural disturbance in an era may become a canonical work in a later one but also synchronically across the cultural spectrum—one culture's noise is another's means of sonic self-affirmation and expression. This variability makes noise, Hegarty continues, "something like a process" rather than a stable element.[13] And as a process, it is at the center of disputes and adjudications that seek to draw a line between the aurally acceptable and unacceptable. These disputes produce at times shifts in the thresholds of audibility ("avant-garde transformation") while at other times end up reinforcing the strictures of the status quo.

The processual character of noise, along with its productivity—even in the negative form of suppressions, curfews, or restrictive legislation—should force us to reevaluate definitions that put the emphasis exclusively on its negative aspects. Christoph Cox has eloquently rejected the frequent characterization of noise as the opposite of signal, language, or form and has defended that it deserves "an ontological place of its own."[14] Sheer negativity places noise in a metaphysical realm where it cannot be accessed and dilutes its concrete materiality and generative effect. Drawing on Gilles Deleuze and Michael Serres, among others, Cox reverses this conception. Rather than the antithesis, or annihilating underside, of sense and meaning, noise is their condition of possibility. It is an all-involving, ever-present aural continuum—a sonic flux—that he describes as "the set of sonic forces that are capable of entering into differential relations with one another in such a way that they surpass the threshold of audibility and become signal."[15] Or to put it differently, noise is not subtractive and lacking, unformed or nonsensical; it is not "*too little*" but "*too much*, overwhelming the system with energy, information, potentiality." Noise is the coexistence of all signals: wideband, white noise, and all frequencies and their differential relations. "It is replete," Cox continues, "with differences, tendencies, attractors, singularities and potential bifurcations."[16] Out of this multiplicity, music, meaningful sound, and speech emerge as singular events. Beyond and around them buzzes an endless acoustic virtuality (to use Deleuze's term) that is occasionally actualized as sense, but that mere sense does not exhaust.

In this regard, the sonic virtual is analogous to what orthodox psychoanalysis described as the domain of the drives: the polymorphously perverse body that becomes socialized, in the course of its development, into intelligible genders and desires. And just as sound does not exhaust the multiplicity of noise, socialized sexuality does not exhaust sexual possibility. Taking his clue from Melanie Klein, Deleuze has recast in sonic terms the narrative of subjective ontogenesis—the mutation of the polymorphous body to the intelligible sexual subject. The body of untrammeled libidinal urges—Klein's oral-anal body—is traversed by noise: "clappings, crackings, gnashings, cracklings, explosions, the shattered sounds of internal objects, and also the inarticulate howls-breaths (*cris-souffles*) of the body without organs that respond to them—all of this forms an oral-sonorous system bearing witness to the oral-anal voracity."[17] Over the anarchy and schizoid dispersion of the oral-anal stage is eventually superimposed the organizing force of the voice: an ordering element that, "comes from above" and that even before it is understood by the infant, communicates order and structure. The voice is the vehicle of language, "conveys tradition," appeals to the child by name, and "demands its insertion" into the social grid.[18] Cox does not invoke this particular reading, but it may be in the background of his consideration that the virtual realm of noise is a material unconscious out of which conscious acoustic events emerge. Like the psychic unconscious of psychoanalysis, the sonic unconscious is an endless combinatorial flow that ordinary hearing represses but becomes noticeable when attention slips and consciousness is off guard or through the effect of the recording media, which capture the noise of the world, both sensical and nonsensical, intentional and involuntary, with a nondiscriminatory ear. In fact, it is through the sound media that the sonic flux becomes perceptible, and that noise is captured and implemented in contemporary music and sound art, where it is no longer a negative determinant but active, generative matter.

Cox restores to noise the complexity and material effectivity that are erased by negative and derivative definitions. He turns noise into a historical variable, partly through his sensitivity to the way in which sound technologies have fostered awareness of the sonic flux and facilitated its use. And he recalls its centrality in perceptual and cognitive processes. But he does not pursue noise's political dimensions. Noise is not merely what lies beyond the threshold of the intelligible, latent on the edges of the perceptual field. It is also what societies actively suppress. "Subjectively," wrote Edgar Varèse, one of its champions in contemporary music, "noise is any sound one does not like"[19]; collectively, Paul Hegarty states, it is "the sounds of 'other people'": those minorities whose expressive styles may question the dominance of leading social groups or offer alternatives to their conceptions of the world.[20]

As the sounds of others—and of otherness—noise is prime political material. Jacques Attali has argued that the organization of the audible is at the core of any political system. States are monopolistic noise emitters and acoustic surveillance systems that set the usable bandwidth and filter out unwanted frequencies.[21] Music is an allegory of the state's regulatory function. As it extracts form from the virtual unformed, music acts out the primal violence through which the social order is constituted and symbolizes the power of

214   EXPERIMENTAL FILM AND QUEER MATERIALITY

the state to impose social coherence and expel what threatens it. Traditional composition employs a range of acceptable sounds (a fundamental tone and the intervals in the overtone series) and combines them according to a set of rules (harmony) that seek to exclude dissonance—or noise. The performance of music stages this power of exclusion and reinforces the cohesion of a community of listeners who gather around a shared harmonic idiom that passes for natural. Because of this, music is always on the side of power: "Its order simulates the social order and its dissonances express marginalities. The code of music simulates the accepted rules of society" (29). Beyond the official tonescape, however, the subterranean strains of the popular—of ecstasy, subversion, Dionysian excess—are occasional disturbances and repositories of future possibilities (16–17).

In Attali's reading, these possibilities of subversion are scattered and submerged under the traditional tonal system of the West, most systematically and influentially codified in Jean-Philippe Rameau's *Traité de l'harmonie* (1722). Orthodox tonality began to break down toward the end of the nineteenth century, when harmonic combinatorics became exhausted and ended up generating dissonant alternatives like serial music and other atonal systems (83). Innovative music and musicians became detached from state power and attached to marginal social groups, such as the Jewish high bourgeoisie that patronized the Second Viennese School or the artistic circles that supported later experiments in aleatory and electronic music and *musique concrète*. A second force that wrested music from the control of state power, and rose simultaneously with the musical avant-garde, was the mass music market, supported by the growth of the broadcast industry, which cut the dependence of music from the elites and turned it into a free-floating commodity.

For Attali, neither experimental music nor the mass music market had much social efficacy in ushering in new aural or social regimes. The "theoretical music" of Cage, Pierre Boulez, and Stockhausen was produced through chance or dehumanized numerical processes and was therefore an exponent of the technocratic rationality of the post-World War II era. And recording and broadcast technologies spread homogenizing repetition—the steady return of the same under the veneer of novelty—dissolved music's festive, sacrificial character, and promoted isolated consumption—"the individualized use of order" (100). Even apparently unruly styles, such as rock and pop, only simulate collective rebellion, while they impose, in fact, solipsistic enjoyment. Only noise, in the sense of proscribed sonority, could rupture this false coherence while asserting difference, autonomy, and marginality and evoking potentials that remain untapped by hegemonic musical modes: "The noise of festival and freedom; a utopia of better times; a new life coming" (133).

These potentials become possible in the sonic order that Attali calls "composition," so-named because it entails "the right to compose one's life," the creation "of one's own relation to the world," and of "new forms of socialization" (134, 132). In his historical scheme, composition rises from the glut of the mass music market. By dint of insistent reiteration, music and "authorized" sound end up meaning nothing at all, and as their hold on the collective imagination loosens, sound technologies and musical styles become available for individual appropriation and reinterpretation. For Attali, composition was still emerging at the time he wrote about it. Some of its possibilities had been foreshadowed in Russolo's and Cage's use of noise, but their work ended up being co-opted by reigning sonic rationality and was unable to change the social relations around music. A more successful attempt was free jazz. Originating in the late fifties, free jazz combined musical experimentation and anti-racist activism and was able to generate a parallel recording and distribution infrastructure, but eventually subsided after being "contained, repressed, limited, censored, expelled" (140). Characteristics of the regime of composition are the blurring of the line between professional and amateur—in the proliferation of amateur orchestras—the recovery of musical traditions, the creation of new instruments—by which he probably means electronic instruments—and improvisation and collective creation.

Sex and the body are central to Attali's composition. They are sources of the (conceptual and literal) dissonance that destabilizes repetition and suggests new ways of living and relating to each other. Composition entails "the production of difference" and "the rediscovery and blossoming of the body," set free by a more open-ended, creative rapport than that allowed by the reified products of the market (142). The rediscovery of the body takes the form of new relational styles in which eroticism is reappropriated and transformed. If traditional music offered an allegory of state power and social cohesion, composition brings into play the noise of the body and highlights music's sexual narrative. It recalls that the body is one of music's main subjects and that a composition offers "a model for amorous relations . . . an exceptional figure of represented or repeated sexual pleasure" (143). While this is evident in some of the classical repertoire—especially in opera, where desire is the main mover of the plot—in composition, the goal is no longer to possess and "mark" (Attali's term) another body, but to enjoy it freely: "to exchange the noises of bodies, to hear the noises of others in exchange for one's own, to create, in common, the codes within which communication takes place." And further: "Any noise, when two people decide to invest their imaginary and their desire in it, becomes a potential relationship, future order" (143). This order is not to be imperialistically imposed on others, but an exercise of personal and communal sovereignty. In addition, the "people," bodies, desires, or relationships that arise from noise are free-floating and unspecified; "potential" and "future," they fulfil what for José Muñoz is one of the defining traits of queerness: being "always on the horizon."[22] A subverter of established order, and a catalyst of disruption and creativity, noise reshuffles the social compact. It favors the acts of "radical self-perception and filiation" that Sedgwick placed at the heart of queerness and opens up "a zone of possibilities" that musicians and filmmakers ventured into in order to imagine how bodies and sounds in combination would reshape perception, materiality, and relationality.

Queer Noise in the Postwar Avant-Garde

Conceptually trenchant, Attali is often vague on historical detail, and his arguments about composition are theoretically intriguing but unfold in a void of historical reference. What, in addition to free jazz, a style that, by Attali's own admission, had been suppressed at the time of his writing, could count as the sound—the noise—of "composition"? Cornelius Cardew's Scratch Orchestra, and Cardew's music generally, exemplify many of its traits—amateurism, improvisation, collective creation—but other examples are possible. In her insightful afterword to the English edition of Attali's *Noise*, Susan McClary points out that the book came out during the explosion of punk—only months before *Never Mind the Bollocks, Here's The Sex Pistols*, in fact.[23] Punk was clearly not on Attali's radar, but its amateurism, musical spareness, political appeal, its way of turning the apparatus of pop music against itself, its foregrounding of the body, not to mention its sheer noisiness, would seem to fulfil many of the traits of composition. And so did, as McClary points out, New York's downtown music scene from the late seventies forward, some of whose most popular developments were directly influenced by punk. Long predating the rise of this movement, the downtown scene had, since the sixties, rejected the academicism of contemporary classical music in the

United States—dominated by Schoenberg's serialism—along with its imperviousness to popular languages and its disregard for communication. Milton Babbitt, a twelve-tone composer, a cofounder of the Columbia-Princeton Electronic Music Center, and a pioneer of computer music, captured the academic attitude in his essay, "Who Cares Who is Listening?" (1958)—an unabashed defense of musical hermeticism.[24] The downtown scene, by contrast, wanted to connect with listeners. Musicians indulged in tonality, recognized the appeal of folk and pop, which they mixed with experimental gestures, used open-ended, improvisatory structures, and performed in alternative venues—art centers, such as The Kitchen, and bars and dance clubs, such as Mudd, Knitting Factory, or CBGB. By the time Attali's book came out, prominent downtown figures were minimalist luminaries, such as Steve Reich and Philip Glass, or unclassifiable musicians, such as Laurie Anderson, Peter Gordon (leader of The Love of Life Orchestra), and Arthur Russell. Russell, a prodigious and idiosyncratic talent who ranged from disco to folk to pop to minimalism, is in many ways a compendium of the downtown musical spirit between the mid-seventies, when he emerged on the scene, and the early nineties, when he passed away. Russell's music, like that of other downtown composers, put into contemporary music the noise of the street, of social difference, of the body, and of sexuality.[25]

But even before then, there were numerous attempts to disrupt reigning tonal regimes while proposing new social and corporeal relations around noise. In Attali's scheme, composition rises after—and from—the deadening repetition of commercial popular music and derives from the ruptures and excesses of the latter, but it may make more historical sense to understand as simultaneous what he conceived as successive stages. After all, unassimilated sonorities—*noise*—that enabled "the production of difference" and heralded a "blossoming of the body" were already at work in the mainstream recording media. The very technologies and distribution networks that underpinned the music market also spread aural and corporeal dissent; they did not only foster deadening vulgarization and solipsistic consumption but also a considerable expansion of sound cultures. The work on electromagnetic fields that made possible radio transmission was also applied to the development of new electronic instruments, such as the Elektrophon, the Theremin, and the Hammond organ, and these were in turn the forbears of the synthesizers that from the early sixties forward introduced unprecedented timbres and dynamics into popular and experimental music. The system of electromechanical recording through microphones and vacuum tube amplifiers patented by Western Electric in the mid-1920s set the basis for the consolidation of the record market but also facilitated the dissemination of a an extremely broad musical spectrum that included blues, folk, and different kinds of "exotica"—such as Javanese gamelan or traditional Indian music. Electronic sounds and non-Western music encouraged the development of alternative tonal and tuning systems and new compositional structures. And the magnetic tape recorders that became household items in the early fifties extended the thresholds of aural inventiveness still further by offering, in Cage's words, "any sound, in any combination, with any parameters."[26]

These developments were often floated for their emancipatory potential. Among designers of new instruments such as Luigi Russolo, Leon Theremin, and Jörg Mager, champions of non-Western music, such as Henry Cowell and Lou Harrison, tape music pioneers like John Cage and Pauline Oliveros, and developers of new tonal systems, such as Harry Partch, the broadly held consensus was that the new sonorities freed the ear from the shackles of aural tradition and blew away old mental habits "like dust."[27] But it has been less often noted that for many of these experimental composers, the liberated ear—open to noise—fostered different forms of corporeal and social freedom. Perhaps the emancipatory aura of "noise"—random and unassimilated sound matter—attracted a considerable number of queer composers and sound innovators, such as Colin McPhee, Cowell, Harrison, Cage, Partch, and Oliveros, to name a few. This is not to say that there was something inherently queer about noise or experimental sound. Pioneer *bruitist* Varèse was not particularly queer-friendly. Tape music innovators Otto Luening and Vladimir Ussachevsky, cofounders of the Columbia-Princeton Electronic Music Center, were blissfully oblivious of the sexual or corporeal resonances of electronic music. And Milton Babbit was attracted to computers for the (fairly unqueer) reason that they permitted absolute control and eliminated the variability that emanated from musicians' bodies and conventional instruments.[28] And while experimentation was not inherently queer, neither were queer composers immediately attuned to the new music. Nadine Hubbs has shown that one of the distinctive idioms of American musical modernism—working in tonal and harmonic orthodoxy—was crafted by gay composers Virgil Thomson, Aaron Copeland, Leonard Bernstein, and Ned Rorem.[29] And yet, despite these caveats and counterexamples, there was a considerable queer investment in the music and sound experiments of the early and mid-twentieth century, experiments that frequently enlisted noise in the development of alternative sonorities.

SYNTHETIC, EXOTIC, MAGNETIC   219

The queer appeal of noise may have resided in its disreputability. In an early statement on the use of noise in contemporary music, Henry Cowell compared noise to sex. Pure tone, he pointed out, was only possible in laboratory conditions. All musical tones contained resident noise—irregular overtones that the ear had become accustomed to filtering out. Yet despite its pervasiveness, noise remained proscribed material: "Although existing in all music, the noise-element has been to music as sex to humanity, essential to its existence, but impolite to mention, something to be cloaked by ignorance and silence."[30] Cowell himself had explored noise through tone clusters, playing inside the piano, and laying objects across the piano strings, and he praised composers George Antheil and Edgar Varèse for using unorthodox sonorities to create a "new chemistry of sound." For John Cage, who was one of Cowell's disciples and a devotee of Varèse's work, noise was not one more ingredient in the musical mix but its very core: "When I really began making music, I mean composing 'seriously,' it was to involve myself with noise, because noises escape power, that is, the laws of counterpoint and harmony."[31] Cage's elision between "power" and "the laws of counterpoint and harmony" encapsulates Attali's contention that conventional music embodies, in its very structure, the aspiration toward homogeneity and the regulation of difference, while noise opens avenues for otherness and dissent. In the immediate postwar years, noise's queer valence was explored through percussion, micro-tonality, and through the incorporation of non-Western scales and structures, especially those borrowed from Balinese gamelan. Cumulatively, these developments queered the aural field: they expanded a soundscape that remained largely circumscribed to traditional tonal systems and brought into music the materiality of the world and the body—particularly of bodies whose sexuality was beyond the pale of the norm.

Percussion, Voice, Exotica

Noise, in Cowell's just-cited essay meant essentially percussion, which produced the least pure tones of all instrumental families, directly addressed the body and the emotions, and gave music, in Cowell's words, "the backbone of entrancement." Percussion was open and expansive, and extended the musical body by incorporating everyday materials. "Strings," Cage claimed, "want to become more and more what they already are, but the [sic] percussion wants to become other than it is."[32] Percussion freed composition from development and resolution, and inspired modular, asymmetrical works that did not orbit around a tonal center and formed aural bodies of uncertain limits. Cage's friend, Lou Harrison, was also interested in percussion as a means to loosen traditional structures and to develop improvisatory works that could be played by amateurs with minimal direction. Early in his career, he gathered ensembles of impromptu musicians who struck found materials, often culled from the rubbish, as a way to test out new tone colors.[33] What started as tinkering became eventually formalized into new instruments. For his *Concerto for Violin with Percussion Orchestra* (1952), Harrison built a "metallophone" with coffee cans, clock coils mounted on the sounding body of a stringless guitar, two galvanized bathtubs, and sets of flower pots and plumber's pipes.[34] For Harry Partch, a mid-century experimentalist who also wrote percussion pieces for instruments of his own design, these material and acoustic conjunctions expressed a supra-human sexuality—a sexuality of things whose erotic convergence produced sound and whose sound appealed to the sexual body. In the documentary about his work *The Dreamer That Remains* (1973),[35] he explains how a particular wooden "tongue" and the cavity in which it was inserted had to vibrate at the same frequency in order to produce resonant tone: "The tongue must couple with the cavity. . . . Acoustics is sexy, music is sexy, nature is sexy."

When practiced on unorthodox instruments or found materials, percussion generated random pitches that hovered between the gradations of the Western chromatic scale. It permitted considerable tonal invention and offered, in Partch's view, "an antidote" to "the monolithic nature of Western musical culture."[36] Percussion filled in sections of the tonal map that remained unattended by composers. These unexplored areas were, for Partch, "a skeleton in a closet . . . without flesh and without a contact of flesh . . . an unmentionable."[37] His compositions and theoretical writings sought to bring the unmentionable out of the closet and restore flesh to the skeleton. He traced some of his dissatisfaction with conventional Western tones to the many types of music he was exposed to as a child. Born to Presbyterian missionaries to China, Harry Partch grew up in Arizona and New Mexico listening to the Chinese lullabies his mother sang for him, to border Mexican music, and Yaqui songs and dances. As a teenager, he played piano and organ in silent movie theaters and, after a brief stint at the University of Southern California's School of Music, he relocated to San Francisco, where he frequented the Mandarin theaters.[38] When contrasted with the rich soundscape in which he came of age, the twelve-tone-to-the-octave seemed to him

SYNTHETIC, EXOTIC, MAGNETIC 221

a "worn-out," limiting system exemplified in the piano keyboard—"twelve black and white bars in front of musical freedom."[39] His own scale fitted forty-three tones to the octave and used just intonation, based on strict numerical ratios rather than on the partly arbitrary steps of the tempered scale. He made himself or commissioned the instruments that could accommodate such tonal refinement.

With his system, Partch tried to restore what he insistently called the "corporeal" character of music. Music, he defended, originated in "speech intonation"; it was a bodily emanation "vital to a time and place, a here and now" and often combined with motion. Like the movements of the body, the voice did not rise and fall in measured tones but in "tonal glide[s]."[40] Strict tone intervals subjected a natural continuum to a rigid, artificial system and eroded "the ancient, lovely and fearless attitude towards the human body."[41] "True music" was "obscured" and suppressed by the reigning harmonic system, but, like Attali, he believed that its strains survived in the West among marginal groups ignored by the musical establishment: blacks, hoboes, vagrants, and scattered folk communities.[42] Partch's early compositions were inspired by the speech of itinerants (*Bitter Music*), hitchhiker inscriptions seen on highway railings (*Barstow*), and the cries of news vendors (*San Francisco*). The marginal groups where "true music" persisted also offered oases of sexual freedom. Such was the case with vagrants and itinerants, whose lifestyle Partch embraced for several years in his youth—forced by necessity but also attracted by its openness, which he frequently evoked in interviews through the rest of his life. "The Letter" (1943), a section of *Bitter Music*, was set to excerpts of a letter from a young vagrant Partch met at a California work camp and with whom he was romantically involved.[43] Tonal freedom for Partch, as for other composers, was not just a matter of the ear but of the whole body—it was the harbinger and conduit of queer corporeal and affective involvement.

Others found such queerness in non-Western traditions—particularly in Javanese gamelan, which became, according to Stevan Key, a gay marker in mid-century Western music and attracted Cowell, Cage, Benjamin Britten, and, especially, Lou Harrison, who ended up combining, in most of his work, Western and Javanese modes and instruments.[44] What clinched gamelan as a queer marker was its metonymic association with queer men; but at the same time, some of its characteristics made it amenable to such appropriation. Gamelan was based on a pentatonic scale alien to the intervals of equal temperament. Canadian composer Colin McPhee, who was partly responsible

222 EXPERIMENTAL FILM AND QUEER MATERIALITY

for introducing it to Western—particularly North American—musicians, found that only some of the tones of the *g'endér*—central instrument in gamelan ensembles—agreed with the piano, while others were "strange and unaccountable as certain tones in the voice of a Negro blues singer."[45] Despite its simpler harmony, gamelan music had considerable timbral nuance and rhythmic sophistication.[46] He praised its "indescribable freshness," flexibility, and freedom, qualities that emanated from the percussive character of this music and from its loose, modular structure.[47]

McPhee discovered gamelan more or less as he did his own homosexuality. Obsessed with this music after hearing it on gramophone records, he travelled to Bali in the early thirties to study it in the field. His wife, anthropologist Jane Belo, who was also engaged in field work in Bali, financed the expedition.[48] It seems the marriage foundered due to his interest in a local man who is featured in his memoir, *A House in Bali* (1944), as his driver and assistant. (The memoir does not mention Belo.) It is possible that the sensuality of the island and the enchantment of the music may have inspired in him a looser attitude toward sexuality, and that this looseness had to do with an understanding of sex as an incidental behavior rather than as a badge of identity full of import and consequence. If this non-identity based notion of sexuality had a soundtrack, it might be gamelan, whose immersive, impersonal character McPhee contrasted favorably to the "personal" and "effusive" character of Western music. Gamelan evokes the sounds of the atmosphere and the weather: hail, rain, "the low sound of wind in the lalang grass"; for its part, Western music is "tempestuous" and "baffling in its emotional climaxes . . . like someone crying," and conveys shrill personal affirmation.[49]

McPhee's praise of a music that evokes the impersonal eventfulness of nature rather than the convolutions of the soul, anticipates Cage's rejection of personal expressiveness, his embrace of chance, and his desire to make "a nothingness"—not musical objects but acoustic ambiences.[50] The point for Cage was to suspend judgment and eliminate one's feelings and volition in order to purge "the things that we know about through Freud . . . guilt, shame, conscience."[51] This was for him a way to avoid labeling or assessing the body and its pleasures and simply "wake up to the very life we are living" without prejudices or expectations.[52] From this perspective, the loose structure of gamelan, Partch's microtones, and the unusual timbres of percussion were means to channel *and* dilute unorthodox bodies and desires: to produce, through sonic means, openness, acceptance, and unlabeled pleasures. These musical means are analogous to other contemporary strategies of queer encipherment that bypassed personality and self-expression and favored instead surface effects, such as the abstraction, blankness, and indirection that critics Jonathan D. Katz, Moira Roth, Gavin Butt, and Kenneth Silver, among others, have studied in the work of pop artists Jasper Johns, Robert Rauschenberg, or Andy Warhol.[53]

Queer experimental film intersected intermittently with the queer noise of postwar musical experimentation. Unusual percussion, odd voices, and non-Western scales and modes occasionally punctuated films that destabilized conventional notions of gender, the body, and sexuality, as did titles by Marie Menken, Sidney Peterson, and Maya Deren.

For all their considerable aesthetic differences, Menken and Peterson shared a taste for odd voices and peculiar instrumentation. For her soundtracks, Menken drew on relatively marginal composers like Lucia Dlugoszewski and Teiji Ito, while Peterson tended to enlist friends and colleagues at the San Francisco School of Art, where most of his films were produced as course projects, even though he also used a Cage composition for *Horror Dream*. Menken's most sonically striking film is her first: *Visual Variations on Noguchi* (1946–47), a dynamic portrait of Isamu Noguchi's sculptures that was initially intended as visual background to Merce Cunningham's ballet *The Seasons* (1945), with music by John Cage (see Figure 8.1). Eventually, Menken decided to add a soundtrack, which she commissioned from Dlugoszewski. Inspired by Cage and Varèse, both of whom she studied with briefly, Dlugoszewski used timbre as her central compositional material and amply experimented with percussion on ordinary objects. For an earlier commission, the sonic background for a Living Theater production of Alfred Jarry's *Ubu the King*, she had used a typewriter, a honk, a drop saw, a kettle whistle, beans rattling inside a jar and poured on a copper sheet, various watery sounds, and rustling and crinkling paper—a recurring timbre in her work.[54] For *Variations*, she used various struck and rubbed metal surfaces, her own version of the prepared piano (which she called "timbre piano"), paper, bubbling water, wood blocks, and whispered voices that are often unintelligible—except for some women's names ("Margaret . . . Ida . . .") and loose words ("began . . . a . . . lithium"). Rather than isolated timbric values, Dlugoszewski favored superimposition and simultaneity. The piece is fast and dense, a rush of rattles, clatters, crinklings, and high-pitched glissandi. Voices, struck wood, and the "timbre piano," on which she played some quick scales—one has a distinct flamenco flavor—occasionally rise from the mix. The rugged, overlapping tone coloring gives

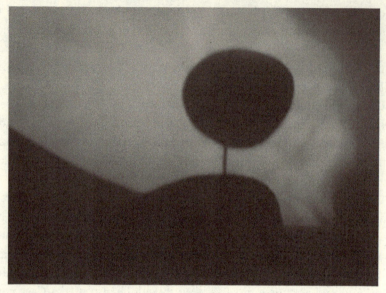

Figure 8.1 Marie Menken, *Visual Variations on Noguchi*, 1947. Frame enlargement.

depth and texture to Noguchi's smooth surfaces, muddles their clarity and finish, and endows them with a complicated animacy that evokes a messy sentience in the inorganic.

Peterson was less invested on percussion than on voice combined with eclectic musical accompaniment. His eccentric soundtracks abound in uncouth, untutored singing and playing and oddly intoned voices whose coarseness and slightly hollow ring suggests that they may have been recorded in a makeshift space rather than at a conventional studio. *The Lead Shoes* (1949), a dreamy narrative evoking fratricide and dismemberment, features two folk ballads that blend in and out of a Dixieland quartet (see Figure 8.2). Both singing and instrumental music were performed by Peterson's students and colleagues at the California School of Fine Arts in San Francisco—school director, Douglas McAgy played drums, for example.[55] The raw ballad-singing and the songs' truculent subject evokes the homegrown surrealism of many of the tracks in Harry Smith's *Anthology of American Folk Music*, which would appear shortly afterward. The jazz sections have a fully urban sound whose roughness matches the folk singing; both roil with a dissonant energy that sits incongruously with the melancholia and despair that dominate the screen. The main visual strand shows

Figure 8.2 Sidney Peterson, *The Lead Shoes*, 1949. Frame enlargement.

a woman ("Mother" in the credits) retrieving what might be construed as the body of her dead son—a deep-sea diver's costume—from the edge of the sea, carting it across town, and hauling it up to her bedroom. Her actions are cross-cut to a young girl playing hopscotch. The recurrence and repetitive nature of the game match the cyclicality of the music. And the alternation between both sets of images mimes the oscillation between two musical languages in the soundtrack. A later film by Peterson, *Mr. Frenhofer and the Minotaur* (1950), similarly mixes peculiar instrumentation and voice. An elusive evocation of an artist's erotic daydreams, it brings together melodic parts for guitar and violin, incidental noise (a screechy violin mimicking a panicked scream, unseen objects crashing), and an absurdist punning voice-over commentary written by Peterson himself in a style reminiscent of *Finnegans Wake*. Spoken by a female voice with a posh, mellifluous cadence, it consistently skirts sense and works instead as one more sonic ingredient in the instrumental mix. The instability of the soundtrack and the slippery commentary rhyme with the elliptical actions of the performers and the anamorphic distortion of the visual track, which blurs and elongates bodies unpredictably.

226 EXPERIMENTAL FILM AND QUEER MATERIALITY

Teiji Ito's scores for Maya Deren are exponents of the contemporary fascination with non-Western modes and, like Dlugoszewski's and Peterson's soundtracks, accompany and amplify dissident corporealities. The soundtrack of *Meshes of the Afternoon* (1943), initially conceived as a silent film, is classically Japanese in feel and instrumentation. The score has parts for tenten and bengaku drums, shô and hichiriki (traditional wind instruments), and koto—replaced in the actual recording by a guitar. The voice parts are inspired by the youkyoku songs of Noh theater, but the structure of the soundtrack departs from Japanese custom since, as Michiko Ogawa has pointed out, it mixes modes—gagaku, nagauta, kabuki, and shômyô—that would hardly coexist in an orthodox composition.[56] Ito recorded these soundtracks by overdubbing the different parts on a multitrack tape recorder. Room tone and open miking produce a slight reverberation, which heightens, in turn, the dreaminess of the film, a quality which arises from the menacing latency of domestic objects and spaces and from the film's uncertain bodies. The menace of dailiness is underscored by dry drumming, brief atonal passages in the upper registers of the shô and hichiriki, and low humming voices matched to particularly ominous shots—a knife on a dinner table or a ghostly figure in an empty alley. In the course of the film, the protagonist shifts from pursued to pursuer, unfolds into three different avatars of herself, and defies spatial logic, when, in four continuous steps, she strides across radically different settings. She eventually takes her own life as if in reaction to a universe intent on rejecting her. The music, which constantly conveys dislocation and unease, magnifies her instability and the hostile radiation of the environment.

If *Meshes of the Afternoon* evoked Japanese classical modes, the soundtrack of *The Very Eye of Night* (1958), which was Deren's last title but her first collaboration with Ito, combines a classical wind trio with percussion passages for metal and wooden gamelan. The sound's uncertain geography, along with its delicacy and airiness, underlines the film's loose spatiality. It is a dance film shown in photographic negative in which the performers, who play different celestial bodies, float across a dark firmament, their movement exquisitely choreographed by Anthony Tudor. At times, they scud across a slowly shifting sky; other times, they rotate in a way that confuses any sense of coordinates or direction, an effect achieved by eliminating the horizon, suspending their bodies from cables, and filming their evolutions from a scaffold. Some dancers stand for different heavenly bodies and deities: the constellation Gemini; Uranus's major moons (Ariel, Oberon, Umbriel, and Titania); and Uranus himself, who condenses the planet, the god, and the entire celestial orb that the god incarnated. In contrast, Urania—in Greek mythology, Uranus's granddaughter—and Noctambulo—etymologically, nightwalker—have no celestial correlatives. They could be regarded as the film's protagonists, since their motion is freer and more individualized than that of the rest, who often appear in group figures that stand for the constellations of which they are a part. Noctambulo drifts alone through the sky and seeks to pry Urania from the embrace of Uranus. His scheme reproduces the archetypal plot of the classical ballet—the pursuit of ideal and elusive beauty. It can also symbolize the chase for knowledge, since Urania is the Greek muse of astronomy, and Noctambulo's attempt to lure her to his side might express a Promethean attempt to pry into nature's secrets. Noctambulo and Uranus vie for Urania's companionship; in repeated *portées*, she is transferred from one to the other while Uranus's moons vie to keep her in her grandfather's orbit. In the end, apparently defeated, Noctambulo drifts across the firmament, alone once again, while Uranus and Urania, surrounded by their four moons, resume their celestial transit with Gemini watching at a distance.

The music dramatizes the film's central struggle. While the wind trio is matched to the disputation over Urania, the gamelan ushers in a calmer rotation and suggests the restoration of order in the heavenly spheres. The alternation of the two scenarios evokes the circularity of celestial motion but also the cyclicality of the search for knowledge, which in the film seems to lead to failure. Started shortly after Deren published her study of Haitian voudon, *Divine Horsemen: The Living Gods of Haiti* (1953), and after she had spent several years filming its rituals, *The Very Eye of Night* transfers to a balletic-mythological scenario many of the themes that she had been exploring in voudon: initiation into arcane knowledge and the power of dance to channel this search. She also imports into this scenario some of the gender and sexual messiness of voudon. Some voudon gods have hermaphroditic features and male and female deities "ride"—or possess—celebrants regardless of their gender, practicing a mystic version of transgender embodiment.[57] In the film, one of Uranus's moons, Umbriel, named after a male gnome in Alexander Pope's *Rape of the Lock*, is incarnated by a female dancer and Gemini act as a couple of self-absorbed male lovers, impervious to the drama unfolding around them.

Queer Electronics

Even more than unorthodox vocal performance, percussion, or exotica synthesized electronic sound projected unmappable corporealities. Electronic instruments fulfilled one of the recurring obsessions of contemporary music: the creation of sliding tones and microtones that did not abide by the steps of the diatonic scale. Jörg Mager, a German engineer and musician who designed several early synthesizers in the 1920s, celebrated that electronics put at the disposal of musicians "the totality of all traditional tones on which the timbre depends."[58] Mager's contemporary, Leon Theremin, boasted that his eponymous invention freed the composer "from the despotism of the twelve-note tempered scale," and went on to report that he was developing an "electronic harmonium" equipped with keys and rotary condenser dials that could produce pitch fluctuations of up to one-hundredth of a tone. Theremin never completed this instrument, but others working on his steps developed versions of it. Just to cite two: in the early thirties, Alfred Lesti and Frederick Sammis developed the "Polytone" or "organ of a trillion tones"; and two decades later, musician and engineer Raymond Scott, completed the Clavivox, which adapted Theremin's technology and could generate a broad number of tones and synthetic sounds that he used to compose advertisement jingles.[59] Neither instrument had much commercial success due to their complexity and relative instability of pitch. In 1962, in the San Francisco Bay Area, Don Buchla created an instrument using ring modulators that were regulated, like Theremin's harmonium, with rotary dials. Two years later, Robert Moog, who in his youth had hand-built and sold theremins, started to commercialize his own synthesizer, also capable of virtually infinite modulation.[60] Through the ethereal medium of electricity, this new family of instruments fulfilled Partch's dream of a "corporeal" music that would range across the entire tonal spectrum. Except that corporeality of synthesized sound was not the earthy, folk kind cultivated by Partch, who used natural materials and drew inspiration from ancient Greek instruments; it was abstract, distributed, of uncertain contours, and slightly monstrous. Not only was it based on a fusion of the organic and electronics; sounds emerged automatically out of a black box without the corporeal gestures and physical exertion that accompanied the playing of conventional instruments; and the resulting timbres lacked correlates in the world of known things. They were the noise of technology, as Andy Birtwistle has suggested,[61] or sound postcards from a still unmapped universe. This was, in fact, the reason

SYNTHETIC, EXOTIC, MAGNETIC   229

why science fiction and horror were the first popular film genres to incorporate synthesized sound. Horror films like *The Red House* (Daves 1946, scored by Miklos Rosza) and *The Spiral Staircase* (Siodmark 1947, scored by Roy Webb) incorporated the theremin, while science-fiction classics *The Day the Earth Stood Still* (Wise, 1951, scored by Bernard Herrmann) and *Forbidden Planet* (Wilcox, 1956) featured, respectively, theremin parts and the first fully electronic soundtrack—by Louis and Bebe Barron.[62]

Electronic instruments prompted a new musical syntax. While electronic tones were often put to the service of traditional music—in Clara Rockwell's virtuoso renditions of classical pieces on the theremin or Wendy de Carlos's hit album, *Switched on Bach* (1968), played on the Moog—their innovative character also seemed to require new structures. In the hands of experimenters, electronic music tended to avoid standard harmonic development and came closer to the modular conception of percussion pieces or to the sonic plateaus of LaMonte Young's early sixties works. Pauline Oliveros, one of the first users of the Buchla, kept her music amelodic and aleatory, based on relatively minimal, slowly shifting variations, as she was less interested in developing musical ideas than in pitching the appropriate sonic backdrop for introspection and meditation.[63] Susan Ciani, who worked in Buchla's workshop before launching her career as a musician, did not build her works as "note music" but as "gestures" and "sweeps" that exploited the connotative resonance of sounds.[64] And long before them, Edgar Varèse had built his compositions as "flows," "shifting planes" and "zones of intensity" of "timbres or colors or different loudnesses"; the different pitches were not tuned to a common fundamental, and rather than move toward resolution, his "sound masses" remained separate, as tectonic plates brushing past each other.[65] The bodies of electronic music, then, are fluid and para-human, alien to identity categories and, therefore, queer. It is not surprising that electronic music was quickly adopted by choreographers that articulated alternative perceptions of the body. Cage's earliest electronic title, *Imaginary Landscape no. 1* (1939), for two variable-speed turntables, frequency recordings, muted piano, and cymbal, was commissioned by Bonnie Bird for a choreography that only showed parts of the performers' bodies lit by a searchlight, while they stood behind black flats in a darkened stage.[66] Cage's composition was also used in Sidney Peterson's film *Horror Dream* (1947) to accompany a choreography by Marian Van Tuyl that was idiosyncratically filmed to highlight immobility and awkward repetition rather than harmonious, proficient motion. And one of the earliest customers for the Moog synthesizer was

230 EXPERIMENTAL FILM AND QUEER MATERIALITY

choreographer Alwin Nikolais,[67] who dressed his dancers in deforming gear, encumbered them with awkward prostheses, blurred their gender, and made them melt into the décor.

In experimental film and elsewhere, electronic sound primarily connoted altered states of consciousness, an association cemented by psychedelic culture's fascination with synthetic sonorities, but it also retained its link to alternative corporealities. The unconventional syntax of electronic music accompanies eccentric bodies that stretch and spill beyond their natural limits, implode and dissolve, or challenge straightforward apprehension. Three examples of this convergence, each with a different orientation and aesthetic, are James Broughton's *Dreamwood* (1972), with music by electronic pioneer Morton Subotnick; Kennth Anger's *Invocation of My Demon Brother* (1969), scored by Mike Jagger; and Barbara Hammer's soundtracks for *Dyketactics* (1975) and *Menses* (1975); all are exponents of Bay Area queer hippiedom.

Broughton's *Dreamwood* depicts a flight from a polluted, dehumanized industrial landscape to a rough but enchanted nature ("the forest of the dream, sacred wood, grove of initiation," declaims the filmmaker off-screen). The camera pans across lovely, wooded hills and valleys populated by sybils, a satyr, stern fairies, and bearded emblems of natural manhood; many of them are prompt to cast off their clothes and tangle up with the protagonist in gruff but no doubt enlightening sensual encounters. Subotnick's synthesized tones lift the protagonist's adventures into the realm of allegory or hallucination. Composed on a Buchla 100, the music has a considerable timbral and rhythmic flexibility. It follows the image in rather conventional fashion, amplifying moods, setting the pace, marking transitions, and underlining peaks and lulls in the action. Its versatility mirrors the adaptative trajectory of the protagonist and his pliable body, which ends up melting into his milieu. At the close of the film, he lies naked on the ground, face down as if copulating with the earth, and the very last shots present him silhouetted against a setting sun with a full moon superimposed on his chest. The flight from civilization culminates in an erotic fusion with the elements, as the hero's body mingles with the planet and is pierced by cosmos. This synthesis is underlined by the unifying character of the music, which envelops the film from start to finish and closely adheres in mood and pace to the visual track.

In contrast with *Dreamwood*, *Invocation of My Demon Brother* evokes dissolution and disintegration. It conjures, at an extremely rapid clip, images of violence and negativity mixed with practices (sex, pot-smoking, music, magic) that might neutralize them but turn out to be as frantic and foreboding as the realities they try to offset. Dark, minimal, and obsessive, Jagger's soundtrack underlines this claustrophobic circularity. It was put together shortly after he learned to use the Moog, at a time when Anger resided in London and was intimate with the band. It consists of a repetitive four-note figure (three identical sustained pitches followed by a descending tone) that recurs throughout with small variations in the length of each note, the ligature between them, and the silences between each iteration. As the film advances, the silences become longer, and the basic repeating figure is overlaid with shots and explosions and with a wheezy parallel four-note pattern that echoes the first and tightens its grip on the film. This closure is corroborated by the variant repetition of several takes—an albino boy holding a glass wand, soldiers jumping out of a helicopter, and Anger running in circles as he performs an "Equinox ritual" at the Haight Theater in San Francisco in September of 1967.[68] The bodies in the film are fragmented by the framing and editing. Naked boys lying together and wrestling in jest are turned upside down and superimposed. The rest are shown in pieces, partly blocked from full view or selectively framed, a headless torso recurs in slightly different attitudes and lighting. Their cut-up quality is characteristic throughout. *Invocation of My Demon Brother* was a salvage piece put together, in Anger's telling, from the remains of what was going to be *Lucipher Rising*. The main part of the footage was stolen by Bobby Beausoleil, Anger's friend and assistant, a musician, and a fixture at the Haight in those years, and it was never recovered. The filmmaker assembled *Invocation* from the extant stock, which may account for the fragmentariness; in turn, the film's somber mood was probably influenced by Beausoleil's betrayal. The music's relentless ostinato further tears the film apart. It undercuts the variety and speed of the visual track with an insistent return of the same that reinforces the film's overall bleakness.

While *Invocation of My Demon Brother* radiates negativity, Barbara Hammer's early seventies shorts exude humor and cheer, qualities also telegraphed by their soundtracks. *Dyketactics* (1974) repeats a simple melodic figure that she created on a Moog synthesizer at Mills College.[69] It accompanies the film's two sequences: in the first, women in nature clown around, lie in the grass, and lather each other in a brook; in the second, a couple—Barbara Hammer and her lover at the time, Ascher Poe—make love at home, bathed in the slanting sunlight that streams through the windows. Sweet and upbeat, the music remains the same in the shift from group to couple and from exterior to interior, uniting both in a continuum of affirmation and enjoyment. Its simplicity and accessibility contrasts with the elaborate superimpositions in the visual track, which sought to convey, in Hammer's testimony, tactile proximity and involvement, and to undermine the equation of looking with detached perspective and distanced control. If *Dyketactics* is celebratory, *Menses* (1974) is satirical, consisting of a series of sketches that break the taboo on representing menstruation. Young women open their legs and let eggs fall and smash on the ground, walk out of supermarkets laden with boxes of sanitary pads, and let blood drip down their legs; they later smear their chests with it and take codeine as a sacrament to neutralize menstrual discomfort. Like other titles of the period such as *Superdykes* (1975), the actions in *Menses* have a performative quality; they are acted out in open spaces and make visible traditionally hidden aspects of women's corporeality. The frontal shooting and straightforward editing foreground this theatricality; at the same time, several segments exploit specifically cinematic techniques like superimpositions, masking, and tinting. For a film that vindicates the naturalness of the body, the soundtrack is patently artificial but chimes with the film's humorous irreverence. It starts with a deadpan female voice stating that menstruation is "ecologically sound" followed by the word "menses" sampled, slowed-down, double-tracked, and phased so that it reverberates cavernously, lowering the feminine voice to a masculine range. Electronic beeps progressively invade the aural field, which is dominated by a driving synthesized pulse through which the word menses occasionally comes through. Toward the end, another off-screen voice recalling the experience of the first period—"I thought I was dying"—is processed with abundant echo and segues into the reverberating repetition of the first syllables of the word "menstruation." In addition to confirming the visual comedy, sound processing undermines the traditional association of women's culture with nature and authenticity—an association that other early films by Hammer seek to cement—bringing it into the realm of the textual, contrived, and performative. In these registers, menstrual blood, electronics, and synthesized sound collude to refigure women's bodies and destabilize their placement in the cultural imaginary.

Magnetic Tape and Queer Plunderphonics

While electronic instruments generated unprecedented sonorities, magnetic tape permitted the capture and playback of the sonic continuum but could also be used to process sound and transform familiar vibrations into unaccustomed tone. Tape became a common aid for musicians and filmmakers after the late forties, when the United States government, which had seized German patents on magnetic recording as part of the War Reparations Act, licensed the technology to companies such as Magnecord, Rangertone, and Ampex, and they, in turn, started to commercialize magnetic tape recorders.[70] Tape was initially used by experimental musicians as a generator of new sonorities.[71] Early tape works by Luening and Ussachevsky used delay and variable playback speed to stretch the sounds of conventional instruments beyond recognition. Warner Jepson, a San Francisco-based pioneer of tape music, followed their cue. He enjoyed "changing reality" by looping, splicing, reversing, and slowing down or speeding up commonplace sounds in pieces that were incorporated into Ann Halprin's choreographies of the late fifties and early sixties and, eventually, into experimental films.[72] Probably on Halprin's recommendation—she was a close friend of James Broughton—Jepson made the soundtracks for Broughton's *The Bed* (1968) and for psychedelic classic *Luminous Procuress* (1972), by Broughton's student Steven Arnold. In both, he used the capabilities of magnetic recorders to defamiliarize ordinary sound. For Arnold's film, he played backward and forward taped conversations in several languages, while for *The Bed*, he double-tracked keyboard parts, phasing them rhythmically, and slowed down recorded guitar chords to generate organ-like tones.

Important as these uses were, queer experimental filmmakers generally saw tape less as a generator of new timbres than as an instrument to appropriate and rework preexisting sound files—a practice that musician John Oswald named "plunderphonics"—with the purpose of reshaping their sexual and gender politics.[73] Two examples of queer plunderphonics are James Tenney—seldom invoked in relation to queer culture—and Oswald himself. Tenney's *Collage #1 (Blue Suede)* (1961) cut up and remixed a popular recording by Elvis Presley, eliminating every trace of melody or progression and drowning the singer's voice in a storm of fuzz, splices, echoes, and dropout. In this way, Tenney disintegrated the illusion of the complete, "lubricated" singing body that pop music seeks to project—the aural vehicle of Elvis's consumable masculinity—and turned it into a synthetic sound fog, hybrid of voice and machine.[74] Decades later, in his first *Plunderphonic* EP (1988), John Oswald altered Dolly Parton's recording of "The Great Pretender" in order to "to take a leisurely tour of the intermediate areas of Ms. Parton's masculinity" and subject her (music) to "a dramatic gender change."[75] He overlayed her singing, phased some of the backup parts, and

234   EXPERIMENTAL FILM AND QUEER MATERIALITY

slowed down the recording to place her delivery in the lower range traditionally associated with male voices.

While Tenney and Oswald queered sound from within, disrupting its acoustic profile and infusing it with noise, experimental filmmakers altered it from the outside, by means of editing. They respected the integrity of different musical pieces but questioned their ideological premises and sexual readability by strategically relocating them in relation to the image and to each other. Kenneth Anger's *Scorpio Rising* (1963), for example, famously edited songs on adolescent love and longing—by Ricky Nelson, Elvis, Ray Charles, and "girl groups," such as The Shirelles or Martha and The Vandellas—that dominated the charts in 1962 and early 1963 to homoerotic images of motorcyclists working on their machines, getting stoned in their rooms, dressing up, and attending a part fascist/part satanic party that culminates in a road crash. Against this visual context, the songs acquire unintended sexual associations. Ricky Nelson asks a biker, framed from behind, to "let this fool rush in"; Little Peggy March's "wind-up doll" could be the bike or the lovingly lit mechanic that tends to it; and Bobby Vinton's blue-velveted "she" turns out to be a succession of "hes" in blue jeans and leather jackets. In turn, the skulls scattered through the bikers' workshops, rooms, and insignia, make the music participate in the flirtation with risk and self-obliteration that underlies the motorcycle mystique and insinuates that death is the endpoint of the energetic eroticism that drives pop music.

Jack Smith and José Rodríguez Soltero took similar advantage of the queer repositioning afforded by tape. They blended classical fragments (Vivaldi in Rodríguez Soltero's *Lupe*, 1966; a Bela Bartok violin concerto in *Flaming Creatures*, 1963) with The Supremes, Kitty Wells, The Everly Brothers, or The Rolling Stones, flattening hierarchies and making the classical tradition into just one more strand of a dense sonic tapestry dominated by pop sounds. The resulting sonic flow accompanies images of drag queens—Mario Montez plays Mexican actress Lupe Vélez in Rodríguez Soltero's film—and gender-indefinite performers—the "creatures" in *Flaming Creatures*—who become the implicit addressees of ostensibly heterosexual pop tunes and classical seriousness. The conjunction opens up some tensions in the music. Bartok's meditative piece adds pathos to the moment in *Flaming Creatures* when the camera surveys a jumble of rubble and dead bodies after the earthquake that takes place halfway through the film, but at the same time, the campy jocularity of the situation undermines the music's earnestness. And in Rodríguez Soltero's *Lupe*, fragments of Vivaldi's concertos escort the protagonist throughout her life—including her passage into the hereafter after her suicide—but the vivid colors and the general farcicality also bring the Italian master down to Lupe's gaudy milieu—the world of a screen goddess of the forties recreated by a cast of queer performers in threadbare settings.

In addition to permitting mobility and collage, tape also captured different kinds of noise. Noise in both films has a resistant character that cuts through the ironies of repositioning and communicates a raw core of unassimilable affect. In the last sequences of Rodríguez Soltero's film, Lupe's partner catches her cheating—with a woman played by Charles Ludlam in drag—and decides to abandon her. Lupe's despondency at their separation is matched to a flamenco tune whose harsh singing (by Niña de los Peines) and coarse registration heighten the pathos of the moment, one of the few unironic ones in the film. The roughness of this particular recording is echoed throughout the soundtrack by frequent slips and gaffes, false starts—already in the first spoken sequence—record scratches, the hiss of tape, and (perhaps involuntary) oscillations in playback speed. These incidents are the sonic counterpart of the pain that plagues Lupe's life—the loneliness and abuse that accompany her rise from streetwalker to star and counterbalance the many jocular moments in the film. The scratchy, noisy soundtrack also underlines the low production values of the image, which openly shows its seams in numerous blank screens and visible edits, and the evident patchwork quality of characters and décor (see Figure 8.3).

Flaming Creatures makes a more sustained use of noise, probably as a result of the collaboration between its director, Jack Smith, and Tony Conrad, who is credited with the film's soundtrack—essentially a collage of found sound and music—and recording. Conrad had received formal training as a musician and, when Smith made his film, he was a member of La Monte Young's experimental ensemble The Dream Syndicate.[76] As a musician, Conrad was interested in the kind of aural debris that, before Cage and Cowell, would have been relegated to music's outside. But Smith was no alien to sonic experimentation or to aural (let alone literal) debris. His impromptu home recordings made in the years leading to *Flaming Creatures* spoofed radio dramas and advertisements and frequently incorporated noise and incidental sound (accidental laughter, falling objects).[77] One of these pieces, "Earthquake Orgy," consists of panicked screams combined with an electronic rumble, probably created by rubbing the needle of a record player's cartridge. The same rumble is used in *Flaming Creatures*'s earthquake scene, where it is overlaid

Figure 8.3 José Rodríguez Soltero, *Lupe*, 1968. Frame enlargement. Courtesy of Film-Makers' Cooperative.

with ringing bells. The film sprinkles its pop-campy soundtrack with various kinds of noise: abundant crackle from well-worn records, false starts (in Kitty Wells's "It Wasn't God Who Made Honky-Tonk Angels" and "Siboney"), and the abrupt entrances and exits of pieces fading in and out (as does Bartok's concerto). Several moments of silence yield still more crackle and hiss. The last part of the film weaves together three Latin pieces: Ernesto Lecuona's "Siboney"—both an instrumental version by the Lecuona Cuban Boys and a vocal version in English—with a *pasodoble* ("España cañí") and Juanita Reina's version of the *copla* "María Amparo." These blend in and out of each other, play simultaneously, and at times lapse into silence, out of which one of them rises again. The apparently chaotic mix—in fact carefully crafted—matches the swirling confusion of the dancers in the film. The melodic nature of these pieces makes the scratches, interruptions, and fading more noticeable and even frustrating, as it is hard to follow any particular tune for long without interference. Their combination radiates the same exuberant energy as do the bodies on the screen, and their constantly blurred limits rhyme with the film's messy materiality, where performers, props, costumes, and debris intermingle in a palpitating whole.

Wet Mixes, Dripping Bodies

The acoustic messiness that haunts these films is the auditory counterpart of what Juliane Rebentisch has discussed as *camp materialism*, a concept that she exemplifies through the visual aspects of Smith's film but that can equally be applied to sound.[78] The soundtracks of Smith and Rodríguez Soltero are camp because of their exuberant affect, their stylistic excess, and the datedness of much of the music—vintage *pasodobles* and *boleros*, old show tunes, faded country numbers.[79] And they are *materialist*, in Rebentisch's sense, for embracing, in their accidental noises and slips, the ephemeral and ruinous, the natural processes of entropic decay to which commodities too are subject. Camp materialism underscores, then, the presence of natural decay within history—the artificial world of commodity production. This is figured iconographically, Rebentisch points out, through images of death and disintegration, in which both *Lupe* and *Flaming Creatures* abound, and through a constant confusion between organic bodies and inert materials—fabrics, ornaments, props—a confusion that indicates "the fate of fugacity shared by both creatures and things."[80] One could argue that camp materialism is further embodied in the degraded surface of the image—the granularity explored in Chapter 7—and in the acoustic indexes of "failure and decay" that recall that recorded sound is vulnerable to aging and obliteration, not least because playback progressively erodes analog recordings. As they are played over time, records, tape, and film are bound to acquire more dust, scratches, and abrasions in a process of gradual ruination. Smith's and Rodríguez Solteros' films embrace these signs of failure and fragility with the same relish that they homage passé Hollywood exotica and the worn-out splendor of faded stars like Maria Montez and Lupe Vélez.

By embracing these signs, *Flaming Creatures*, *Lupe*, and other titles from the period, side deliberately with the imperfect and impure. Garble, scratches, slips, poor splices, and static dirty up the sound mix and deliberately flaunt the seams in the aural collage. Warhol's sound films from the mid-sixties are similarly awash in the noise of imperfect registration. Rather than on collage, his soundtracks rely on lengthy unedited live takes that are analogous to his long shots, which often stretched for the duration of entire thirty-three minute film reels. Sound was either directly recorded on the optical track of the 16mm Auricon camera he used at the time or taped and later added to the film. Open miking and poor environmental acoustics yielded a muddy tone, heightened by the narrower range of optical sound, the overlapping voices of the performers, and ever-present ambient noise—room tone, steps, ringing telephones, car horns in the street outside, and conversations taking place off-screen but within microphone range. The films from late 1966 forward were often taped on a magnetic recorder synchronized with the camera; stopping and starting the camera and tape recorder at the same time produced "strobe cuts": a clear frame, a double-exposed frame and a characteristic "bloop" in the soundtrack that was often repeated for rhythmic purposes or for sheer relish in its comically pneumatic quality.[81] The shower scene that opens *Bike Boy* (1967) is a characteristic example. The titular character's naked body is proffered for lengthy contemplation, but constant cuts and shifts in framing, along with accompanying bloops, interfere with the spectacle and impede candid apprehension.

By deliberately cultivating these extraneous sounds, underground filmmakers were countering industry standards. The recording industry had traditionally favored transparency, fidelity, and immersion, and had envisioned the evolution of technology as a steady progression toward exact reproduction. These ideas were symptomatic of the tendency endemic to modernity: to perfect the different types of sensory input in isolation from each other. The end result was a perceptual segmentation that Carolyn A. Jones has labeled "the bureaucratization of the senses."[82] Art and technology both reinforced and embodied this bias. They offered intensely targeted inputs that compartmentalized the human sensorium by engaging its separate perceptual streams, and they disembodied perception by focusing on fidelity to the real while seeking to attenuate the presence of the material mediations required by such pursuit. The search for perfect sensorial input was not alien to gender politics. Keir Keightley has shown that the tendency to purify aural perception and to isolate it from its material particulars was consistently masculinized in postwar audiophile culture, whose heyday was the years spanning from the introduction of the high-fidelity long-playing record by Columbia in 1948 to the spread of home stereo equipment in the late fifties, which popularized hi-fi, attenuating its exclusivity. Before then, while hi-fi and stereo were still relatively up-market, their enjoyment became a mark of cultural distinction particularly cultivated by men. "Women," *Life* magazine asserted in a feature on the phenomenon, "don't like high fidelity."[83] Publications pandering to the hi-fi craze of the times associated fidelity with control, technological proficiency, and the attempt to isolate the (male) listener from his domestic milieu—the domain of obstreperous women and children disrespectful toward the inviolability of pristine sound. By contrast, "feminine" listening was presumed to be non-immersive, participatory, lower-volume, and integrated in domestic environs as part of everyday tasks. In this context, the sound of much queer underground sixties is deliberately feminine. Ostentatiously murky and flaunting technological mediation—scratchy recordings, hissing tape—it implicitly spurns the (male) fascination with perfect sound and recreates instead a low-fi, domestic mode of audition that incorporates interruptions, mismatches, and flaws as part of the listening experience and no longer as an outsider that threatens its integrity.

In addition to being femininized and domestic, low-fi sound was aligned with messy corporealities. The unstable, falling, excreting bodies of the Kuchar films, explored in Chapter 4, are aurally framed by deliberately imperfect collages of pop, classic movie soundtracks, bland instrumentals, and histrionic off-screen narration. And Gustavus Stadler has connected Warhol's fascination with mono recording and "wet" (i.e. murky) sound with a jocular fascination with the sounds of dripping and excreting bodies that threaten to spill beyond their confines.[84] Stadler does not turn to the Factory films in his discussion, but they amply support his insight. They offer an intermittent archive of bodies enmeshed in foreign substances, dripping with fluids, and enveloped in screechy sound. A quick run-through would include the food fight in *Loves of Ondine* (1967) and the bathing and shower scenes in *Bike Boy, Tarzan and Jane Regained . . . Sort Of* (1963), *Tub Girls* (1967), and *Blue Movie* (1968), to name a few.

Perhaps *My Hustler* (1965) offers the most sustained alignment of the dripping, fluid body and the leaky sound mix. It depicts the tiff of several characters over a blond hustler that one of them procured through a telephone escort service. The action, set at seaside cottage, is accompanied by a constant aquatic murmur. In the first part of the film, the watery sound comes from the ocean, as the hustler in question lies on the beach, while his suitors, the owner of the beach house and two uninvited guests who drop in at the start of the film, sit on the porch and tease each other with their eyes on the prize. The camera pans back and forth between the talkers and the hustler on the sand. The second half of the film takes place in a bathroom, where one of the house guests, a former hustler himself, tries to seduce his younger colleague while they shower, shave, brush their teeth, apply lotion, piss, and comb interminably. The scene is punctuated by constant squirts, sprays, trickles, sloshes, and drips that occasionally cover up the dialogue. This acoustic ambience brings the film into the orbit of contemporary sound experiments in which liquids—at times emanating from bodies—played a

240   EXPERIMENTAL FILM AND QUEER MATERIALITY

prominent part. Fluxus actions, for example, often involved fluid discharges. Maciunas's *Duet for Full Bottle and Wine Glass* (1962) consisted in pouring liquid out of a bottle, drinking, gargling, sipping, rinsing one's mouth, and spitting. And Nam June Paik's *Fluxus Champion Contest* (1962)—part of his PHYSICAL MUSIC [*sic*] series—required several performers to stand in a circle and piss into a container while singing their respective national anthems.[85] There is gargling and pissing in *My Hustler* (but no anthems) as well as repeated aquatic immersion—into the ocean and the shower. But liquidity affects the film at a semantic level as well, rendering it fluid and uncontainable. Characters' motivations and identities are often uncertain, conversations are plagued by equivocation and misunderstanding, and the outcome of the film is unsure—who will fill in the "my" in the title? Whose hustler will this be? And, finally, the action revolves around a different kind of flow: cash, the money that buys company and sex and that the hustler's would-be seducers dangle in front of him. Cash is the ultimate, and unstable, referent of the hustler's body and of the dance of enticement unfolding around him; it washes and dribbles around the action as much as liquid does in the soundtrack.[86]

Break, Malfunction, Escape

Noise remains integral to experimental film after the heyday of the underground—during the reemergence of its styles and modes in punk and post-liberation queer subcultures. It was also cultivated in experimental music just as sound technologies incorporated noise reduction systems and new portable devices, such as the Sony Walkman—introduced in 1979—provided listeners with new means for isolated, concentrated listening. As mainstream sound moved toward polish, discrimination, and immersiveness, experimental acoustics—musical genres ranging from punk, post-punk, dance, and rap, to minimalism and different strands of electronic music—harked back to monaurality, distortion, glitch, and impurity.[87] Especially in popular culture, these qualities were often aligned with different types of corporeal dissent—the androgyny of punk, the homoeroticism of dance and techno, or the ethnic defiance of rap. Experimental film continued to intersect with sound experimentation and borrowed amply from this musical spectrum when it did not fuse with it. Examples of this symbiosis are New York "No Wave" film and the London-based

"New Romantics": two lively experimental scenes of the late seventies and early eighties that borrowed their names from local rock and pop trends.[88] Noise is the ingredient of avant-pop and experimental music that most frequently carried over into film. Breaks, scratch, and the sound of malfunction remained not just circumstantial additions to queer visuality but also foundational components of its sonic envelopes.

In the post-underground decades, these accidents no longer signified camp materialism, the rebuke of masculine audiophilia, or the fascination with corporeal spillage, but different kinds of rupture. For filmmakers such as Lionel Soukaz, noise and aural debris convey traumatic fracture. They bespeak the vulnerability of queer bodies to different kinds of homophobic aggression and to the systemic violence that the spread of AIDs unveiled. In other cases, glitch and malfunction helped to interrupt the dominant visual imaginary, especially as it concerned the representation of gender and sexuality, as in Abigail Child's eighties series *Is This What You Were Born For?* (1981–89). But noise is not always associated to negativity and critique. In Ashley Hans Scheirl's films, break and scratch have a reparative function. Cheerfully disruptive and creative, they accompany the corporeal reinvention of those who blithely cross gender and sexual lines and refuse to function—paraphrasing Legacy Russell—inside a social machine that was not made for them.[89] Overall, the work of this small transnational group of filmmakers is symptomatic of three uses of noise that I find characteristic of the closing decades of the twentieth century and the beginning of the new millennium—traumatic, critical, and reparative.

Lionel Soukaz's collage film *Ixe* (1980) is largely built on the interruptive break—both visual and aural. An autobiographical testimony of the post-liberation decade, it is also a brooding generational account and a reflection on the tug-of-war between liberation and reaction in French society since the sixties, a conflict that, in the film's outlook, is being won by the forces of conservatism. By the time Soukaz made *Ixe*, whose title—the letter "x" in French—evokes both the X used to classify porn film and the cross of censorship, Soukaz had made several films in a similar fragmentary style. The most sustained is *Sexe des anges* (1978), a series of sketches of explicit sex acts and humorous satires of gay stereotypes that also included incisive reflections about the marginalization of homosexuals. But Soukaz was best known at the time for the suppressed *Race D'Ep* (1979), cowritten with theorist and activist Guy Hocquenghem, an essay film about the development of homosexual culture since the late nineteenth century. The censorship of *Race d'Ep* suggested

Ixe's title, which seems both to anticipate and call forth a new act of suppression through its unabashed depictions of sex and drug use.[90]

Ixe arcs from the primping, dancing, and gleeful sex of early segments to violence and heavy drug-taking in the last part of the film. Its final sequences depict the knifing of the "protagonist"—Soukaz himself—in a dark alley, shown several times and cross-cut with the killing of Julius Cesar in the Hollywood production *Cleopatra* (1963). It is as if the environmental tensions that the film flags throughout—images of police repression, militarism, and war—had eventually compounded to disrupt the joys of gay liberation. As chronicle of "the disco years"—in Lawrence Schehr's words[91]—*Ixe* is built on some of the principles of disco—particularly the cut and the mix of multiple layers to create a dense, driving track. But what in disco usually yields a smooth, danceable mix, in *Ixe* produces a heterogeneous collage of quickly changing moods. The film's music runs from the celebratory to the somber to the inane. The innocence of Richard Anthony's pop hit "Les enfants qui pleurent" (1964) prepares the way for the exhilarating energy of techno— by Belgian band Telex—that is edited to dancing and sex, metonymies for seventies gay liberation. The sounds of liberation are interrupted by some reactionary fare: Luis Mariano singing a forties romantic ballad or Soeur Sourire's "Dominique" (1963), a hymn to the patron saint of the Dominican religious order that became a runaway hit. Gustav Mahler's *Symphony no. 1* (1889) accompanies young men shooting up spliced with images of rocket launches—an obvious joke on getting high. Sounds and images are often cut off as soon as they are introduced, and looped and distorted by deliberately faulty edits whose repetition takes on a rhythmic value.

The cuts suggest the precariousness of the private pleasures that sexual liberation earned and the ultimate vulnerability of queer lives, easily ruptured by homophobia and violence.[92] While the film has autobiographical elements and prominently features its maker—who soon afterward started an exhaustive project of self-documentation on analog video that continued for decades—Soukaz's testimony has a collective character as well, in part through the generational narrative from liberation to self-implosion, and in part through the insistent use of the colors of the French flag. Sequences depicting state functions are tinted red and blue in order to suggest that the nation, a concept that invites sameness and conformity, is one of the agencies of environmental violence, an idea already present in *Sexe des anges*. The sonic and visual ruptures that punctuate the film are effects of this ideology: they are scars left by a confining idea of nation but also cracks on its surface. Through these cracks one may glimpse those queer lives pushed to the margins which the film wants to portray, while the rough sound edits that accompany them and other incidental noise keep alive the memory of trauma.

Abigail Child's eighties work uses noise less as a marker of subjective circumstance than as a vehicle for cultural critique. Her seven-film cycle, *Is This What You Were Born For?* mixes found footage with Child's own images in order to examine and disrupt the bodily tropes that have dominated visual culture since the beginning of the century. As she put it: "In the 80s, I was engaged in a project to uncover the historical models through which we exist in a body; to collect, destroy, and reconstruct the vocabulary of the body—exploring how gesture means and engaging that vocabulary in play, critique, and creative structures."[93] In order to do so the series engages a broad image repertoire, from silent cinema, thirties pornography and fifties home movies to industrial film, advertisements, travelogues, nature films, sequences acted by downtown performers in Child's orbit, and segments of Child's early seventies documentaries. The series examines the apparatus of cinema as a "technology of gender"—Teresa de Lauretis's term—in a way that is similar to, and directly influenced by, the feminist film critiques of the time—by Laura Mulvey, Mary Ann Doane, Kaja Silverman, and de Lauretis, among others. Except Child's project is informed by a stronger awareness of the pleasures of the image and by a firmer desire to engage the filmic apparatus on its own terms: "I wanted to undo the Model. To display the functions of the splendiferous illusion machine that is the movies—to engage the mechanization of pleasure/seduction (not merely emotional identification but the physicality of the cut, sensuousness of the image, vortex of movement) *and* pull the carpet out from under our illusions, to participate and interrogate."[94] Her complicity with and affection toward the same iconography that she was seeking to undo also brings her close to the artists of the so-called Pictures generation, with whom her work has important connections that have seldom been acknowledged.[95] Like Cindy Sherman, Jack Goldstein, Robert Longo, Richard Price or Troy Brauntuch, Child's work acknowledges the seductive appeal of preexisting images—often culled from the visual archive of their shared postwar childhood—which she seeks to destabilize and critique by laying bare their ideological underpinnings. Her main procedure, just like theirs, was, in Douglas Crimp's influential formulation, citing, "performing," or "staging" preexisting images with the purpose of uncovering in them "strata of signification" and exploring how their

244 EXPERIMENTAL FILM AND QUEER MATERIALITY

repositioning—their "quoting"—affects their perception and sense.[96] In fact, Crimp continues, citing and repositioning, even more than image generation, are the crucial procedures in their work, and define as well the artistic logic of postmodernism.

Sound—or rather noise—is a crucial part of Child's process. "Sound is where my work comes together formally, or rather my interest in changing the image is enacted," she states in a recent interview.[97] She employs a broad variety of sounds in the *Born For* series: idiosyncratic percussion, disrupted speech, decontextualized voice-over, clichés of classical film scoring (stingers and mickey-mousing), experimental music, electronic sounds, snippets of educational and industrial film soundtracks, and a rich panoply of Foley effects. Some of the musical experiments included in the series consist in abrasively noisy interventions, such as Shelley Hirsch's extended vocal techniques, Polly Bradfield's improvisations on amplified violin in *Mutiny*, and the abstract soundtracks that Christian Marclay, Zeena Parkins, John Zorn, and Charles Noyes improvised for *Mayhem* and *Perils*. Other times, sound is pushed toward unintelligibility by deliberate mismatch or by pulverizing speech or musical cues through an onslaught of splices (in *Mutiny* and *Mayhem*, for example). These sonic disturbances disrupt the smooth transmission of the dominant spectacle, which Child describes as "a partial world where 'noise,' imagination, and the body do not enter," and they open up this very spectacle to reuse and scrutiny.[98] Noise also hinders narrative linearity: a "patriarchal ordering of consciousness" and a "synthetic flow" that marginalize dissident energies. Against this standardizing flow, film has to be, Child claims, "the poem of the cunt"[99]: the recreation of unbound corporeal energies that exceed narrative regulation and belong to a corporeal and material unconscious that conventional cinema represses. Rather than insert images into a forward-moving storyline, Child's works seeks to recreate the energy fields around them, as she is more interested in intensive moments than in linearity: "Is time a linear progression of things? Or is it an energy, an energy field, that's everywhere, acting on everything simultaneously."[100] Willfully desynchronized sound and noise heighten the tension and charge the energy field around the image track. They also recall the material conduit for such radiating force: "the body below the surface," untrammeled by conventional narrative or visual coding. Noise is the main catalyst in this pursuit. It disrupts the surfaces that hold this energy down, suspends the linear storytelling that streamlines it, and recasts the iconography that keeps bodies in thrall to a traditional gender economy.

SYNTHETIC, EXOTIC, MAGNETIC 245

Emancipation from received gender and corporeal configurations is central to Hans (now Ashley) Scheirl's films, made in the eighties and nineties, often in collaboration with Ursula Pürrer. Influenced by punk and post-punk, VALIE EXPORT's feminist actionism, and schlocky pop culture, Scheirl and Pürrer developed alternative bodily imaginaries in a number of shorts and in the features *Flaming Ears* (*Rote Ohre fetzen durch Asche* 1991, cosigned with Pürrer) and *Dandy Dust* (1998), a solo project by Scheirl initiated after he started to identify himself as transgender and initiated a testosterone regime.[101] Noise plays a prominent part in their work, where it has less a critical than an affirmative character, as it is less tied to disruption of the surrounding visual ecology than to the generation of new imaginaries.[102] Their fascination with noise is partly biographical—since Scheirl and Pürrer were part of Vienna's noise music scene through their participation in the bands 8 oder 9 and Ungünstige Vorzeichnen—and partly conceptual, since noise's disruptive materiality augments the messy embodiment and disorienting visual style of their films.

The otherworldly aurality of their feature length projects—trash-horror-sci-fi fantasies *Flaming Ears* and *Dandy Dust*—communicates the strangeness of their settings and the fragmentariness of the bodies that inhabit them. In the post-apocalyptic city of Asche, in *Flaming Ears*, sounds ring hollow and the air is thick with radio static, the clatter of helicopters, and the drone of distant factories (see Figure 8.4). In the interplanetary milieu of *Dandy Dust*, space travel and teleportation are accompanied by cartoonish swooshes and sighs, and aliens, cyborgs, intelligent insects, and humanoids have oddly resonant voices and bodies that squeak and crack when they move. For all its odd coloring, however, sound, like music, works in both films in fairly conventional ways, providing affective accents and acoustic anchorage for the visual dynamics. Noise is often synchronized to violence and mutilation—to bodies that are pummeled, burned, sliced, liquified, pierced, or bitten to pieces but somehow recompose themselves and keep on the move. Nun and Volly, the fractious protagonist couple in *Flaming Ears*, respectively played by Scheirl and Pürrer, are shot at, knifed, and bombed, but endure through it all; at the end, however, a jealous Volly emits a radiation that turns Nun's body into a cardboard flat, which is promptly folded up and carried away by Volley's chauffer. And Dandy Dust (played by Scheirl), in the eponymous film, is repeatedly tortured, eviscerated, and raped as he flees his evil stepmother across the galaxy, but keeps recovering his corporeal outline and traveling in search of freedom. By punctuating these accidented

Figure 8.4 Ashley Hans Scheirl, *Flaming Ears* (*Rote Ohren fetzen durch Asche*), 1992. Frame enlargement. Courtesy of Ashley Hans Scheirl.

metamorphoses, sound corroborates the corporeal plasticity envisioned in both films, and clinches the notion that bodies lack intrinsic organic shape and can be regarded instead as mere equipment whose parts could be altered and replaced at will.

The shorts of the eighties and early nineties confirm this conception in nonnarrative contexts and through a less conventional use of sound.[103] Sound is synchronized in *Super-8 Girl Games*, where it follows lines hand-scratched on the emulsion that represent bodily fluids and affects (anger, resentment, defiance) rebounding between Scheirl and Pürrer, dressed in athletic tank tops and framed against flat backdrops. In most other shorts, sound unfolds at a tangent to the images. These often show unaccountable milieus strewn with odds and ends in which the filmmakers and other performers exhibit their bodies and carry out enigmatic, ritualistic actions. *Body-Building* (1984) shows Pürrer and other women flexing their muscle for the camera to intermittent rattles, sighs, and groans. In *Das Schwartze Hertz Tropft* (1985) a black heart made out of cloth, a green paper plant, and a yellow cardboard drip and squirt in a cluttered studio. Halfway through the film, brief shots of electrical transformers, cables, and jacks are interspersed with close-ups of the filmmakers wearing geometrical face ornaments. Shortly afterward, the filmmakers, naked and with their facial ornaments on, solemnly carry away a stretcher with little white mounds of what might be salt or sugar bathed in a bluish light. The soundtrack bristles with unplaceable scratches, rumbles, and whirrs; a brief burst of song recurs twice: a scrappy tune played on a Moroccan raita, whose lyrics mention a padded plant that drips. Sound and image offer odd aggregates where one can connect nothing with nothing. In the notes to *Das Schwartze Hertz*, which is in many ways exemplary of the eighties' shorts, Scheirl and Pürrer proclaim their wish to cross to the other side of metaphor and metonymy ("verqueren Metaphor und Metonimie") in order to "discover the speech of homemade objects."[104] Yet more than a "speech" which suggests grammatical regulation and semantic coherence, what they seem to discover is flickering intensities in image and sound. The fragmentariness of the soundtracks underlines that of the visual track and of the enigmatic bodies that populate the films. Like the props and the backdrops, these bodies are jerry-built and impermanent, and in their androgyny and oddness, they escape ready-made gender ascriptions. They also live beyond "metaphor and metonymy"; not members of pregiven categories nor stand-ins for a species, they remain radically irreducible singularities.

While *Body-Building*, *Das Schwartze Hertz*, and others, communicate their dissident corporealities through the "speech of things" and visual and sonic abstraction, *Halbe Frösche Ficken Fink* (1992), resorts to sports, sex, psychotronic film, and dance music. Early on, boxing and sex provide moments of corporeal plenitude, but they are constantly snagged, distorted, and interrupted through abrupt cuts, thick graininess, and white screens. Severed heads, exploding bodies, and crumbling buildings culled from horror titles shot off the television monitor take over the second half of the film. The iconography of disintegration replaces corporeal affirmation. But exuberant destruction does not undercut the enjoyment of earlier moments but recodes them in the register of breakup and collapse. Dissolution may be as pleasurable as affirmation, as it redeems the body of meaning and shunts it to basic materiality and scattered intensity, to an existence beyond "metaphor and metonymy." Later scenes operate a sort of synthesis between the affirmative and the entropic, fullness and emptiness. Two half-frog, half-human figures have sex (see Figure 8.5). They are both unified and fragmented; their pleasure may lie in the cut that both divides and joins each of them; that detaches them from their original shape but also attaches them to others, extending their potentialities for pleasure, sentience, and cognition. The soundtrack is similarly based on the disjunctive cut and conveys the pleasures of the full and the empty, the affirmative and fragmentary, both separately and in combination. Bits of dance tracks are skillfully synchronized to the movement of the bodies on screen and oscillate between the two poles that structure the film. They swell with melodic and rhythmic effusiveness, but are also constantly damaged and scratched, and steadily revert to noise, just as the bodies on the screen and the film itself, with its textural changes from Super-8 to grainy VHS to TV noise, its whiteouts and black screens.

* * *

Last in this survey, Scheirl's work is far from the last to explore the queer valence of noise in experimental film, but I will leave to others to map further work in celluloid, video, digital and mixed formats. The chapter appropriately ends with Scheirl, since the motivation for writing it rose from my encounter with the joyful materiality of Scheirl's and Pürrer's Super-8 films and with Scheirl's riotous, noise-drenched performances with Jakob Lena

Figure 8.5 Ashley Hans Scheirl, *Halbe Frösche ficken flink*, 1994. Frame enlargement. Courtesy of Ashley Hans Scheirl.

SYNTHETIC, EXOTIC, MAGNETIC 249

Knebl, Andreas Riegler, and das Em in the early 2010s. From them I worked backward to conceptual and historical antecedents that pumped up the noise in queerness and queered up noise, and on through the *bruitist* streak of queer experimental film. In a way, this exploration seems coextensive with the history of experimental film itself. This is hardly surprising, since experimental film has often been synonymous with conceptual and visual dissonance and, as has already been noted, filmmakers and visual artists rather than musicians were often the most appreciative audiences for music and sound experiments. Possibly since the inception of sound film, the presence of noise in experimental cinema spiked after the late forties, when home film and audio equipment—magnetic tape in particular—became easily available. And it has remained a central ingredient of the experimental screen ever since, persisting in a variety of technological supports and through the different queer ecologies of the last decades of the twentieth century and forward into the present.

Noise consistently works to de-linearize and destabilize the visual field. If the purpose of conventional soundtracks was to provide, in Michel Chion's terms, an orientating sonic vector through the film and, in Mary Ann Doane's, "a oneness of appeal," centering spectators and confirming their epistemic dominance, noise routinely thwarts linearity and oneness.[105] It opens up sidelines and lateral connections—fields of tension, in Abigail Child's words—introducing extraneous matter and foiling smooth transmission and capture. In particular, it hinders the straightforward conduction of gender and sexuality. Mary Ann Doane, Kaja Silverman, Katryn Kalinak, and Caryl Flynn have differently demonstrated the subservience of sound and music in classical film to a binary gender economy and to the heterosexual appeal of the image. Voices and musical cues stabilize the gender and sexual identity of characters and impel an anthropomorphic, intersubjective, and heterosexist ecology of desire. Voices in particular were clearly attached to bodies and helped to position and make them intelligible, they dominated over music and sound—a characteristic Chion named "vococentrism"—and bore the dramatic and narrative weight of the film.[106] Whether originating in unruly matter, electronic generation, low-fidelity, or malfunction, noise displaces the authority of the intelligible voice and attenuates vococentrism and human-centeredness. It places the body alongside a network of material attachments and post- and para-human linkages or directly dissolves it into them. And when noise retains human reference, it encourages a plurality of sexual and affective investments that bypass conventional gender morphology and libidinal pathways.

Another way of putting this would be to say that noise glitches automatized corporeal, gender, and sexual protocols. It obstructs recognizability and breaks down the automatism that expects bodies to reply when they are hailed as belonging to a particular gender, sex, or ontological status. A piece of "socio-cultural malware," in Legacy Russell's words, glitch counters the imperative to be visible, countable, and operative, and offers instead disappearance, breakdown, and blip. While Russell locates glitch in the digital realm, noise is its incarnation in the analog sphere, where it has always haunted data storage, transmission, and playback. Queer experimental film provides an ample record of its disruptive work. But disruption is also a concept generator and the trigger of new possibilities: "In these breaks and system failures," Russell claims, "we find new beginnings."[107] As Florence Okoye points out, glitch may also be "a way of seeing the unseen."[108]

Stable throughout these histories has been noise's instability—the variability of its senses and lines of attachment. These have comprised from archaic and folk resonances to the futurism of synthesized sonorities, from the tones of urban subcultures to different kinds of exotica, from camp materialism to low-fi liquidity, and from mystic environmentalism and magical conjuration to political critiques and dreamy lyricism. Such fantastic variability has made noise less a mark of identity than a vanishing point and a line of escape. It has worked as a conduit for different varieties of corporeal and social differences that are often precariously localized and remain, for that reason, in the realm of the unseen and unspoken. Since noise is relative, context-dependent, and contingent, it channels, as Brandon LaBelle has recently pointed out, a politics of the emergent, coming collectivities, and inchoate desires.[109] The abstract nature of hearing, he continues, and particularly of noise, I would add, fosters awareness of impulses and demands that lie beyond recognizability, beyond current words and vision, but point the way toward coming communities, impending insurrections, untraveled routes, and looming futures. Most examples examined in this chapter worked in exactly this manner. Before there was an explicit politics of gender equality and sexual liberation, many of their demands were latent, if unformalized, in the noisiest frequencies of films by Peterson, Menken, Deren, or Anger. And once those political fronts were articulated, their limits and aporias were sonographed in Soukaz's and Child's collaged soundtracks, but also their untapped possibilities. Likewise, the excitement of corporeal discovery buzzes through Scheirl's and Pürrer's work of the eighties, announcing promises that may or may not be fulfilled but whose mere intuition—as a subtle pulse buried deep in the mix—makes our refusals more pointed and precise and our pending utopias more daring and imaginative.

Finally, noise reminds us that we never do it alone. Material and technologically mediated, noise is the product of interfaces and posthuman conjunctions—of forces and things, electronics, and bodies—and so is sexuality. Because, paraphrasing Bruno Latour, one does not make the sexual with sexuality alone—we need things, images, substances, surfaces, and spaces as channels and supports.[110] Noise is another name for the manner in which sexuality attaches to and spreads across intricate configurations that bring together the human and nonhuman.

The dynamics of this spread and the messiness of these configurations have been the focus of this book. In a way, the materialist and materializing urges that have driven this writing have become inevitable in our profoundly ironic present. The progressive virtualization of cultural and social practice impelled by digital culture has drawn attention to the complexities of thingness and objecthood. And deepening environmental crises, widespread pollution, the accumulation of unassimilable residue, and the increasing scarcity of elemental resources such as clean air and water have forced us to attend to matter's trenchant exigencies. Tuning into the vibrancy of matter and its thick histories, affective valences, and plural investments may have been triggered by the awareness that what was once taken for granted or thought inert has turned out to be neither assured nor lifeless. I can only hope that this book contributes to the ongoing critique of the arrogant disregard for the material and inorganic that have marked much action and thought since early modernity with what now reveal themselves as catastrophic results. I hope it also shows that much of this critical impulse has long driven experimental film and its radical redefinition of sexuality, images, matter, and their multiple interactions.

Notes

Chapter 1

1. See, for example, Jerry Tartaglia, "The Gay Sensibility in American Avant-Garde Film," *Millennium Film Journal* 4, no. 5 (Summer/Fall 1979), 53–58; Richard Dyer, *Now You See It: Studies on Lesbian and Gay Film* (New York: Routledge, 1990); Tom Waugh, *Hard to Imagine: Gay Male Eroticism in Photography and Film From their Beginnings to Stonewall* (New York: Columbia University Press, 1996); Juan A. Suárez, *Bike Boys, Drag Queens, and Superstars: Avant-Garde, Mass Culture, and Gay Identities in the 1960s Underground Cinema* (Bloomington: Indiana University Press, 1996); Marc Siegel, "Documentary That Dare/Not Speak Its Name," in *Between the Sheets, In the Streets: Queer, Lesbian, and Gay Documentary*, eds. Cynthia Fuchs and Chris Holmlund (Minneapolis: University of Minnesota Press, 1996); J. Hoberman, *On Jack Smith's* Flaming Creatures *(and Other Secret Flix of Cinemaroc)* (New York: Granary Books, 2001); Matthew Tinkcom, *Working Like a Homosexual: Camp, Capital, Cinema* (Durham: Duke University Press, 2002), esp. 73–188; Douglas Crimp, *Our Kind of Movie: The Films of Andy Warhol* (Cambridge: MIT Press, 2012); Ara Osterweil, *Flesh Cinema: The Corporeal Turn in American Avant-Garde Film* (Manchester: Manchester University Press, 2014); Marc Siegel, ed. *Criticism* 56, no. 2, special issue: "Jack Smith: Beyond the Rented World"(2014).
2. Janet Steiger, "Finding Community in the Early 1960s: Underground Cinema and Sexual Politics," in *Perverse Spectators: The Practices of Film Reception* (New York: New York University Press, 1992), 125–160.
3. I am taking the term "animacy" in part from Mel Y. Chen, *Animacies: Micropolitics, Racial Mattering, and Queer Affect* (Durham: Duke University Press, 2012). Initially a linguistic concept, "animacy" has been described, recalls Chen, "variously as a quality of agency, awareness, mobility, and liveness" (2). Acknowledging—and celebrating—the term's slipperiness and cross-disciplinary use, Chen uses the term to explore its use "as an often racialized and sexualized means of conceptual and affective mediation between human and inhuman, animate and inanimate, whether in language, rhetoric or image" (10). While fully in agreement with Chen's important work, I use the term in this book in a way that is closer to its original use in linguistics, as another way of designating the vibratory, animated character of matter.
4. See, for example, Stacy Alaimo and Susan Hekman, eds. *Material Feminisms* (Bloomington: Indiana University Press, 2007), 400–424; Karen Barad, *Meeting the Universe Halfway: Quantum Physics and the Entanglement of Matter and Meaning* (Durham: Duke University Press, 2007), 132–187; Elizabeth Grosz, *Time Travels: Feminism, Nature, Power* (London: Allen and Unwin, 2005); Judith Halberstam

254 NOTES

and Ira Livingstone, eds. *Posthuman Bodies* (Bloomington: Indiana University Press, 1995); Jeffrey J. Cohen, *Stone: An Ecology of the Inhuman* (Minneapolis: University of Minnesota Press, 2015); Chen, *Animacies*. Thinking at a "distance from the anthropic" comes from Susan Stryker, "Transing the Queer (In)Human," *GLQ: Journal of Lesbian and Gay Studies* 21, nos. 2–3 (2015): 227–230, special issue "Queer Inhumanisms," edited by Mel Y. Chen and Dana Luciano.

5. Judith Butler, *Gender Trouble: Feminism and the Subversion of Identity* (New York: Routledge, 1990), esp. 163–180, and *Bodies That Matter: On the Discursive Limits of "Sex"* (New York: Routledge, 1993), esp. 93–119 and 223–236; Michel Foucault, *History of Sexuality, Volume One: The Will to Knowledge*, trans. R. Hurley (New York: Vintage, 1980); Gayle Rubin, "Thinking Sex: Notes for a Radical Theory of the Politics of Sexuality," in *The Lesbian and Gay Studies Reader*, eds. Henry Abelove, Michèle Aina Barale, and David Halperin (New York: Routledge, 1993), 3–44.

6. Since the bibliography on these various branches of queer studies has grown immensely, the following titles may be taken as indicative: José E. Muñoz, *Disidentifications: Queers of Color and the Performance of Politics* (Minneapolis: University of Minnesota Press, 1999); Robert F. Reid-Pharr, *Black Gay Men: Essays* (New York: New York University Press, 2002); Roderick A. Ferguson, *Aberrations in Black: Towards a Queer of Color Critique* (Minneapolis: University of Minnesota Press, 2003); E. Patrick Johnson and May G. Henderson, eds. *Black Queer Studies: A Critical Anthology* (Durham: Duke University Press, 2005); Lisa Henderson, *Love and Money: Queers, Class and Cultural Production* (New York: New York University Press, 2013); Elizabeth Freeman, *Time Binds: Queer Temporalities, Queer Histories* (Durham: Duke University Press, 2010); David Bell and Gill Valentine, eds. *Mapping Desire* (London: Routledge, 1995); Yolanda Retter, Anne-Marie Bouthillette, and Gordon Brent Ingram, eds. *Queers in Space: Communities, Public Spaces, Sites of Resistance* (Seattle, Washington: Bay Press, 1997); Eithne Lubhéid and Lionel Cantu, eds. *Queer Migrations: Sexuality, U. S. Citizenship and Border Crossings* (Minneapolis: University of Minnesota Press, 2005); Jasbir Puar, *Terrorist Assemblages: Homonationalism in Queer Times* (Durham: Duke University Press, 2007); Gayatri Gopinath, *Impossible Desires: Queer Diasporas and South Asian Public Cultures* (Durham: Duke University Press, 2005); Arnaldo Cruz-Malavé and Martin F. Manalansan IV, eds. *Queer Globalizations: Citizenship and the Aftermath of Colonialism* (New York: New York University Press, 2002); Jennifer Terry, *An American Obsession: Science, Medicine, and Homosexuality in Modern Science* (Bloomington: Indiana University Press, 1999).

7. Jeffrey J. Cohen, *Medieval Identity Machines* (Minneapolis: University of Minnesota Press, 2003), 40.

8. Sara Ahmed, *Queer Phenomenology: Orientations, Objects, Others* (Durham: Duke University Press, 2006).

9. Dana Luciano and Mel Y. Chen, "Introduction: Has the Queer Even Been Human?" *GLQ: Journal of Lesbian and Gay Studies* 21, nos. 2–3 (2015): 182–209; esp. 185–188.

10. Michel Foucault, "Friendship as a Way of Life," in *Foucault Live: Collected Interviews, 1961–84*, ed. Sylvère Lotringer, trans. Lysa Hochroth and John Johnston (New York: Semiotext(e), 1996; 2nd edition), 308–312.

NOTES 255

11. "The problem is not to discover in oneself the truth of one's sex, but, rather, to use one's sexuality henceforth to arrive at a multiplicity of relationships." Foucault, "Friendship as a Way of Life," 308.

12. Ahmed, *Queer Phenomenology*, 170.

13. Butler, *Bodies That Matter*, 1–2; further references are given in the text.

14. On the bio-centrism of queer critique, see Jeffrey J. Cohen, "Queering the Inorganic," in *Queer Futures: Reconsidering Ethics, Activism, and the Political*, eds. Elahe Hashemi Yekani, Eveline Kilian, and Beatrice Michaelis (Farnham, Surrey: Ashgate, 2013), 149–164, esp. 152–153.

15. Of Miller's voluminous bibliography, see, for example, *Material Cultures*, ed. Daniel Miller (Chicago: University of Chicago Press, 1998); Daniel Miller, *The Comfort of Things* (Cambridge: Polity, 2008); and Daniel Miller, *Stuff* (Cambridge: Polity, 2010). To be totally fair, in *Bodies That Matter*, Butler makes some gestures toward actual material in relation to the transferability of the phallic function to fetishes and "purposefully instrumentalized body-like things" (88) and in her remarks on the theatricality of AIDS-derived mourning and rage (233, 236).

16. "[If] there is an occupation and reversal of the master's discourse, it will come from many quarters, and those resignifying practices will converge in ways that scramble the self-replicating presumptions of reason's mastery. For if the copies speak, or if what is merely material begins to signify, the scenography of reason is rocked by the crisis on which it was always built." Butler, *Bodies That Matter*, 52

17. Walter Benjamin, *The Arcades Project*, ed. Rolf Tiedemann, trans. Howard Eiland and Kevin McLaughlin (Cambridge: Harvard/Belknap Press, 1999), 79.

18. Roland Barthes, *Mythologies: The Complete Edition*, trans. Anette Lavers and Richard Howard (New York: Hill and Wang, 2013); Jean Baudrillard, *The System of Objects*, trans. James Benedict (New York: Verso, 1996 [1968]).

19. Henry Lefebvre, *Everyday Life in the Modern World*, trans. Sacha Rabinovitch (New York: Harper and Row, 1971 [1968]), 7–8.

20. Andy Warhol and Pat Hackett, *POPism: The Warhol 1960s* (New York: Harcourt Brace Jovanovich, 1980), 291.

21. Esther Newton, *Mother Camp: Female Impersonators in America* (Chicago: University of Chicago Press, 1979), 102.

22. Susan Stryker, "Transsexuality: The Postmodern Body and/as Technology," in *The Cybercultures Reader*, eds. Barbara M. Kennedy and David Bell (London: Routledge, 2000), 588–597; see also, Stryker, "My Words to Victor Frankenstein Above the Village of Chamounix," *GLQ: A Journal of Lesbian and Gay Studies* 1, no. 3 (1994): 237–254, reprinted in *The Transgender Studies Reader*, eds. Susan Stryker and Stephen Whittle (New York: Routledge, 2006), 244–256; Beatriz Preciado, *Testo Yonqui* (Madrid: Espasa, 2008), English version: *Testo Junkie: Sex, Drugs, and Biopolitics in the Pharmacopornographic Era*, trans. Bruce Berenson (New York: The Feminist Press at CUNY, 2013).

23. Bruno Latour, *We Have Never Been Modern*, trans. C. Porter (Cambridge: Harvard University Press, 1993), 136–138.

256 NOTES

24. Michael Warner, *The Trouble with Normal: Sex, Politics, and the Ethics of Queer Life* (New York: The Free Press, 1999), 11.

25. Michel Serres, *The Parasite*, trans. L. R. Schehr (Minneapolis: University of Minnesota Press, 2007), 61–65; Bruno Latour, *We Have Never Been Modern*.

26. Bruno Latour, "The Berlin Key," in *Matter, Materiality, and Modern Culture*, ed. P. M. Graves-Brown (London: Routledge, 2000), 19.

27. Jane Bennett, *Vibrant Matter: A Political Ecology of Things* (Durham: Duke University Press, 2010), ix.

28. Sigmund Freud, *The Psychopathology of Everyday Life*, trans. and ed. James Strachey (New York: W. W. Norton, 1989).

29. Sigmund Freud, "Fetishism" (1927), in *The Collected Papers of Sigmund Freud. Volume 5: Miscellaneous Papers 1888–1938*, trans. and ed. James Strachey (London: Hogarth, 1950), 198–204.

30. Sigmund Freud, "Analysis of a Phobia in a Five-Year Old Boy" (1909), in *The Sexual Enlightenment of Children*, ed. P. Rieff (New York: Collier, 1976; 7th printing), 47–183.

31. Melanie Klein, *Love, Guilt, and Reparation and Other Works 1921–1945. The Writings of Melanie Klein, Volume I* (New York: The Free Press, 1975), 59–105.

32. Ernest Jones, "The Theory of Symbolism," *British Journal of Psychology* 9, no. 2 (October 1918), 181–229, esp. 198–202.

33. In this respect I find particularly productive Leo Bersani's reading of sublimation in *The Freudian Body* (New York: Columbia University Press, 1986), 29–50.

34. Sigmund Freud, "Three Essays on the Theory of Sexuality," in *The Standard Edition of the Complete Psychological Works of Sigmund Freud. Vol VII*, ed. J. Stratchey (London: The Hogarth Press and the Institute for Psychoanalysis, 1953), 123–246; see esp. 150–151.

35. Freud, "Three Essays," 147–148.

36. Freud, "Three Essays," 150–151, 161–162.

37. Jacques Lacan, *Le Seminaire, Livre XX. Encore*, ed. Jacques-Alain Miller (Paris: Seuil, 1975), 14–15, 17.

38. Tim Dean, *Beyond Sexuality* (Chicago: University of Chicago Press, 2000), 213–268.

39. Gilles Deleuze and Félix Guattari, *The Anti-Oedipus. Capitalism and Schizophrenia*, trans. R. Hurley, M. Seem, and H. Lane (Minneapolis: University of Minnesota Press, 1983; 1st French ed. 1972), 270. Subsequently cited as *AO* in the text.

40. Gilles Deleuze, *Cinema 1: The Movement-Image*, trans. Hugh Tomlinson and Barbara Habberjam (University of Minnesota Press, 1986 [Editions de Minuit: 1983]), 194–196.

41. Gayle Rubin with Judith Butler, "Sexual Traffic, Interview," in *Feminism Meets Queer Theory*, ed. Elizabeth Weed and Naomi Schor (Bloomington: Indiana University Press, 1997), 85.

42. Gilles Deleuze and Félix Guattari, *A Thousand Plateaus. Capitalism and Schizophrenia*, trans. Brian Massumi (Minneapolis: University of Minnesota Press, 1987), 278.

43. Deleuze and Guattari, *A Thousand Plateaus*, 217.

44. Deleuze and Guattari, *A Thousand Plateaus*, 229–231.

NOTES 257

45. Guy Hocquenghem, *Homosexual Desire*, trans. Daniela Danghoor, with a new introduction by Michael Moon. Preface by Jeffrey Weeks (Durham: Duke University Press, 1993), 94, 106.

46. Eve Kosofsky Sedgwick, *Touching Feeling: Affect, Pedagogy, Performativity* (Durham: Duke University Press, 2002), 8–9.

47. Amber Jamilla Musser, "Objects of Desire: Toward an Ethic of Sameness," *Theory and Event* 16, no. 2 (2013), unpaginated.

48. See Jennifer Terry, "Loving Objects," *Trans-Humanities* 2, no. 1 (2010): 33–75.

49. Pat Califia, "Beyond Leather: Expanding the Realm of the Senses to Latex," *Public Sex: The Future of Radical Sex* (San Francisco: Cleis Press, 1994), 199–208; quoted text 204–205.

50. Chen, *Animacies*, 202–203.

51. Chen, *Animacies*, 211.

52. In addition to the references given above (to Muñoz, Ferguson, Reid-Pharr, Puar, and E. Patrick Johnson and Mae G. Henderson), a thumbnail sample of this important body of work would include: David Eng, Jack Halberstam, and José E. Muñoz, eds. *Social Text* 23, nos. 3–4 (2005), special issue: "What's Queer about Queer Studies Now?"; Roderick Ferguson and Grace Hong, eds. *Strange Affinities: The Gender and Sexual Politics of Comparative Racialization* (Durham: Duke University Press, 2011); E. Patrick Johnson, *Appropriating Blackness: Performance and the Politics of Authenticity* (Durham: Duke University Press, 2003); David Eng and Alice Y. Hom, eds. *Q & A: Queer in Asian America* (Philadelphia: Temple University Press, 1998); David Eng, *The Feeling of Kinship: Queer Liberalism and the Racialization of Kinship* (Durham: Duke University Press, 2010); Nguyen Tan Hoang, *View from the Bottom: Asian American Masculinity and Sexual Representation* (Durham: Duke University Press, 2014).

53. Chen, *Animacies*, 89–126 and 211–220; Zakkiyah Iman Jackson, *Becoming Human: Matter and Meaning in an Antiblack World* (New York: New York University Press, 2020); Uri McMillan, "Objects, Avatars, and the Limits of the Human," *GLQ: Journal of Lesbian and Gay Studies* 21, nos. 2–3 (2015): 224–227; and Uri McMillan, *Embodied Avatars: Genealogies of Black Feminist Art and Performance* (New York: New York University Press, 2015).

54. José E. Muñoz, "Ephemera as Evidence: Introductory Notes to Queer Acts," *Women & Performance* 8, no. 2 (1996): 5–16.

55. Muñoz, "Ephemera as Evidence," 10.

56. Ann Cvetkovich, *An Archive of Feelings: Trauma, Sexuality, and Lesbian Public Cultures* (Durham: Duke University Press, 2003), 285. See also, Sara Ahmed, *The Cultural Politics of Emotion* (Edinburgh: University of Edinburgh Press, 2004).

57. Bruno Latour, *Reassembling the Social: An Introduction to Action-Network Theory* (London and New York: Oxford University Press, 2004), 252–253.

58. Kobina Mercer, "Black Hair / Style Politics," *New Formations* 1, no. 3 (Winter 1987): 33–54; reprinted in Kobina Mercer, *Welcome to the Jungle: New Positions in Black Cultural Studies* (London: Routledge, 1994), 97–130; Susan Bordo's "Cassie's Hair," in *Material Feminisms*, ed. Alaimo and Hekman, 400–424. More

258 NOTES

generally, Benedict Anderson has discussed the material supports of nationalism: *Imagined Communities: Reflections on the Origins and Spread of Nationalism* (London: Verso, 1983).

59. Susanne Bost, "From Race/Sex/Etc to Glucose, Feeding Tubes, and Mourning: The Shifting Matter of Chicana Feminism," in *Material Feminisms*, eds. Alaimo and Hekman, 349.

60. Oskar Negt and Alexander Kluge, *Public Sphere and Experience: Toward an Analysis of the Bourgeois and Proletarian Public Sphere*, trans. Peter Labanyi (Minnesota: University of Minnesota Press, 1993), 45.

61. See also, Theodor W. Adorno, *Negative Dialectics*, trans. E. B. Ashton (London: Routledge, 1973), 191. This idea runs through Theodor W. Adorno and Max Horkheimer, "Elements of Anti-Semitism: The Limits of Enlightenment," in *The Dialectics of Enlightenment*, trans. J. Cumming (London: Continuum, 1988 [1944]), 168–208. For example: "The unconditional realism of civilized humanity, which culminates in Fascism, is a special case of paranoiac delusion which dehumanizes nature and finally the nations themselves" (193).

62. Adorno, *Negative Dialectics*, 191.

63. Karen Barad, "Posthuman Performativity: How Matter Comes to Matter," *Signs* 28, no. 2 (2003): 801–832; the quotations are from p. 817 and p. 821. A further reworking of this essay is Barad, "Agencial Realism: How Material-Discursive Practices Matter," in *Meeting the Universe Halfway*, 132–187.

64. Vicki Kirby, *Quantum Anthropologies* (Durham: Duke University Press, 2011), 84, 88. On the creativity of nature, see also Elizabeth Grosz, *Becoming Undone: Darwinian Reflections on Life, Politics, and Art* (Durham: Duke University Press, 2011). A view of nature's articulateness and creativity based on bifurcations and the unpredictability of strange attractors is described in Manuel De Landa, "Non-Organic Life," in *Incorporations*, eds. Jonathan Crary and Sanford Kwinter (New York: Zone, 1992), 129–167.

65. Bennett, *Vibrant Matter*, 109. See also Bruno Latour, "The Parliament of Things," *We Have Never Been Modern*, 142–145.

66. Chen, *Animacies*, 212–214.

67. Barad, *Meeting the Universe Halfway*, 384.

68. "We move unfailingly toward noise, but we come from noise." Serres, *The Parasite*, 72; see also 126–128.

Chapter 2

1. Kenneth Anger's birth is usually dated 1930, but according to Anger's biographer Bill Landis, the correct year is 1927: Bill Landis, *Anger: The Unathorized Biography of Kenneth Anger* (New York: HarperCollins, 1995), 5. On the making of *Fireworks*, see 44–46.

2. Lewis Jacobs, "Experimental Cinema in America, 1921–1947," in *The Rise of the American Film: A Critical History* (New York: Columbia Teacher's College, 1974),

543–582, originally published as a two-part article in Hollywood Quarterly 7, nos. 2 and 3 (Winter 1947–48 and September 1948). Siegfried Kracauer, "Filming the Subconscious," in American Writings: Essays on Film and Popular Culture, eds. Johannes von Moltke and Kristy Rawson (Berkeley and Los Angeles: University of California Press, 2012), 57–61. Similarly, critic Parker Tyler posited the dream as the basic structure of experimental film at the time Parker Tyler, Three Faces of the Film: The Art, The Dream, the Cult (New York and London: Thomas Yoseloff, 1960), 66, 70 and passim.

3. P. Adams Sitney, Visionary Film: The American Avant-Garde, 1943–2000, 3rd edition (New York: Oxford University Press, 2002), 10–11, 14–15, 27–28.

4. Richard Dyer, Now You See It: Studies in Lesbian and Gay Film (New York: Routledge, 1990), 104.

5. Sitney, Visionary Film, 136.

6. Tyler, Three Faces of the Film, 62.

7. Beatriz Colomina, Domesticity at War (Cambridge: MIT Press, 2007) and Beatriz Colomina, ed. Cold War Hot Houses: Inventing Cold War Culture from Cockpit to Playboy (Cambridge: MIT Press, 2009).

8. Henry Miller, The Air-Conditioned Nightmare (New York: New Directions, 1945), 24.

9. "Storage Walls," Life Magazine 18, 22 January 1945, 63–71; citation is from 64. For an insightful commentary on the series, see Jeffrey Meikle, Design in the USA (New York: Oxford University Press, 2005), 136–138.

10. Meikle, Design in the USA, 144. Justus Nieland, Happiness by Design: Modernism and Media in the Eames Era (Minneapolis: University of Minnesota Press, 2020).

11. Eve Kosofsky Sedgwick, "Queer and Now," in Tendencies (Durham: Duke University Press, 1993), 3. "Futulitarian" is in Miller, The Air-Conditioned Nightmare, 42. The sentence is: "I am stopping at the gay Detroiter, the Mecca of the futilitarian salesman."

12. Kevin Lynch, Wasting Away. An Exploration of Waste: What It Is, Why We Fear It, How to Do It Well (San Francisco: Sierra Club Books, 1990), 49–50, 91–97.

13. Kenneth Jackson, Jr. The Crabgrass Frontier: The Suburbanization of the United States (New York: Oxford University Press, e-book edition, 2010 [1985]), 380–415. For a recent reassessment of the phenomenon that places it in global perspective, see Robert A. Beauregard, When America Became Suburban (Minneapolis: University of Minnesota Press, 2006).

14. Marshall Berman, All That Is Solid Melts Into Air: The Experience of Modernity (London: Verso, 1982), 290–312.

15. An authoritative account of these changes is Robert A. M. Stern, Thomas Mellins, and David Fishman, New York 1960: Architecture and Urbanism Between the Second World War and the Bicentennial (New York: Monacelli Press, 1995), especially 61–134, and 895–943.

16. Landis notes that the house where the Anglemyers lived on Holly Drive was razed down for the construction of the L. A. Freeway: Landis, Anger, 7. The sector of the Freeway that intersects with Holly Drive was opened in 1954; by that time Anger's family had relocated in Pacific Palisades. On the L. A. Freeway, see Richard Simon, "Hollywood Freeway Spans Magic and Might of L. A." Los Angeles Times, Dec 19,

260 NOTES

1994, accessed May 20, 2022, https://www.latimes.com/archives/la-xpm-1994-12-19-mn-10830-story.html.

17. An incisive contemporary description of the suburbs is William H. Whyte, *The Organization Man* (Philadelphia: University of Pennsylvania Press, 2002, epub edition [New York: Simon and Schuster, 1956)], esp. Section VII: "The New Suburbia: Organization Man at Home."

18. Ezra Pound, *The Spirit of Romance* (London: J. M. Dent and Sons, 1910), vi.

19. James Longenbach, *The Modernist Poetics of History: Pound, Eliot, and the Sense of the Past* (Princeton: Princeton University Press, 1987), pp. 109–13

20. Lynch, *Wasting Away*, 27.

21. On the possible cross-dressing in this scene, see Stan Brakhage, *Film at Wit's End: Eight Avant-Garde Filmmakers* (Kingston, NY: McPherson and Co, 1989), 54.

22. Broughton provides information about these locations in his memoir: James Broughton, *Coming Unbuttoned* (San Francisco: City Lights, 1994), esp. chapters 6 and 7, on his forties and fifties films.

23. Rice provides a first-hand account of the film's production in: Mary Batten, "Ron Rice Interview," *Film Comment* 1, no 3 (1962): 32–35.

24. While he was not a theorist of garbage, Bataille's ideas on taboo and transgression are quite applicable in this context: George Bataille, *Erotism: Death and Sensuality*, trans. Mary Dalwood (San Francisco: City Lights, 1962 [Editions de Minuit, 1957]), esp. 63–71, 129–147; Mary Douglas, *Purity and Danger: An Analysis of Concepts of Pollution and Taboo* (New York: Routledge, 2001 [London: Routledge and Kegan, Paul, 1966]); Kevin Lynch, *Wasting Away*, 49–50; Michael Thompson, *Rubbish Theory. The Creation and Destruction of Value* (Oxford University Press, 1979), esp. 77–102; John Scanlan, *On Garbage* (London: Reaktion, 2005).

25. Mary Douglas, *Purity and Danger*, 36.

26. Allen Ginsberg, *Howl and Other Poems* (San Francisco: City Lights, 2005 [1955]), 9–10.

27. For Smith's ideas on the old and outdated, see Gerard Malanga, "Interview with Jack Smith," *Film Culture* 45 (Summer 1967): 9–13; Jack Smith and Sylvére Lotringer, "Uncle Fishhook and the Sacred Baby Poo-Poo of Art," *Semiotext(e)* 3, no 2 (1978): 192–203; reprinted in Jack Smith, *Wait for Me at the Bottom of the Pool: The Writings of Jack Smith*, ed. J. Hoberman and E. Leffingwell (New York/London: High Risk Books/P. S. 1, 1997), 107–135.

28. On Smith and Jacobs's collaboration, see Ken Jacobs, "Unpublished Letter to the *Village Voice*, November 1991," in J. Hoberman, "Jack Smith and His Secret Flix." Program Notes. American Museum of the Moving Image, third revised edition, January 1998, 71–75; and Ara Osterweil's brilliant commentary, *Flesh Cinema: The Corporeal Turn in American Avant-Garde Film* (Manchester: Manchester University Press, 2014), 1–10.

29. John Scanlan comments on the paradoxical duality of trash as material that is disengaged from its intended backdrop, and therefore singularized, but also massed indistinctly into a continuum of refuse: *On Garbage*, 15–17 and ff.

NOTES 261

30. Jonathan Rosembaum, "Looking Back in Anger," *The Chicago Reader*, February 27, 2004, accessed December 9, 2020, https://jonathanrosenbaum.net/2022/10/looking-back-in-anger/.

31. Parker Tyler, *Underground Cinema: A Critical History* (New York: Da Capo, 1995 [1969]), 79.

32. Theodor Adorno, *Minima Moralia. Reflections from Damaged Life*, trans. E. F. N. Jephcott (London: Verso, 1978), 227–228.

33. Sigmund Freud, "Character and Anal Eroticism" (1908), *The Standard Edition of the Complete Psychological Works of Sigmund Freud. Volume 9*, ed. James Strachey (London: Hogarth and The Psychoanalytic Institute, 1954), 167–176.

34. Until the late 2000s, the only extended explorations of Menken's work, besides Jonas Mekas's brief review in *Movie Journal*, were Stan Brakhage, "Marie Menken," in *Film at Wit's End: Eight Avant-Garde Filmmakers* (Kingston: McPherson and Company, 1989), 32–47 and Stan Brakhage, "On Marie Menken," *Film Culture* 78 (Summer 1994): 1–9, transcript of a lecture at the Innis Film Society in 1992. More recent work is: P. Adams Sitney, "Marie Menken and the Somatic Camera," in *Eyes Upside Down: Visionary Filmmakers and the Heritage of Emerson* (New York: Oxford University Press, 2008), 21–48; Melissa Ragona, "Swing and Sway: Marie Menken's Filmic Events," in *Women's Experimental Cinema*, ed. Robin Blaetz (Durham: Duke University Press, 2007), 20–44; Caroline Guo, "Work-in-Progress: Marie Menken and the Mechanical Representation of Labor," *Jump-Cut* 54 (Fall 2012), accessed November 12, 2021, https://www.ejumpcut.org/archive/jc54.2012/GuoMenken/index.html; Juan A. Suárez, "Myth, Matter, Queerness: The Cinema of Willard Maas, Marie Menken, and the Gryphon Group, 1943–1969," *Grey Room* 36 (August 2009): 58–87.

35. Sitney, "Interview with Marie Menken," 10.

36. Sitney, "Interview with Marie Menken," 11. According to David Revill, *The Seasons* was Cage's first work for orchestra and the first of his scores directly influenced by Eastern philosophy—in particular, by the writings of Ananda Coomaraswamy and Sry Ramakrishna. David Revill, *The Roaring Silence. John Cage: A Life* (New York: Arcade, 1992), 91–92.

37. Sitney, "Interview with Marie Menken," 10.

38. Stan Brakhage, "Letter to Gerard Malanga," *Filmwise* 5–6 (1967): 20.

39. Even if such ordinariness is culturally and ideologically conditioned, as Brakhage would later argue in *Metaphors on Vision* (New York: Film Culture, 1963); originally published as a special issue of *Film Culture* (Fall 1963) and reprinted by Anthology Film Archives and Light Industry (2017).

40. Stan Brakhage, "On Marie Menken," 1–9.

41. Brakhage, "On Marie Menken," 4.

42. Parker Tyler, *Underground Cinema: A Critical History* (New York: Dutton 1995 [1969]), p. 159–160.

43. Sitney, "Interview with Marie Menken," 11. Brakhage offers a hyperbolically hetero-normative, homophobic reading of the film in *Film at Wit's End*, 39.

262 NOTES

44. Gilles Deleuze, "He Stuttered," *Essays Critical and Clinical*, trans. Daniel W. Smith and Michael A. Greco (Minneapolis: University of Minnesota Press, 1997), 107–114.
45. Sitney, "Interview with Marie Menken," 11.
46. On Harry Smith's biographical background—often heavily mythologized by himself—see P. Adams Sitney, "Harry Smith Interview," in *Film Culture Reader*, ed. P. Adams Sitney (New York: Praeger, 1970), 263, and John Cohen, "A Rare Interview with Harry Smith," *Sing Out! The Folk Song Magazine* 19, nos. 1–2 (1969), reprinted in Paola Igliori, *American Magus, Harry Smith* (New York: Inanout Press, 1996), 125–144.
47. Walter Benjamin, "Surrealism, The Last Snapshot of the European Intelligentsia," *One-Way Street and Other Writings*, trans. Edmund Jephcott, Kingsley Shorter (London: New Left Books, 1979), 228.
48. Arthur Evans, *Witchcraft and the Queer Counterculture* (Boston: FAG RAG, 1978). See also Richard Cavendish, *The Black Arts* (New York: Perigee Books, 1967), 11–13, 140–141.
49. This and the following quotations are Harry Smith's descriptions of his own films, in Sitney, *Visionary Film*, 235–236.
50. The recurrence of the empty head has prompted Noel Carroll to read the film as an allegory of perception: Noel Carroll, "Mind, Medium and Metaphor in Harry Smith's Heaven and Earth Magic," *Film Quarterly* 31, no. 2 (Winter 1977–78).
51. Sitney, *Visionary Film*, 254. Annette Michelson has read the film as a representation of the two successive stages Melanie Klein established in human psychogenesis: the paranoid-schizoid stage, when the infant preys aggressively on the mother's body for nurture and protection, and the reparative moment, when the infant recognizes its dependence on the mother and seeks to restore her to wholeness. The actions of the small man, often directed toward hitting and dismembering the Victorian ladies, are the focus of her attention. Annette Michelson, "The Mummy's Return: A Kleinian Film Scenario," in *Meaning in the Visual Arts: Views from the Outside. A Centennial Commemoration of Erwin Panofsky (1892-1968)*, ed. Irvin Lanvin (Princeton, NJ: Institute for Advanced Study, 1995), 335–350.
52. Sitney, "Harry Smith Interview," 272.
53. Benjamin, "Surrealism," 229.
54. André Breton, "Foreword," in Max Ernst, *The Hundred Headless Woman (La Femme 100 Têtes)*, trans. Dorothea Tanning (New York: Brazillier, 1981 [1929]), 8.
55. Hal Foster has interpreted Ernst's collages from this perspective: enactments of the return of a repressed sexuality and of the invasion of the bourgeois interior by the industrial commodity: *Compulsive Beauty* (Cambridge: MIT Press, 1995), 178–182.
56. Harry Smith, "Queens Museum of Art Talk, 11 November 1978," in *Harry Smith: The Avant-Garde in the American Vernacular*, eds. Andrew Perchuk and Rani Singh (Los Angeles: Getty Research Institute, 2010), 115.
57. Sitney, "Harry Smith Interview," 272.
58. Aleister Crowley, *Liber 777 and Other Qabalistic Writings of Alestair Crowley*, ed. Israel Regardie (York Beach, Maine: Samuel Weiser, 1975).

NOTES 263

59. Crowley's quotation is: "Nature is a continuous phenomenon, though we do not know in all cases how things are connected" in *Magick in Theory and Practice* (New York: Dover, 1976 [1929]), xv.

60. Gershom Scholem, *Kabbalah* (New York: Meridian, 1974), 104

61. S. L. MacGregor Mathers, "Introduction," to Christian Knorr von Rosenroth's *Kabbala Denudata: The Kabbalah Unveiled*, ed. and trans. by S. L. MacGregor Mathers (Leeds: Clephaïs Press, 2003 [1887]), 50–51; Scholem, *Kabbalah*, 115–116.

62. Michel Carrouges, *Les Machines celibataires* (Paris: Editions du Chêne, 1976 [1954]).

63. Harald Szeeman, ed. *The Bachelor Machines* (Venice: Alfieri Edizioni d'Arte/ New York: Rizzoli, 1975). The inclusion of Smith's film in Szeeman's show has been mentioned by Sitney and Stephen Fredman, without pointing out the implications of this inclusion for the sexual politics of the film. P. Adams Sitney, "Harry Smith, Bibliophile and the Origins of the Cinema," and Stephen Fredman, "Forms of Visionary Collage: Harry Smith and the Poets," both in *Harry Smith: The Avant-Garde in the American Vernacular*, 109 and 247.

64. Karl Marx, "The Fetishism of Commodities and the Secret Thereof," in *The Marx–Engels Reader*, ed. Robert Tucker (New York: Norton, 1978), 319, 321ff.

65. Smith's friend Lionel Ziprin has described him as "a Berkeley Marxist" at the time of his arrival in New York, in 1950. Shortly afterward, Smith started to explore the Kabbalah and Jewish mysticism. He befriended Ziprin's grandfather, Rabbi Naftali Zvi Margolis Abulafia and made recordings of him singing songs in honor of Reb Shimon Bar Yocha, purported author of the *Zephir*, the first written exposition of the Kabbalah, written in the second century: C. E. Igliori, *American Magus*, 47–49.

66. Marcel Mauss, *A General Theory of Magic*, trans. Robert Brain (New York: Norton, 1975 [1902–03]), 20.

67. Mauss, *A General Theory of Magic*, 111, 107.

68. See, for example, *The Sears, Roebuck and Co. Catalogue*, no. 112 (Chicago: Sears, Roebuck and Co, 1903), 121.

69. Adrienne Rich, "Compulsive Heterosexuality and Lesbian Existence," *Bread, Blood, and Poetry: Selected Prose, 1979–1985* (New York: Norton, 1985); it was originally published in *Signs* (1980).

70. On the song's composition and context in John Latouche's life, see Howard Pollock, *The Ballad of John Latouche: An American Lyricist's Life and Work* (Oxford University Press, 2017), 240–241. Pollock notes the nuances that Holman and White's own history adds to the song.

71. On Holman, see Jon Bradshaw, *Dreams That Money Can Buy: The Tragic Life of Libby Holman* (New York: Murrow, 1985).

72. For an overview of Arledge's life and work, see Irene Tsatsos, *Sara Katryn Arledge: Serene for the Moment* (Los Angeles: Armory Center for the Arts, 2020).

73. The biographical information, with details on the making of *Introspection*, comes from Terry Cannon, "Sara Kathryn Arledge: *Introspection* (1941–46)," in *Unseen Cinema: Early American Avant-Garde Film, 1893–1941*, ed. Bruce Posner (New York: Black Thistle Press/Anthology Film Archive, 2001), 75–76.

264 NOTES

74. Cannon, "Sara Katryn Arledge, *Introspection* (1941–46)," 76. On the Whitney brothers' pioneering methods of optical printing, see John Powers, "A DIY Come-On: A History of Optical Printing in Avant-Garde Cinema," *Cinema Journal* 57, no. 4 (2018): 71–95; esp. 77–78.

75. Program announcement for Art in Cinema's Second Series, March 1947, in MacDonald, ed. *Art in Cinema*, 64. Her name is spelled Sarah Catherine Arledge.

76. Cannon, "Sara Kathryn Arledge, *Introspection* (1941–46)," 76; a pocket history of hubcaps is Don H. Krug, "Hubcaps," in *The Guide to US Popular Culture*, eds. William Labov, Ray B. Browne, and Pat Browne (Madison: University of Wisconsin Press, 2001), 416.

77. My gratitude to Jon Shibata and Michael Campos-Quinn, at Berkeley Art Museum/Pacific Film Archive, for access to Arledge's films and archival materials (consulted remotely in early October 2020).

78. Jim Davis, *The Flow of Energy*, edited with an introduction by Robert A. Haller (New York: Anthology Film Archives, 1992), 1, 96.

79. Jim Davis, Letter to Frank Stauffacher, 2/21/50, in MacDonald, ed. *Art in Cinema*, 210–11.

80. Davis, Letter to Frank Stauffacher, 2/21/50, in MacDonald, ed. *Art in Cinema*, 211.

81. Davis's influence on this scene has been detailed by Henning Engelke, *Metaphern Einer Anderen Filmgechichte: Amerikanischer Experimental Film, 1940–1960* (Marburg: Schüren Verlag, 2018), 193–206.

82. Davis, *The Flow of Energy*, 59.

83. He wrote in his journals: "But often, and perhaps too frequently, I destroy my work because I am *afraid* . . . of revealing too clearly those things in myself that are '*taboo*' in our social, legal, religious, etc. order." *The Flow of Energy*, 72.

84. Davis, *The Flow of Energy*, 79.

85. Davis, *The Flow of Energy*, 80.

86. I have not had access to this footage, so I cannot speak of it authoritatively. During the writing of this volume (April 2020 to December 2022), Anthology Film Archives, where Jim Davis's films are deposited, was closed to researchers, and my inquiries about conducting further research there have remained unanswered.

87. "Not only that but, to me, the handsome youthful male, in the nude, is the *most* beautiful of all of nature's creations." Davis, *The Flow of Energy*, 56.

88. Bruce Friar, "Jim Davis Interviewed about his Films in 1966," in *On Jim Davis: Horizons of Light*, ed. Robert A. Haller (Paris: Re:Voir and Anthology Film Archives, 2006), 20.

89. Lex Morgan Lancaster, "Queer Abstraction," *ASAP Journal*, July 19, 2019, access: January 18, 2023, https://asapjournal.com/queer-abstraction-lex-morgan-lancaster/; see also Lancaster's *Dragging Away: Queer Abstraction in Contemporary Art* (Durham: Duke University Press, 2022); David Getsy, "Ten Queer Theses on Abstraction," in *Queer Abstraction*, ed. J. Ledesma (Des Moines: Des Moines Art Center, 2019), 65–75.

90. See Jonathan D. Katz, "The Sexuality of Abstraction: Agnes Martin," in *Agnes Martin*, eds. L. Cooke, K. Kelly, and B. Schröder (Dia Art Foundation/Yale University Press, 2011), 93–120; Jonathan D. Katz, "John Cage's Queer Silence, Or How to Avoid

NOTES 265

Making Matters Worse," *GLQ: Lesbian and Gay Quarterly* 5, no. 2 (1999): 231–252. See also, Carolyn Jones's kindred argument in relation to silence: "Finishing School: John Cage and the Abstract Expressionist Ego," *Critical Inquiry* 19, no. 4 (Summer 1993): 628–665.

91. Davis, *The Flow of Energy*, 63.

92. Plexiglas was one of the brand names of an acrylic glass developed in Germany since the late 1910s as a glass substitute for its transparency and resistance. Lumarith was a first-generation thermoplastic: cellulose acetate molded by a combination of heat and pressure, used also from the 1940s onward for injection molding. An early assessment of this material is "Molding the Newer Plastics," *American Machinist* 74 (April 30, 1931): 671–673. In the United States it was commercialized mainly by Celanese Plastics. It was easily colored and laminated in translucent colored sheets and widely used in lamp shade manufacture. See full-page advertisement, *Life Magazine*, April 15, 1946, 58. Acetate was often commercialized in thin, flexible transparent or metalized sheets. Silver acetate was highly reflective and could work as a lightweight, soft mirror. Davis worked with these substances when they were relatively new in the market, at a time when the plastics industry was consolidating and polishing its image and corporate identity. For the broader context and impact of these inventions, see Jeffrey L. Meikle, *American Plastic: A Cultural History* (New Brunswick, NJ: Rutgers University Press, 1995), esp. 91–124 and 153–181.

93. A succinct review of these shows in the context of the time is in Meikle, *Design in the U. S. A.*, 148–151. See also Russell Lynes, *Good Old Modern: An Intimate History of the Museum of Modern Art* (New York: Atheneum, 1973), 180–182. Press releases and photographic documentation of these shows are available at https://www.moma.org/calendar/exhibitions/1714? accessed January 4, 2021.

94. Shelley Nickles, "More is Better: Mass Consumption, Gender, and Class Identity in Postwar America," *American Quarterly* 54, no. 4 (December 2002): 581–622.

95. Adolf Loos, "Ornament und Verbrechen [1908]," in *Ornament & Verbrechen*, ed. Peter Stuibler (Wien: Metroverlag, 2012).

96. Nickles, "More is Better," 609.

97. An excellent introduction to this group is Michael Duncan, Kristine McKenna, Stephen Fredman, eds. *Semina Culture: Wallace Berman and His Circle* (Santa Monica: DAP/Santa Monica Museum of Art, 2015).

Chapter 3

1. Beatriz (Paul B.) Preciado, *Testo Yonqui* (Madrid: Espasa Calpe, 2008), 252–253, my translation; English version: Paul B. Preciado, *Testo Junkie: Sex, Drugs, and Biopolitics in the Pharmacopornographic Era*, trans. Bruce Benderson (New York: Feminist Press, 2013).

2. William Burroughs and Daniel Odier, *The Job. Interviews with William Burroughs* (Harmondsworth, Middlesex, England: Penguin, 1989 [1970]), 128–160.

266 NOTES

3. John Barker, "Intensities of Labor: From Amphetamine to Cocaine," *Mute*, March 7, 2008, accessed October 12, 2022, https://www.metamute.org/editorial/articles/intensities-labour-amphetamine-to-cocaine.

4. Jack Halberstam, *In a Queer Time and Place: Transgender Bodies, Subcultural Lives* (New York: New York University Press, 2004), 4–5.

5. Andy Warhol and Pat Hackett, *POPism: The Warhol Sixties* (New York: Harcourt Brace Jovanovich 1980), 64. Subsequently cited as *P* in the text.

6. Danny Fields: "The trip books were a big thing. You worked on them when you were on amphetamines. You'd fill in the blank pages . . . little poems, decorations . . . Beautiful drawings. A collage of photographs from the *National Geographic.* A piece of cotton pasted in. Somebody's pubic hair. Toothpicks. Spangles. Blotches of color. The books got so fat they wouldn't close." Jean Stein, ed., with George Plimpton, *Edie: American Girl* (New York: Grove Press, 1982), 216.

7. In addition to Warhol's memoir, *POPism*, the standard Warhol biographies have much, often overlapping, information on the three: Victor Bockris, *Andy Warhol: The Biography* (New York: Da Capo, 1997); Steven Watson, *Factory-Made: Warhol and the Sixties* (New York: Pantheon, 2003); and (my own favorite) Tony Scherman and David Dalton, *The Genius of Andy Warhol* (New York: HarperCollins 2009).

8. On Ondine's theatrical career, see Stephen J. Bottoms, *Playing Underground: A Critical History of the 1960s Off-Off Broadway Movement* (Ann Arbor: The University of Michigan Press, 2006), 283–286 and 323–324. Agenoux's play was the subject of the 33-minute reel, *A Christmas Carroll* (1967), included in the 24-hour program **** (1967). Callie Angell, *The Films of Andy Warhol: Part II* (New York: Whitney Museum of American Art, 1994), 31; Callie Angell, *Andy Warhol Screen Tests: The Films of Andy Warhol Catalog Raisonné* (New York: Abrams/Whitney Museum of American Art, 2006), 149.

9. Jonas Mekas's filmography of Warhol's films mentions another title with Herko: *Salome and Delilah* (1963), in David Coplans, ed., *Andy Warhol* (New York: New York Graphic Society, 1971). On these films, see Bruce Jenkins's entries "*Haircut no.1,*" "*Haircut no. 2,*" "*Dance Movie,*" and "*Jill and Freddy Dancing,*" in John Hanhardt, ed. *The Films of Andy Warhol. Catalogue Raisonné, 1963–1965* (New Haven: Yale University Press, 2021). On Herko, see Donald McDonagh, "The Incandescent Innocent," *Film Culture* 45 (Summer 1967): 55–60, which contains a description of what might have been *Dance Movie*; Warhol and Hackett, *POPism*, 55–57, 84 and passim; and, more recently, José E. Muñoz, "A Jeté Out of the Window: Fred Herko's Incandescent Illumination," in *Cruising Utopia: The Then and There of Queer Futurity* (New York: New York University Press, 2010), 147–167.

10. Lynne Tillman and Stephen Shore, *The Velvet Years: Warhol's Factory, 1965–67* (New York: Thunder's Mouth Press, 1995), 112.

11. On Danny Williams, see Esther B. Robinson's documentary *Walk into the Sea: Danny Williams and the Warhol Factory* (2007).

12. On Dean and her passage through the Factory world, see Ara Osterweil, "The Last World: Dorothy Dean and Black Fugitivity in Andy Warhol's *My Hustler,*" *Art Journal* 78, no. 4 (2019): 58–75.

NOTES 267

13. Nicolas Rasmussen, *On Speed: The Many Lives of Amphetamine* (New York: New York University Press, 2008), 177–178

14. Rasmussen, *On Speed*, 177–178.

15. Marissa A. Miller, "History and Epidemiology of Amphetamine Abuse in the US," in Hilary Klee, ed. *Amphetamine Misuse: International Perspectives on Current Trends* (Amsterdam: Harwood Academic Publishers, 1997), 115–116.

16. For a history of the clinic, which is at the same time an extraordinary slice of sixties social history, see David E. Smith and John Luce, *Love Needs Care: A History of San Francisco's Haight-Ashbury Free Medical Clinic and Its Pioneering Role in Treating Drug Abuse Problems* (Boston: Little Brown, 1971). See the Free Clinic's *Journal of Psychedelic Drugs* Special Issue: "Speed Kills: A Review of Amphetamine Abuse," 2, no. 2 (1969) for information on patterns of abuse in the mid-to-late 1960s.

17. Roger C. Smith, "Compulsive Methamphetamine Abuse and Violence in the Haight-Ashbury District," in *Current Concepts in Amphetamine Abuse*, eds. E. Ellingwood and S. Cohen (Rockville, MD: Department of Health, Education, and Welfare; NO(HSM) 72–9085, 1972), 205–216.

18. Warhol and Hackett, *POPism* 33; Scherman and Dalton, *The Genius*, 146–47; Bockris, *Warhol*, 132.

19. Parker Tyler, "Dragtime and Drugtime, Or Film á la Warhol," *Evergreen Review* 11, no. 46 (1967); reprinted in Michael O'Pray, ed. *Andy Warhol: Film Factory* (London: British Film Institute, 1989), 94–103.

20. Michael Angelo Tata, "Andy Warhol: When Junkies Ruled the World," *Nebula* 2, no. 2 (June 2005): 76–112, accessed August 12 2012, http://www.nobleworld.biz/images/Tata.pdf.

21. Chelsea Weathers, "Drugtime," *Criticism* 56, no. 3 (Summer 2014).

22. Tata, "When Junkies," 80.

23. Tyler, "Dragtime," 103.

24. William Burroughs, *Naked Lunch* (New York: Grove, 1980 [1958; 1962]), 22.

25. Matthew Tinkcom, *Working Like a Homosexual: Camp, Capital, Cinema* (Durham: Duke University Press, 2002), 12–13.

26. Tinkcom, *Working Like a Homosexual*, 77–81.

27. Homay King, "Girl Interrupted: The Queer Time of Warhol's Cinema," *Discourse* 28, no. 1 (Winter 2007): 98–120.

28. Rasmussen, *On Speed*, 6–24.

29. Herbert Hunkie, "An Oral History of Benzedrine Use in the USA," *The Herbert Hunkie Reader* (London: Bloomsbury, 1997), 340–42.

30. Rasmussen, *On Speed*, 91.

31. Rasmussen, *On Speed*, 31–40.

32. Betty Friedan, *The Feminine Mystique* (New York: Dell, 1973 [W. W. Norton, 1963]), 170.

33. Smith and Luce, *Love Needs Care*, 17.

34. Marshall McLuhan, "Notes on Burroughs," *The Nation*, December 28, 1964, 517–19; reprinted in Jennie Skerl and Robyn Lyndenberg, eds. *William S. Burroughs at the*

268 NOTES

Front: Critical Reception, 1959-1989 (Carbondale: Southern Illinois University Press, 1991), 69–73.

35. See Antonio Negri and Michael Hardt, *Empire* (Cambridge: Harvard University Press, 2001), 285–294, and, very especially, Preciado, *Testo Junkie.*

36. Andy Warhol, "What is Pop Art?" Interview by G. R. Swanson, *Artnews* 62 (1963); reprinted in Kenneth Goldsmith, ed. *I'll Be Your Mirror: The Selected Andy Warhol Interviews* (New York: Carroll & Graf, 2004), 18. Warhol's actual words are: "The reason I'm painting this way is because I want to be a machine. Whatever I do, and do machine-like, is because it is what I want to do." The full transcript of the interview has been recently unearthed by Jennifer Sichel, "What is Pop Art? A Revised Transcript of Gene Swenson's 1963 Interview with Andy Warhol," *Oxford Art Journal* 41, no. 1 (2018): 85–100. On the context of this interview and Swenson's trajectory and importance, see Jennifer Sichel, "Is Pop Art Queer? Gene Swenson and Andy Warhol," *Oxford Art Journal* 41, no. 1 (2018): 59–83. For an extraordinarily far-reaching reading of the machinic aspects of Warhol's art, see Jonathan Flatley, "Art Machine," in *Like Andy Warhol* (Chicago: University of Chicago Press, 2017), 89–137.

37. Harvey Cohen, *The Amphetamine Manifesto* (Paris: Olympia Press, 1972), 110–111.

38. John Tytell, *Naked Angels: The Lives and Literature of the Beat Generation* (New York: Grove, 1976), 140–209; Marcus Boon, *The Road of Excess: A History of Writers on Drugs* (Cambridge: Harvard University Press, 2002), 197–99.

39. Jack Kerouac, *On the Road: The Original Scroll Edition* (New York: Penguin, 2008), 145.

40. Jack Kerouac, *Visions of Cody* (New York: McGraw-Hill, 1972).

41. James Agee, *Let Us Now Praise Famous Men* (Boston: Houghton Mifflin, 1980 [1941]), xiv.

42. Kerouac, *Visions of Cody,* 98.

43. Béla Balázs, *Theory of the Film,* trans. Edith Bone (New York: Arno, 1972 [1951]). According to Balázs the sound film could do for acoustic phenomena what the silent film had done to optics: it could "reveal to us our acoustic environment . . . the speech of things and the intimate whisperings of nature" (197). Such revelations were for him always on the side of meaning, not symptoms of the opaque materiality that opens up to the speed user and the media.

44. Kerouac, *Visions of Cody,* 99.

45. Jonas Mekas, "Notes on Reseeing Andy Warhol's Films," in *Andy Warhol: Film Factory,* 28–41.

46. Friedrich A. Kittler, *Discourse Networks 1800/1900,* trans. Michael Metteer, with Chris Cullen (Stanford: Stanford University Press, 1988), 186, 188.

47. Lester Grinspoon and Peter Hedblom, *Speed Culture: Amphetamine Use and Abuse in America* (Cambridge: Harvard University Press, 1975), 106–108. More recent, and also an extremely useful introduction to the pharmacology, history, and effects of amphetamine, is Leslie Iversen, *Speed, Ecstasy, Ritalin: The Science of Amphetamines* (London: Oxford University Press, 2008).

NOTES 269

48. Rasmussen, *On Speed*, 76. The flicker threshold of 40 flashes per second is given in "Tony Conrad on 'The Flicker.' From a letter to Henry Romney, dated November 11, 1965," *Film Culture* 41 (Summer 1966): 2.

49. Kerouac, *Visions of Cody*, 15.

50. Douglas Crimp, "Early Films by Andy Warhol. Introduction to the Film Program at Dia:Beacon. Summer of 2005," *Dia's Andy. May 2005–April 2006* (New York: Dia Art Foundation, 2005), 73.

51. Gregory Battcock, "Four Films by Andy Warhol," *Film Culture* 45 (Summer 1968), reprinted in *Andy Warhol: Film Factory*, 48; Mekas, "Notes on Reseeing Andy Warhol's Films," in *Andy Warhol: Film Factory* 39; Stephen Koch, *Stargazer: Andy Warhol's World and His Films* (New York: Marion Boyards, 1972), 91.

52. Paul Taylor, "Andy Warhol: The Last Interview," *Flash Art* 133 (April 1987): 43; reprinted in Goldsmith, ed. *I'll be Your Mirror*, 389.

53. Jonathan Flatley has pointed out the parallel between Warhol and Sol Lewitt's conceptualism, also traversed by a tension between the pristine conception of the work (10000 lines not straight, not touching, incomplete open cubes, etc.) and its actual overwhelming apprehension. See Flatley, *Like Andy Warhol*, 122–124.

54. Warhol and Hackett, *POPism*, 294.

55. My thanks to Ashley Swinnerton, Collections Specialist, and to the staff of the MoMA Film Study Center for making this experience retrievable and allowing me to screen many of these early titles at the speed for which they were intended on repeated visits in February 2013, April 2016, and March 2018.

56. Not only inspired by speed it was also induced by it. Giorno: "I looked over and there was Andy in the bed next to me, his head propped up on his arm, wide-eyed from speed, looking at me." John Giorno, *You've Got to Burn to Shine* (New York: Serpent's Tail, 1994), 130. A more recent, fuller account of the experience is: John Giorno, *Great Demon Kings: A Memoir of Poetry, Sex, Art, Death, and Enlightenment* (New York: Farrar, Straus, Giroux, 2020), 48–75.

57. Branden Joseph, "The Play of Repetition: Andy Warhol's *Sleep*," *Grey Room* 19 (2005): 35.

58. Claude E. Shannon and Warren Weaver, *The Mathematical Theory of Communication* (Urbana and Chicago: University of Illinois Press, 1998 [1949]), 14–15, 32.

59. Angell, *The Films of Andy Warhol: Part II*, 20.

60. For Geldzahler's account of the experience, see John Wilcock, *The Autobiography and Sex Life of Andy Warhol* (New York: Trela Media, 2010 [1971]), 65. What I take to be reversal of the body and face into inert matter, Geldzahler reads as "self-revelation": "I could see from viewing the film later that it gave me away completely." For a more extensive discussion of the film, see Juan A. Suárez, "The Face in Flight: Andy Warhol's Henry Geldzahler," *JCMS: Journal of Cinema and Media Studies* 58, no. 4 (Summer 2019): 112–133.

61. Roy Grundmann, *Andy Warhol's Blow Job* (Minneapolis: University of Minnesota Press, 2002), 71–72.

62. Adriano Aprá, spoken introduction to *Blow Job* in *Andy Warhol: Four Silent Movies* (Minerva Pictures Group SpA: Univideo, 2004).

270 NOTES

63. Douglas Crimp, *Our Kind of Movie: Essays on Andy Warhol's Films* (Cambridge: MIT Press, 2012), 7–8.

64. Gretchen Berg, "Andy Warhol: My True Story," in *I'll Be Your Mirror*, ed. Goldsmith, 85–96; the quotation is on p. 90.

65. Crimp, *Our Kind of Movie*, 109.

66. Crimp, *Our Kind of Movie*, 15.

67. Tom Waugh, "Cockteaser," in *Pop Out: Queer Warhol*, eds. Jennifer Doyle, Jonathan Flatley, and José Esteban Muñoz (Durham, Duke University Press, 1996), 51–77.

68. Linda Nochlin, "'Sex is so Abstract.' The Nudes of Andy Warhol," in *Andy Warhol Nudes*, ed. John Cheim (New York: Robert Miller Gallery, 1995). Nochlin does not give any source for the Warhol quotation that gives the essay its title; Bob Colacello reports it in *Holy Terror: Andy Warhol Close Up* (New York: Harper Collins, 1990), 338, 341, 343.

69. In this respect, Warhol seems in agreement with the Freud of the *Three Essays on the Theory of Sexuality*.

70. Grinspoon and Hedblom, *Speed Culture*, 96–102.

71. I am appropriating here J. C. Flügel's notion of cutaneous eroticism; see J. C. Flügel, *La psicología del vestido*, trans. A. Kornblit (Buenos Aires: Paidós, 1964); Spanish version of J. C. Flügel, *The Psychology of Clothes*, London: Hogarth, 1930. On the heightening of tactile sensation under amphetamine, see Grinspoon and Hedblom, *Speed Culture*, 107.

72. Warhol, *a, a novel* (New York: Grove, 1998), 66.

73. Warhol, *a, a novel*, 66.

74. Warren Sonbert, "Letter to Gerard Malanga," *Film Culture* 45 (Summer 1967): 40.

75. While Sonbert used these words to describe his following film, *Where Did Our Love Go?*, they are also quite appropriate for *Amphetamine*. Sonbert, "Letter to Gerard Malanga," 40.

76. Andy Warhol, *THE Philosophy of Andy Warhol, from A to B and Back Again* (New York: Harcourt Brace Jovanovich, 1975), 63.

77. Amy Taubin, "Hot Heads," *Village Voice*, December 1990, 20; cited in Waugh, "Cockteaser," 61.

78. Juan A Suárez, "Structural Film: Noise," in *Still Moving: Between the Cinema and Photography*, eds. Karen Beckman and Jean Ma, eds. (Durham, NC: Duke University Press, 2008), 62–89.

79. David Joselit, *Feedback: Television Against Democracy* (Cambridge: MIT Press, 2007), 63.

80. Preciado, *Testo Yonqui*, 15.

81. Jonathan Flatley has thoroughly explored this dimension of Warhol's art: *Like Andy Warhol*, esp. 1–52.

82. Berg, "Andy Warhol: My True Story," 93.

NOTES 271

Chapter 4

1. Kuchar, "The Old Days," in *To Free the Cinema: Jonas Mekas and the New York Underground*, ed. David James (Princeton: Princeton University Press, 1992), 49–50.
2. See Jack Stevenson, *Desperate Visions: Camp America. John Waters. George and Mike Kuchar* (London: Creation Books, 1996), and *Deathtripping: The Cinema of Transgression* (London: Creation Books, 1995). With the occasion of a "Kuchar Film Festival" at the Lighthouse Cinema, New York, in June 1996, Michael Atkinson wrote "Over 30 years later, the Kuchars are still fathering renegade film culture—check out any edition of the New York Underground Film Festival if you need proof." Michael Atkinson, "Kuchar Film Festival," *The Village Voice*, June 18, 1996, 51.
3. J. Hoberman, "Desire under the El: How the Kuchar Brothers Found Hollywood in the Bronx," *The Village Voice*, December 8, 1975, 18, 20; David James, *Allegories of Cinema* (Princeton: Princeton University Press, 1989), 143–149; Paul Arthur, "History and Crass Consciousness: George Kuchar's Fantasies of Un-power," *Millennium Film Journal* 20, no. 21 (1988–89): 151–158; Scott MacDonald, "George Kuchar. Interview," in *A Critical Cinema* (Berkeley: University of California, 1988), 297–316; Chuck Kleinhans, "Taking out the Trash," in *The Politics and Poetics of Camp*, ed. Moe Meyer (New York: Routledge, 1996), 157–173; Steve Reinke, "Excrements of Time: A Brief Introduction to *The World of George Kuchar*," and Gene Youngblood, "Underground Man," brochure for the DVD pack *The World of George Kuchar* (Video Data Bank, 2006).
4. Youngblood, "Underground Man" (no page number).
5. Mark Finch, "George Kuchar: Half the Story," in *Queer Looks: Perspectives on Lesbian and Gay Film and Video*, eds. Martha Gever, John Greyson, and Pratibha Parmar (New York: Routledge, 1993), 76–85; Raymond Murray, *Images in the Dark: An Encyclopedia of Gay and Lesbian Film and Video* (New York: Plume, 1996), 80–81.
6. Thomas Hine, *Populuxe* (New York: Alfred A. Knopf, 1986); Alison J. Clarke, *Tupperware: The Promise of Plastic in 1950s America* (Washington, DC: Smithsonian, 2001).
7. Sara Ahmed, *Queer Phenomenology: Orientations, Objects, Others* (Durham: Duke University Press, 2006); Jennifer Terry, "Loving Objects," *Trans-Humanities* 2, no. 1 (June 2010): 33–75; Scott Herring, "Material Deviance: Theorizing Queer Objecthood," *Postmodern Culture* 21, no. 2 (January 2011), accessed October 18, 2022, http://www.pomoculture.org/2013/09/03/material-deviance-theorizing-queer-obj ecthood/; Scott Herring, *The Hoarders: Material Deviance in Modern Material Culture* (Chicago: University of Chicago Press, 2014); "Queer Inhumanisms," special issue of *GLQ: A Journal of Lesbian and Gay Studies*, eds. Dana Luciano and Mel Y. Chen, 25, no. 1 (2015).
8. Karl Schoonover, "Divine: Towards an 'Imperfect' Stardom," in *Screen Stars of the 1970s*, ed. James Morrison (New Brunswick: Rutgers University Press, 2010), 158–181; Rosalind Galt, *Pretty: Film and the Decorative Image* (New York: Columbia University Press, 2011), esp. ch. 2, "Colors: Derek Jarman and Queer Aesthetics"; Lucas Hilderbrand, *Inherent Vice: Bootleg Histories of Videotape and Copyright*

272 NOTES

(Durham: Duke University Press, 2011), esp. 161–193, Rosalind Galt and Karl Schoonover, *Queer Cinema in the World* (Durham: Duke University Press, 2016).

9. J. Hoberman describes these "nabes" in "Desire under the El," 18.

10. Sheldon Renan, "Interview with the Kuchar Brothers," *Film Culture* 45 (1967): 47–50; Michael Reynolds, "Talking Trash with Director George Kuchar, Parts 1 and 2," *Berkeley Barb* 540 and 541 (1975).

11. These figures come from the US Senate Interim Report of the Committee on the Judiciary, 1955–56, "Comic books and juvenile delinquency," 3–4, Congress Catalogue Card Number 77–90720, accessed December 18, 2020, http://www. thecomicbooks.com/1955senateinterim.html. On this era in comic book history, see David Hajdu, *The Ten-Cent Plague: The Comic-Book Scare and How It Changed America* (London: Picador, 2009); Bradford W. Wright, *Comic Book Nation: the Transformation of Youth Culture in America* (Baltimore: Johns Hopkins University Press, 2003), esp. 86–153.

12. Covers for numbers 15, 19, 23, and 24, published February–March 1953 and August–September 1954. The covers may be consulted in the complete run of the magazine, *The EC Archives: Shock SuspenStories. Three-Volume Boxed Set* (White Plains: Russ Cochran Publishing, 1981).

13. Fredric Wertham, *The Seduction of the Innocent* (New York: Rinehart, 1954), 177.

14. Wertham, *The Seduction of the Innocent*, 173–93 and passim; analysis of the Batman comics, 189–191.

15. Wertham, *The Seduction of the Innocent*, 209–210.

16. US Senate, "Comic books and juvenile delinquency," 18–20.

17. US Senate, "Comic books and juvenile delinquency," 20.

18. Matthew Tinkcom, *Working Like a Homosexual: Camp, Capital, Cinema* (Durham: Duke University Press, 2002), 27–28.

19. Renan, "Interview," 49.

20. Often attributed to Theodor W. Adorno and Max Horkheimer's analysis of the culture industry, *The Dialèctics of Enlightenment*, trans. J. Cummins (New York: Continuum, 1988), the formula seems to stem from Leo Löwenthal. See Miriam Bratu Hansen, *Cinema and Experience: Siegfried Kracauer, Walter Benjamin and Theodor W. Adorno* (Berkeley: University of California Press, 2011), 227.

21. Jacques Rancière, "Falling Bodies: Rossellini's Physics," *Film Fables*, trans. Emiliano Battista (London: Berg, 2006), 125–141. Siegfried Kracauer is among the critics who remarked on the unhospitable materiality of silent film; see Miriam Hansen, "'With Skin and Hair': Kracauer's Theory of Film, Marseille 1940," *Critical Inquiry* 19 (1993): 437–469.

22. Dominique Laporte, *Historia de la mierda*, trans. N. Pérez de Lara (Valencia: Pre-Textos, 1980); Spanish version of *Histoire de la merde* (Paris: Christian Bourgeois, 1978).

23. Sigmund Freud, "On the Transformation of Instincts with Special Reference to Anal Eroticism" (1917), in *Character and Culture*, ed. Phillip Rieff (New York: Collier Books, 1963), 202–209.

NOTES 273

24. George Kuchar, "George Kuchar Speaks on Films and Truth," *Film Culture* 33 (1964): 14.

25. Handwritten program notes, undated. Mike Kuchar clipping file, Anthology Film Archives, New York. Consulted August 2008.

26. George and Mike Kuchar, *Reflections from a Cinematic Cesspool* (Berkeley: Zanja Press, 1997), 53.

27. George and Mike Kuchar, *Reflections from a Cinematic Cesspool*, 75.

28. Jack Smith, "Uncle Fishhook and the Sacred Baby Poo-Poo of Art," *Wait For Me at the Bottom of the Pool: The Writings of Jack Smith*, eds. J. Hoberman and E. Leffingwell (London: Serpent's Tail, 1997), 115.

29. Film-Makers' Coop online catalogue, accessed December 18, 2014, http://film-mak erscoop.com/rentals-sales/search-results?fmc_authorLast=&fmc_title=Eclipse+of+ the+Sun+Virgin&fmc_description=&x=61&y=10.

30. Victoria O'Donnell, "Science Fiction Films and Cold War Anxiety," in *The Fifties: Transforming the Screen, 1950–59*, ed. Peter Lev (New York: Charles Scribner's, 2003), 169–196; Hajdu, *Ten Cent Plague*, 177–178 Wright, *Comic Book Nation*, 109–153.

31. Mikhail Bakhtin, *Rabelais and His World*, trans. Heléne Iswolsky (Bloomington: Indiana University Press, 1984), 336.

32. Referenced in the filmography in George and Mike Kuchar, *Reflections*, 176–177, as *Dream Quest of the Ju-Ju Cult*, and in various programs and catalogues (including the can of the film at Film-Makers' Coop, New York), as *Death Quest of the Ju-Ju Cult*.

33. Laporte, *Historia de la mierda*, 86–92.

34. Sigmund Freud, *Civilization and Its Discontents*, trans. and ed. James Strachey (New York: W. W. Norton, 1961), 51–52, 58–60.

35. A self-avowed Kuchar disciple, John Waters has gone furthest in the attempt to import smell into the cinema in his "Odorama" film *Polyester* (1981).

36. For much of what follows, I am drawing on Jeffrey L. Meikle, *American Plastic: A Cultural History* (New Brunswick: Rutgers University Press, 1995), 63–91.

37. Hine, *Populuxe* passim.

38. Jeffrey L. Meikle, "Material Doubts: The Consequences of Plastic," *Environmental History* 2, no. 3 (July 1997): 278–300, esp. 280–281.

39. Reyner Banham, "The Triumph of Software," *New Society*, October 1968; reprinted in Banham, *Design by Choice* (New York: Rizzoli, 1981), 133–136.

40. In Pierre Restany, *Plastics in the Arts* (Paris: Leon Amiel, 1974).

41. Richard Hamilton, "An Exposition of $he," in *Pop Art Redefined*, eds. John Russell and Suzi Gablik (London: Thames and Hudson, 1969), 73.

42. Andy Warhol and Pat Hackett, *POPism: The Warhol 1960s* (New York: Harcourt Brace Jovanovich, 1980), 291.

43. For a glimpse into this subculture in New York, see Avery Willard, *Female Impersonation* (New York: Regiment Publications, 1971).

44. Mike Kuchar, typed, undated hand program. Mike Kuchar clipping file; Anthology Film Archives, New York. Consulted August 2008.

45. Bakhtin, *Rabelais and His World*, 174–175.

274 NOTES

46. Sigmund Freud, "On the Sexual Theories of Children" (1908), in *The Sexual Enlightenment of Children*, ed. Philip Rieff (New York: Collier, 1976), 25–40.

47. A recent review of this work is Julia Robinson, ed., *New Realisms: 1957–1962. Object Strategies Between Spectacle and Ready-Made* (Cambridge: MIT Press, 2010).

48. Meikle, *American Plastic*, 88–90.

49. Claes Oldenburg, "Environment, Situation, Spaces," in *Store Days* (New York: The Something Else Press, 1967); reprinted in *Pop Art Redefined*, 97–99.

50. Carolee Schneemann, *Parts of a Body House* (Devon: Beau Geste, 1972); reproduced in *Correspondence Course: An Epistolary History of Carolee Schneemann and Her Circle*, ed. Kristine Stiles (Durham: Duke University Press, 2010), plates 8–11.

51. Program, *Fluxusfest. In and Around Fluxus. September 19–October 11, 1992* (New York: Anthology Film Archives, 1992).

52. George Maciunas, "Manifesto" (1963). Accessed July 4, 2022, http://georgemaciunas.com/about/cv/manifesto-i/. See also George Maciunas, "Letter to Tomas Schmit," in *Theories and Documents of Contemporary Art: A Sourcebook of Artists' Writings*, eds. Kristine Stiles and Peter Selz (Berkeley: University of California Press, 2012), 726–727.

53. Scott MacDonald, *Avant-Garde Film: Motion Studies* (Cambridge: Cambridge University Press, 1993), 22–27.

54. Allan Kaprow, *Assemblages, Environments and Happenings* (New York: Harry N. Abrams, 1966), 168–170.

55. Miles Orvell, *The Real Thing: Imitation and Authenticity in American Culture, 1880–1940* (Chapel Hill: University of North Carolina Press, 1989), 287–299.

56. Sally Banes, *Greenwich Village 1963: Avant-Garde Performance and the Effervescent Body* (Durham: Duke University Press, 1963), 189–204.

57. Georges Bataille, *Visions of Excess: Selected Writings, 1927–1939*, trans. and ed. Allan Stoekl (Minneapolis: University of Minnesota Press, 1986), 97.

58. Bataille, *Visions of Excess*, 99.

59. Bataille, *Visions of Excess*, 101.

60. For a cogent, psychoanalytically informed discussion of the queerness of excrement, see Tim Dean, *Beyond Sexuality* (Chicago: University of Chicago Press, 2000), 264–268.

61. Sigmund Freud, *Three Essays on the Theory of Sexuality*, trans. Joan Riviere (London: Tavistock, 1973); "Character and Anal Eroticism" (1908); and "On the Transformation of Instincts with Special Reference to Anal Eroticism" (1917), *Character and Culture*, 27–33 and 202–209.

Chapter 5

1. Todd Haynes, "Preface," in *Glam! Bowie, Bolan, and the Glitter Revolution*, ed. Barney Hoskyns (New York: Pocket Books, 1998), x–xi.

2. Michelle White, *Producing Women: The Internet, Traditional Femininity, Queerness, and Creativity* (New York: Routledge, 2015), 169–70.

NOTES 275

3. Gordon Hall, "Object Lessons: Thinking Gender Variance Through Minimalist Sculpture," *Art Journal* 72, no. 4 (Winter 2013): 46–57; quotation page 47.

4. Haynes, "Preface," *Glam!*, xi.

5. José E. Muñoz, "Ephemera as Evidence," *Women & Performance: A Journal of Feminist Theory* 8, no. 2 (1996): 5–16.

6. Aja Magnum, "Glitter: A Brief History," *New York Magazine*, October 4, 2007, http://nymag.com/shopping/features/38914/

7. Caity Weaver, "What is Glitter?" *The New York Times*, December, 21, 2018, accessed April 23, 2021, https://www.nytimes.com/2018/12/21/style/glitter-factory.html; print version: Caity Weaver, "Glitter Secrets," *The New York Times*, ST 1, December 23, 2018.

8. "Glittering Windows for Christmas Still Possible Despite Dim-Out," *The New York Times*, December 20, 1942, 72.

9. Susan Ward, "Eyeglasses," *Encyclopedia of Clothing and Fashion, Volume 1*, ed. Valerie Steele (New York: Scribner's, 2005), 232–234.

10. Angela Taylor, "Evening Make-Up Is Made to Dazzle. Flecks of Silver, Gold, and Pearls Are Put into Cosmetics," *The New York Times*, December 28, 1963, 14.

11. "Shop Talk. Make-Up and Boyish Bob Evoke Feeling of Thirties," *The New York Times*, July 14, 1964, 30. "Fall Brings Beauty Aids in Profusion," *The New York Times*, October 23, 1964, 44.

12. "1964—The Year When Everyone Had Fun with Fashion," *The New York Times*, January 1, 1965, 23.

13. "The Cover Look," *Vogue*, December 1, 1964, 3. "Beauty Bulletin. Predictions '65," *Vogue*, 1 January, 1965, 100. The "jeweled eye" look is credited to Pablo Manzoni—usually referred to as "Pablo"—the Italian makeup artist who was Elizabeth Arden's creative director between 1964 and 1979.

14. Joel Lobenthal, *Radical Rags: Fashions of the Sixties* (New York: Abbeville Press, 1990), 96.

15. Joel Lobenthal, "Space Age Styles," *Encyclopedia of Clothing and Fashion, Volume 2*, ed. Valerie Steele (New York: Scribner's, 2005), 199–200.

16. See, for example, Patricia Peterson, "The Plastic Girl," *The New York Times*, April 3, 1966, 326; Mary Ann Crenshaw, "Glitter Girls," *The New York Times*, May 8, 1966, 323.

17. Lobenthal, *Radical Rags*, 78–104.

18. Andy Warhol and Pat Hackett, *POPism: The Warhol Sixties* (New York: Harcourt, Brace, Jovanovich, 1980), 64–65.

19. "Shop Talk. Make-Up and Boyish Bob Evoke Feeling of Thirties," *The New York Times*, July 14, 1964, 30.

20. Patricia Peterson, "The Spirit of '65," *The New York Times*, August 22, 1965, 378.

21. Patricia Peterson, "The Flapper Frugs," *The New York Times*, September 18, 1965, 19, 198, 200.

22. Patricia Peterson, "Off the Silver Screen," *The New York Times*, October 24, 1965, 132, 144.

23. J. Jack Halberstam, *Gaga Feminism: Sex, Gender, and the End of Normal* (Boston: Beacon Press, 2012), 58.

276 NOTES

24. Warhol and Hackett, *POPism*, 163.

25. Nan Ickeringill, "And Here's . . . Cheetah. A Roar in the Concrete Jungle," *The New York Times*, April 28, 1966, 47.

26. See "Wild New Flashy Bedlam of the Discothèque," *Life* 60, May 27, 1966, 72–77, which opens with a photograph of The Velvet Underground on stage; Robert A. M. Stern, Thomas Mellins, David Fishman, *New York 1960: Architecture and Urbanism between the Second World War and the Bicentennial* (New York: Monacelli, 1995), 531–535. On Cerebrum, see Gene Youngblood, *Expanded Cinema* (New York: Dutton, 1970), 354–360.

27. Francesco Guzzetti, "Ye-yé style. Les night-clubs en France et en Italie. Artistes, architectes et culture de la jeunesse dans les années 1960," *In Situ. Revue des patromoines* 32 (2017): 1–17. The Institute of Contemporary Art devoted an exhibition to this architectural trend: "Architecture and Nightlife in Italy, 1965–1975," ICA, London, December 8, 2015–January 10, 2016. See also Fabrizio Capolei, "Radical Disco: The 1965 Piper Club Experience," accessed March 26, 2021, https://archive.ica.art/bulletin/radical-disco-1965-piper-club-experience.

28. Warhol and Hackett, *POPism*, 177.

29. Willoughby Sharp, "Luminism and Kineticism," in *Minimal Art: A Critical Anthology*, ed. Gregory Battcock (New York: Dutton, 1968), 317–318.

30. Gregory Bateson, "Cybernetic Explanation," *Steps to an Ecology of Mind* (New York: Ballantine Books, 1972), 399–410.

31. Warhol and Hackett, *POPism*, 58.

32. Warhol and Hackett, *POPism*, 128.

33. Warhol and Hackett, *POPism*, 58.

34. Dan Sullivan, Review of *The White Whore and the Bit Player*, *The New York Times*, February 2, 1967, cited in Stephen Bottoms, *Playing Underground: A Critical History of the Off-off Broadway Movement* (Ann Arbor: University of Michigan Press, 2004), 57.

35. Cited in Bottoms, *Playing Underground*, 90.

36. David Kaufman, *Ridiculous! The Theatrical Life and Times of Charles Ludlam* (New York: Applause, 2002), 101–111.

37. I am using the female pronoun to refer to Curtis's drag persona; in life, he oscillated between male and female identifications. See Craig Highberger's documentary and book *Superstar in a Housedress: The Life and Legend of Jackie Curtis* (New York: Penguin/Chamberlain Bros., 2005).

38. Video documentation is available at Craig Highberger's YouTube channel: https://www.youtube.com/c/CraigHighberger/videos.

39. Highberger, *Superstar in a Housedress*, 109. Woodlawn's costume further included pasties with miniature antlers covered in glitter.

40. Jimmy Camicia, *My Dear, Sweet Self: My Hot Peach Life* (New York: Fast Books, 2013), 78.

41. Stefan Brecht was touched by their peculiar charm: "Using lighting (colored, dim) and costume (scintillating with glitter, say), [Ree] does dancing that is powerful and

NOTES 277

moving as seen [sic]." Stefan Brecht, *Queer Theater: The Theater of the City of New York* (Frankfurt: Suhrkamp Verla, 1978), 134.

42. Other versions claim The Cockettes premiered on Halloween of 1969. See the documentary *The Cockettes* (dir. David Weissman and Bill Weber, 2001), in which different members give either of the two dates.

43. A brief bio of Harris appears in the scandal-mongering piece: Anthony Driscoll, "Cockettes Crumble. Hibiscus Tells All," *The Berkely Barb* 330, December 10–16, 1971, 1–2. Driscoll claims Harris drove west with the Orlovskys. The documentary *The Cockettes* claims he traveled west with Irving Rosenthal, poet, novelist, editor (creator of Haruman books), and artist. He was friends with Jack Smith and appears in *Normal Love*.

44. Pam Tent, *Midnight at the Palace: My Life as a Fabulous Cockette* (Los Angeles: Alyson Books, 2004), 33, cited in Craig J. Peariso, "It's not Easy Being 'Free,'" in *Hippie Modernism: The Struggle for Utopia*, ed. Andrew Blauvelt (Minneapolis: Walker Art Center, 2004), 83.

45. "I never wore anything made after World War II," states Cockette Kreemah Ritz in David Weissman and Bill Weber's documentary on the troupe: *The Cockettes* (2002).

46. Alexandra Jacopetti Hart, *Native Funk and Flash*, with photographs by Jerry Wainwright (Bloomington, IN: Trafford Publishing, 2013 [1974]), 46–47. Julia Bryan-Wilson explores the gender politics of The Cockettes' clothing: *Fray: Art and Textile Politics* (Chicago: University of Chicago Press, 2017), 60, 67–68.

47. Irina Averkieff, *The Success of Excess: The Life and Art of Billy Bowers* (Scott Valley, CA: Createspace Independent Publishing Platform, 2015).

48. Sylvester and Pam Tent are cited in Bryan-Wilson, *Fray*, 71.

49. Kaufman, *Ridiculous!*, 66.

50. On Smith's use of second-hand clothing, see Ron Gregg, "Fashion, Thrift Stores, and the Space of Pleasure in the 1960s Queer Underground Film," in *Birds of Paradise: Costume as Cinematic Spectacle*, ed. Marketa Uhlirova (London: Walter Koenig, 2013), 293–304.

51. Brecht, *Queer Theater*, 10, 21. See also Jonas Mekas, "Jack Smith, or the End of Civilization," *Movie Journal. The Rise of the New American Cinema, 1959–1971* (New York: Macmillan, 1972), 388–397. On Smith's use of refuse as part of his gift economy, see my "Drag, Rubble, and 'Secret Flix': Jack Smith's Avant-Garde Against the Lucky Landlord Empire," *Bike Boys, Drag Queens, Superstars: Avant-Garde, Mass Culture, and Gay Identities in 1960s Underground Cinema* (Bloomington: Indiana University Press, 1996), 181–214.

52. Brecht, *Queer Theater*, 19.

53. Jack Smith, "The Perfect Film Appositeness of Maria Montez," *Wait for Me at the Bottom of the Pool: The Writings of Jack Smith*, eds. J. Hoberman and Edward Leffingwell (New York: Serpent's Tail, 1997), 25–36; first published in *Film Culture* (Winter 1962/1963).

54. See the sources Stefan Brecht cites for *Grand Hotel* and *The Conquest of the Universe*, *Queer Theater*, 46–47.

278 NOTES

55. Rosalyn Regelson, "Not a Boy, Not a Girl, Just Me," *The New York Times*, November 2, 1969, 178–185.

56. Marc Siegel and Arnaldo Cruz-Malavé have attended to the importance of fervor and belief in camp: Arnaldo Cruz-Malavé, "Between Irony and Belief: The Queer Diasporic Underground Aesthetic of José Rodríguez-Soltero and Mario Montez," *GLQ* 21, no. 4 (2015): 585–615; Marc Siegel, "Lensable Belief," *A Gossip of Images* (Duke University Press, forthcoming 2025). My thanks to Marc Siegel for sharing this text.

57. Reported in Bryan-Wilson, *Fray*, 63–64.

58. On the spiritual connotations of shine in aesthetics and philosophy, see Thomas Leddy, "Sparkle and Shine," *British Journal of Aesthetics* 37 (July 1997): 263–269.

59. Gilles Deleuze, "Immanence: A Life," in *Pure Immanence: Essays on A Life*, trans. Anne Boyman, with an introduction by John Rajchman (New York: Zone, 2004), 25.

60. Mike Kelley, "Cross Gender/Cross Genre," *PAJ: Performing Art Journal* 22, no. 1 (2000): 1–9.

61. Ingrid Hotz-Davies, Georg Vogt, Franziska Bergmann, "'The Dirt Does Not Get Any Worse': The Alliance of Camp and Dirt," *The Dark Side of Camp Aesthetics: Queer Economies of Dirt, Dust, and Patina*, eds. I. Hotz-Davies, G. Vogt, and F. Bergmann (New York: Routledge, 2018), 1–11. The volume has essays on Jack Smith and John Waters, but there is no mention of Kelley's insightful and pioneering intervention on "black camp."

62. Kelley, "Cross Gender/Cross Genre," 6.

63. See Vaccaro's intervention in the documentary *Jack Smith or the Destruction of Atlantis* (Mary Jacobs 2006).

64. Regelson, "Not a Boy, Not a Girl, Just Me," 185.

65. Brecht, *Queer Theater*, 66.

66. For an analysis of the collaboration, see Gerald Rabkin, "Kenneth Bernard and John Vaccaro: A Collaboration," *Performing Arts Journal* 3 (Spring-Summer 1978): 43–54.

67. Geoffrey Lokke, "The Theater of Andy Warhol: *Pork* in New York and London," *PAJ: A Journal of Performance and Art* 41 (January 2019): 62.

68. Vaccaro interviewed in Guillian McCain and Legs McNeil, *Please Kill Me: The Uncensored History of Punk* (New York: Grove Press, 1996), 89.

69. Kemp has provided an account of the production and of his early friendship with Bowie in "Pierrot in Turquoise," in *The Bowie Companion*, eds. Elizabeth Thomson and David Gutman (London: Macmillan, 1993), 29.

70. Brian Monahan's 1970 version of the show for Scottish television, accessed March 3, 2023, https://vimeo.com/249177678.

71. J. Hoberman, *On Jack Smith's* Flaming Creatures *(and Other Secret-Flix of Cinemaroc)* (New York: Granary Books, 2001), 102–107.

72. J. Hoberman, *On Jack Smith's* Flaming Creatures, 105.

73. For a wonderful survey of the film and Arnold's artistic milieu at the time, see Steve Seid, "Illumination Procured: Steven Arnold and the Body Eclectic," accessed on March 26, 2021, https://bampfa.org/page/illumination-procured-steven-arnold-and-body-eclectic.

NOTES 279

74. Wong's "design show" and Christmas specials are advertised in the film and theater listings of various local publications: *San Francisco Good Times* 3 (47), November 26, 1970; *Berkeley Tribe*, November 20, 1970; *Berkeley Tribe*, December 18, 1970. This last announces "Special Christmas show for children. Chinese fairy tale 'Monkey Subdues White Bone Demoness,' costumed and directed by Kaisik Wong. Recently performed as Midnight Show with great success." It was supplemented with the film *The Fabulous World of Jules Verne*, by Czech animator Karel Zemen and "rare cartoons, vintage Mickey Mouse, and other delightful surprises." Kaisik Wong is reported in Jacopetti's *Native Funk and Flash* as one of the local designers who are poised "to make it in the high fashion world" (58). Dead in 1990 at forty due to AIDS-related health problems, he was the object of an exhibition at the M. H. de Young Memorial Museum, in San Francisco, in late 1995 and early 1996 and has remained the object of growing scholarly interest. In 2002, Balenciaga's designer Nicolas Ghesquière was discovered to have plagiarized a design from Wong: Cathy Horyn, "Is Copying Really a Part of the Creative Process?" *The New York Times*, April 9, 2002, B: 10.

75. In his survey of the contribution of the SFAI to the local film scene, Steve Anker recalls Arnold's "spirited, iconoclastic work." Steve Anker, "Radicalizing Vision: Film and Video in the Schools," in *Radical Light: Alternative Film and Video in the San Francisco Bay Area, 1945–2000*, eds. Steve Anker, Kathy Geritz, Steve Said (Berkeley: University of California Press, 2010), 152–163.

76. Amos Vogel described it as: "A haunting, genuinely decadent work about mannequins that may be real and girls that may be models journeying through strange universes towards possible self-discovery." *Film as a Subversive Art* (New York: Random House, 1974), 60.

77. Alberto Berzosa, *Cine y sexopolítica* (Madrid: Brumaria, 2021), 57–78. I am indebted to Berzosa's research of Comas and the Barcelona Super-8 film scene in much of what follows.

78. The best assessment of Ocaña's influence is Pedro G. Romero and Carles Guerra, eds. *Ocaña: 1973–1983. Acciones, actuaciones, activismo* (Barcelona: Polígrafa, 2011). For great anecdotal information on Ocaña and, generally, on the Barcelona underground at that time, see Nazario, *La vida cotidiana del dibujante underground* (Barcelona: Anagrama, 2016), 139–182.

79. Warmest thanks to Eike Dürrfeld, from the Thomas Schulte Gallerie, Munich, and to Studio 111a, Düsseldorf for providing access to the film.

80. Jean-Claude Amman, *Transformer: Aspekte der Travestie* (Luzerne: Kunstmuseum Luzerne, 1974). Amman used a photograph by Sieverding for the catalog's cover.

81. Colin Lang, "Celluloid Drag, Sonic Disguise: Katharina Sieverding, Kraftwerk, and Glam," *Art Bulletin* 99, no. 1 (2017): 160–179.

82. On the eroticism of gems, see Jeffrey J. Cohen, "Queering the Inorganic," *Queer Futures: Reconsidering Ethics, Activism, and the Political*, eds. Elahe Haschemi Yekani, Evelyn Killian, and Beatrice Michaelis (New York: Routledge, 2013), 149–163.

83. Dominique Noguez, "Un école du corps?" *Politique hebdo* 287, October 31–November 6, 1977; reprinted in Nicole Brenez and Christian Lebrat, eds. *Jeune, dure et pure!*

280 NOTES

Une histoire de cinéma d'avant-garde et expérimental en France (Milano: Gabrielle Mazzotta/Cinémathèque française, 2001), 393.

84. *L'Art corporel* was consecrated at the show of the same name curated by François Pluchart at the Gallerie Stadler, in Paris, in 1975, a show that also included Sieverding's work. An early, comprehensive study is Lea Vergine, *Il corpo come linguaggio: Body art e storie simili* (Milano: Giampaolo Prearo, 1974).

85. The Collectif Jeune Cinema program for June 14, 1977, lined up tapes of actions by Gina Pane and Michel Journiac, a video by Arnulf Reiner, and Michel Nedjar's *Le Gant de l'autre* (1977) *Cinema Different* 11–12 (May–June 1977): 32 (back cover). Raphaël Bassan explores at some length the links between Marti and Journiac in "Les cités corporelles de Stéphane Marti," *Jeune, dure et pure!*, 417–419.

86. Noguez, "Un école du corps?" *Jeune, dure et pure!*, 393.

87. See the materials compiled in Christian Lebrat and Deke Dusinberre, eds. *MétroBarbèsRochechou Art* (Paris: Paris Experimental, 2005).

88. Bassan, "Les cités corporelles de Stéphane Marti," *Jeune, dure et pure!*, 418.

89. Biographical information is drawn from Xochitl Camblor-Macherel, "Le Banquet de Teo (Teo Hernandez)," *Jeune, dure et pure!*, 405–408.

90. On Hernández's *Estrellas del ayer*, see Manuel Ramos, "The Most Beautiful Film Ever Made," *MIRAJ: Moving Image Review and Art Journal* 11, no. 2 (2022): 88–97; on Hernández's activity in Tangiers, see my "Sexualidad, exilio y frontera en el cine *underground* español de los 70," in *Reimaginar la disidencia sexual en la España de los 70. Redes, vidas, archivos*, eds. A. Berzosa, L. Platero, J. A. Suárez, and G. Trujillo (Barcelona: Bellaterra, 2019), 310–355.

91. Teo Hernandez, "Carnets de Téo Hernández," in *Téo Hernandez: Trois gouttes de mezcal dans une coupe de champagne*, ed. Jean-Michel Bouhours (Paris: Éditions du Centre Pompidou, 1997), 110. (My translation).

92. Presumably to save wear and tear on the film and to be able to screen it without having to run the projection himself, Hernández blew up *Salomé* to 16mm in 1982, preserving its slowed-down pace. This is the version that circulates today.

93. Joseph Morder and Gerard Courant, "Entretien avec Teo Hernandez," carried out in 1979; first published as program notes for a retrospective of Hernández's films, Cinémathèque Française, 27 November – 4 December 1979, accessed May 5, 2021, http://derives.tv/entretien-avec-teo-hernandez/.

94. Eliza Steinbock, *Shimmering Images: Trans Cinema, Embodiment, and the Aesthetics of Change* (Durham: Duke University Press, 2019), 8, 11–12.

95. On "transing"—and its relation to "queering"—as a platform for critical work that explores and brings about new ontologies, see Susan Stryker, Paisley Currah, and Lisa Jean Moore, "Introduction: Trans-, Trans, or Transgender," *Women Studies Quarterly* 36 nos. 3–4 (Fall-Winter 2008): 11–22.

96. Jacqueline Lichtenstein, *Eloquence of Color: Rhetoric and Painting in the French Classical Age*, trans. Emily McVarish (Berkeley: University of California Press, 1993), 138–168.

97. Rosalind Galt, *Pretty: Film and the Decorative Image* (New York: Columbia University Press, 2011).

NOTES   281

Chapter 6

1. 16mm was introduced by Eastman Kodak in association with Bell and Howell in 1923; and 8mm, in the format of double 8mm, started to be marketed roughly a decade later, also by Kodak, as a cheap substitute for 16mm. Lenny Lipton's technical primers contain much information on the development of different stocks: Lenny Lipton, *Independent Filmmaking* (San Francisco: Straight Arrow Books, 1972) and *The Super 8 Book* (New York: Simon and Schuster, 1975).

2. Eric Barnouw, *Tube of Plenty. The Evolution of American Television*, 2nd edition (New York: Oxford University Press, 1990 [1975]), 288–289.

3. http://www.kodak.com/US/en/corp/researchDevelopment/whatWeDo/technology/chemistry/silver.shtml Last accessed May 24, 2018; no longer available.

4. Jonas Mekas, *Movie Journal: The Rise of a New American Cinema, 1959–1971* (New York: Macmillan, 1972), 196.

5. The main exception is Lucy Fife Donaldson's brief discussion of "film (celluloid) texture" in *Texture in Film* (Basingstoke; New York: Palgrave Macmillan, 2014), 33–37.

6. The original formulation of this trend is P. Adams Sitney, "Structural Cinema," *Film Culture* 47 (Summer 1969); reprinted in a slightly different version in P. Adams Sitney, ed. *The Film Culture Reader* (New York: Anthology Film Archives, 1970), 326–348; and in *Visionary Film: The American Avant-Garde* (New York: Oxford University Press, 2002; first edition: 1975), 347–371. Just as generative was Peter Gidal's inflection (and rejection) of Sitney's definition: Peter Gidal, "Theory and Definition of Structural/Materialist Film," in *Structural Film Anthology*, ed. Peter Gidal (London: British Film Institute, 1976), 1–19.

7. Dorsky would disclaim any connection of this title—or of its companion title *Alaya*—with structural cinema: see his introduction to the film at La casa encendida, Madrid, June 1, 2011. https://vimeo.com/26471344CCCB

8. In Peter Gidal's account, grain was one of the main means to heighten the dialectical tension between film's material conditions and its representational content: "The dialectic of the film is established in that space of tension between materialist flatness, grain, light, movement, and the supposed reality that is represented." And he further placed "grain" in the middle of the tension between the image and its granular configuration: "grain to image, image dissolution to grain." Gidal, "Theory and Definition of Structural/Materialist Film," 1–2.

9. Stan Brakhage, "At Oneness," section in Donna Cameron, "Pieces of Eight: Interviews with 8mm Filmmakers," in *Big as Life. An American History of 8mm Films*, ed. A. Kilchesty (San Francisco: Museum of Modern Art / San Francisco Cinematheque, 1998), 60–61.

10. Fred Camper, "The Qualities of Eight," in *Big as Life*, 27.

11. Eric Schaefer, "Plain Brown Wrapper: Adult Films for the Home Market, 1930–1970," in *Looking Past the Screen: Case Studies in American Film History and Method*, eds. Jon Lewis and Eric Smoodin (Durham: Duke University Press, 2007), 201–226.

12. Bradley Eros, "atomic cinema," in *Big as Life*, 31–37.

282   NOTES

13. In this regard, the work of David Getsy, Lex Lancaster, and Gordon Hall, for example, has a paradigm-shifting quality. See, for example, David Getsy, *Abstract Bodies: Sixties' Sculpture in the Expanded Field of Gender* (New Haven: Yale University Press, 2015); David Getsy, "Ten Queer Thesis on Abstraction," in *Queer Abstraction*, ed. Jared Ledesma (Des Moines: Des Moines Art Center, 2019); Lex Morgan Lancaster, "The Wipe: Sadie Benning's Queer Abstraction," *Discourse* 39, no. 1 (2017): 92–116; Gordon Hall, "Object Lessons: Thinking Gender Variance Through Minimalist Sculpture," *Art Journal* 72, no. 4 (Winter 2013): 47–56.

14. Filmmaker and archivist Jim Hubbard is, to my knowledge, the sole writer to point out their convergence in filmmakers such as Roger Jacoby, Laurence Brose, Abigail Child, Su Friedrich, Barbara Hammer, and Hubbard himself. Jim Hubbard, "Introduction: A Short, Personal History of Lesbian and Gay Experimental Cinema," *Millennium Film Journal* 41 (2003): 3–15. More recently, Maud Jacquin has explored the feminist materialism of Jean Matthees, Vicky Smith, and Anabel Nicholson, among others, in the context of the London Filmmakers Cooperative during the 1970s and 1980s. Maud Jacquin, "From Reel to Real—An Epilogue: Feminist Politics and Materiality at the London Filmmakers Co-operative," *Moving Image Review and Art Journal* 6, nos. 1–2 (2017): 80–88.

15. A general overview of the history and technology of halftone printing is Dusan C. Stulik and Art Kaplan, *Halftone* (Los Angeles: The Getty Conservation Institute, 2013).

16. "Benjamin H. Day, Obituary," *The New York Times*, August 31, 1913, 9. The obituary calls his method for "tinting drawings for photographic reproduction" the "Ben Day tint."

17. Vachel Lindsay, *The Art of the Moving Picture* (New York: Liveright, 1970 [1915]), 21–22.

18. John Coplans, "Talking with Roy Lichtenstein," *Artforum* (May 1967): 34–39.

19. G. R. Swenson, "Interview with Andy Warhol," in *Pop Art Redefined*, eds. John Russell and Suzi Gablik (London: Thames and Hudson, 1969), 116–119. The interview first appeared in the two-part series of conversations: Gene Swenson, "What Is Pop Art? Answers from 8 Painters," *Art News* 67, no. 7 (November 1963) and *Art News* 67, no. 8 (February 1964). For the complete transcript see Jennifer Sichel, "'What is Pop Art?' A Revised Transcript of Gene Swenson's 1963 Interview with Andy Warhol," *Oxford Art Journal* 45, no. 1 (2018): 85–100; see also Sichel's commentary on the interview and the figure of Swenson in the same issue: "Is Pop Art Queer? Gene Swenson and Andy Warhol," 59–83.

20. Alexander R Galloway, "Pixel," in *The Object Reader*, ed. Fiona Candlin and Raiford Guins (New York: Routledge, 2009), 499–502.

21. Hal Foster has described an analogous dialectic of return and revision in the relationship between the historical avant-garde and the neo avant-gardes of the sixties. His thesis is that the neo avant-gardes helped to clarify and distill the original project of the historical avant-garde rather than dilute it through acritical repetition. Hal Foster, "Who is Afraid of the Neo Avant-Garde?" *The Return of the Real: The Avant-Garde at the End of the Century* (Cambridge: MIT Press, 1996), 1–35.

22. Bela Julesz, *Foundations of Cyclopean Perception* (Chicago: University of Chicago Press, 1971).

NOTES   283

23. Eugene Youngblood noted them in his discussion of computer-generated moving images: *Expanded Cinema* (New York: Dutton, 1970), 249–250.

24. Mara Mills has brilliantly mapped the history and cultural consequences of this field: see, for example "On Disability and Cybernetics: Hellen Keller, Norbert Wiener, and the Hearing Glove," *differences* 22, nos. 2–3 (2011) 74–112; and Mara Mills, "Deaf Jam: From Inscription to Reproduction to Information," *Social Text* 102 (Spring 2010): 35–58.

25. Norbert Wiener, *Cybernetics, Or Control and Communication in the Animal and the Machine* (Cambridge: MIT Press, 2002 [1948, 2nd rev. ed MIT 1965]), 92–93.

26. H. F. Mayer, "Principles of Pulse Code Modulation," *Advances in Electronics and Electron Physics* 3 (1951): 221–260.

27. On cybernetics' claim to universality and the rhetorical strategies that accompanied this claim, see Geoff Bowker, "How to Be Universal: Some Cybernetic Strategies, 1943–1970," *Social Studies of Science* 23 (1993): 107–127.

28. As Bowker has pointed out, this was a frequent claim: In his introduction to the proceedings of the First International Conference on Cybernetics, which took place in Namur in 1956, Pierre Auger wrote: "Now after the age of materials and stuff, after the age of energy, we have begun to live the age of form," cited in Bowker, "How to Be Universal," 111.

29. Wiener, *Cybernetics,* 13–14; Norbert Wiener, *I Am a Mathematician* (Garden City: Doubleday, 1956), 263–265.

30. Wiener, *I Am a Mathematician,* 263.

31. György Kepes, *The New Landscape in Art and Science* (Chicago: Paul Theobald, 1963), 173. While the book's main argumentative line is by Kepes, the volume has brief essays by noted contemporary artists and thinkers: Jean Arp, Naum Gabo, Walter Gropius, Fernand Léger, Richard Neutra, and Norbert Wiener, among others.

32. Kepes, *The New Landscape in Art and Science,* 173.

33. Wiener, *Cybernetics,* 5–8. On the implications of the war effort as a starting point for Wiener's cybernetics, see Peter Galison, "The Ontology of the Enemy: Norbert Wiener and the Cybernetic Vision," *Critical Inquiry* 21, no. 1 (Autumn 1994): 228–266.

34. Kepes, *The New Landscape in Art and Science,* 205.

35. Kepes, *The New Landscape in Art and Science,* 207.

36. Karl Deutsch, "Review: A New Landscape Revisited by György Kepes." Manuscript. April 1960, Karl Deutsch Papers, HUGFP, 141–150, manuscripts and research materials ca. 1940–90, Harvard University Archives. Cited in Orit Halpern, *Beautiful Data: A History of Vision and Reason since 1945* (Durham: Duke University Press, 2015), 15.

37. See, for example, the show "New Realisms, 1957–1962: Object Strategies, Between Ready Made and Spectacle," Museo Nacional Centro de Arte Reina Sofía, Madrid, June 16–October 4, 2010; curator: Julia Robinson. See the exhibition catalogue: Julia Robinson et al., *Nuevos realismos, 1957–1962: Estrategias del objeto, entre el ready-made y el espectáculo* (Madrid: Museo Nacional Centro de Arte Reina Sofía, 2010).

38. The proposal is in Yoko Ono, *Grapefruit: A Book of Instructions and Drawings* (New York: Simon and Schuster, 2000), unpaginated. First published in 1964.

39. Thomas Hess, cited in Pamela Lee, *Chronophobia: On Time in the Art of the 1960s* (Cambridge: MIT Press, 2004), 189.

284 NOTES

40. This is one of the central ideas in Foster's discussion of Hamilton and Warhol in Hal Foster, *The First Pop Age. Painting and Subjectivity in the Art of Hamilton, Lichtenstein, Warhol, Richter, and Ruscha* (Princeton: Princeton University Press, 2011).

41. Foster, *The Return of the Real*, 134–136.

42. Foster, *The First Pop Age*, esp. 42–60.

43. It was published by The Letter Edged in Black Press as part of the S. M. S. portfolio in an edition of c. 1500–2000. Accessed January 20, 2022, https://gerrishfineart.com/product/to-mother/.

44. Richard Hamilton, *Collected Words, 1953–1982* (London: Thames and Hudson, 1982), 68.

45. Youngblood, *Expanded Cinema*, 223.

46. Youngblood, *Expanded Cinema*, 225.

47. Suranjan Ganguly, "Interview," in *Stan Brakhage: Interviews*, ed. Suranjan Ganguly (Jackson: University Press of Mississippi, 2019), 67.

48. Bela Julesz, *Dialogues on Perception* (Cambridge: MIT Press, 1995); Jimmy Soni and Rob Goodman, *A Mind at Play: How Claude Shannon Invented the Information Age* (New York: Simon and Schuster, 2014), 134–136.

49. Ganguly, "Interview," 67.

50. In a letter of June 8, 1963, he describes to Gregory Markopoulos a visit with Tenney to the Labs, where he experienced digitally generated pure color: Stan Brakhage, *Metaphors on Vision* (New York: Film Culture, 1963), 80. The volume was initially printed as a regular issue of *Film Culture*, and I am citing this source. While it is unpaginated, I am referencing the page on which the quotations may be found counting from the cover. On Brakhage's brush against computer music, largely through his friendship and attempted collaborations with Tenney, see Eric Smigel, "Metaphors on Vision, James Tenney and Stan Brakhage, 1951–64," *American Music* 30, no. 1 (Spring 2012), 61–100, esp. 75–86.

51. Brakhage, *Metaphors on Vision*, 32–33.

52. Brakhage, *Metaphors on Vision*, 29.

53. Brakhage, *Metaphors on Vision*, 36.

54. Carolee Schneemann, *Imaging Her Erotics: Essays, Interviews, Projects* (Cambridge: The MIT Press, 2002), 159.

55. Schneemann, *Imaging Her Erotics*, 160.

56. Carolee Schneemann, "The Obscene Body/Politic," *Art Journal* 50, no. 4 (Winter 1991): 28–35.

57. Carolee Schneemann, *Imaging Her Erotics*, 134.

58. Schneemann, *Imaging Her Erotics*, 47–48.

59. Schneemann, *Imaging Her Erotics*, 76.

60. Scott MacDonald, "Interview with Carolee Schneemann," in *A Critical Cinema: Interviews with Independent Filmmakers* (Berkeley and Los Angeles: University of California Press, 1988), 150–151.

61. Carolee Schneemann, "What Matters," *Performing Arts Journal* 122 (2019): 16–17.

62. On the fragility of this home-movie-like set up, see MacDonald, "Interview with Carolee Schneemann," 149–150.

NOTES 285

63. MacDonald, "Interview with Carolee Schneemann," 139.
64. Jack Halberstam, *The Queer Art of Failure* (Durham: Duke University Press, 2012).
65. Gregory Bateson, *Steps to an Ecology of Mind* (San Francisco: Chandler Publishing, 1972), 410.
66. J. Hoberman, *Jack Smith's* Flaming Creatures *(and Other Secret Flix of Cinemaroc)* (New York: Granary Books / Hips Road, 2001), 10–17.
67. Jack Smith, "The Perfect Film Appositeness of Maria Montez," *Wait for Me at the Bottom of the Pool. The Writings of Jack Smith*, eds. J. Hoberman and Edward Leffingwell (London/New York: Serpent's Tail/High Risk Books, 1997), 25–35; originally published in *Film Culture* 27 (1962–63).
68. See Giorno's account of the circumstances of the film: John Giorno, *Great Demon Kings: A Memoir of Poetry, Sex, Art, Death, and Enlightenment* (New York: Farrar, Straus, Giroux, 2020), 48–75.
69. Douglas Crimp, *"Our Kind of Movie": The Films of Andy Warhol* (Cambridge: MIT Press, 2013), 7.
70. Carolee Schneemann, "Istory of a Girl Pornographer," *More Than Meat Joy: Performance Works and Related Subjects* (Kingston: McPherson, 1979), 193–195.
71. Carolee Schneemann, *Imaging Her Erotics*, 45.
72. Ara Osterweil, *Flesh Cinema: The Corporeal Turn in American Avant-Garde Film* (Manchester: University of Manchester Press, 2014), 165.
73. Kate Haug, "Interview with Carolee Schneemann," in *Imaging Her Erotics*, 33.
74. Kate Haug, "Interview with Carolee Schneemann," in *Imaging Her Erotics*, 42.
75. On Markopolous's circle, see Scott MacDonald, "Interview with P. Adams Sitney," in *A Critical Cinema 4: Interviews with Independent Filmmakers* (Berkeley and Los Angeles: University of California Press, 2005), 29–32. The best document on Chomont's trajectory is his interview with Scott MacDonald: Scott MacDonald, "Tom Chomont," *A Critical Cinema* (1988), 152–173. Mike Hoolboom's film *Tom* (2002) is a beautiful homage. My thanks to Jim Hubbard for facilitating access to Chomont's films.
76. MacDonald, "Tom Chomont," *A Critical Cinema*, 164.
77. Sally Banes, *Greenwich Village 1963: Avant-Garde Performance and the Effervescent Body* (Durham: Duke University Press, 1993).

Chapter 7

1. Kim Knowles, *Experimental Film and Photochemical Practices* (London: Palgrave Macmillan, 2020); Jonathan Walley, *Cinema Expanded: Avant-Garde Film in the Age of Intermedia* (New York: Oxford University Press, 2020).
2. Hito Steyerl, "In Praise of the Poor Image," *e-flux* 10 (November 2009): accessed November 5, 2021, https://www.e-flux.com/journal/10/61362/in-defense-of-the-poor-image/.

286 NOTES

3. Douglas Crimp, *Melancholia and Moralism: Essays on AIDS and Queer Politics* (Cambridge: MIT Press, 2002), especially the essays "How to Have Promiscuity in an Epidemic" (1987), 43–81, "Portraits of People with AIDS" (1992), 83–107, and "De-Moralizing Representations of AIDS" (1994) 253–272; Gregg Bordowitz, *The AIDS Crisis is Ridiculous and Other Writings, 1986–2003* (Cambridge: MIT Press, 2004); Alexandra Juhasz, *AIDS TV: Identity, Community, and Alternative Video* (Durham: Duke University Press, 1996). The exception to this tendency is Roger Hallas, who discusses both celluloid-based and video work in *Reframing Bodies: Bearing Witness and the Queer Moving Image* (Durham: Duke University Press, 2009).

4. Particularly odd is their absence from Tom Gunning's survey of eighties' "minor cinema," even though they share many of its characteristics, such as the textured surface, the use of small gauge, the fascination with the interlacing of private and collective memory, the examination of the medium, and their foregrounding of situated, personal perspective. See Tom Gunning, "Towards a Minor Cinema: Fonoroff, Herwitz, Ahwesh, Lapore, Klahr, and Solomon," *Motion Picture* 3, nos. 1–2 (Winter 1989–90): 2–5. See also Paul Arthur, *A Line of Sight. American Avant-Garde Film Since 1965* (Minneapolis: University of Minnesota Press, 2005), 133–150; Lucas Hilderbrand, Alexandra Juhasz, Debra Levine, and Ricardo Montez, "Downtown's Queer Asides," in *Downtown Film and TV Culture, 1975–2001*, ed. Joan Hawkins (Chicago: Intellect, 2015), 241–258.

5. D. N. Rodowick, *The Virtual Life of Film* (Cambridge: Harvard University Press, 2007), 19–20. For a provocative argument that posits the fragility of celluloid as the very condition of film history see, Paolo Cherchi Usai, *The Death of Cinema: History, Cultural Memory, and the Digital Dark Age* (London: British Film Institute, 2001), 59–60 and ff.

6. On the growing popularity of hand-processing among experimental filmmakers, see Chris Gehman, "Toward Artisanal Cinema: A Filmmaker's Movement," in *Process Cinema: Handmade Film in the Digital Age*, eds. Scott MacKenzie and Janine Marchessault (Montreal: McGill-Queens University, 2019), 178. On the use of the optical printer as a means of aesthetic intervention, see John Powers, "A DIY Come-On: A History of Optical Printing in Avant-Garde Cinema," *Cinema Journal* 57, no. 4 (Summer 2018): 71–95, and John Powers, *Technology and the Making of Experimental Film Culture* (New York: Oxford University Press, 2023), 113–150.

7. Walter Benjamin, "Theses on the Philosophy of History," (1939) in *Illuminations: Essays and Reflections*, trans. Harry Zohn (New York: Schocken, 1969), 253–264. The text alluded to is in Thesis V: "The true picture of the past flits by. The past can be seized only as an image which flashes up at the instant when it can be recognized and is never seen again. . . . For every image of the past that is not recognized by the present as one of its own concerns threatens to disappear irretrievably" (255).

8. Joel Schlemowitz, "Interview with Jim Hubbard," *Incite! Journal of Experimental Media*. November 12, 2016, accessed August 2, 2021, http://www.incite-online.net/hubbard.html.

NOTES   287

9. Roger Hallas, "The Resistant Corpus: Queer Experimental Film and Video and the AIDS Pandemia," *Millennium Film Journal* 41 (Fall 2003): 8. See Douglas Crimp, "Mourning and Militancy," in *Melancholia and Moralism*, 129–149; first published in *October* 51 (Winter 1989).

10. Gregg Bordowitz, "The AIDS Crisis is Ridiculous," in *The AIDS Crisis is Ridiculous* (Cambridge: MIT Press, 2006), 43–68.

11. The same could be said of Hubbard's extraordinary *Homosexual Desire in Minnesota* (1980–85), a record of his and Jacoby's life in Minneapolis in 1980 and 1981. With scenes devoted to anti-homophobic protest, parties, drag shows, cruising, friends, and love interests, the film is a multi-tonal record of the moment before the catastrophe. It refuses to settle comfortably on any single mood—certainly not on nostalgia or celebration—and shows that homophobia, but also pleasure, community-building, and resilience determined queer life even before AIDS. My thanks to Hubbard for making his film available to me.

12. On the making of the film, see Jerry Tartaglia, "Ecce Homo," in *Queer Looks: Perspectives on Lesbian and Gay Film and Video*, eds. Martha Gever, John Greyson, and Pratibha Parmar (New York: Routledge, 1993), 204–208.

13. See, for example DIVA's video *Like a Prayer* (1989), which documents the "Stop the Church!" action at Saint Patrick's Cathedral, in New York, in 1989. https://vimeopro.com/deepdishtv/diva-tv-spring-1990/video/178261617.

14. David Wojnarowicz, *Close to the Knives. A Memoir of Disintegration* (New York: Vintage, 1991), 58.

15. On the circumstances of the journey, see Cynthia Carr, *A Fire in the Belly. The Life and Times of David Wojnarowicz* (New York: Bloomsbury, 2013, ebook version), 658–668.

16. Wojnarowicz describes this statue, without giving the name of the deity, in *Close to the Knives*, 74.

17. Wojnarowicz, *Close to the Knives*, 69.

18. Eve Kosofsky Sedgwick, "Paranoid Reading and Reparative Reading, Or, You Are So Paranoid You Probably Think This Essay Is About You," in *Touching Feeling: Affect, Pedagogy, Performativity* (Durham: Duke University Press, 2003), 123–153.

19. Benjamin Ogrodnik, "The Theatricality of the Emulsion: Queerness, Tactility, and Abstraction in the Hand-Processed Films of Roger Jacoby," *Screen Bodies* 4, no. 2 (Winter 2019): 17.

20. Simon Watney insightfully analyzed this mainstream sensationalism and vapid moralism as "the spectacle of AIDS": Simon Watney, "The Spectacle of AIDS," in *AIDS: Cultural Analysis / Cultural Activism*, ed. Douglas Crimp (Cambridge: MIT Press, 1989), 71–86, first published in *October* 43 (1987). See also Crimp, "Portraits of People with AIDS," and "De-Moralizing Representations of AIDS," in *Melancholia and Moralism*, 83–109 and 253–272.

21. Hallas, *Reframing Bodies*, 185–216.

22. Steyerl, "In Praise of the Poor Image."

23. Tess Takahashi, "After the Death of Film: Writing the Natural World in the Digital Age," *Visible Language* 42, no. 1 (2008): 44–69.

24. Steyerl, "In Praise of the Poor Image."

288   NOTES

25. Silt is cited in Kathy Geritz, "I Came into an 8mm World," in *Big as Life: An American History of 8mm Films*, ed. A. Kilchesty (San Francisco: Museum of Modern Art/San Francisco Cinematheque, 1998), 43, 45.

26. George Bataille et al., *Encyclopaedia Acephalica* (London: Atlan Press, 1995), 42–43. This is a compilation and translation of texts written by Bataille and writers associated with him and his "Acéphale" group for the *Dictionnaire Critique* section of Bataille's journal *Documents* (1929–30) and for the *Da Costa Encyclopédie*, published anonymously in Paris in 1947–48.

27. Pip Chodorov, "Artist-Run Film Labs," *Millennium Film Journal* 60 (Fall 2014): 28–37, reprinted in MacKenzie and Marchessault, eds., *Process Cinema*, 170.

28. Kim Knowles, "Self-Skilling and Home Brewing: Some Reflections on Photochemical Film Culture," *Millennium Film Journal* 60 (Fall 2014): 20–27; reprinted in MacKenzie and Marchessault, eds., *Process Cinema*, 75.

29. Lucas Hilderbrand, *Inherent Vice: Bootleg Stories of Videotape and Copyright* (Durham: Duke University Press, 2009), 193–194.

30. https://www.williamejones.com/portfolio/all-male-mash-up/, accessed November 11, 2021.

31. Elizabeth Freeman, *Time Binds: Queer Temporalities, Queer Histories* (Durham: Duke University Press, 2010), 13 and ff.; see also 1–3.

32. My reading of Rosenfeld's film, like my argument in this section, is indebted to Greg Youmans, "Performing Essentialism: Reassessing Barbara Hammer's Films of the 1970s," *Camera Obscura* 81 (2012): 100–136.

33. Genet was in Chicago as part of an unconventional reporting team that also included Terry Southern at the height of his fame and William Burroughs; they had been commissioned by *Esquire* magazine to report on the convention. Genet's piece was published as "The Members of the Assembly," trans. Richard Seaver, *Esquire*, November 1968, 86–89. See Robert Sandarg, "Jean Genet in Chicago," *Romance Quarterly* 38, no. 1 (Fall 1991): 39–48. Moffet's video is scrupulously researched and recreates closely Genet's movements during the convention. My thanks to Lucas Hilderbrand for suggesting Frédéric Moffet's work.

34. Genet's fragments come from "The Members of the Assembly," "A Salute to 100,000 Stars," trans. Richard Seaver, *Evergreen Review* (December 1968), and from short biographical pieces compiled in Jean Genet, *L'Ennemi declaré. Textes et entretienes choisis (1970–83)* (Paris: Folio, 2010).

35. Filmmaker Sandra Lahire, who was Pucill's partner, wrote an insightful and poetic commentary of the film: Sandra Lahire, "The Fairies' Banquet," *Coil* 7 (1998), accessed November 20, 2021, http://www.luxonline.org.uk/articles/fairies_banquet%281%29.html.

36. See Richard Dyer's classic intervention: "Queer Noir," *The Culture of Queers* (New York: Routledge, 2004), 90–114.

37. Steven Shaviro, "Decomposing: Peggy Ahwesh's *The Color of Love*," *Stranded in the Jungle*: accessed December 4, 2021, http://www.shaviro.com/Stranded/17.html.

38. Elena Gorfinkel, "Arousal in Ruins: The Color of Love and the Haptic Object of Film History," *World Picture* 4 (Spring 2010): accessed December 4, 2021, https://www.

academia.edu/5423852/Arousal_in_Ruins_The_Color_of_Love_and_the_Haptic_Object_of_Film_History.

39. Artist's statement: accessed December 4, 2021, https://vimeo.com/35139986.

40. Roberta Smith, "Luther Price, Experimental Artist and Filmmaker, Dies at 58," *The New York Times*, July 19, 2020, B10. While Price's work was often reviewed, it has not been the object of much sustained academic study. An excellent survey is Ed Halter, "Remains Luther Price," *International Kurtzfilmtage Oberhausen 2013* (Oberhausen: 2013), 266–269, accessed December 6, 2021, http://edhalter.com/59_Katalog_LutherPrice.pdf.

41. "I feel like a lot of things revolve around the fact that I was shot in 1985. I went to Nicaragua during the Sandinista revolution [sic] and I got mortally injured there. I went to see what was going on, with a bunch of artists." Donna Cameron, "'I Want to Keep Truth.' Interview with Luther Price," in *Big as Life: An American History of 8mm Films*, ed. A. Kilchesty (San Francisco: Museum of Modern Art/San Francisco Cinematheque, 1998), 68–71.

42. Cameron, "'I Want to Keep Truth,'" 71.

Chapter 8

1. Michel Chion, *Audiovision: Sound on Screen*, trans. Claudia Gorbman (New York: Columbia University Press, 1994), 95–122.

2. Luigi Russolo, *The Art of Noises*, ed. and trans. Barclay Brown (New York: Pendragon Press, 1986), 27.

3. Thomas Y. Levin, "'Tones from Out of Nowhere': Rudolph Pfenninger and the Archeology of Synthetic Sound," *Grey Room* 12 (Summer 2003): 32–79; Douglas Kahn, *Noise Water Meat: A History of Sound in the Arts* (Cambridge: MIT Press, 2002), 123–156; William Moritz, *Optical Poetry: The Life and Work of Oskar Fischinger* (Bloomington: Indiana University Press, 2004), 39–44.

4. Michel Foucault, *The History of Sexuality, Volume 1: An Introduction*, trans. Robert Hurley (New York: Random House, 1978), 158.

5. Karen Bijsterveld, "The Diabolical Symphony of the Mechanical Age," in *The Auditory Cultures Reader*, eds. Michael Bull and Les Black (London: Berg, 2003), 165–189.

6. George M. Beard, *American Nervousness: Its Causes and Consequences* (New York: G. P. Putnam and Sons, 1881), 106–107.

7. Jennifer Terry, *An American Obsession* (Chicago: University of Chicago Press, 1999), 49–50.

8. Jonathan Ned Katz, ed. *Gay American History: Lesbians and Gay Men in the U. S. A.*, 2nd ed (New York: Meridian, 1992), 52.

9. Eve Kosofsky Sedgwick, "Queer and Now," in *Tendencies* (Durham: Duke University Press, 1993), 9.

10. "Zone of possibilities" is Lee Edelman's term: *Homographesis: Essays on Queer Literature and Cultural Theory* (New York: Routledge, 1994), 114; on queerness as

290 NOTES

utopian aspiration, José E. Muñoz has been greatly generative: *Cruising Utopia: The Then and There of Queer Futurity* (New York: New York University Press, 2009); see, for example, chapter 1: "Queerness as Horizon: Utopian Hermeneutics in the Face of Gay Pragmatism," pp. 19–31.

11. On the political agency of the "empty signifier," see Ernesto Laclau and Chantal Mouffe, *Hegemony and Socialist Strategy: Towards a Radical Democratic Politics* (London: Verso, 1986), 129–130 and ff.

12. Paul Hegarty, *Noise/Music: A History* (London: Bloomsbury, 2007), 4.

13. Hegarty, *Noise/Music*, 5.

14. Christopher Cox, "Sound Art and the Sonic Unconscious," *Organized Sound* 14, no. 1 (2009): 20; see also Christopher Cox, *Sonic Flux: Sound, Art, and Metaphysics* (Chicago: University of Chicago Press, 2018), 15–18.

15. Cox, "Sound Art and the Sonic Unconscious," 22.

16. Cox, *Sonic Flux*, 47.

17. Gilles Deleuze, *The Logic of Sense*, trans. Mark Lester with Charles Stivale (New York: Columbia University Press, 1993), 192–193.

18. Deleuze, *Logic of Sense*, 193–194.

19. Edgar Varèse, "The Electronic Medium" (1962), in *Audio Culture. Readings in Modern Music*, revised edition, eds. Christopher Cox and Daniel Warner (London: Bloomsbury, 2017), 44.

20. Hegarty, *Noise/Music*, 4.

21. Jacques Attali, *Noise: The Political Economy of Music*, trans. Brian Massumi (Minneapolis: University of Minnesota Press, 1984), 6–7. From now on, cited between brackets in the text.

22. Muñoz, *Cruising Utopia*, 10.

23. Susan McClary, "Afterword: The Politics of Silence and Sound," in Attali, *Noise*, 149–158.

24. The essay is reprinted in Elliot Schwartz and Barney Childs with ed. Jim Fox, *Contemporary Composers on Contemporary Music*, expanded edition (New York: Da Capo, 1998 [1967]), 373–383.

25. Tim Lawrence, *Hold on to Your Dreams: Arthur Russell and the Downtown Music Scene, 1973–1992* (Durham: Duke University Press, 2009).

26. John Cage, *Silence: Lectures and Writings* (Hanover: Wesleyan University Press, 1961), 8–9. Attali makes a similar point: "The consumer, completing the mutation that began with the tape recorder and photography, will thus become a producer and will derive at least as much of his satisfaction from the manufacturing process itself as from the object he produces. He will institute the spectacle of himself as the supreme usage." *Noise* 144.

27. Cage, *Silence*, 16.

28. Robin Maconie, "Care to Listen: Milton Babbitt and Information Theory in the 1950s," *Tempo* 65, no. 258 (October 2011): 20–36.

29. Nadine Hubbs, *The Queer Composition of America's Sound* (Berkeley: University of California Press, 2004); Hubbs comments on Varèse's homophobia on 156–158. On Varèse's superciliousness towards Cage, for reasons other than his sexuality,

see Robert H. Brown, *Through the Looking Glass: John Cage and Avant-Garde Film* (New York: Oxford University Press, 2019): 42–43.

30. Henry Cowell, "The Joys of Noise," *Essential Cowell: Selected Writings on Music*, ed. Dick Higgins (Kingston: McPherson, 2002). Digital version, accessed 8 February 2022, http://www.henrycowell.org/joys.html.

31. John Cage and Daniel Charles, *For the Birds* (Boston: Marion Boyars, 1981), 187.

32. Richard Kostelanetz, *Conversing with Cage*, 2nd edition (New York: Routledge, 2005), 10.

33. Lita Miller and Frederic Lieberman, "Lou Harrison and the American Gamelan," *American Music* 17, no. 2 (Summer 1999): 146–178.

34. On the metallophone and its use in *Concerto for Violin with Percussion Orchestra*, see Lita Miller and Frederic Lieberman, *Lou Harrison* (Urbana: University of Illinois Press, 2006), 44 and ff.

35. *The Dreamer that Remains* (1976), dir. Stephen Pontiot, prod. Betty Freeman.

36. Harry Partch, "The Ancient Magic" (1959), in *Bitter Music. Collected Journals, Essays, Introductions, and Librettos*, ed. with an introduction by Thomas McGeary (Urbana: University of Illinois Press, 2000), 185–186.

37. Partch, "Show Horses in the Concert Ring" (1948), *Bitter Music*, 174.

38. Harry Partch, *Genesis of a Music* (New York: Da Capo, 1974 [1949]), viii–ix.

39. Partch, *Bitter Music*, 12.

40. Partch, *Genesis of a Music*, 8–9, 45.

41. Partch, *Genesis of a Music*, 19.

42. Partch, *Bitter Music*, 183.

43. Partch recreates the relation rather obliquely in his journal "Bitter Music," *Bitter Music*, 17–21, 83.

44. Stevan Key is cited in Philip Brett, "Eros and Orientalism in Britten's Operas," in *Queering the Pitch: The New Gay and Lesbian Musicology*, 2nd edition, eds. Philip Brett, Elizabeth Wood, and Gary C. Thomas (New York: Routledge, 1995), 238.

45. Colin McPhee, *A House in Bali* (New York: John Day, 1944), 42–43.

46. "Drums beat in cross-rhythms, negating the regular flow of the music, disturbing the balance, adding a tension and excitement which came to rest only with the cadence that marked the end of a section in the music." McPhee, *A House in Bali*, 38.

47. McPhee, *A House in Bali*, 38.

48. Carol J. Oja, *Colin McPhee: Composer in Two Worlds* (Washington: Smithsonian Institution Scholarly Press, 1990), 58–64 and 65–78. On the circulation of gamelan in post-war gay musical milieus, see Philip Brett, "Eros and Orientalism in Britten's Operas," 235–255.

49. McPhee, *A House in Bali*, 43, 115.

50. Peter Dickinson, *Cage Talk: Dialogues with and about Cage* (Rochester: University of Rochester Press, 2006), 178, 192–193.

51. Dickinson, *Cage Talk*, 188.

52. Cage, *Silence*, 12.

53. Jonathan D. Katz, "John Cage's Queer Silence, or How to Avoid Making Matters Worse," *GLQ* 5, no. 2 (1999): 231–254; Moira Roth, "The Aesthetic of Indifference,"

292 NOTES

Artforum (November 1977): 46–53, reprinted in *Difference/Indifference*, ed. Jonathan D. Katz (New York: Routledge, 1999); Gavin Butt, *Between You and Me: Queer Disclosure in the New York Artworld, 1948–1963* (Durham: Duke University Press, 2005); Kenneth Silver, "Modes of Disclosure: The Construction of Gay Identity and the Rise of Pop Art," in *Hand-Painted Pop: American Art in Transition, 1955–1962*, ed. Russell Ferguson (Los Angeles: Museum of Contemporary Art, 1992), 179–203.

54. For the context of this collaboration, and for Dlugloszewski's music in general, see Amy C. Beal, *Terrible Freedom: The Life and Work of Lucia Dlugloszewski* (Berkeley: University of California Press, 2022), 58–60.

55. "Dixieland" is Peterson's characterization of the music: Sidney Peterson, *The Dark of the Screen* (New York: Anthology Film Archives, 1980), 24, 31. On the context of these productions, see Steve Anker, "Radicalizing Vision: Workshop 20 and Art Movies," in *Radical Light: Alternative Film and Video in the San Francisco Bay Area, 1945–2000*, eds. Steve Anker, Kathy Geritz, and Steve Seid (San Francisco: University of California Press, 2010), 39–47.

56. For the Ito-Deren collaboration, I am very indebted to Michiko Ogawa's pioneering research on Ito: See Michiko Ogawa, "Searching for the Cosmic Principle: Transcribing and Performing the Music of Teiji Ito," Unpublished PhD Dissertation, University of California, San Diego, 2019.

57. Maya Deren, *Divine Horsemen: The Living Gods of Haiti* (Kingston: Documentext/McPherson, 1991 [1953]), 111.

58. Cited in Albert Glinsky, *Theremin: Ether Music and Espionage* (Urbana: University of Illinois Press, 2005), 54, 56–58.

59. On Scott's invention, see Irving Chusid and Jeff Winner, eds. *Artifacts from the Archives. Raymond Scott's Electronic Music Inventions, 1940s–70s* (Aalsmer: Basta Music ·and Reckless Night Music, 2017), 177–199. A rich trove of materials, this book is published as a companion to Raymond Scott compilations: *Three Willow Park* (Basta Music, 2017), *Manhattan Research Inc.* (Basta Music, 2000), and *Soothing Sounds for Baby* (Basta Music, 2017), accessed May 3, 2023, https://www.raymondscott.net/artifacts/.

60. Trevor Pinch and Frank Trocco, *Analog Days: The Invention and Impact of the Moog Synthesizer* (Cambridge: Harvard University Press, 2009), 41–43.

61. Andrew Birtwistle, *Cinesonica: Sounding Film and Video* (Manchester: Manchester University Press, 2010), 136.

62. Timothy D. Taylor, "The Avant-Garde in the Family Room: American Advertisement and the Domestication of Electronic Music in the 1960s and 1970s," *The Oxford Handbook of Sound Studies*, eds. Trevor Pinch and Karin Bijsterveld (New York: Oxford University Press, 2012), 387–409.

63. Finch and Trocco, *Analog Days*, 161.

64. Finch and Trocco, *Analog Days*, 168.

65. Varèse, "New Instruments and New Music" (1936), in *Audio Culture*, 41–43.

66. Dickinson, *Cage Talk*, 72.

67. On Nicholais as first buyer of a Moog synthesizer: Finch and Trocco, *Analog Days*, 29.

NOTES 293

68. The event was reviewed in *The San Francisco Oracle. The Psychedelic Newspaper of the Haight-Ashbury, 1966–68.* Reprint, CD-Rom digital edition. Regent Press and the Estate of Allen Cohen, 2008.

69. Initially, Hammer set *Dyketactics* to music by folk singer Alix Dobkin, but as Dobkin refused to grant permission, Hammer composed a second soundtrack after David Heinz, at Mills College, gave her access to a Moog. Years later, Dobkin relented, and Hammer made a second version of her film—*Dyketactics X 2*—with both soundtracks. Barbara Hammer, Oral History Interview by Svetlana Kitto, March 15–17, 2018. Smithsonian Archives of American Art, https://www.aaa.si.edu/collections/interviews/oral-history-interview-barbara-hammer-17555

    The music is uncredited in the film, but is confusingly attributed to Dobkin in the filmography in Barbara Hammer, *HAMMER: Making Movies out of Sex and Life* (New York: The Feminist Press, 2010), 321.

70. Overviews of these developments are in Andre Millard, *America on Record: A History of Recorded Sound* (Cambridge: Cambridge University Press, 1995), 195–198; Donald Morton, *Off the Record: The Technology and Culture of Sound Reproduction in America* (New Brunswick: Rutgers University Press, 2000), 136–151.

71. Alvin Lucier, "Tape Recorders," in *Music 109. Notes on Experimental Music* (Middletown: Wesleyan University Press, 2012), 103–108.

72. Warner Jepson, "Warner Jepson's Autobiography," accessed June 17, 2022, http://www.wjepson.com/warner/bio/index.htm.

73. For examples of Oswald's appropriations and writing, accessed May 4, 2023, http://www.plunderphonics.com/. For the wider context of plunderphonics—without mention of its queer potentials—see musician Chris Cutler's "Plunderphonia," in *Audio Culture: Readings in Modern Music. Revised Edition*, eds. Christoph Cox and Daniel Warner (London: Bloomsbury, 2017), 197–217; first published in *Musicworks* 60 (1994).

74. "Lubricated body" is Roland Barthes's term: Roland Barthes, *S/Z. An Essay*, trans. Richard Miller (New York: Farrar, Straus and Giroux, 1975 [1970]), 52, 64.

75. Liner notes to *Plunderphonic*, accessed May 4, 2023, http://www.plunderphonics.com/xhtml/xnotes.html.

76. On this phase of Conrad's career, see Branden W. Joseph, *Inside the Dream Syndicate: Tony Conrad and the Arts after Cage* (New York: Zone Books, 2008), 213–279.

77. Conrad edited these recordings in CD format in the late nineties: *Jack Smith. 56 Ludlow Street, 1962–64. Volume I Les Evening Gowns Damnées; Volume II. Silent Shadows on Cinemaroc Island* (Table of the Elements, 1997), accessed September 21, 2022, https://www.discogs.com/release/727518-Jack-Smith-Silent-Shadows-On-Cinemaroc-Island-56-Ludlow-Street-1962-1964-Volume-II.

78. Juliane Rebentisch, "Camp Materialism," *Criticism* 56, no. 2 (Spring 2014): 235–248.

79. Already Susan Sontag's originating essay on camp singles out datedness as one of the mode's characteristics: "Notes on Camp," in *Against Interpretation* (New York: Farrar, Straus and Giroux, 1966), 175–192. See also Andrew Ross, "The Uses of Camp," in *No Respect: Intellectuals and Popular Culture* (New York: Routledge, 1991), 135–170;

294   NOTES

Philip Core, *Camp: The Lie that Tells the Truth* (New York: Delilah Books, 1984); David Bergman, "Strategic Camp: The Art of Gay Rhetoric," in *Camp Grounds: Style and Homosexuality* (New York: Routledge, 1993), 92–110. On "camp" sound in queer film, see my "The Music and Sound of Queer Experimental Film," in *The Music and Sound of Experimental Film*, eds. Holly Rogers and Jeremy Barham (New York: Oxford University Press, 2017), 241–245.

80. Rebentisch, "Camp Materialism," 242.

81. I am borrowing Callie Angell's description of the strobe cut. According to Angell, *Bufferin* (1966) was the first film in which Warhol experimented with the strobe cut. Angell, *The Films of Andy Warhol: Part II* (New York: The Whitney Museum of American Art, 1994), 28.

82. Caroline A. Jones, *Eyesight Alone: Clement Greenberg and the Bureaucratization of the Senses* (Chicago: University of Chicago Press, 2006), 407 and ff.

83. Keir Keightley, "'Turn It Down! She Shrieked': Gender, Domestic Space, and High Fidelity," *Popular Music* 15, no. 2 (1996): 149–172; the *Life* feature is cited on p. 150.

84. Gustavus Stadler, "'My Wife': The Tape Recorder and Andy Warhol's Queer Ways of Listening," *Criticism* 56, no. 3 (Summer 2014): 425–456.

85. Douglas Kahn reviews these events in *Noise Water Meat*, 260–288.

86. Barthes proposes that since in contemporary societies money is "a sign"—based on differential relations and unanchored in real value—it ushers "metonymic confusion": "the limitless process of equivalences, representations, that nothing will ever stop, orient, fix, sanction." Barthes, *S/Z*, 39–40.

87. In addition to Hegarty, *Noise/Music* (especially, 89–193), see, for example, Simon Reynolds, *Generation Ecstasy: Into the World of Techno and Rave Culture* (Boston: Little Brown and Company, 1998); Simon Reynolds, *Rip It Up and Start Again: Post-Punk, 1978–1984* (New York: Penguin, 2005); Steven Blush, *American Hardcore: A Tribal History* (Port Townsend: Feral House, 2001); Caleb Kelly, *Cracked Media: The Sound of Malfunction* (Cambridge: MIT Press, 2009).

88. A recent survey of No-Wave and its context is Joan Hawkins, ed. *Downtown Film and TV Culture, 1975–2001* (New York: Intellect, 2015); on the New Romantics, see: Michael O'Pray, "'New Romanticism' and the British Avant-Garde Film in the Early '80s," in *The British Cinema Book*, ed. R. Murphy (London: British Film Institute, 2001), 256–262; A. L. Rees notes the occasional overlap of the New Romantics with the rise of music video, *A History of Experimental Film and Video* (London: BFI, 1999), 96–98.

89. Legacy Russell, *Glitch Feminism* (London: Verso, 2020), 145.

90. Vivien Sica, "Le Réinvestissement de la censure comme forme cinématographique dans l'oeuvre de Lional Soukaz," in *Homosexualité. Censure et Cinema*, ed. Christophe Triollet (Paris: Lettmotif, 2019), 141–156. Other commentaries of the film and its contexts are: James S. Williams, "From Gay Visibility to Queer In/Visibilities," in *The French Cinema Book*, 2nd edition, eds. Michael Temple and Michael Witt (London: Bloomsbury, 2019), 313–320; see also, Hélène Fleckinger, "'Nous sommes un fléau social': Cinéma, vidéo et luttes homosexuelles," in *Queer Sexualities in French and Francophone Literature and Film*, ed. James Day (Amsterdam and New York: Rodopi, 2007), 145–161.

NOTES 295

91. Lawrence Schehr, "Soukaz in a Staccato Mode," in *Hexagonal Variations: Diversity, Plurality, and Reinvention in Contemporary France*, eds. Jo McCormack, Murray Pratt, and Alistair Roles (Amsterdam: Rodopi, 2011), 244–257.

92. For Schehr, *Ixe* questions "the progress narrative of the political," "Soukaz in a Staccato Mode," 248; Nick Rees-Roberts places the film between "the personal intimacy of gayness and the public nature of homophobic discourse," or "between *cinéma affectif* and *cinéma militant*." *French Queer Cinema* (Edinburgh: Edinburgh University Press, 2008), 130–131.

93. Abigail Child, *This Is Called Moving. A Critical Poetics of Film* (Tuscaloosa: University of Alabama Press, 2005), 20–21.

94. Child, *This Is Called Moving*, 22.

95. The usual contextual frame for Child's work has (understandably) been Language Poetry. The fragmentariness of much of her seventies and eighties work is quite cognate to Language's aesthetic. As a poet, she contributed to Language-identified periodicals, and she is mentioned in the preface to Ron Silliman's monumental anthology *In the American Tree* (1986), a freeze frame of the movement at the time, as a poet whose main medium, however, is cinema, which explains her exclusion from the anthology. (Ron Silliman, ed. Silliman, "Language, Realism, Poetry" *In the American Tree* (Orono: National Poetry Foundation, 1986), xxi. She had close personal ties with Charles Bernstein and Ron Silliman, who can be briefly glimpsed in *Mutiny*. And poets Steve Benson and Carla Herriman contributed to the soundtrack of *Covert Action*. P. Adams Sitney offers a compelling analysis of her work in this connection: *Eyes Upside Down: Visionary Filmmakers and the Heritage of Emerson* (New York: Oxford University Press, 2008), 271–295.

96. Douglas Crimp, "Pictures," *October* 8 (Spring 1979): 75–88.

97. Sebastian Weidmann, "Interview with Abigail Child," *hambre* (October 2014): 2, accessed September 1, 2022, https://hambrecine.files.wordpress.com/2014/10/abigail-child.pdf. Even in this respect is her work close to the Pictures artists, some of whom were also interested in citing and "staging" found sound. Crimp points out that Jack Goldstein made sound pieces splicing fragments of found recordings from a broad variety of sources "paralleling his use of stock footage to make films." Crimp, "Pictures," 78.

98. Child, *This is Called Moving*, 134.

99. Child, *This is Called Moving*, 44.

100. Child, *This is Called Moving*, 137; see also 31.

101. Stella Rollig and Hans Scheirl, "Ten Questions to Hans Scheirl," *h_dandy body_parts* (Vienna: Schlebrügge, 1994), 122–129.

102. Scheirl's "manifesto for the dada of the cyborg embryo," a contribution to Sue Golding's edited volume *the eight technologies of otherness*, is included in the section "noise." Less about noise than about cyborg bodies, it is a noisy intervention in itself, with its constant typographical changes and its refusal of straightforward argumentation. Sue Golding, ed. *the eight technologies of otherness* (London: Routledge, 1997), 46–57.

296 NOTES

103. There is scant commentary on this body of film; see, for example, Alice Kuzniar, "Scheirl's Hermaphroditic Cinema: From *Super 8 Girl Games* (1985) to *Dandy Dust* (1999)," in *[Cyborg.Nets/z] Catalogue on / Katalog zu* Dandy Dust, ed. Andrea B. Braidt (Vienna: BKA Filmbeirat/BM:WV, 1999), 54–58; Kuzniar discusses Scheirl and Pürrer's work in the context of other queer experimental film in her book *The Queer German Cinema* (Stanford: Stanford University Press, 2000), 186–234.

104. *Scheirl/Pürrer Super-8 Girl Games* DVD. Vienna, Index DVD Edition, 2005. Accompanying brochure, p. 11.

105. Michel Chion, *Film: A Sound Art*, trans. C. Gorbman (New York: Columbia University Press, 2009), 40–55; Mary Ann Doane, "The Voice in the Cinema: The Articulation of Body and Space," in *Film Sound: Theory and Practice*, eds. John Belton and Elizabeth Weiss (New York: Columbia University Press, 1985), 162–176.

106. Michel Chion, *The Voice in the Cinema*, trans. C. Gorbman (New York: Columbia University Press, 1999), 5–6.

107. Russell, *Glitch Feminism*, 102.

108. Cited in Russell, *Glitch Feminism*, 140.

109. Brandon LaBelle, *Sonic Agency: Sound and Emergent Forms of Resistance* (London: Goldsmiths Press, 2018), 1–27.

110. Latour's sentence is: "It is because the social cannot be constructed with social that it needs keys and locks." Bruno Latour, "The Berlin Key, or How to Do Words with Things," in *Matter, Materiality, and Modern Culture*, ed. P. M. Graves-Brown (London: Routledge, 2000), 10–21; quotation is on page 19.

Index

For the benefit of digital users, indexed terms that span two pages (e.g., 52–53) may, on occasion, appear on only one of those pages.

Adorno, Theodor W., 19, 36–37
Agee, James, 73–74
Agenoux, Soren, 64, 65, 125–26
Ahmed, Sara, 5–6, 17, 115
Ahwesh, Peggy, 203–4
AIDS activist film, 181–93
  and memory, 183–87
  and the reparative, 191–94
amphetamine
  aesthetics of, 122–23
  eroticism of, 83–85
  at the Factory, 63–67
  in Jack Kerouac's writing, 74
  and mechanical registration, 75–76
  medical uses of, 70–71
  in postwar United States, 71–72
  recreational use of, 71–72
Anger, Kenneth, 3–4, 25–26, 27–29, 30, 38–
    39, 43, 96–97, 102–3, 209–10, 250–51
  and dark camp, 130–31
  Fireworks, 1–2, 24–25
  Hollywood Babylon, 130–31
  Invocation of My Demon
    Brother, 230–32
  Scorpio Rising, 234
  use of pop music, 230–31, 234
Anzaldúa, Gloria, 17–18
Aragon, Louis, 45–46
Arledge, Sara Kathryn, 21, 25–26, 27–
  28, 50–55
Arnold, Steven, 118–19, 133, 135–
  37, 232–33
Art in Cinema series (San Francisco), 52, 55
Attali, Jacques, 213–17

Babbitt, Milton, 216–17, 218
Bakhtin, Mikhail, 103–4, 111–12

Balász, Béla, 74
Banham, Reyner, 108
Barad, Karen, 3, 19–20
Barthes, Roland, 7–8, 148, 233–34
Bataille, Georges, 34, 113–15, 195–96
Bateson, Gregory, 169
Badaud, Gäel, 175–76
Baudrillard, Jean, 7–8
Beard, George M., 210–11
Ben Day dots, 22, 77–78, 149–50, 154–
  56, 162–63
Benglis, Lynda, 111–12
Benjamin, Walter, 7–8, 38, 43, 45–46,
  74, 183–84
Bennett, Jane, 9–10, 20
Berlin, Brigid, 64–65, 66, 85–86
Berman, Wallace, 43, 60–61
Bernard, Kenneth, 131–32
Bordo, Susan, 18–19
Bordowitz, Gregg, 181–82, 186–87
Bowie, David, 116, 117–18, 132
Brakhage, Stan, 38
  on Marie Menken, 41–42
  Metaphors on Vision, 164–66
  use of grain, 152–53, 164, 169
Brecht, Stefan, 125–26, 128, 131–32
Breton, André, 43, 45–46
Brose, Lawrence, 181–82, 189–90
Broughton, James, 22–23, 25–26, 27–28,
  31–33, 55, 209–10, 230, 232–33
Buchla, Don, 228–29
Buchla synthesizer, 230
Burroughs, William S., 45, 62, 63, 68–69,
  72, 88–89, 198
Butler, Judith, 6–7

Caffé Cino, 124–26

298 INDEX

Cage, John, 38–39, 73–74, 209–10, 223–24
  electronic sound, 214–19, 229–30
  interest in non-Western music, 221–22
  and noise, 88–89, 215, 219, 235–36
  and queer abstraction, 57–58, 222–23
  and randomness, 58
  view of percussion, 219–20
Cale, John, 81–82
Califia, Pat, 15
Cameron, Marjorie, 43
Camp, 69–70, 92, 97, 116, 124–25, 126,
  135–36, 146, 186–87, 198–99
  camp materialism, 237
  camp sound, 234–36
  "dark" camp, 130–33
  spirituality and, 127–29
Cardin, Pierre, 120
Carrouges, Michel, 48
Cassady, Neil, 73–74
Centola, Jimmy, 126–27. *See also* Hot
  Peaches, The
Chen, Mel Y., 3, 5–6, 15–16, 20, 93
Child, Abigail, 9–10, 22–23, 209–
  10, 243–44
Chion, Michel, 208, 249–50
Chomont, Tom, 3–4, 174, 175–76, 178, 193
Ciani, Susan, 229–30
Cinéma corporel, 142–43, 175–76
Cockettes, The, 21–22, 126–27, 129–30,
  135–37
Cocteau, Jean, 110
Cohen, Jeffrey J., 3, 5–6
Comas, Carles, 9–10, 21–22, 117–18,
  133, 137–39
Comics, 94–96, 97, 99–100, 103–4,
  137–38
Conrad, Tony, 88–89, 235–36
Courrèges, André, 120
Cowell, Henry, 218–20, 221–22, 235–36
Cox, Christopher, 212–13
Crimp, Douglas, 76, 80, 82–83, 170–71,
  181–82, 186, 243–44
Crowley, Aleister, 43, 46–47
Cunningham, Merce, 38–39, 223–24
Curtis, Jackie, 125–26, 131–32
Cvetkovich, Ann, 17
Cybernetics, 22, 88–89, 149–50, 154–55,
  158–61, 164, 169, 178

Darling, Candy, 125–26
Davis, Jim, 3–4, 21, 25–26, 27–28, 50–
  52, 54–59
Dean, Dorothy, 66
Deleuze, Gilles, 12–5, 42, 48, 212–13
  See also Guattari, Félix
Deren, Maya, 25–26, 199–200, 209–10,
  223, 226–8, 250–51
Dine, Jim, 35–29, 54–55, 112–13
Discothèques, 121–17
Dlugoszewski, Lucia, 223–24
Domingo, David, 200–181, 202–3
Dorsky, Nathaniel, 152–53, 174
Douglas, Mary, 34, 37
Duchamp, Marcel, 48, 51
Dyer, Richard, 2–3, 26

Eliot, Thomas Stearns, 30–31
Ellis, Havelock, 210–11
Engel, Morris, 30
Ernst, Max, 45–26, 51
Excrement
  aesthetics of, 101–92, 112–13
  and the body, 102, 103–93
  as heterology, 113–93
  as queer material, 92–93
  and regression, 105–95, 115
Exploding Plastic Inevitable, 30,
  121–19

Fashion
  electric dresses, 120
  glitter in, 119–21
  vintage clothing, 120–21, 125–16,
  127
  shiny fabrics, 120–21
  "space age," 120
Foucault, Michel, 5, 6, 8–9, 210–11
Freud, Sigmund, 1–2, 13, 36–37, 156–57,
  197, 222–23
  on the excremental, 42, 101,
  105, 111–12
  on sexual desire, 10–11
Friedan, Betty, 71–72

Galt, Rosalind, 149
Gamelan music, 217–18, 219, 221–23,
  226–27

INDEX 299

Garbage, 34. *See also* junk
  as artistic material, 34–36
  and childhood regression, 36–37
  and sexual anarchy, 37
Gehr, Ernie, 88–89, 152–53, 157
Genet, Jean, 132, 142, 187–88, 198–99
George, Carl M., 189
Gernreich, Rudi, 119–20
Gidal, Peter, 27–28, 152–54, 168
Ginsberg, Allen, 59, 66–67, 73–74, 126–
  27, 129, 198
Giorno, John, 170–71
glam rock, 21–22, 116, 117–18, 141–42, 143
glitter
  and camp, 116–17, 130–33
  in experimental film, 133–48
  in fashion, 119–21
  history, 118–19
  and transcendence, 127–29
  in underground performance, 124–33
Gryphon Group, 25–26
Guattari, Félix, 12–15, 48
  See Deleuze, Gilles
Gysin, Brion, 88–89

Halberstam, Jack, 3, 62, 116, 169
Hall, Gordon, 116–19, 150
Hamilton, Richard, 108–9, 161, 162–63,
  169, 178
Hammer, Barbara, 3–4, 197–98
  and queer memory, 181–82, 183–
  85, 187–88
  and sound, 208, 230, 231–32
Harrington, Curtis, 25–26
Harrison, Lou, 209–10, 218, 219–
  20, 221–22
Hegarty, Paul, 211–12, 213
Herko, Freddy, 21–22, 64, 85–87, 124–25
Hernández, Teo, 9–10, 21–22, 117–18,
  133, 175–76
  and *cinema corporel*, 142–43
  Corps aboli, 176
  Salomé, 145–48
Hibiscus (George Harris, III), 126–27,
  129–30, 138–39, 148–49
high fidelity sound, 238–39
Hoberman, J. 91–92
Hoolboom, Michael, 191–94

Hot Peaches, The, 126–27. *See also*
  Centola, Jimmy
Hubbard, Jim, 185–87

Ito, Teiji, 211–12

Jackson, Zakkiyah Iman, 15–16
Jacobs, Ken, 21, 25–26, 27–28, 29–30, 50–
  51, 88–89, 91, 96–97, 152
  collaborations with Jack Smith, 34–37
Jacoby, Roger, 181–82, 186, 191–
  92, 193–94
Jarman, Derek, 93
Jepson, Warner, 232–33
Jones, William E., 196–97
Judson Church Gallery, 112–13
Judson Dance Theater, 64, 124
Judson Poet's Theater, 112–13, 126–27
Julesz, Béla, 157, 164–65
junk, 34. *See also* garbage
  as artistic material, 34–36
  and childhood regression, 36–37
  and sexual anarchy, 37

Kabbalah, The, 43–44, 46–47
Kaprow, Alan, 60–61, 112–13
Kelley, Mike, 130–31
Kemp, Lindsay, 132–33, 146–48
Kepes, György, 159–60, 178
Kerouac, Jack, 73–76
Kessler, Chester, 30
kineticism, 123–24
Kittler, Friedrich, 75–76
Klein, Melanie, 10–11, 212–13
Kluge, Alexander, 18–19
Kracauer, Siegfried, 26
Kuchar, George, 98–100, 101–2, 110–11
  and classical Hollywood, 96–97
  and the comics, 94–96
  and contemporary experimental
  art, 112–15
  8mm films, 91, 94
  excrement in, 101–6
  plastics in, 106–12
  sexuality in, 92–93, 97–99
  sound in, 239
  and underground cinema, 91, 96–97,
  102–3

300 INDEX

Kuchar, Mike, 91, 96, 98–100, 110–11
  and classical Hollywood, 96–97
  and the comics, 94–96
  and contemporary experimental
    art, 112–15
  8mm films, 91, 94
  excrement in, 101–6
  plastics in, 106–12
  sexuality in, 92–93, 97–99
  sound in, 239
  and underground cinema, 91, 96–97,
    102–3
Kusama, Yayoi, 161, 169, 178

LaBelle, Brandon, 250–51
Lacan, Jacques, 11
Laporte, Dominique, 101, 105
Latour, Bruno, 8–9, 17–18, 251
Lee, Russell, 30
Lefebvre, Henri, 7–8
Léger, Ferdinand, 27–28, 50–52
Lichtenstein, Jacqueline, 149
Lichtenstein, Roy, 78, 156, 162–63
Lipton, Lenny, 151–52
low-fidelity sound, 76, 238–40, 249–50
Ludlam, Charles, 125–26, 235
  and excremental aesthetics, 112–13, 114–15
  and recycled clothing, 126–27
  and recycling of mass culture, 128–29,
    131–32
Luening, Otto, 218, 232–33
luminism, 123–24
Lynch, Kevin, 31–33, 34

Maas, Willard, 1–2, 25–26, 27–28, 38–39,
    56, 57–58
  parodied by George Kuchar, 110–11
  use of urban ruins, 29–31
McClary, Susan, 216–17
MacDonald, Scott, 91–92, 167–68
Maciunas, George, 112–13, 239–40
McLuhan, Marshall, 72, 89
McPhee, Colin, 218, 221–23
Mager, Jörg, 218, 228–29
magic, 1–2, 21, 250–51
  in Harry Smith, 43–45, 46–47, 48–50
  in Kenneth Anger, 24–25, 27–28, 230–31
  theory of, 49
Malanga, Gerard, 39–40, 79–80, 84–85

Markopoulos, Gregory, 25–26, 28–29,
    102–3, 153–54, 174, 175–76
Martin, Agnes, 58
Marx, Karl, 18–19, 48–49
Mauss, Marcel, 49
Mead, Taylor, 33, 112–13, 138–39
Mekas, Jonas, 38, 75, 128, 152–53
Menken, Marie, 1–2, 25–26, 27–28
  materials, 41
  queerness, 41–42
  visual style, 38–40
Mercer, Kobina, 17–18
Miller, Henry, 26–28
Moffet, Frédéric, 198–99
Montez, María, 96–97, 128–29, 237
Montez, Mario, 97, 125–26, 128, 134–35,
    234–35
Moog, Robert, 228–29
Moog synthesizer, 229–32
Moore, Ben, 26, 110
Mulvey, Laura, 127–28, 243–44
Muñoz, José Esteban, 16–17, 117–18, 215–16
Murrin, Tom (The Alien Comic), 131–32
Musser, Amber Jamilla, 15

Name, Billy (William George Linich),
    63–64, 66
Nedjar, Michel, 142–43, 145, 175–76
Negt, Oskar, 18–19
Newton, Esther, 8
Nguyen, Tan Hoang, 197–98
Nico (Christa Päffgen), 81–83
Noguchi, Isamu, 38–39, 41–42, 223–24
Noguez, Dominique, 142–43, 145

off-off-Broadway theater, 63, 124–26
Oldenburg, Claes, 35, 60–61, 111–13
Oliveros, Pauline, 218, 229–30
Ondine (Robert Olivo), 64, 66, 81, 83, 84,
    85–86, 239
Ono, Yoko, 99–100, 112–13, 161–62, 169, 178
Osterweil, Ara, 167–68, 172
Oswald, John, 233–34

Paik, Nam June, 88–89, 112–13, 239–40
Partch, Harry, 219–21, 228–29
Peterson, Sidney, 22–23, 55
  collaborations with James Broughton,
    25–26, 31–33

use of sound, 209–10, 223, 224–26, 229–30

plastics, 1–2, 4–5, 21, 27–28, 92–93, 121–22, 148–49. *See also* glitter
  in clothing, 120, 121–22
  in discotheque design, 121–22
  in Fernand Léger's film, 51
  in Jim Davis's films, 55–56, 58–59
  in the Kuchars' films, 108–12
  in Marie Menken's films, 40–41
  in midcentury's material culture, 7–8, 27
  in people's sex lives, 108–9
  in performance, 35–36, 125–26, 172
  "Tupperware modernity," 106–8

Pound, Ezra, 30–31
Preciado, Paul B., 8–9, 62, 89
Price, Luther, 204–5, 206
Pucill, Sarah, 199–200, 202–3
punk, 216–17, 240–41
Pürrer, Ursula, 245–48

queer abstraction, 55–58, 170–71, 172, 204–6, 222–23, 247–48. *See also* Davis, Jim

Rabanne, Paco, 120
Rancière, Jacques, 100–1
Rauschenberg, Robert, 35–36, 114–15, 222–23
Rebentisch, Juliane, 237
Ree, Larry, 126
Reed, Lou, 141, 143–44
Reeves, Jennifer, 202, 204–6
Rice, Ron, 3–4, 21, 25–26, 27–28, 37, 50–51, 73, 208
  The Flower Thief, 30
  The Queen of Sheeba Meets the Atom Man, 33
Ridiculous Theatrical Company, 125–26, 128–29, 131
Riley, Bridget, 161, 162
Rodríguez Soltero, José, 234–35, 237
Rosenfeld, Liz, 197–98
Rosenthal, Irving, 129, 134–35
Rubin, Gayle, 5, 13
ruins
  as artistic material, 30
  in modernism, 30–31

landscapes of fantasy, 31–33
urban, 28–29
Russell, Arthur, 216–17
Russell, Legacy, 250
Russolo, Luigi, 208, 215, 218

Saarinen, Eero, 27–28, 106–7
Scheirl, Ashley Hans, 3–4, 9–10, 22–23, 209–10, 241, 245–49
Schneemann, Carolee
  and excremental aesthetics, 112–13, 114–15
  and film grain, 164, 166–69
  Fuses, 171–74
Scholem, Gershon, 46–47
Schoonover, Karl, 93
Schreber, Daniel Paul, 1–2, 44
Sedgwick, Edie, 65–66, 85–86, 87
Sedgwick, Eve Kosofsky, 14, 27–28, 191–92, 211, 215–16
Serra, M. M., 202
Serres, Michel, 8–9, 212
Shannon, Claude, 22, 78–79, 158–59
Sharp, Willoughby, 123–24
Sieverding, Katharina, 133, 139–42, 143–44, 148–49
Smith, Harry, 1–2, 3–4, 9–10, 21, 25–26, 50–51, 60–61, 208
  Anthology of American Folk Music, 224–25
  and Art in Cinema series, 55
  Heaven and Earth Magic, 43–49
  and magic, 27–28, 43, 46–47, 49–50
  and mysticism, 43–44, 46–47
  and surrealism, 45–46
  as a queer film, 47–48
Smith, Jack, 3–4, 9–10, 21–22, 25–26, 96–97
  collaborations with Ken Jacobs, 34–37
  Flaming Creatures, 136–37, 169–70, 237
  No President, 134–35
  performances, 35–36, 128, 133–34
  Reefers of Technicolor Island (aka *Jungle Island*), 133–34
  Scotch Tape, 29–30
  use of glitter, 117–18, 134–35
  use of junk, 34–37, 101–2
  use of sound, 234–36
Sonbert, Warren, 84–85, 174

302 INDEX

Soukaz, Lionel, 9–10, 22–23, 142, 209–10, 241–43
Stauffacher, Frank, 54–55
Steinbock, Eliza, 148–49
Steyerl, Hito, 180–81, 195–96
Stryker, Susan, 3, 8

Tartaglia, Jerry, 181–82, 187–89, 192–93
Tavel, Ronald, 64, 65, 126–27, 131
Tenney, James, 165–66, 167–68, 171, 172–74, 233–34
Terry, Jennifer, 15, 93, 210–11
Theremin, Leon, 217–18, 228–30
Tinkcom, Matthew, 69–70, 97
trash culture, 94, 101–2, 128–29, 192–93
Tyler, Parker, 26, 36–37, 41–42, 68–69

Ussachevsky, Vladimir, 212, 232–33

Vaccaro, John, 21–22, 64, 125–26, 130–32
Varèse, Edgar, 213, 218, 219, 223–24, 229–30
Velvet Underground, The (band), 81–82, 121–22

Warhol, Andy, 1–2, 8, 21, 56–57
a, a novel, 64–65, 66, 75, 76, 78–79, 84–85
and amphetamine, 67–68
Blow Job, 80
camera style in, 80–82

Empire, 78–79
film grain in, 77–79, 162–63
film speed in, 77
Haircut, 79–80, 86–87
Kiss, 79–80
in Marie Menken's films, 39–40
"mis-fitting" relationality, 82–83
My Hustler, 87–88, 239–40
performance styles in Warhol's films, 79–80, 85–87
sexuality in Warhol's films, 83–85
Sleep, 170–71
Taylor Mead's Ass, 112–13
The Velvet Underground and Nico, 81–82
The Velvet Underground in Boston, 121–22
use of sound, 237–38, 239–40
Warner, Michael, 8–9
Watson, James Sibley, 52
Webber, Melville, 52
Whitney, James, 164
Whitney, John, 52, 164
Wiener, Norbert, 158–59, 160
Wojnarowicz, David, 181–82, 190–92

Young, LaMonte, 81–82, 229–30, 235–36
Youngblood, Eugene, 91–92, 164

Zappa, Frank, 66–67, 131
Zulueta, Iván, 176–77